Für Professor Georg Iggers
mit herzlichen Grüßen
Ihr Benedikt Stuchtey

British and German Historiography, 1750–1950

Studies of the German Historical Institute London

GENERAL EDITOR: Peter Wende

British and German Historiography

1750–1950

Traditions, Perceptions, and Transfers

EDITED BY
BENEDIKT STUCHTEY
AND
PETER WENDE

GERMAN HISTORICAL INSTITUTE LONDON
OXFORD
UNIVERSITY PRESS

OXFORD
UNIVERSITY PRESS

Great Clarendon Street, Oxford OX2 6DP

Oxford University Press is a department of the University of Oxford.
It furthers the University's objective of excellence in research, scholarship,
and education by publishing worldwide in

Oxford New York

Athens Auckland Bangkok Bogotá Buenos Aires Calcutta
Cape Town Chennai Dar es Salaam Delhi Florence Hong Kong Istanbul
Karachi Kuala Lumpur Madrid Melbourne Mexico City Mumbai
Nairobi Paris São Paulo Singapore Taipei Tokyo Toronto Warsaw
with associated companies in Berlin Ibadan

Oxford is a registered trade mark of Oxford University Press
in the UK and in certain other countries

Published in the United States
by Oxford University Press Inc., New York

© The German Historical Institute London 2000

The moral rights of the authors have been asserted
Database right Oxford University Press (maker)

First published 2000

All rights reserved. No part of this publication may be reproduced,
stored in a retrieval system, or transmitted, in any form or by any means,
without the prior permission in writing of Oxford University Press,
or as expressly permitted by law, or under terms agreed with the appropriate
reprographics rights organization. Enquiries concerning reproduction
outside the scope of the above should be sent to the Rights Department,
Oxford University Press, at the address above

You must not circulate this book in any other binding or cover
and you must impose this same condition on any acquirer

British Library Cataloguing in Publication Data
Data available

Library of Congress Cataloging in Publication Data
Data applied for

ISBN 0–19–920235–4

1 3 5 7 9 10 8 6 4 2

Typeset in Baskerville by
Cambrian Typesetters, Frimley, Surrey

Printed in Great Britain
on acid-free paper by
Biddles Ltd., Guildford and King's Lynn

Foreword

This volume is based on a conference on British and German historiography from the eighteenth to the twentieth centuries held at Cumberland Lodge in July 1996. To mark the twentieth anniversary of its foundation, the German Historical Institute London convened a gathering of historians from the United Kingdom, Germany, the United States, and Israel. As promoting contacts and collaboration between British and German historians is one of the GHIL's principal aims, we thought it appropriate to go back into the history of their relationship and trace its roots.

The present essays reflect on the scope and impact of transfers, the potentials of mutual perceptions, and the power and influence of national traditions. To a certain extent they demonstrate the different scientific approaches of two different historical academes, whether in the past or in the present. They document the profound competition between the British and the German scholarly communities, and show how these also profited from each other while it was often not easy to build bridges. The one and only meeting between Lord Macaulay and Leopold von Ranke illustrates the potentials and limits of historiographical transfers. As the Greville Diary of 16 October 1843 tells us, the expected 'first-rate literary talk between such luminaries as Ranke and Macaulay' did not materialize because the two had no common language in which to converse. Thus 'there never was a greater failure' than this 'babel of a breakfast'.

None the less, as the author of an article on Ranke and Macaulay published in the *Historische Zeitschrift* of 1867 wrote, these historians were the most celebrated masters in their respective countries. Although they were very different from each other, their historiographical talent was equal. Consequently, he claimed, it was 'in fact no little pleasure to immerse oneself in the peculiarities of their different approaches to research, views, combinations, and accounts'. This is exactly the aim of the present volume. The comparison between the two historiographical cultures, and the investigation into the success or failure of transfers, opens up new views both for an assessment of the intellectual relationship between the two countries, and for an evaluation of the achievements of each historical tradition. This volume is among the first to address these aspects. It takes the long perspective from the Enlightenment to the middle of the twentieth century.

I should like to take the opportunity to thank a number of individuals who helped to make our conference a success. Professor Ernst Breisach, Professor Notker Hammerstein, Professor Georg Iggers, Professor Ernst Schulin, and Dr Stuart Wallace greatly stimulated the discussions which they chaired. Expert and indispensable advice was given by Professor John Burrow and Professor Jürgen Osterhammel who, together with the editors of this volume, formed the steering committee. I especially wish to thank Professor John Burrow for his valuable help when editorial questions arose. The critical comments of Mr Patrick Bahners, Dr Willibald Steinmetz, and Dr Gerrit Walther were very helpful. Special thanks must go to Dr Angela Davies who translated three German essays into English. In her usual precise manner, she revised the English of all other texts, and helped in editing the volume. The relationship between the GHIL and Oxford University Press is a long and fruitful one; many thanks to Ms Anne Ashby for her expertise. Finally, however, the main credit for organizing the conference and for editing this volume is due to Dr Benedikt Stuchtey, and I should like to express my thanks to him.

Peter Wende

London
December 1998

Contents

1. Introduction: Towards a Comparative History of Anglo-German Historiographical Traditions and Transfers   1
   BENEDIKT STUCHTEY and PETER WENDE

2. Universal History and National History: Eighteenth- and Nineteenth-Century German Historians and the Scholarly Community   25
   ULRICH MUHLACK

3. Adam Ferguson's Histories in Germany: English Liberty, Scottish Vigour, and German Rigour   49
   FANIA OZ-SALZBERGER

4. Gibbon and German Historiography   67
   WILFRIED NIPPEL

5. Niebuhr in England: History, Faith, and Order   83
   NORMAN VANCE

6. Stubbs, Maitland, and Constitutional History   99
   JAMES CAMPBELL

7. 'A place among the English Classics': Ranke's *History of the Popes* and its British Readers   123
   PATRICK BAHNERS

8. Lord Acton and German Historiography   159
   HUGH TULLOCH

9. Views and Reviews: Mutual Perceptions of British and German Historians in the Late Nineteenth Century   173
   PETER WENDE

Contents

10. Historicism and the 'Noble Science of Politics' in Nineteenth-Century Germany 191
    GANGOLF HÜBINGER

11. The Historicization of Political Economy? 211
    KEITH TRIBE

12. English Positivism and German Historicism: The Reception of 'Scientific History' in Germany 229
    ECKHARDT FUCHS

13. Historicism and Social Evolution 251
    JOHN BURROW

14. 'Peoples without History' in British and German Historical Thought 265
    JÜRGEN OSTERHAMMEL

15. 'Westward the course of empire takes its way': Imperialism and the Frontier in British and German Historical Writing around 1900 289
    BENEDIKT STUCHTEY

16. The Role of British and German Historians in Mobilizing Public Opinion in 1914 335
    HARTMUT POGGE VON STRANDMANN

17. British Conservative Historiography and the Second World War 373
    REBA N. SOFFER

18. The Web and the Seams: Historiography in an Age of Specialization and Globalization 401
    PETER BURKE

Select Bibliography 410
Notes on Contributors 422
Index of Names 427

I

Introduction

Towards a Comparative History of Anglo-German Historiographical Traditions and Transfers

BENEDIKT STUCHTEY AND PETER WENDE

I

Writing about the beginnings of historical science in eighteenth-century Britain, the German historian Manfred Schlenke pointed out in 1976 that there was little British history of historiography worth mentioning.[1] Since then, however, a number of important pioneering studies have been published in this field, among others by John Kenyon, John Burrow, P. B. M. Blaas, Christopher Parker, Rosemary Jann, Philippa Levine, J. P. von Arx, and Colin Kidd on the Scottish case.[2] Yet to the present day, the study of the history

---

[1] Manfred Schlenke, 'Anfänge einer wissenschaftlichen Geschichtsschreibung in Großbritannien im 18. Jahrhundert', in Karl Hammer and Jürgen Voss (eds.), *Historische Forschung im 18. Jahrhundert: Organisation, Zielsetzung, Ergebnisse* (Pariser Historische Studien 13; Bonn, 1976), 315: 'One must conclude that, in contrast to France and Germany, Britain has a considerable backlog in the field of the history of historiography.' However, as a counter-example to Schlenke's argument we could refer to one of Herbert Butterfield's influential studies which tried to establish Anglo-German links by focusing on Lord Acton, cf. *Man on his Past: The Study of the History of Historical Scholarship* (Cambridge, 1955).

[2] John Kenyon, *The History Men: The Historical Profession in England since the Renaissance* (London, 1983); John Burrow, *A Liberal Descent: Victorian Historians and the English Past* (Cambridge, 1981); id., *Whigs and Liberals: Continuity and Change in English Political Thought* (Oxford, 1988); Piet B. M. Blaas, *Continuity and Anachronism: Parliamentary and Constitutional Development in Whig Historiography and the Anti-Whig Reaction between 1890 and 1930* (The Hague, 1978); Christopher Parker, *The English Historical Tradition since 1850* (Edinburgh, 1990); Rosemary Jann, *The Art and Science of Victorian History* (Columbus, Oh., 1985); Philippa Levine, *The Amateur and the Professional: Antiquarians, Historians and Archaeologists in Victorian England, 1838–1886*

of historiography in Britain has not gained the status of a special branch of historical science to the same extent as in Germany.[3] But in Britain as well as in Germany, where the study of historiography possesses such a long and strong tradition, few attempts have been made at comparative studies going beyond the framework of the national context.[4] Although the study of historiography is currently enjoying remarkable popularity, and several encyclopaedias have been published relatively recently,[5] relations between British and German historical scholarship have not been extensively explored. Nor have the modes of mutual perception, or the ways and means of academic transfers between the two academic communities in the field of history, been studied.[6]

This, of course, is mainly because the evolution of modern

(Cambridge, 1986); Jeffrey Paul von Arx, *Progress and Pessimism: Religion, Politics and History in Late Nineteenth-Century Britain* (Cambridge, Mass., 1985); Colin Kidd, *Subverting Scotland's Past: Scottish Whig Historians and the Creation of an Anglo-British Identity, 1689–c.1830* (Cambridge, 1993). For the wealth of recent literature on this subject, cf. the bibliography at the end of this volume.

[3] The theoretically highly stimulating series *Theorie der Geschichte: Beiträge zur Historik*, 6 vols. (Munich, 1977–90) has been of particular influence in Germany; see also the more recent series edited by Wolfgang Küttler, Jörn Rüsen, and Ernst Schulin, *Geschichtsdiskurs*, 5 vols. (Frankfurt am Main, 1993–9); indispensable for the biographical background are the nine volumes edited by Hans-Ulrich Wehler, *Deutsche Historiker* (Göttingen, 1971–82); see also Ernst Schulin, *Traditionskritik und Rekonstruktionsversuch: Studien zur Entwicklung von Geschichtswissenschaft und historischem Denken* (Göttingen, 1979).

[4] A highly acknowledged work that transcends both national and chronological frontiers is Ernst Breisach, *Historiography: Ancient, Medieval, and Modern* (Chicago, 1983); the classic account of the evolution of German historicism is Friedrich Meinecke, *Die Entstehung des Historismus*, 2 vols. (Munich, 1936); also still valuable is G. P. Gooch's broad overview *History and Historians in the Nineteenth Century* (1913; 2nd edn., London, 1958).

[5] Cf. Michael Bentley (ed.), *Companion to Historiography* (London, 1997); Volker Reinhardt (ed.), *Hauptwerke der Geschichtsschreibung* (Stuttgart, 1997); Kelly Boyd (ed.), *Encyclopedia of Historians and Historical Writing*, 2 vols. (London, 1999).

[6] The few exceptions are relatively old, cf. Klaus Dockhorn, *Der deutsche Historismus in England: Ein Beitrag zur englischen Geistesgeschichte des 19. Jahrhunderts*, with a foreword by G. P. Gooch (Göttingen, 1950); id., *Deutscher Geist und angelsächsische Geistesgeschichte. Ein Versuch der Deutung ihres Verhältnisses* (Göttingen, 1954); Duncan Forbes, 'Historismus in England', *Cambridge Journal*, 4 (1951), 387–400; Charles E. McClelland, *The German Historians and England: A Study in Nineteenth-Century Views* (Cambridge, 1971); Manfred Messerschmidt, *Deutschland in englischer Sicht. Die Wandlungen des Deutschlandbildes in der englischen Geschichtsschreibung* (Düsseldorf, 1955). But see the interesting and thorough book by Rosemary Ashton, *The German Idea: Four English Writers and the Reception of German Thought, 1800–1860* (Cambridge, 1980).

historical science has been closely linked with the rise of nationalism and the ascendancy of the modern nation-state since the beginning of the nineteenth century. Language and tradition, public interest and political implications all made the historian concentrate on his nation's history in the first place. But the great European *res publica litteraria* still existed, that international intellectual community which, in the Middle Ages, had been attached to the church of Christ and which, since the Renaissance and especially during the Enlightenment, had become a transnational congregation of men of letters. Out of this tradition, still vigorous in nineteenth-century Europe, grew numerous contacts, mutual perceptions, and transfers which contributed to the formation of modern historical science in the age of nationalism.

The special achievements of national historiographies can be properly judged only when put into an international context. This volume therefore concentrates on this intricate web of connections. It examines certain aspects and sectors of the relationship between British and German historiography, and particular trends in it.[7] The evolution of modern historical science in both countries coincided with a period of intermittently intense mutual perception. The transfers resulting from this were by no means one-way, but directions changed and gradients varied. By studying the history and typology of intellectual transfers we become aware of the paths and limits of such transfers in the field of historical scholarship.

Moreover, differences between the English and the German paths become apparent, and we find that members of each national tradition idealized the other. German historians of the pre-March period, for example, praised the English model of constitutional freedom, but Prussian historians in Treitschke's political environment, by contrast,

---

[7] This volume is based on a conference held in July 1996. See the Conference Report by Benedikt Stuchtey in *Bulletin of the German Historical Institute London*, 19/1 (May 1997), 82–90. Any possible relations between German and Irish, as distinct from British, historiography still need to be explored. For a general overview see Joseph Lee, 'Some Aspects of Modern Irish Historiography', in Ernst Schulin (ed.), *Gedenkschrift Martin Göhring: Studien zur europäischen Geschichte* (Wiesbaden, 1968), 431–43, and more recently Benedikt Stuchtey, *W. E. H. Lecky (1838–1903): Historisches Denken und politisches Urteilen eines anglo-irischen Gelehrten* (Göttingen, 1997), 119–38.

became increasingly Anglophobic.[8] As Bernd Weisbrod has suggested, the portrait of the other was, to a great degree, a mirror of one's own background. Thus the construction of the history of other nations depended largely on current circumstances at home.[9] The essays in the present volume attempt to elaborate the role of both traditions, and to describe the workings of the motor of transfer. The comparative method is essential to this undertaking. Finally, a third category, that of perception, needs to be examined. This itself is rooted in the cultural conceptions (and ideologies) of one's own national history. Butterfield called this the 'Whig Interpretation of History' in England, and Prussian historians produced the German equivalent for the Kaiserreich.[10]

II

The prelude to the evolution of modern historical science coincided with the climax of the European Enlightenment. The great examples set by Voltaire's *Essai sur les mœurs et l'esprit des nations* and Montesquieu's *De l'esprit des lois* were accepted, admired, and imitated everywhere in Western Europe,[11] but it was English and especially Scottish historians who created new models of historiography. Authors such as Hume and Gibbon, Robertson and Ferguson regarded historiography not only as a civilized recreation, but also as a tool for moral and political instruction, or as the starting point for philosophical reflection of universal relevance.[12] Yet

---

[8] Wolfgang J. Mommsen, 'Zur Entwicklung des Englandbildes der Deutschen seit dem Ende des 18. Jahrhunderts', in Lothar Kettenacker *et al.* (eds.), *Studien zur Geschichte Englands und den deutsch-britischen Beziehungen: Festschrift für Paul Kluke* (Munich, 1981), 375–97.

[9] Bernd Weisbrod, 'Der englische *Sonderweg* in der neueren Geschichte', *Geschichte und Gesellschaft*, 16 (1990), 233–52, here 234.

[10] Bernd Faulenbach, *Ideologie des deutschen Weges: Die deutsche Geschichte in der Historiographie zwischen Kaiserreich und Nationalsozialismus* (Munich, 1980).

[11] Hans-Peter Jaeck, 'Montesquieu als Historiker', *Rechtshistorisches Journal*, 12 (1993), 513–59.

[12] Cf. Kenyon, *History Men*, 41 f.; see also Hermann Gogarten, 'David Hume als Geschichtsschreiber: Ein Beitrag zur englischen Historiographie des 18. Jahrhunderts', *Archiv für Kulturgeschichte*, 61 (1979), 120–53, and the standard work

while they searched for truth among the examples set by history and tried to uncover the constant principles governing human nature by examining men in a variety of historical situations, these historians also looked for methods to verify the results of their efforts in a scientific way. For this end, the historians of the age of Enlightenment also made use of the achievements of antiquarian research, or even adopted its methods.[13] These methods for the critical examination of source material had been developed in the field of classical scholarship since the Renaissance. The sole aim of the antiquarians had been to establish facts beyond doubt, not to construct historical narratives dealing with 'eternal truths' which could never be the subject of critical studies.

Those historians who presented *historia* as *magistra vitae* made sporadic use of the results of the antiquarians' endeavours to corroborate the truths they claimed to have distilled from history. This was even more the case with a historian such as Hume, who wanted to prove a political point.[14] Aspiring to literary success in order to arouse intellectual interest, Hume had set out to demolish the reigning Whig view of seventeenth-century English history not only by the strength of his arguments, but also by producing documentary evidence. Thus he combined the method of the antiquarian with a literary style.[15] By placing the achievements of traditional antiquarianism into the context of narrative history, he produced 'the first national history that was both critical and readable'.[16]

---

on Hume by Nicholas Phillipson (New York, 1989); on Gibbon cf. John Burrow, *Gibbon* (Oxford, 1985), and Roy Porter, *Gibbon: Making History* (London, 1988); on Robertson, Manfred Schlenke's essay is still instructive: 'Aus der Frühzeit des englischen Historismus: William Robertsons Beitrag zur methodischen Grundlegung der Geschichtswissenschaft im 18. Jahrhundert', *Saeculum*, 7 (1956), 107–25.

[13] Ulrich Muhlack, 'Von der philologischen zur historischen Methode', in Christian Meier and Jörn Rüsen (eds.), *Theorie der Geschichte, Beiträge zur Historik: Historische Methode*, v (Munich, 1988), 168.

[14] Jürgen Osterhammel, 'Nation und Zivilisation in der britischen Historiographie von Hume bis Macaulay', *Historische Zeitschrift*, 254 (1992), 281–340.

[15] Ulrich Muhlack, *Geschichtswissenschaft im Humanismus und in der Aufklärung: Die Vorgeschichte des Historismus* (Munich, 1991), 395; see also Joseph M. Levine, *Humanism and History: Origins of Modern English Historiography* (Ithaca, NY, 1987).

[16] V. G. Wechsler, *David Hume and the 'History of England'* (Philadelphia, 1979), 101.

The rise of British historiography during the second half of the eighteenth century was stimulated by a huge demand among a growing reading public with a strong interest in history. It flourished in a free market which guaranteed the liberty of the press, and where this demand could be met by a rapidly expanding editing and printing industry. These were the conditions which facilitated the monumental achievements of Gibbon and Hume, who provided the towering models for historians all over Europe. In this context of intellectual transfers from west to east during the Enlightenment, British and especially Scottish historical scholarship also gained a strong readership in Germany.

Here the evolution of historical science had taken a different path. The driving force behind its formation originated in the peculiar conditions of political particularism within the German Empire. During the eighteenth century historical scholarship had served as a handmaiden to public law and politics. Whenever evidence was needed in the many legal disputes between the Estates of the Empire, it had to be drawn from history. Therefore history became an important part of the study of public law at the numerous German universities, especially, at first, at Halle, and then at Göttingen. Here the tools were acquired for gaining and critically assessing historical facts, which were gathered and then published in learned handbooks and compendia. Though little historiography was written with an eye to a wider public, the means for scholarly precision had been developed, and they could also be applied in the wider context of historical science proper.[17]

The impact of the great works of the historians of the Scottish Enlightenment (for example, Gibbon, Hume, and Robertson) has to be judged against this background of nascent historical erudition.[18] Though these were read and

---

[17] Notker Hammerstein, *Jus und Historie: Ein Beitrag zur Geschichte des historischen Denkens an deutschen Universitäten im späten 17. und im 18. Jahrhundert* (Göttingen, 1972), 377.

[18] The influence of the Enlightenment on 19th-century English historiography has now been pointed out by P. R. Ghosh, 'Macaulay and the Heritage of the Enlightenment', *English Historical Review*, 112 (1997), 358–95. For the importance of 18th-century literature in the particular case of Macaulay cf. Mark Phillips, 'Macaulay, Scott and the Literary Challenge to Historiography', *Journal of the History of Ideas*, 1 (1989), 117–33.

greatly appreciated by a small but growing intellectual readership, they did not stimulate German historians to follow their example. Perceptions do not necessarily inaugurate transfers in the manner of an import-export business, the more so as intellectual perception, especially in the field of historiography, is conditioned by national differences in political and scholarly culture which normally determine and control aspects and points of view, and canalize transfers.[19]

Fania Oz-Salzberger, writing in this volume, demonstrates this in the case of the Scottish philosopher-historian Adam Ferguson. Though his works, especially his *Essay on the History of Civil Society* and the *History of the Progress and Termination of the Roman Republic*, were avidly read by German intellectuals, the author's underlying republicanism was either overlooked, ignored, regretted, or even treated with hostility, as it did not fit into the conceptual framework of contemporary German political thought. As the former book fell into the genre of 'universal history' which was beginning to be cultivated with growing self-confidence by German historians, political criticism was presented in the guise of historiographical critique. Thus Ferguson's German translator annotated the work in such a way as to present the author's republicanism as the result of a partial selection and biased reading of his sources. Moreover, Ferguson's influence on the German discourse was felt not only in the historiographical area, but also in political thinking, and moral philosophy. While his 'Scottishness' was valued by his German recipients because it was seen as offering a stimulating political and cultural model, Ferguson's 'Englishness' was rejected.

The extent to which self-confident erudition provided a critical filter for transfers is demonstrated by *The Universal History from the Earliest Account of Time to the Present Compiled from the Original Authors*, which was published in Britain in thirty-eight volumes between the years 1736 and 1765. Scholars at the University of Göttingen soon took notice of this compilation, and started to translate a considerable

[19] Rudolf Muhs, Johannes Paulmann, and Willibald Steinmetz (eds.), *Aneignung und Abwehr. Interkultureller Transfer zwischen Deutschland und Großbritannien im 19. Jahrhundert* (Bodenheim, 1998).

number of its many volumes.[20] But at the same time it provoked criticism which expressed the aspirations of nascent German historicism. The learned Johann Christoph Gatterer, for example, pointed to its lack of coherence and called it a mere addition of individual national narratives without unifying thought or principle, a compendium without sustaining philosophical ideas.[21]

In contrast to the universal histories produced hitherto, Gatterer launched an idea for a philosophical framing of world history. Accordingly, his history of humanity followed one scientific principle: the historical. As an admirer of French and British historiography, especially Voltaire and Montesquieu, Hume and Robertson, Gatterer paved the way both for debate and for transfer. This can be traced in the way he kept his distance from mere political and diplomatic, Reich-centred history. Instead he advocated a cultural and social history which also took moral, religious, and many other aspects into account. This was the beginning of a new, historicist approach. In his attempt to give history a theoretical basis, and to define the historian's aim as that of understanding rather than teaching or illustrating, Gatterer was an important mediator between the late eighteenth and early nineteenth centuries.[22] In this context history was primarily a means of rationally assessing the past without drawing moral lessons or aiming for educational objectives; history was seen as a value in itself, and therefore scientific history henceforward needed to be distinguished from the philosophy of history.

German historians such as Gatterer not only envied but also sharply criticized the elegant narratives of the great historians of the western Enlightenment. The art of the historical narrator was contrasted with a passion for establishing the truth by scientific methods. As Wilfried Nippel

---

[20] The present volume does not contain an essay specifically devoted to the ambivalence and possible misunderstandings that can arise from translations. However, this problem is addressed in a number of essays in this volume.

[21] Hammerstein, *Jus und Historie*, 367.

[22] In general see Peter Hanns Reill, *The German Enlightenment and the Rise of Historicism* (Berkeley and Los Angeles, 1975); for Gatterer see id., 'History and Hermeneutics in the *Aufklärung*: The Thought of Johann Christoph Gatterer', *Journal of Modern History*, 45 (1973), 24–51.

shows, this was the case with the German perception of Edward Gibbon. Though critics praised his *Decline and Fall* as a great work of art, the Göttingen historian Spittler, for example, pointed out in 1788 that it fell short of German standards of profound and exact scholarship, especially with regard to its treatment of sources. Unlike Ferguson, Gibbon has never really been accepted by German historians to the present day, and a complete German translation of his masterpiece is still not available. Instead, Niebuhr counted from the start as one of the founding fathers of German ancient history, indeed of historicism, although this view certainly undervalued the significance of the studies of Antiquity dating from the sixteenth to the eighteenth centuries upon which Gibbon had built.[23] According to Norman Vance, there is a long history of perception and reception of Niebuhr in Britain, and his *Römische Geschichte* immediately influenced his British colleagues. From Thomas Arnold's studies of Roman history at the beginning of the nineteenth century to Macaulay's *Lays of Ancient Rome* and Seeley's vision of Britain's imperial mission which was based on Niebuhr's account of the Roman Empire, many English works revealed a debt to Niebuhr. The liberal Anglicans (including Hare, Thirlwall, Whately, and Milman) welcomed his work on the early history of Rome and were fascinated by his presentation of Roman mythology. Niebuhr had questioned the origins of traditional political and religious notions, supplying contemporary Homeric and biblical critics with arguments in the process. Niebuhr must therefore be seen as having played an important part in English revisionism. In the context of the religious debate his ideas were reminiscent of those of the deist John Toland, of whose work, however, he was presumably unaware.[24]

---

[23] The standard work on Niebuhr is now Gerrit Walther, *Niebuhrs Forschung* (Stuttgart, 1993).
[24] See Ulrich Muhlack, 'Die deutschen Einwirkungen auf die englische Altertumswissenschaft am Beispiel George Grotes', in Mayotte Bollack and Heinz Wismann (eds.), *Philologie und Hermeneutik im 19. Jahrhundert: Philologie et herméneutique au 19ème siècle*, ii (Göttingen, 1983), 376–93.

III

If historicism is defined as the decisive stage in the formation of modern historical science, the beginnings of this process in Germany can be traced back to the period before the French Revolution.[25] Yet it was the impact of this revolution which produced the final impetus for the take-off in this development just as it was the French Revolution that motivated the study of both history and nation. The evolution of historical science in Germany was subjected to influences from two different directions. History, as Edmund Burke had demonstrated, provided defensive weapons against the assault of revolutionary doctrines on the one hand.[26] On the other, it showed the Germans an alternative route to the cherished goal of the nation-state.

Whereas the French Revolution made visible the all-consuming power of a modern nation based on the *volonté générale*, the Germans tried to reassemble a glorious national history from the broken pieces of a turbulent past in order to provide a focus for national identity. This would prove to be a most demanding task, and was to keep German historians immensely busy for more than a century.[27] During this process scholars such as Niebuhr refined the tools for assessing truth among the tangled mass of historical traditions, and others critically examined sources for the collections of the *Monumenta Germaniae Historica*. In striving to accomplish the great national task German historians, as Ulrich Muhlack argues in this volume, at the same time contributed decisively to the universal task of establishing history as a science and an academic discipline. And to the extent to which the achieve-

---

[25] Despite the polemics by Nietzsche, Popper, and other enemies of historicism, this phenomenon has always attracted great attention and stimulated important controversies among different camps (including politically different ones); for new assessments cf. Annette Wittkau, *Historismus: Zur Geschichte des Begriffs und des Problems* (Göttingen, 1992); Friedrich Jaeger and Jörn Rüsen, *Geschichte des Historismus: Eine Einführung* (Munich, 1992); Jörn Rüsen, *Konfigurationen des Historismus: Studien zur deutschen Wissenschaftskultur* (Frankfurt am Main, 1993).

[26] Some stimulating ideas can still be drawn from John C. Weston, 'Edmund Burke's View of History', *Review of Politics*, 23 (1961), 203–29.

[27] Ernst Schulin, 'Fortschrittsdrang und Renaissance der Vergangenheit: Die Veränderung des Kulturbewußtseins in Aufklärung und Historismus', *Freiburger Universitätsblätter*, 126 (Dec. 1994), 53.

ments of German historicism culminate in the works of Ranke, most of these were contributions to universal history, or at least the history of the European system of states.

Finally, historicism meant not only the evolution of historical science, but also, according to Ernst Troeltsch, the fundamental historicization of human thought and culture.[28] Hegel established the identity of history and philosophy, and in his system of historical materialism Marx based revolution on history. Muhlack also points to the problem of the polarization of German historiography in the nineteenth century between universality and the republic of scholars on the one hand, and nationality and patriotic thinking on the other. Ultimately, this dichotomy was overcome not only by the idea of a national mission and the notion that German historians were destined for historicist thinking, not least because of the German language, but also by the idea that to study the history of a particular nation is to study the history of mankind in its concrete reality.

The relations between German and British historians during the nineteenth century were governed by the paradox that at a time when the focus of historical interest narrowed and concentrated on national history in Britain, it was also open to influences from abroad, especially from Germany.[29] Now the tables were turned between British and German historians; the direction of transfer had changed. In England as a consolidated nation-state which had successfully resisted and finally defeated French aggression, the impact of the French Revolution was different. Historiography flourished as it turned to national history in order to tell a rapidly growing reading public the heroic success story of the rise of Great Britain. And there was no need critically to scrutinize a long-gone past in order to make it the starting point of national tradition.[30] There was no demand

---

[28] Ernst Troeltsch, *Der Historismus und seine Probleme* (*Gesammelte Schriften*, iii; Tübingen, 1922; new edn., Aalen, 1972), 102.

[29] Jürgen Osterhammel, 'Epochen der britischen Geschichtsschreibung', in Küttler, Rüsen, and Schulin (eds.), *Geschichtsdiskurs*, i. 157.

[30] Hedva Ben-Israel, *English Historians on the French Revolution* (Cambridge, 1968); Barton R. Friedman, *Fabricating History: English Writers on the French Revolution* (Princeton, 1988).

for this, and Britain lacked institutions capable of developing academic scholarship in the field of history.

Academies did not yet exist, and at the universities, as a pamphlet stated in 1856, 'there is practically no study of history . . ., a fact almost incredible in a country which has produced so many good historians'.[31] The Regius chairs at Oxford and Cambridge were sinecures, and did not involve any genuine obligation to teach history. Nor did the Scottish universities serve as centres for research. Thus John Stuart Blackie, Professor of Classics at Edinburgh, complained in 1855: 'The historical department of our Scottish universities is either blanc or a farce (whereas) Berlin has Ranke, and every petty German academia can tell her men of profound historical research by the dozen.'[32] Soon Sir John Robert Seeley would state that 'as a rule good books are in German',[33] and in George Eliot's *Middlemarch* the eminent scholar Casaubon is doomed to intellectual failure because he has not studied the works of the appropriate German scholars. The fact that in England public records had been kept at the State Paper Office since 1578 did not stimulate archival research, and when the *Rolls Series* was started in 1857 it was only a crude imitation of the *Monumenta Germaniae Historica* on which it was consciously modelled. The continuing success of the gentleman-historian also to a certain extent obstructed the development of a modern historical science based on meticulous scholarship. Macaulay and Carlyle were succeeded by Froude, Freeman, Buckle, Lecky, and Green who 'were deaf to the dictates of Ranke and his German colleagues'.[34] The story of the slow and, in the European context, belated professionalization (and institutionalization) of history in Britain, where

---

[31] Quoted in Schlenke, 'Anfänge', 321.   [32] Ibid.
[33] John Robert Seeley, *Lectures and Essays* (London, 1870), 235; the basic book on Seeley is still Deborah Wormell, *Sir John Seeley and the Uses of History* (Cambridge, 1980).
[34] Kenyon, *History Men*, 97. Freeman's ideas were particularly strong in this field. See *The Methods of Historical Study: Eight Lectures Read in the University of Oxford in Michaelmas Term, 1884* (London, 1886). However, a counter-example is the Catholic historian John Lingard, whose interpretation of the Reformation remained very influential throughout the 19th century. See Donald F. Shea, *The English Ranke: John Lingard* (New York, 1969). On the connections between historiography and modernity cf. J. A. Schmiechen, 'The Victorians, the Historians, and the Idea of Modernism', *American Historical Review*, 93 (1988), 287–316.

even in 1891 there was not a single historian among the sixty Fellows of Trinity College, Cambridge, has been told in several well-known studies.[35] It has therefore not been chosen as a topic for the present volume. The problem is inherent in many of the essays in any case, and certainly the contrast between scholars as civil servants (as in Germany) and as amateur 'men of letters' (as in England) was not only a historiographical one, but also had social and political dimensions.

When the influential British magazines took notice of Ranke and published lengthy reviews, German historical scholarship achieved a kind of breakthrough, as the contributions by Patrick Bahners and Peter Wende show. And when Stubbs initiated the translation of Ranke's *Englische Geschichte* by six Oxford colleagues his intention was to set up a signpost showing British historians the way towards true scholarship. Though he was disappointed by the reaction of the general reading public, which treated 'his [Ranke's] work as on the same plane with those of the ephemeral writers whose reputation is so carefully nursed in what is called literary society',[36] the Oxford school of history he established was to become an important access door for the scholarly techniques and academic institutions of German historicism.

The same applies to Cambridge where Acton and Seeley were Regius Professors of History. The second half of the nineteenth century thus marked the climax of transfers and the influence in Britain of German scholarly achievements

---

[35] Felix Gilbert, 'The Professionalization of History in the Nineteenth Century', in John Higham, Leonard Krieger, and Felix Gilbert (eds.), *History* (Englewood Cliffs, NJ, 1965), 335 f.; for the case of Oxford see Reba Soffer, 'Nation, Duty, Character and Confidence: History at Oxford, 1850–1914', *Historical Journal*, 30 (1987), 77–104; see also Peter Slee, *Learning and a Liberal Education: The Study of Modern History in the Universities of Oxford, Cambridge and Manchester 1800–1914* (Manchester, 1986); Doris S. Goldstein, 'The Professionalisation of History in Britain in the Late Nineteenth and Early Twentieth Century', *Storia della storiographia*, 3 (1983), 3–27; ead., 'History at Oxford and Cambridge: Professionalization and the Influence of Ranke', in Georg G. Iggers and James M. Powell (eds.), *Leopold von Ranke and the Shaping of the Historical Discipline* (Syracuse, NY, 1990), 141–53.

[36] William Stubbs, 'On the Present State and Prospect of Historical Study' (1876), in *Seventeen Lectures* (Oxford, 1900), 65.

in the field of history.[37] As soon as the *English Historical Review*, the last of the great national periodicals, was founded in 1886, intellectual interchange became institutionalized as mutual perception by the reviewing of each other's books, the subject of Peter Wende's contribution to this volume. The first numbers of the *Historische Zeitschrift* (1859) and the *EHR* laid the foundations for a lively history of mutual reception which was interrupted only by the outbreak of the First World War. While German historians were interested in English history in general, the British side displayed more interest in the methodology and organization of German historiography.

As regards the subject matter of histories, there were close contacts with Germany in the study of English medieval history, which played a central part in the development of historical science in Britain. In his essay James Campbell discusses how Stubbs and Maitland made the study of constitutional history an Anglo-German enterprise. Here the influence of German historicism was particularly effective. Stubbs's famous *Constitutional History of England*, which owed a debt to the German *Historische Rechtsschule*, is not only one of the most influential works of British historiography, but its source criticism also adopted the criteria developed by continental historians. Initially, it evoked a greater response in Germany than in England. Like Stubbs, Maitland enjoyed a positive reception in Germany, for example, by Otto Brunner. Other scholars including Savigny, Grimm, Waitz, Liebermann, Pauli, and Gierke also made many valuable contributions, but to try to trace their influence in British works at every point would be 'an immense and probably unrewarding undertaking'.[38]

IV

The fact that historians such as Freeman, for example, deliberately played down their debt to German historicism[39] leads

---

[37] Cf. especially Burrow, *Descent*, ch. 5.
[38] Burrow, *Descent*, 120.
[39] Ibid.

to the important question of barriers to transfers and limits to perception, a question addressed by many of the contributors to this volume.

As a general rule, British historians adopted historicism only so far as its technical and practical side was concerned, while its philosophical or even political basis was, on the whole, ignored.[40] But there are notable exceptions. According to James Campbell, Stubbs's idea of progress in the manner of the self-realization of the state, and Maitland's concept of the reification and personalization of the nation-state, were developed in the spirit of historicism. And in his seminal work *The Growth of British Policy*, Seeley, the most 'German' of British historians,[41] related how in the course of its history Britain came, as John Burrow demonstrates, to consciousness and the realization of its national individuality in a manner which can be seen as a movement of Hegel's 'World Spirit'. Seeley was a historian with a political mission which could fit into the framework of the philosophy of German idealism. Most of his British colleagues who kept on writing history according to the ancient notion that history teaches life adopted the modern techniques developed by critical historical scholarship, but they stopped short of subscribing to the essence of historicism, that is, the idea of the autonomy of historical judgement.

As Hugh Tulloch suggests in this volume, Lord Acton's famous article 'German Schools of History' in this respect forms a singular landmark in the context of perceptions and transfers between British and German scholars in the nineteenth century. When Acton separated the techniques of German historical scholarship from its philosophical and political implications, his criticism was provoked by the involvement of German historicism with German nationalism, and by what he regarded as the amoral relativism of the historians' impartiality.[42] Acton criticized the nationalism espoused by German historians after 1848 as a force counteracting the church and individual conscience; accordingly,

---

[40] Osterhammel, 'Epochen', 161. [41] p. 256 below.
[42] Cf. Owen Chadwick, *Acton, Döllinger and History* (The 1986 Annual Lecture of the German Historical Institute London; London, 1987).

he observed the political significance of historicism with suspicion, which set him apart from Froude, Seeley, and Maine. His specifically liberal system, which aimed to combine the scientific nature of German historiography with a model of freedom built on an ethical foundation, aspired to overcome German historical relativism such as Ranke's, for example. Probably not many other British historians before G. P. Gooch and Herbert Butterfield had displayed so much interest in German historiography. Seeley and Stubbs are certainly exceptional here, famously objecting to English insularity. The same holds true for G. W. Prothero, editor of the *Quarterly Review* from 1899, who had been a student at Sybel's seminar at Bonn, and A. W. Ward who had studied history in Saxony.[43]

The example of German perceptions of the Scottish philosophical and political Enlightenment has already demonstrated that influences can operate via adequate appreciation and understanding of foreign examples as well as through misunderstandings or distorted views. And in the field of historiography, models can be adopted and transfers can take place only within a range of receptivity delimited by cultural preconceptions and political conditions. Thus Acton was not the first to qualify the achievements of German historicism by criticizing the deficiencies of its moral dimension. Aspects of Niebuhr's influence on English critical revisionism in the early nineteenth century, such as the reception of his criticism of the traditional myths of ancient Rome, were from the very start drawn into the great debate between traditionalists and progressives. This kind of historical criticism was regarded as a direct challenge to traditional religiosity whose faith was based on the most sacred of all ancient texts, the Bible. The impact of religiousness on nineteenth-century British thought erected a firm barrier to the methodological and philosophical implications of historicism.

This also applies to Ranke, as Patrick Bahners points out, despite the fact that some British contemporaries, such as

---

[43] Reba N. Soffer, *Discipline and Power: The University, History and the Making of an English Elite, 1870–1930* (Stanford, Calif., 1994), 75.

Macaulay, were prepared to give his *History of the Popes* 'a place among the English classics'. This work, four different English translations of which were published between 1840 and 1846, was highly praised because it displayed the main achievements of modern German historical scholarship—meticulous study of the sources and calm impartial judgement. Liberal Protestants and liberal Catholics alike approved of this approach, while the orthodox wing accused Ranke of not committing himself clearly to one side or the other. This very objectivity was criticized on the grounds of contemporary religious policy, and when some reviewers accused Ranke of having a blind spot for the forces of religion in general and the policies of the popes in particular, they argued from the basis of the English tradition of propagating and exercising the moral function of history against Ranke's 'sovereignty of history, the exclusion of all external interference'.[44] Ranke's critics associated the secular interpretation of religious history with the rationalism of German Bible criticism, thus preparing their objections to the moral relativism of historicism. Again, the perception of the historian's œuvre can be regarded as part of a contemporary religious and political discussion. In England, Ranke's *History of the Popes* must be seen against the background of the Oxford Movement and Catholic emancipation. Ranke's teleological, progress-orientated principle had historicized the papacy, which no longer posed a threat to Protestant Europe.

In addition to dams, dykes, and locks which to a certain extent regulate the flow of transfers, there are bypasses and twisted byways which allow unexpected influences in unexpected places. This aplies to the study of economics and economic history as discussed by Keith Tribe in this volume. The German historical school of economics originated in a decided reaction against the classical school of British political economy. The writings of Roscher and Hildebrand were studied in England, but this did not lead to the establishment of economics as a British historical enterprise. Their influence was, instead, limited to contributing to the formation of the academic discipline of economic history as a

[44] p. 133 below.

subdiscipline of history, as the careers of William Cunningham and William Ashley demonstrate. Cunningham's pioneering *The Growth of English Industry and Commerce* (1882–1910) was itself a critique of the political economics of Alfred Marshall. And when Cliffe Leslie, for example, advocated economic historicism, this was the result not of his having read Roscher but rather of the influence of Leslie's academic teacher, Henry Maine, whose historicism derived from Savigny and the German Historical School of Law.[45]

V

Even during the age of historicism, when the impact of German historical science on its British counterpart was exceptionally strong, there were clear limits to transfers. Moreover, these transfers were not unidirectional. In certain aspects Germany, too, was at the receiving end. British historians, whose art of history-telling attracted a wide reading public, continued to set standards for German historiography as Peter Wende shows. To write history in the Macaulayan fashion remained the ambitious goal of many of his German colleagues, and in 1867 Rudolf Köpke praised his teacher Ranke because he 'certainly bears comparison with the great men of other nations'.[46] The national political mission of historiography, as postulated in the age of the formation of the German nation-state, meant that German historians would continue to regard authors such as Macaulay or Froude as their role models.

Further barriers to the influence of historicism were erected by the inherent limits of historicism itself—not only with regard to its philosophical or simply moral implications, but in view of its limited subject matter. This centred, as is evident from Ranke's work, on the evolution of the modern

---

[45] Cf. Gerard M. Koot, *English Historical Economics, 1870–1926* (Cambridge, 1987); for historicism in the German discipline of economics see Bertram Schefold, 'Karl Bücher und der Historismus in der deutschen Nationalökonomie', in Notker Hammerstein (ed.), *Deutsche Geschichtswissenschaft um 1900* (Stuttgart, 1988), 239–67.

[46] p. 28 below.

European state and the formation of the European system of states. History was, in the first place, the history of politics: High Politics and Foreign Politics. Henry Thomas Buckle's *History of Civilization in England* (1857, 1861) therefore owed nothing to German influences, but was heavily indebted to Auguste Comte and French positivism.[47] Nevertheless, it was immediately translated into German, although its translator, Arnold Ruge, an ardent disciple of Hegel, found fault with its underlying philosophy.[48] And although Droysen later savagely criticized the book,[49] Eckhardt Fuchs suggests in his essay that it stimulated debates on alternatives to historicism which, in Germany, prepared the theoretical and methodological ground for the famous Lamprecht controversy starting in 1891.[50] German historiography, therefore, was not untouched by positivist 'scientific history' as proposed by Buckle. Consequently, positivism should not be seen as an irreconcilable contrast with historicism, but rather as a complement that even helped to popularize historicism.

The extent to which the limits of historicism shaped influences and transfers from Britain to Germany is illustrated by Jürgen Osterhammel's contribution on 'Peoples without History'. After 1800, Enlightenment interest in the histories of non-Western, non-European civilizations continued to thrive in Britain, to a large extent, of course, in the wake of the expansion of the second British Empire. In Germany, even 'world history' focused mainly on Europe as the allegedly decisive, driving force in the history of mankind. Therefore, the great Eastern civilizations aroused only marginal interest among German historians, and the so-called 'primitive races' none at all. This blind spot, on the other hand, left space in Germany for the development of new disciplines, namely

[47] Cf. T. R. Wright, *The Religion of Humanity. The Impact of Comtean Positivism on Victorian Britain* (Cambridge, 1986); but see also Christopher Parker, 'English Historians and the Opposition to Positivism', *History and Theory*, 22 (1983), 120–45.

[48] *Geschichte der Zivilisation in England von H. T. Buckle*, trans. Arnold Ruge, 2 vols. (Leipzig, 1860), i. 61.

[49] Johann Gustav Droysen, 'Die Erhebung der Geschichte zum Rang einer Wissenschaft', *Historische Zeitschrift*, 9 (1863), 1–22.

[50] For this context the standard work is by Roger Chickering, *Karl Lamprecht. A German Academic Life (1856–1915)* (Atlantic Highlands, NJ, 1993).

ethnology and historical geography, which tried to overcome the Eurocentricity of classical European historiography.[51] Lewis Henry Morgan's cultural history, *Ancient Society*, was translated into German in 1877 as *Die Urgesellschaft* and was of considerable significance at a time when the German Society for Anthropology, Ethnology, and Ancient History was founded in Berlin. Links with the cultural history of both Buckle and Lamprecht may be drawn here, thereby closing the circle as regards the role of positivism.

But as neither Buckle's positivism nor the continuing Enlightenment tradition in British historiography represented serious challenges to the tenets of historicism, it was evolutionism which could be regarded as its extreme opposite. While historicism was associated with the idea of the individuality of various peoples, social evolution was related to universal theories of stages. However, as John Burrow indicates, Herbert Spencer's philosophy, for example, is linked to historicism by, among other things, the influence of German *Naturphilosophie*. Yet evolutionism of Anglo-Saxon origin was taken up not so much by German historians or even anthropologists as by German socialists.

VI

A closer look at perceptions and transfers does not reveal simple relations in the manner of give and take, but an intricate network of complex cross-fertilizations. On the one hand, obvious connections might be broken by hidden counter-currents; on the other hand barriers can be overcome or circumvented in a similar manner. But 'international relations' in the field of historical science were at all times dominated and regulated by the traditions of political culture, and the great tasks and problems of the national politics of the countries involved. The fact that historiography as well as historical science is either directly or indirectly always linked to politics, is in any case the

---

[51] In Britain the rise of anthropology played a similarly important role, cf. George W. Stocking, *Victorian Anthropology* (New York, 1987).

essential prerequisite for intellectual contacts and relationships.[52]

Even when history finally became established at British universities, as part of the academic curriculum it had to contribute to the process of forming the English élite. Teaching national values ranked above research; England's history, according to its Whiggish viewpoint, was to be shown as continuous political and constitutional progress, because, as Edward Pusey put it: 'We make not books but men.'[53] Especially in the historiography of imperialism, political missions prevailed, as Benedikt Stuchtey argues in this volume in his comparison of British and German historical writing around 1900. Starting from the frontier thesis put forward by the American historian Frederick Jackson Turner, Stuchtey suggests that the British Empire can be presented as a living organism and its expansion described in terms of drawing a cultural boundary between civilization and the wild. Like Turner, British imperial historians tended to concentrate on white colonization. This holds true not only for those who interpreted the expansion of Empire in terms of the expanding frontier of Anglo-Saxon civilization, but also for Seeley, whose *Expansion of England* must be seen as an important contribution to the political education of his contemporaries in matters of Empire.

Thus the historian who replaced the dramatic narrations of heroic deeds with an account of causes and effects did not, as Trevelyan complained in 1913, 'sacrifice the tradition of English history' at 'German shrines'.[54] The same applies to the German side. Although as a rule professional historians in Germany adhered to the ideal of objectivity achieved in total political independence, the study of history was conceived of as the study of political progress defined in

---

[52] See the classic essay by John Roach, 'Liberalism and the Victorian Intelligentsia', *Historical Journal*, 13 (1957), 58–81; the best recent studies are by Stefan Collini, especially his *Public Moralists: Political Thought and Intellectual Life in Britain, 1850–1930* (Oxford, 1991), and id. with J. Burrow and D. Winch, *That Noble Science of Politics: A Study in Nineteenth-Century Intellectual History* (Cambridge, 1983).

[53] Soffer, *Discipline and Power*, 14; further see, for an earlier period, Olive Anderson, 'The Political Uses of History in Mid Nineteenth-Century England', *Past and Present*, 36 (1967), 87–105.   [54] Soffer, *Discipline and Power*, 125.

terms of the formation of the German nation-state.[55] At the same time, as Gangolf Hübinger shows in his essay, German historicism was closely linked with the formation of modern political science, especially from the 1830s onwards when Dahlmann's *Politik*, for example, was first published.

Finally, power politics dealt a shattering blow to Anglo-German relations in the domain of history.[56] The relationship had begun to deteriorate at the end of the century with escalating political rivalry until the First World War cut links almost completely for a considerable time.[57] The war turned many pro-German British historians and their Anglophile German colleagues into ardent nationalists, making them close ranks with their governments' policies and actively join in a war of pamphlets against each other. In October 1914 nearly all of Germany's university professors signed a joint declaration justifying Germany's military engagement,[58] and in July 1915, 1,347 German intellectuals, including many historians, expressly encouraged the German government in its radical war aims.[59] Hartmut Pogge von Strandmann shows that from the start, nationalist historians in Britain were busy

---

[55] Cf. Georg G. Iggers, *The German Conception of History: The National Tradition of Historical Thought from Herder to the Present* (Middletown, Conn., 1968).

[56] Cf. in general Walter Laqueur and George L. Mosse (eds.), *Historians in Politics* (London, 1974); for Germany see Fritz K. Ringer, *The Decline of the German Mandarins: The German Academic Community, 1890–1933* (Cambridge, Mass., 1969).

[57] There is a large amount of recent literature on this topic: for example, Jean-Jacques Becker, Jay M. Winter, Gerd Krumeich, Annette Becker, and Stéphane Audoin-Rouzeau (eds.), *Guerre et cultures 1914–1918* (Paris, 1994); Gerhard Hirschfeld, Gerd Krumeich, Dieter Langewiesche, and Hans Peter Ullmann (eds.), *Kriegserfahrungen: Studien zur Sozial- und Mentalitätsgeschichte des Ersten Weltkriegs* (Essen, 1997); Wolfgang J. Mommsen (ed.), *Kultur und Krieg: Die Rolle der Intellektuellen, Künstler und Schriftsteller im Ersten Weltkrieg* (Munich, 1996). See also the account by Fritz Stern, 'Die Historiker und der Erste Weltkrieg. Eigenes Erleben und öffentliche Deutung', in id., *Verspielte Größe: Essays zur deutschen Geschichte des 20. Jahrhunderts* (Munich, 1996), 37–68.

[58] 'Erklärung der Hochschullehrer des Deutschen Reiches', reprinted in Bernhard vom Brocke, 'Wissenschaft und Militarismus: Der Aufruf der 93 "An die Kulturwelt!" und der Zusammenbruch der internationalen Gelehrtenrepublik im Ersten Weltkrieg', in William Calder, Hellmut Flashar, and Theodor Lindken (eds.), *Wilamowitz nach fünfzig Jahren* (Darmstadt, 1985), 717.

[59] e.g. the historian Dietrich Schäfer in his speech: 'Rede in der Versammlung des "Unabhängigen Ausschusses für einen Deutschen Frieden"', in id., *Durch deutschen Sieg zum deutschen Frieden: Fünf Reden zur Lage* (Berlin, 1917), 8–13.

discussing the 'war guilt question'. Many went into government service. The analysis of the Oxford War Pamphlets sheds light on how British scholars differed from German scholars by actually educating the public for war. Conservative and liberal historians united, and identified with the state and the government much more strongly than was the case after 1945, for example, and in this context the enduring impact of the Boer War of 1899 to 1902 was still felt.[60]

After this watershed in Anglo-German scholarly relations the gulf was not bridged again until after the Second World War. The final defeat of nationalism on the German side as well as the repercussions of the gruesome experience of the war in general also shaped the understanding and writing of history after 1945 in Britain, as Reba Soffer explains in her analysis of Herbert Butterfield's Christian conservatism. He regarded this as a necessary prerequisite for the historian dealing with the roots and results of human evil.[61] In a way, Butterfield took up the theme Lord Acton had developed in his dialogue with German historicism. Soffer argues that British historians had been able to triumph after 1918. Their political scepticism, inherent in conservatism, was strengthened by the rise of fascism and communism in Europe. After 1945, by contrast, British historians showed symptoms of insecurity as a result of the loss of the Empire and the electoral victory of the Labour Party. Butterfield's *Whig Interpretation of History* (1931) was a polemic against liberal values; by 1944, his *The Englishman and his Past* revealed a conservative standpoint. What remained was distrust of all governments and a conservative disillusionment.

It goes without saying that today academic relations in the field of historical science are not limited to the form of a nineteenth-century dialogue between two countries. Rather, they are part of the globe-spanning international

---

[60] Stuart Wallace, *War and the Image of Germany: British Academics 1914–1918* (Edinburgh, 1988).
[61] Cf. Geoffrey R. Elton, 'Herbert Butterfield and the Study of History', *Historical Journal*, 27 (1984), 729–43.

discussion among historians in the age of numerous and often huge conferences, and ever-expanding communications via the modern media.[62] In this respect the national character of nineteenth-century historiography was much less conducive to scholarly co-operation than the more international character of the discipline in both the eighteenth and the twentieth centuries.[63]

The many 'varieties of historiography' and the tension between globalization and specialization are addressed by Peter Burke in the concluding essay. These are described as consequences of two ruling principles. Centripetal forces are visible in the context of the globalization of an increasingly interlinked world; centrifugal forces, by contrast, lead to the fragmentation of the historical discipline (the history of everyday life, micro-history, etc.) and a more and more complicated particularization that makes colleagues become specialists among specialists. Since the end of the Cold War there no longer seem to be any obstacles to the establishment of a worldwide *res publica litteraria*.

---

[62] Cf. Karl Dietrich Erdmann, *Die Ökumene der Historiker: Geschichte der Internationalen Historikerkongresse und des Comité International des Sciences Historiques* (Göttingen, 1987).

[63] For the 18th century see Ernst Schulin, 'Historie und internationale Wissenschaftsbeziehungen im 18. Jahrhundert', *Informationen der Historischen Kommission zu Berlin*, Supplement 16 (Berlin, 1992).

2

Universal History and National History

Eighteenth- and Nineteenth-Century German Historians and the Scholarly Community

ULRICH MUHLACK

This essay examines the position occupied by German historians within the international community of historians in the late eighteenth and nineteenth centuries. It is interested less in drawing up a comparative balance sheet of achievements or in the numerous 'transfers' that took place between German and non-German history, than in the subjective side. It looks at how German historians saw their place in the international scholarly community of their discipline, in other words, at their awareness of their position.

A universal community of historians can exist only if history claims to present universal truth. Anyone who feels committed to this claim belongs to that community, regardless of where he comes from. This community is the place that brings like-minded people together. It is the public to which they appeal, and the authority to which they submit. This sort of community came into being when the foundations of modern historical scholarship were laid in the fifteenth and sixteenth centuries, and was firmly established by the eighteenth century. It was part of the *res publica litteraria* created by the Humanists, essentially going back to the tradition of the great historians of classical Antiquity, and long used Latin as the lingua franca of scholarship. From the

Trans. Angela Davies, GHIL.

beginning of modern historiography, however, specific national traditions emerged, as demonstrated by the increase in the number of history books written in the vernacular. But essentially, these differences remained within the framework of common goals: nationality was subordinated to universality, the fatherland to the international community.

During the period covered by this essay, this changed decisively in response to two opposing developments. First, since the end of the eighteenth and beginning of the nineteenth centuries, when modern historical thought culminated in so-called historicism, the discipline's development into a human science (*Verwissenschaftlichung*) had taken off in an unprecedented way, enormously enhancing its claim to universality. History became a professionally organized, independent discipline everywhere. The fact that the first international conference of historians was held at the end of the nineteenth century is consistent with this development. Secondly, at that time history entered into the service of the modern national idea which, permeating all areas of life, was of a different quality from all earlier forms of national thinking. The result was a strict polarization: universality and nationality diverged, as did the international community and the fatherland. As Leopold von Ranke wrote in his *Entwurf zu einer Geschichte der Wissenschaft in Deutschland* in 1859, history acquired 'a national and general character at the same time'.[1] This essay explores the problem of how German historians coped with this dualism.

At first glance it seems that they could simply sidestep the dilemma through ingenuity: scholarly universality and German nationality could simply be equated. To make this possible, three things had to coincide: the obvious leadership of German scholars in the renewal of history, their national pride produced by this, coming together with the idea, which had been current since the mid-eighteenth century, of a German cultural nation.

This is not the place to recapitulate the development of modern German historicism and the history of its interna-

---

[1] Leopold von Ranke, *Zur eigenen Lebensgeschichte*, ed. Alfred Dove (Leopold von Ranke, *Sämmtliche Werke*, liii–liv) (Leipzig, 1890), 685.

tional triumph. Suffice it to say that the French Revolution also revolutionized historical thinking in Germany, that this revolutionary change gradually spread to all the disciplines which today would be called the humanities, the social sciences, and the cultural sciences, including, ultimately, also history in the narrow sense, and that these developments were accompanied by the establishment of new forms of historical teaching and research at the German universities. Suffice it to say, too, that not only German but also contemporary non-German voices testified to the fact that German historiography had, for the time being, taken the lead internationally—as demonstrated by Lord Acton's famous essay 'German Schools of History', published in the *English Historical Review* which began in 1886, modelled on the *Historische Zeitschrift*.[2]

In order to assess the impact of this on the self-confidence of German scholars, we need to look back further. Lord Acton, who acknowledged German supremacy in the nineteenth century, said simply: 'Before this century the Germans had scarcely reached the common level even in the storage of erudition.'[3] This is confirmed by the contemporary German writers whose opinions Franz von Wegele summarized in his *Geschichte der Deutschen Historiographie* of 1885,[4] and it explains the resentment or feeling of inferiority which German historians of the early modern period felt when confronted by foreign work. From the period of Humanism to the Enlightenment, German texts reverberated with complaints about the inferiority of German historiography, even if it was only that their authors felt that they had to defend themselves against allegedly unjustified

---

[2] Reprinted in J. E. E. D. Acton, *Historical Essays and Studies* (London, 1907), 344–92. Similarly J. Monod, 'Du progrès des études historiques en France depuis le XVIe siècle', *Revue historique*, 1 (1876), 5–38, at 27 ff.

[3] Acton, *Historical Essays*, 344 f.

[4] Franz X. von Wegele, *Geschichte der Deutschen Historiographie seit dem Auftreten des Humanismus* (Geschichte der Wissenschaften in Deutschland. Neuere Zeit 20; Munich, 1885). In the foreword he spoke of the 'wretched state' of historiography 'during that period' (p. v). In the passage cited Lord Acton referred to Wegele and criticized the structure of his history of historiography: 'Nine-tenths of his volume are devoted to the brave men who lived before Agamemnon, and the chapter on the rise of historical science, the only one which is meant for mankind, begins at page 975, and is the last' (Acton, *Historical Essays*, 344).

attacks by foreign writers.[5] All their efforts were directed towards imitating the work of the great foreign historians: first the Italians, then the French, and finally the British. This aspiration on the part of German historians lasted well into the nineteenth century, the heyday of German historicism. In 1867 the highest praise which Rudolf Köpke could give his teacher Ranke, at that time at the height of his fame, was to say that he 'certainly bears comparison with the great men of other nations'.[6] Continuous comparison with British or French historiography kept alive the centuries-old trauma of intellectual inferiority.[7]

But at the end of the eighteenth and beginning of the nineteenth centuries, this resentment gave way to a feeling of self-confidence which developed into the conviction of a national mission. This change originated in a discussion about the place of German literature in Johann Gottfried Herder's *Briefe zu Beförderung der Humanität* (1793–7). In the

---

[5] Cf. also Johann Christoph Gatterer, 'Vom historischen Plan, und der darauf sich gründenden Zusammenfügung der Erzählungen' (1767), in Horst Walter Blanke and Dirk Fleischer (eds.), *Theoretiker der deutschen Aufklärungshistorie*, ii (Fundamenta Historica 1, pt. 2; Stuttgart, 1990), 621–62, at 621 f. and 630. Gatterer admitted that 'the muse which governs history has not been particularly kind to our German geniuses', but rejected the 'criticism which foreigners make ... of our nation', that 'its class of historical writers consists merely of translators and compilers'.

[6] Rudolf Köpke, 'Ranke—Fest' (1867), in id., *Kleine Schriften zur Geschichte, Politik und Literatur*, ed. F. G. Kiessling (Berlin, 1872), 780–91, at 781. Similarly Wilhelm Giesebrecht, 'Die Entwicklung der modernen deutschen Geschichtswissenschaft: Habilitationsrede gehalten zu Königsberg am 19. April 1858', *Historische Zeitschrift*, 1 (1859), 1–17, at 2: 'It is often said that we Germans have only recently produced a historical literature that can match up to that of the English and the French.'

[7] This experience or memory is also reflected in the fact that the new genre of history of historiography conventionally presented its subject as a competition between European nations in which first one, then another, and finally the German nation prevailed. One early and one late example: Ludwig Wachler, *Geschichte der historischen Forschung und Kunst seit der Wiederherstellung der litterärischen Cultur in Europa*, i, pt. 2 (*Geschichte der Künste und Wissenschaften seit der Wiederherstellung derselben bis an das Ende des achtzehnten Jahrhunderts. Fünfte Abteilung*, i, pt. 2; Göttingen, 1812), p. vii: he planned to follow the 'course of historical research and art' since the Renaissance 'by individual nations'; and Wegele, *Geschichte*, 339: throughout, he was concerned to compare 'German historiography to related, contemporary literature of the other civilized nations (*Kulturvölker*) of the West'. On Wachler, Horst Walter Blanke, *Historiographiegeschichte als Historik* (Fundamenta Historica 3; Stuttgart, 1991), 201.

seventh and eighth collections of these letters Herder undertook a 'comparison between the poetry produced by various peoples in the past and the present'.[8] He concluded that because Germany had so far been backward, it would in future take the lead. In this he was responding to a double criticism which he transformed into double praise. The criticism was that the Germans had been 'too late', and that as a consequence they had been forced merely to 'imitate' foreign 'original forms'.[9] For Herder, belatedness meant rejuvenation: 'We still have a lot to do while others rest because they have achieved what they set out to do.'[10] And for him imitation provided the chance to make use of what others had done, 'by appropriating the best produced by all other peoples'.[11] In his view their language permitted the Germans to do this, 'a language of reason, of power, and truth'.[12] The German language, he believed, 'allows the imitation of foreign idioms in every expression, in every transition'. 'It is unbelievably flexible in adapting to the expression and idiom, the spirit and even the syllables of foreign languages, including those of the Greeks and the Romans.' 'By treating every original spirit it becomes, as it were, a new language unique to him.'[13] In his fragment *Deutsche Größe*, dating from the time when the peace of Lunéville and the peace of Amiens were concluded, Friedrich Schiller developed these ideas into a veritable eschatological cultural programme.[14] Herder and Schiller did not explicitly mention history, but it was obviously the ultimate goal of all their deliberations. The belatedness, the retrospective position, the ability to 'appropriate the best

---

[8] Johann Gottfried Herder, *Briefe zu Beförderung der Humanität*, ed. Hans Dietrich Irmscher (Johann Gottfried Herder, *Werke*, vii; Frankfurt am Main, 1991), no. 107, 572.

[9] Ibid., no. 100, 549. [10] Ibid., no. 101, 550.
[11] Ibid. 551. [12] Ibid., no. 57, 337. [13] Ibid., no. 101, 552.
[14] Friedrich Schiller, *Sämtliche Gedichte*, ii, ed. Herbert G. Göpfert (Friedrich Schiller, *Sämtliche Werke*, ii) (Munich, 1965), 226 ff. A few quotations: 'the slowest people will catch up with all the quick, hasty ones' (ibid. 227); the German language expresses 'everything': 'the most profound things and the most fleeting, the spirit, the soul', 'the youthful Greek and the modern ideal' (ibid. 227 f.); the Germans are called 'to bring humanity, general humanity, to completion within themselves, and to unite in one garland the most beautiful blossoms from all peoples', to preserve 'the treasures of centuries' (ibid. 229 f.).

produced by all other peoples', the 'unbelievable flexibility' of the German language: in the end, all this amounted to seeing the Germans as having an exclusive mission to interpret the world historically, a mission to think historically, a mission for historicism. In this regard, national awareness coincided with a universal awareness of history, national determination with a universal claim to science, and the German nation with the scholarly community.

One of the first writers to interpret this German mission for historical writing was Wilhelm von Humboldt. In 1796–7, during a visit to Paris, he criticized the French for their inability, when assessing historical phenomena, 'to go beyond . . . the standpoint of their time and their nation for a single moment'. 'We, by contrast, are accustoming ourselves to studying the peculiarities of every period and every nation, to entering into them as far as possible, and to making this knowledge the central point of our assessments.' As far as international communication between scholars was concerned, he concluded that the French kept 'the other nations in servility' and made 'it difficult for others to associate with them', while the Germans 'need to waken and gather together all their forces'.[15] Accordingly Humboldt saw himself as an ambassador for German scholarship in Paris. With French acquaintances, for example, he organized a conference on contemporary German philosophy. Throughout, however, he saw himself and them as 'inhabiting two different worlds'.[16] From that time on a constant succession of scholars declared the new historical thinking to be the German nation's mission to the world. In his *Reden an die Deutsche Nation* of 1808, Johann Gottlieb Fichte identified the 'Germanness of a people' with his philosophical-historical thinking;[17] at the beginning of his *Historik* (1857)

[15] Wilhelm von Humboldt, 'Das achtzehnte Jahrhundert', in id., *Werke*, ed. Andreas Flitner and Klaus Giel, i (Darmstadt, 1960), 376–505, at 456 f.

[16] Wilhelm von Humboldt, *Tagebücher*, ed. Albert Leitzmann, i (Wilhelm von Humboldt, *Gesammelte Schriften*, xiv; reprint Berlin, 1922), 483 ff., quotation on 486.

[17] Johann Gottlieb Fichte, *Reden an die Deutsche Nation*, ed. Fritz Medicus, (Hamburg, 1955), 121 f., esp. 122: 'Anyone who believes in the intellect, in the freedom of this intellect, and in the eternal development of this intellect through freedom is one of us, wherever he may have been born and whatever language he speaks. He belongs to us and will join us. Anyone who believes in

Johann Gustav Droysen, with reference to Humboldt, expressed his expectation that 'we Germans' will accomplish the 'task' 'of developing a theory of history';[18] and even at the beginning of the First World War, Ulrich von Wilamowitz-Moellendorff, the classical philologist, was still able to assert with undiminished self-confidence: 'We Germans will not take lightly the responsibilities that come with being leaders in the humanities and sciences; the others are aware of this, although they won't admit it.'[19] In 1914 the 'others', however, saw this claim as nothing more than a pan-German diktat.[20]

The emergence of this scholarly nationalism points to the well-known fact that the modern German nation constituted itself not as a political nation but, definitely during the Enlightenment, as a cultural one. The intellectuals who made up this nation led an unpolitical existence in the sense, too, that their relationship with German politics and with the state in general was an extremely distanced one. Moreover, they regarded this as placing them above all other nations, and so far as they were aware of political problems, they immediately transformed them into cultural ones. All this was radicalized to an enormous extent after 1789. German intellectuals reacted to the French Revolution by producing new aesthetic, philosophical, and scholarly concepts; they proclaimed a cultural revolution to be set against the political revolution of the French. This pushed the renunciation of practical politics even further and nourished the German intellectuals' feeling that they were marked out from all other nations. The German cultural revolution disputed the French Revolution's character as

stagnation, going backwards, and going around in circles, or who places dead nature at the helm of the world government is unGerman, wherever he may have been born and whatever language he speaks. He is a stranger to us, and it is desirable that he should separate himself from us completely, and the sooner the better.'

[18] Johann Gustav Droysen, *Historik*, ed. Peter Leyh, i (Stuttgart, 1977), 53.

[19] Quoted in Karl Dietrich Erdmann, *Die Ökumene der Historiker: Geschichte der Internationalen Historikerkongresse und des Comité International des Sciences Historiques* (Abhandlungen der Akademie der Wissenschaften in Göttingen, Philologisch-historische Klasse, 3rd series, 158; Göttingen, 1987), 98 f.

[20] Ibid. 99.

cosmopolitan, laying claim to this quality for itself. The emergence of historicism was the central element in this cultural revolution and its cosmopolitan programme, and thus moved to the heart of the cultural nation's self-image. Another reference to Schiller's fragment of 1801–2 may be helpful in documenting this context.[21] Schiller did, of course, suffer under Germany's continued humiliation during the revolutionary wars. Thus there was a strong element of compensation in his profession of the German cultural nation's historicist world mission. This points forward to the politicization of the German national idea, initially directed against Napoleonic supremacy. On the other hand it was crucial that the original cultural impetus was kept up as the process of politicization took place. The political nation remained a cultural nation and thus a nation of scholars—at least this is how it was seen by the German intellectuals, who now began to turn towards politics.

This continuity, however, should not conceal the fact that the emergence of a political national consciousness created a completely new situation among German historians. Political nationalism may have absorbed scholarly nationalism, but it also opened up a whole new area with quite different values. The world mission of the German cultural nation was relativized by the idea of the nation-state; the German nation, hitherto seen as the quintessence of humanity, was from now on related to itself, to its own particular existence. German historians took part in this process. The interest in 'studying the peculiarities of every period and every nation' gave way to an interest in history written 'from the standpoint of their time and their nation'. Naturally this 'national historiography' did not emerge fully-fledged overnight. It developed in the course of the nineteenth century, from the Wars of Liberation to the Wilhelmine period. Nor did it establish itself as a monolithic school. Rather, it provided a framework which permitted

---

[21] Schiller, *Sämtliche Gedichte*, ii. 226 ff.: the poet began from the lost revolutionary wars and foresaw the imminent collapse of the Reich, but based 'German greatness' on the cultural nation which was independent of this fate. From this he derived Germany's international significance, which was brought to completion in his eschatological cultural programme, this call to a historical world examination. The formation of the cultural nation led over into the formation of historicism.

a large number of approaches depending on the different regional, confessional, and party political positions of individual writers. Finally, it was by no means uncontroversial, but needed constant justification. When the Königsberg historian Hans Prutz attempted a provisional summing up in 1883, he asked straight out: 'Do we have a national historiography? Could we have one? And if not—how could this be? And how can this situation be remedied?'[22] We can answer anyway that during the nineteenth century 'national historiography' became a general problem of history in Germany that affected almost all historians, regardless of their position. Prutz explained it more precisely by attempting to define 'the concept and nature of national historiography as such'. One of his key points was that 'although it cannot dispense with a scholarly foundation, national historiography is neither exclusively nor even predominantly scholarly. Rather, its purpose is general, practical political, or national educational.'[23]

This obviously represented a restriction on the truth claims of history. 'National historiography' was created in response to the political needs of the nation. It started with the nation, took its side, and was addressed to it. Heinrich von Sybel went so far as to claim that historiography must 'take a particular stance on the great earth-shattering questions of religion, politics, and nationality'.[24] Even mother tongue became an organ and a symbol of peculiarity and difference. In 1857 the Tübingen historian Hermann Bischof, for example, was not content with praising, like Herder, the 'natural harmony' of the German language,[25] but finally identified it with national partiality and national separation;[26] he remarked on the long

[22] Hans Prutz, 'Über nationale Geschichtschreibung: Rede zur Feier von Kaisergeburtstag (am 17. März 1883), gehalten in der Aula der Albertus-Universität zu Königsberg', *Die Grenzboten*, 42 (1883), 667–81, at 669.

[23] Ibid.

[24] Heinrich von Sybel, 'Ueber den Stand der neueren deutschen Geschichtschreibung (Marburg, 1856)', in id., *Kleine historische Schriften*, i (3rd edn., Stuttgart, 1880), 349–64, at 355.

[25] Hermann Bischof, 'Die Regeln der Geschichtschreibung und Deutschlands Historiker im 19. Jahrhundert', *Deutsches Museum*, 7 (1857), 713–23, 754–66, 796–806, and 827–39, at 805.

[26] He saw 'a people's language' as being 'inextricably intertwined with its intellectual individuality'. 'Each people speaks differently from the rest because it thinks differently' (ibid. 802).

predominance of Latin in German historiography: 'This method alienates history from national interests and gives the scholarly caste a monopoly on its use.'[27]

It is also clear that in espousing this restrictive interpretation German historians distanced themselves from the scholarly community. The place that brought like-minded people together, the public to which they appealed, and the authority to which they submitted was now primarily the political nation. Sometimes this attitude led to scepticism about whether international historiography could exist at all, and even to open rejection. When Heinrich von Treitschke had read Ranke's most recent work in 1872, he could hardly restrain himself in a letter to Droysen: 'This pussyfooting around, saying nothing about the most important issues, is dreadful. Ranke should stay in England or Italy; there his greatness can be admired without reservation.'[28] Ranke will be dealt with again at the end of this essay.

In 1903 Berlin historians including Otto Hintze, Max Lenz, Eduard Meyer, Theodor Mommsen, and Dietrich Schäfer tried to prevent a conference of international historians from being held in the Reich capital as planned. They declared that the 'idea of holding an international historical conference' was 'misconceived', 'because history—apart from that of Antiquity—even if it is interpreted in the universal sense, is too strongly influenced by political and national differences for any common ground to be assumed as the basis for international understanding'.[29] Even Adolf von Harnack, who was in favour of the conference, qualified his view of international historiography as follows: 'It does not, of course, encompass the deepest knowledge, and it

---

[27] Ibid. 801; Johann Wilhelm Loebell, 'Ueber die Epochen der Geschichtsschreibung und ihr Verhältnis zur Poesie: Eine Skizze', *Historisches Taschenbuch*, NS, 2 (1841), 277–372, at 349: 'This historiography, therefore, had to renounce the great right to renew itself out of the life of the people, and to renew and elevate this in turn. It could only operate in the circle of initiates; it could only put down its roots in the milieu of a scholarly education, which never matches national developments in freshness and powers of creativity.'

[28] Treitschke to Droysen, 24 Dec. 1872, in Johann Gustav Droysen, *Briefwechsel*, ed. Rudolf Hübner, ii (Deutsche Geschichtsquellen des 19. Jahrhunderts 26; reprint, Osnabrück, 1967), 905.

[29] Quoted in Erdmann, *Ökumene*, 66.

makes no value judgements. None the less, it is a possession of the highest value—a collection of historically attested facts.'[30]

In 1883, when Prutz discussed the 'concept and nature of national historiography as such', he included the 'form, content, and intention' of historiography.[31] In the following, this essay will concentrate on 'content' to illustrate the new situation, namely on the fact that 'national historiography' increasingly turned towards the history of its own nation: the German nation itself.

When Herder, Schiller, and Humboldt had announced the German cultural nation's world mission for historicism around 1800, they had had no particular interest in German history. Indeed, their universalist, cosmopolitan attitudes led them to look outwards, in quest of the general. They called for foreign cultures and nations to be researched, for a balance sheet to be drawn up of human development as a whole, and for a new interpretation of universal history. The German nation was more or less to be absorbed in its ability to achieve this global knowledge; as the subject of historical investigation, it played at most a subordinate role. The scholarly productions of early historicism largely accorded with these views. Except for the philosophy of history, this new type of historiography first became apparent in the study of classical Antiquity, that universal historical discipline *par excellence*. In studying the Greeks, Friedrich August Wolf was interested in the 'history of humanity',[32] while Barthold Georg Niebuhr, looking at Roman history, dealt with a 'great world revolution' in the 'course of world history'.[33] In 1858–9 Wilhelm Giesebrecht summed up: 'Yes, it is our undisputed

---

[30] Quoted ibid. 65. Hermann Heimpel, incidentally, used a similar expression after the Paris Conference of 1950: 'For all its will to be international, historiography, unlike science and medicine, for example, simply does not possess a common language of symbols', in 'Internationaler Historikertag in Paris (1950)', in id., *Aspekte: Alte und neue Texte*, ed. Sabine Krüger (Göttingen, 1995), 272–6, at 272.

[31] Prutz, 'Über nationale Geschichtschreibung', 669.

[32] Friedrich August Wolf, *Darstellung der Altertumswissenschaft nach Begriff, Umfang, Zweck und Wert* (1807), ed. Johannes Irmscher (Berlin, 1985), 134.

[33] B. G. Niebuhr, *Römische Geschichte*, i (Berlin, 1811), 15; on this see Gerrit Walther, *Niebuhrs Forschung* (Frankfurter Historische Abhandlungen 35; Stuttgart, 1993), 311 and 434 ff.

glory: German research has enriched and explained the history of all the peoples of Europe. All nations must be grateful for German thoroughness, impartiality, and love of truth.'[34] At the same time he hinted at what the future held: 'As German historiography was seized by the national idea with irresistible force, it was only natural that the lack of a history of its own nation became painfully obvious.' 'This was a thought that the cosmopolitan school of philosophical historiography had unduly rejected.'[35]

'National historiography' did not simply turn away from universal history. In 1903 the Berlin historians quoted above emphasized the influence of 'political and national differences' on history, even 'if it is interpreted in the universal sense'. One of them, Dietrich Schäfer, published his *Weltgeschichte der Neuzeit* in 1907. This was a typical example of a universal history 'more or less limited to power politics',[36] well suited to the tastes of an imperialist, neo-Rankean period. In the same declaration the Berlin historians claimed that Ancient History was excepted from the national perspective, but they can easily be refuted. The accuracy of Giesebrecht's claim that Niebuhr had already revealed a 'national standpoint' may be doubted.[37] But in his *Römische Geschichte* (1854–6, 1885) Theodor Mommsen, one of the signatories to the Berlin declaration of 1903, certainly produced a model of a democratic-national approach.[38] Similarly unmistakable was the national element in Droysen's first work, his *Geschichte Alexanders des Großen* published in 1833.

Nevertheless, the shift towards German history lay within the logic of 'national historiography'. This historiography was most effective where the nation was led to look at its own

---

[34] Giesebrecht, 'Die Entwicklung', 14.
[35] Ibid. 8 f. Similarly Adalbert Heinrich Horawitz, *Zur Entwickelungsgeschichte der Deutschen Historiographie: Ein Versuch* (Vienna, 1865), 4.
[36] Ernst Schulin, 'Universalgeschichtsschreibung im zwanzigsten Jahrhundert' (1974), in id., *Traditionskritik und Rekonstruktionsversuch: Studien zur Entwicklung von Geschichtswissenschaft und historischem Denken* (Göttingen, 1979), 163–202, at 183.
[37] Giesebrecht, 'Die Entwicklung', 10.
[38] On this see Alfred Heuß, 'Theodor Mommsen als Geschichtsschreiber', in Notker Hammerstein (ed.), *Deutsche Geschichtswissenschaft um 1900* (Stuttgart, 1988), 37–95, esp. 59 ff. and 73 ff.

past: 'where it is a matter of celebrating Germany's past, and conferring about its future.'[39] Here, therefore, the relativizing of history's claim to present the truth and its distancing from the scholarly community appears to have advanced furthest, in the starkest contrast to the world historical interests of the cosmopolitan writers of early historicism. The new programme of a German national history was not completely without precedent. It had had precursors in the early modern period, from humanist accounts of German history through to the eighteenth-century legal histories of the Reich. It is certainly no coincidence that first of all German legal history was studied in the nineteenth century, following the tradition of Reich history. Yet the real breakthrough took place in the study of German language and literature, that is, in the subject dealing with the primary or original contents of the new German national consciousness. Historians in the narrow sense were last of all on the scene; a continuous history of the genre did not begin until after the 1848–9 revolution.

In September 1846 representatives of the three groups, 'scholars of law, history, and language', met in Frankfurt am Main. There they took stock of their disciplines in order to arrive at preliminary definitions of their subjects. The most interesting aspects of their discussions are reflected in the following quotations from the keynote speech given by Jacob Grimm, who chaired the assembly. Grimm subsumed all of these disciplines under the concept of the 'inexact sciences', which he distinguished from subjects such as mathematics, chemistry, and physics, but also to some extent from classical philology with its fixed rules of textual criticism.[40] In his view the value of the inexact sciences lay in the fact that they deal with subjects that affect us more directly than any others: 'We stand much more firmly on the earth of the fatherland and embrace all feelings from home much more sincerely'; 'we think that anything that is discovered in the history of our fatherland must stand it in

---

[39] G. Waitz, 'Deutsche Historiker der Gegenwart', *Allgemeine Zeitschrift für Geschichte*, 5 (1846), 520–35, at 535.
[40] *Verhandlungen der Germanisten zu Frankfurt am Main am 24., 25. und 26. September 1846* (Frankfurt am Main, 1847), 59, 62, and 104.

good stead'.[41] As for the 'exact sciences', however, he said that while they 'extend over the whole earth and also benefit the foreign scholar, they do not touch the heart'.[42] Grimm went on to define the particular value of each of the three disciplines. At the head he placed German philology: it explores the 'mighty feeling for language' which 'has always given man his first initiation and equipped him for every eventuality',[43] and can thus be studied only in 'one's own native language'.[44] German legal research was given the task of exposing the roots of indigenous law, which had been obscured by Roman law. Thus Grimm strengthened the position taken by traditional Reich history against the 'Roman legal scholars, the so-called *Civilisten*': 'These live in a magnificent building, even if it is in the foreign style.'[45] And the duty of German historical research in the narrow sense was 'to develop politics out of history': 'Of course, our history is also concerned with general history, and cannot be confined within the borders of present-day Germany. But this is, after all, our primary concern.'[46] These quotations express everything that is the matter here: the distancing of German history from traditional universal history, and thus the separation of 'national historiography' from the historicist world mission of the Germans, of nationality from scholarly universality, and the fatherland from the academic community. Grimm was not only recapitulating the development of Germanic studies so far, but also indicating the direction which future developments were to take. And although he had reason to criticize the relative backwardness of historiography by comparison with philology or law, he was soon to experience the beginning of an upswing which would make it match up fully to his expectations. Treitschke, who wanted Ranke banished to Italy or England, set himself only one goal in his *Deutsche Geschichte* of 1879,

---

[41] Ibid. 60.
[42] Ibid.; cf. also ibid. 62: 'This is also the simple key to why our meetings, without questioning the successes achieved by the leading gatherings of German scientists and classical philologists, nevertheless evoke, of course, almost exclusively before a German public, more lasting participation and give greater satisfaction.'
[43] Ibid. 11.   [44] Ibid. 60.   [45] Ibid. 16.   [46] Ibid. 51 f.

namely, to awaken the Germans' 'pleasure in their fatherland'.[47]

Yet while 'national historiography' turned its back on scholarly universality and thus on the academic community, there is no doubt that its writers felt part of and committed to both. They served the political nation, but at the same time were filled with the academic nationalism that they had inherited from the early days of historicism. Droysen started publishing his *Geschichte der preußischen Politik* in 1855, and from 1857 gave lectures on the theory of history as the 'task' allotted to 'us Germans'. The Germans wrote history from a national perspective while fully aware of the academic standards which they needed to uphold. Indeed, they based their national-political aspirations upon it. This was still true of Treitschke, who wanted to use academic historiography to awaken 'pleasure in the fatherland'. While they had reservations about the academic community, they certainly did not leave it: the controversial Berlin conference was held in 1908.[48] In his *Geschichte der Deutschen Historiographie*, a paean to German historicism, Wegele brought everything into a 'harmonious unity' of 'scholarly, universal, and national motives': 'historiography, humanity, and German nationality'.[49]

Of course, this harmonization is suspect. There was obviously a dichotomy here, if not an opposition or contradiction. On the one hand there was a political nationalism which was sufficient unto itself, the national relativization of historiography, and the restriction of history to the horizons of the fatherland, and on the other, a cosmopolitan scholarly

---

[47] Heinrich von Treitschke, *Deutsche Geschichte im Neunzehnten Jahrhundert*, i (Leipzig, 1927), p. ix. Special praise was reserved for those who cleansed German history of the alleged distortions of foreign historians. In 1846 Droysen found it intolerable that no German sources on the most recent German history were yet available: 'We have to read them out of the reports of foreigners, as if our memory were to remain under foreign rule.' (J. G. Droysen, *Vorlesungen über die Freiheitskriege*, i (Kiel, 1846), foreword.) Häusser's research in German archives leading to the 'annihilation' of the French approach and method was therefore praised all the more as 'a national achievement' (Wegele, *Geschichte*, 1073).

[48] 'Justice demands that we point out that the sceptics did not merely submit to the inevitable, did not put a good face on what they could not change, but did their utmost to make the best of it' (Erdmann, *Ökumene*, 68).

[49] Wegele, *Geschichte*, 976 and 1081.

nationalism, the appeal to general scholarly standards and participation in the scholarly community which was based on these standards. How can this be reconciled?

Some of the answers to this question have already been mentioned in passing. They all suggest that there was a complementary relationship between German nationality and scholarly universality, which could be ascribed to two strictly delimited areas between which a sort of peaceful coexistence was possible. Prutz differentiated between the 'national educational trend' and 'the scholarly foundation' of 'national historiography'; Bischof between 'national interests' and the 'scholarly caste'; Harnack between 'value judgements' and a 'collection of historically attested facts'. Thus they all distinguished between studying and interpreting the sources, between collecting and evaluating historical facts. The former was the realm of scholarly universality, the latter that of German nationality. The historian belonged to the scholarly community on the one hand, and to his fatherland on the other. This explanation can be completed with a quotation from Sybel, who contrasted the 'writer's attitude to the state' with 'the circle of the academic and scholarly apparatus'.[50] In essence, all these statements aimed to draw a line between historical research and the writing of history. This had consequences for the language. To some extent historical research approached the 'exact sciences', and although it lacked an international scientific language, it seemed capable of rising above the special quality of mother tongue. The writing of history, by contrast, took over the genuine task of developing the peculiarities and specific features of the vernacular. This difference was expressed in an open letter which Heinrich Ritter, a philosopher from Göttingen, wrote to Ranke, his former colleague and friend in Berlin, in 1867. Ritter called historical research 'Geschichtskunde', which he identified with 'Geschichtswissenschaft'. He wrote that it 'follows only rules which are generally valid; among all people, of all races, it strives to achieve the same form'. History-writing, by contrast, he classed among the 'fine arts'. An author's writing of history,

---

[50] Sybel, 'Ueber den Stand', 363 f.

he suggested, 'will remain characteristic of him and carry a national colouring; it will depend on his national language, on the taste of his people'.[51]

This complementary relationship did not, of course, remove the dichotomy between universality and nationality. On the contrary, it reinforced it. However, the German historians did not stop there. Ritter concluded his open letter by placing history-writing in the service of historical research: 'Peoples may compete with each other as to which of them can best explain in words, to themselves and to other rivals, the science and the meaning of history.'[52] Thus instead of separating nations, history-writing was to facilitate academic communication between them. Ritter found this solution by trying to keep the national element, which he saw as permeating history-writing, as free as possible of politics.[53] It can be shown, however, that 'national historiography' with its political dimension was by no means a diversion from the universal claims of historicism.

Everything depended on the concept of individuality, which since Herder had been the central category of the historicist theory of history. From the start nations were in the foreground; history presented itself essentially as a cosmos of national individualities. The writers of early historicism regarded this cosmos as a world of objects to which they had direct access. Their own national individuality was for them simply another word for the objective vision which they claimed to possess. The 'national historians' went beyond this in that they transferred national individualization from the world of objects to their subjective perspective. For them national individuality signified writing history

[51] Heinrich Ritter, *An Leopold von Ranke über deutsche Geschichtschreibung: Ein offener Brief* (Leipzig, 1887), 14 f.; he concluded: 'If I were pursuing strict science I would have to forget that I am a German; as an artist working on my life's work, or on some other work of art, I must not omit to put my personality and my nationality into the scales of my choice' (ibid. 76). [52] Ibid.

[53] 'We are told to consider our national state; that establishing it and putting it on a secure footing should be our main aim; and that history, too, is to sacrifice its general scholarly character to this purpose. It seems that our patriotism is considered so weak that our love of our disciplines could damage it unduly' (ibid. 63). See also ibid. 75, where Ritter was in general against 'German history-writers aspiring to have a practical impact on present-day politics', 'because I reject any contemporary tendency in works that have a scholarly basis and are executed in an artistic way'.

from a specifically German standpoint. Droysen, after Sybel, derived from this a general maxim that outstripped all previous assumptions about the perspectivism of historical knowledge,[54] thus taking the historicist concept of individuality to a logical conclusion. So a straight path led from the historicist theory of history to 'national historiography'.

It may be doubted whether the claim to be a universal science could be reconciled with this sort of individualization and nationalization. Such doubts would be justified if it were merely a matter of history being fragmented into individual phenomena. But individuality as a historicist category was built upon a completely different idea, namely, that the general is immanent or inherent in the individual, and thus that universal knowledge is inherent in specific knowledge. Individuality lies at the centre because universal knowledge is possible only through it. As 'national historiography' pushed individualization forward into an unprecedented perspectivization of historical knowledge, this universal dimension was retained. To identify history with the historian's national position was not necessarily to sacrifice universal truth to national truth. What was sacrificed was the illusion that a universal truth could be achieved directly; the 'idea that the writer of history belonged to no nation' and was 'free of all the ties of nationality'.[55] Instead, they achieved the insight that historians could not rid themselves of these 'ties', and that universal truth could be achieved only in the light of particular problems arising in present-day national life. Thus illusion was to be replaced by the possibility, and therefore the reality, of universal truth. The historicist idea of immanence also applied to the relationship between universal history and national history. If the general was inherent in the individual, then every individual history was always also universal history, or conversely, individual histories contained universal history within themselves. If they could be distinguished at all, then it was only in an external sense.

[54] Droysen, *Historik*, 238: 'in that I look at the destinies of the world from the standpoint and the idea of my state, my people, and my religion.'
[55] Wilhelm Wachsmuth, *Entwurf einer Theorie der Geschichte* (1820), ed. Hans Schleier and Dirk Fleischer (Wissen und Kritik 1; Waltrop, 1992), 126; on this see Droysen, *Historik*, 236.

Seen in this light, there was little point in drawing the distinction encountered earlier between national history-writing and universal historical research, between the 'writer's attitude to the state' and 'the circle of the academic and scholarly apparatus', between the 'national educational trend' and 'the scholarly foundation', between 'value judgements' and a 'collection of historically attested facts'. To put a national perspective on historical knowledge meant that these two things were connected, in that the former determined the latter; that the 'writer's attitude to the state' determined the use of the 'academic and scholarly apparatus', that the 'national educational trend' prefigured the 'scholarly foundation', and that 'value judgements' laid down the framework within which 'historically attested facts were collected', in other words, that history-writing structured historical research. It was crucial that the universal character of historical research was not thereby abandoned, but was actually to be made achievable for the first time. Universal historical research was realized in a specific way within the horizons of national history-writing. In essence, the two were identical; one was inconceivable without the other.

What became of the scholarly community in all this? In the course of historicist individualization and nationalization it took on a new aspect. And it is only seemingly paradoxical that 'national historiography' could claim to have contributed to its formal re-establishment. The early historicists aspired to communicate internationally in the awareness of their innate superiority. They themselves made up the scholarly community; foreign scholars were accepted if they achieved German standards. This attitude was widespread among German historians even during the period of 'national historiography'. But another model developed in parallel to it: the model of national rivalry for universal truth. To put a national perspective on historical knowledge meant that there could be no scholarly community standing above each individual fatherland. This did not, however, mean that the scholarly community fell apart into national disciplines. On the contrary, only at this time, it seemed, was the scholarly community truly constituted. Every nation was to go its own way, but in achieving a goal which it had in common with all other nations: that is, to gain knowledge which could stand up to the criteria of scholarly universality. Nations competed with each other as to which was best able to achieve this goal. Each nation was therefore forced to compare itself with, and be compared with, others. This involved processes of reception between the nations. It was not a matter of one nation simply imitating another. While this might have been possible to a certain extent within 'the circle of the academic and scholarly apparatus', and in the 'collection of historically attested facts', it did not apply to the particular national perspectives upon which, ultimately, that apparatus and those facts depended. What could become established as a pattern was the ability of a nation to extract universal truth from its specific situation. This was the task which all nations faced, and upon which the unity of the scholarly community was based. There was probably no better witness to this than Karl Lamprecht, who kept his distance from historicism and worked towards a universal history in the style of the Enlightenment and positivism: 'In the natural sciences, method is the same throughout the world, and national peculiarities produce only tiny differences. But in the humanities, and history in particular, this is certainly not yet the case to the same extent. American method, for example, is quite different from German. . . It is desirable, however, that studies of universal history should make use of the advantages of all methods.'[56] Of course, behind this lay the beginnings of a new idea of regulating historiographical universality and the scholarly community.

There is one striking indication that the writers of 'national historiography' took seriously their notion of the scholarly community, namely, the fact that when they were developing and implementing their own programme, they studied the work of foreign historians. It was a commonplace among them that 'German historiography should learn from the national historiographies of the French and the English';[57] the traditional zeal to match up to the admired

[56] Karl Lamprecht, *Alternative zu Ranke. Schriften zur Geschichtstheorie*, ed. Hans Schleier (Leipzig, 1988), 406.
[57] Prutz, 'Über nationale Geschichtschreibung', 678.

foreign masters was here directed at a new goal.[58] German historians were not sparing with their criticism. They found fault with political one-sidedness and the tendency towards novelistic effects which they found associated with it: 'national historiography in the worst sense'.[59] Such passages reverberated with inherited pride in the 'very high degree of objective love of truth' which, in their view, was characteristic of German historiography.[60] But they did acknowledge that English and French historians had produced models of 'committed historiography'.[61] The high esteem in which Thomas Babington Macaulay's *History of England* was held in Germany is an indication of this.

There was, of course, also criticism. Droysen was scornful of 'Macaulay's stylistic pretensions',[62] and Treitschke commented disparagingly that Macaulay saw the whole of world history as a Whig.[63] But these views were in the minority. Sybel stressed the 'healthy, but at the same time comfortable and proud' awareness of the state that 'goes through Macaulay's works', and felt politically close to him.[64] And for all his animosity, Droysen valued the 'feeling of attachment to home' that Macaulay conveyed,[65] and recognized that the 'lively interest with which Macaulay is received among us' revealed a 'deep need for practical politics in our nation'.[66] Treitschke, too, recognized that it was essential for a histo-

---

[58] Cf. Giesebrecht, 'Die Entwicklung', 2: 'It is often said that we Germans have only recently produced a historical literature that can match up to that of the English and the French. And we cannot deny that we have not long had history-writers who compete with the French in the brilliance of their accounts, or that we possess few historical works which, like those produced by the English, are pervaded by the fresh breath of a national life based on the state, and which strengthen and lift a manly spirit.' Similarly, Horawitz, *Zur Entwickelungsgeschichte*, 45.   [59] Prutz, 'Über nationale Geschichtschreibung', 678.
[60] Treitschke to his father, 19 Nov. 1864, in *Heinrich von Treitschkes Briefe*, ed. Max Cornicelius, ii (Leipzig, 1913), 351.   [61] Heuß, 'Theodor Mommsen', 40.
[62] Droysen to Wilhelm Arendt, 8–9 June 1859, in *Briefwechsel*, ii. 605; on this see Heuß, 'Theodor Mommsen', 39 f.
[63] Treitschke to his father, 19 Nov. 1864, in *Briefe*, ii. 352.
[64] Sybel, 'Ueber den Stand', 359 f. and 362.
[65] Droysen to Sybel, 5 Aug. 1853, in *Briefwechsel*, ii. 169; on this see Heuß, 'Theodor Mommsen', 40.
[66] Droysen to Arendt, 8 May 1857, in *Briefwechsel*, ii. 450; on this see Heuß, 'Theodor Mommsen', 40.

rian to declare his 'party-political affiliation'.[67] At times it seemed as if the only goal the 'national historians' were pursuing was to write a work that could stand comparison with Macaulay's: 'The need was felt for a German Macaulay.'[68] In any case, they were particularly committed to the international historiography to which the early historicists had seen themselves as superior.

Finally, to look briefly at Ranke makes sense not because he took a different position on the problem which is the subject of this essay, as Treitschke's attack on 'Ranke's pussyfooting around' would suggest, but because his work brought together the different elements which have been discussed here, and because he defined the position of German historiography in a way which is ideal for summing up.

Ranke grew up with the German cultural nation's historicist world mission, and remained committed to it his whole life long. In all his writing, from his first attempts to his late works, he produced universal history: the prehistory and history of the European system of states. But in this context he was also receptive to 'national historiography'. From the July Revolution his writing pursued epistemological interests that arose out of developments in Prussian-German politics, and his universal history gradually acquired more and more national colour.[69] Ranke also increasingly devoted himself to German history. Although the long-planned overview from the beginnings to the present day never materialized,[70] he did write a number of separate parts, most importantly *Deutsche Geschichte im Zeitalter der Reformation* (1839–47), which was a significant influence on other historians. It is also

---

[67] Treitschke to his father, 19 Nov. 1864, in *Briefe*, ii. 351.
[68] Heuß, 'Theodor Mommsen', 39.
[69] See, finally, Ranke's comment, dictated in November 1885, printed in *Zur eigenen Lebensgeschichte*, 56–76, at 76: 'Then followed the two great wars which changed the fate of the world, the Austro-Prussian war and the Franco-Prussian war. Their main consequence was that political conditions developed on a level field. The universal prospects for Germany and the world then prompted me to devote my last strength to a book on world history, and I am still working on it.'
[70] On this see Ernst Schulin, 'Universalgeschichte und Nationalgeschichte bei Leopold von Ranke', in Wolfgang J. Mommsen (ed.), *Leopold von Ranke und die moderne Geschichtswissenschaft* (Stuttgart, 1988), 37–71, at 39 and 59 ff.

noticeable that since the founding of the Reich, Ranke's interest in German history had grown enormously. In all these aspirations he more or less personified the scholarly community; Treitschke's comment referred to Ranke's repeated journeys to Italy, England, and France. In Paris and London he enjoyed the recognition that he regarded as his due as a representative of the new German historical science. But he also tried to learn, in particular, studying examples of 'committed historiography'. In March 1857 Ranke wrote to Clara Ranke, reporting a conversation he had had with Macaulay: 'I told him that I admired the form of his writings, and especially the way in which he explains the present through the past, although I did not agree with him on every point.'[71] 'Form' is the epitome of what, in the name of national historiography, streamed from nation to nation.

On 20 February 1867 Ranke celebrated the fiftieth anniversary of his graduation as a Doctor of Philosophy. His wife Clara, daughter of a barrister, Graves, from Dublin, sent her family at home a detailed account of the activities of the day, from the school choir in the morning to the celebratory dinner at night. She stressed the countless letters 'from all parts of Europe', not omitting to mention that 'he got no letter of congratulation from England—but it is not English fashion to regard such jubilees'.[72] Ranke, inspired by this almost unanimous international acclamation, rounded off the day with an after-dinner speech which he called his 'historical testament'. This is the speech which, when it was published, provoked Ritter into writing his open letter to Ranke.

In it, Ranke compared contemporary German with foreign historiography. He started by acknowledging that foreign historiography enjoyed 'not inconsiderable advantages'. The Italians, the English, and the French, he said, took the present moment as their starting point in every-

---

[71] Ranke to Clara Ranke, 26 Mar. 1857, in Leopold von Ranke, *Das Briefwerk*, ed. Walther Peter Fuchs (Hamburg, 1949), 415. On this see C. v. Noorden, 'Ranke und Macaulay', *Historische Zeitschrift*, 17 (1867), 87–138.

[72] Extract from Madame von Ranke's letter giving an account of the jubilee in Berlin on 20 Feb. 1867, *Syracuse Scholar*, 9 (1988), no. 1: *Leopold von Ranke*, 68 f.

thing: 'we can say of them and of the others that they are entirely national. That is their advantage over us.' However, there was another side in which the Germans, he claimed, outdid them: 'We are superior to them in looking at the whole in a universal-historical way.' 'Our national view is more universal, something which they have yet to develop.' Ranke continued: 'What we lack is the power to seize the fullness of the moment, but we will achieve that too. I always envisaged it as associated with that general direction. And when I see the strength and industriousness with which the younger generation in particular is treading this path and seeking to seize the moment, then I should like to say: I am looking, like Moses, at the promised land of a future German historiography, even if I do not live to see it, a land in which what I have spent my life striving for, and what I have tried to convey to others, will be achieved.'[73]

What Ritter objected to in this speech was the national tone. He, by contrast, insisted on the international nature of historiography, played the universal off against the national, while of course moving towards a mediation between the two. Ranke himself, looking at his own work and the course of German historiography as a whole, was concerned to achieve exactly this sort of mediation. Here are, in the most concentrated form, all the problems and aspects, all the approaches and lines of development in the chapter of intellectual history that is the concern of this essay. This 'historical testament' can be seen as a summary of the ways in which German historians at the end of the eighteenth and in the nineteenth centuries tried to define their position within the scholarly community.

[73] Leopold von Ranke, *Abhandlungen und Versuche: Neue Sammlung*, ed. Alfred Dove and Theodor Wiedemann (Leopold von Ranke, *Sämmtliche Werke*, li–lii) (Leipzig, 1888), 590 f.

3
Adam Ferguson's Histories in Germany
English Liberty, Scottish Vigour, and German Rigour

FANIA OZ-SALZBERGER

I

Schiller called him 'a great sage of our century'; for Friedrich Heinrich Jacobi he was 'the great noble Ferguson'; Gotthold Ephraim Lessing opened one of his most interesting letters with the words: 'I would like to make a real study of Ferguson now.'[1] Abundant praise, even by eighteenth-century standards, was heaped on the Scottish thinker Adam Ferguson as his works were read in Germany during the last three decades of the century. Each of Ferguson's major works was considered a triumph by German readers, and his overall success surpassed that of most of the other central writers of the Scottish Enlightenment.[2]

Ferguson's appeal to German readers at that time stemmed first and foremost from the fact that he was a Scot. The Scottish Enlightenment affected its German counterpart in several important ways; intellectual traffic in the opposite direction acquired momentum only in the early nineteenth century. Scottish learning was well appreciated by an expanding

---

[1] F. Schiller, 'Philosophy of Physiology' (1779), in K. Dewhurst and N. Reeves, *Friedrich Schiller: Medicine, Psychology and Literature* (Oxford, 1978), 150; F. H. Jacobi, 'Etwas das Lessing gesagt hat' (1782), in *Werke*, ii (Leipzig, 1815), 359; G. H. Lessing to Mendelssohn, 9 Jan. 1771, in *Briefe von und an Lessing*, ed. H. Kiesel *et al.* (Frankfurt am Main, 1988), 144.
[2] Fania Oz-Salzberger, *Translating the Enlightenment: Scottish Civic Discourse in Eighteenth-Century Germany* (Oxford, 1995), ch. 5 and *passim*.

German readership during the second half of the eighteenth century. Until recently this reception was often blurred into the general vista of 'English literature' in Germany. However, it is now becoming clear that Scottish scholarship gained the lion's share of what contemporary German intellectuals termed 'Anglophilia'.[3]

The reception of Scottish books was an important part of the growing German appreciation of British culture during the second half of the eighteenth century. Scottish authors were increasingly seen by alert German readers as the intellectual vanguard of the British philosophical tradition. David Hume's role in awakening Kant from his dogmatic slumber has become a commonplace, but this token link was by no means unique. The common-sense philosophy of Thomas Reid and James Beattie had a powerful impact in Germany, and James Steuart and Adam Smith were hailed as dependable alternatives to French economic theorists. While these authors were often dubbed 'Englishmen', their Scottishness was nevertheless acknowledged and attracted a special brand of admiration.[4] Observant visitors such as the writer Johann Wilhelm Archenholz made much of Scotland's excellence. 'There is more true learning to be found in Edinburgh', Archenholz informed his readers, 'than in Oxford and Cambridge taken together.'[5] On the Scottish side, the traveller James Macdonald wrote: 'The Scotch are perhaps more like the Germans, especially in their faults, than any other nation of Europe. We have the same courting of that seductive harlot who promises much and performs nothing, metaphysics.'[6]

---

[3] The best overview is Michael Maurer, *Aufklärung und Anglophilie in Deutschland* (Göttingen, 1987); for the Scottish–German links see Norbert Waszek, 'Bibliography of the Scottish Enlightenment in Germany', *Studies on Voltaire and the Eighteenth Century*, 230 (1985), 283–303.

[4] Manfred Kuehn, *Scottish Common Sense in Germany, 1768–1800: A Contribution to the History of Critical Philosophy* (Kingston, 1987); Norbert Waszek, *The Scottish Enlightenment and Hegel's Account of Civil Society* (Dordrecht,1988); Keith Tribe, *Governing Economy: The Reformation of German Economic Discourse 1750–1830* (Cambridge, 1988).

[5] Quoted by P. E. Matheson, *German Visitors to England 1770–1795 and their Impressions* (Oxford, 1930), 23.

[6] Quoted by Alexander Gillies, *A Hebridean in Goethe's Weimar: The Reverend James Macdonald and the Cultural Relations between Scotland and Germany* (Oxford, 1969), 74–5.

Macdonald's 'seductive harlot' indeed exposed the Scottish edge over the English. As early as 1772 Herder was able to point out that 'the spirit of British philosophy seems to be situated beyond Hadrian's wall, in a little group of its own adherents in the Scottish mountains'.[7] By the early nineteenth century both Hegel and Goethe were well aware that German thought in the preceding decades had been nourished by Scottish rather than English thinkers. Goethe wrote of the appreciation of the Germans, striving after *Bildung* (education), for 'the merits of worthy Scottish men'. Hegel put it more sharply: 'One can no longer speak of English philosophers,' he opined. Germans were indebted to the moral philosophy of the 'learned, thinking men' of Scotland.[8] Significantly, the only two Britons elected as members of the Royal Prussian Academy of Sciences and Arts in the late eighteenth century were Scots: Adam Ferguson, the historian of mankind, and Sir John Sinclair, the agriculturist and author of the celebrated *Analysis of the Statistical Account of Scotland*.[9]

This nuanced reception of the Scottish literary and philosophical culture as different from—and more interesting than—its English counterpart owed a great deal to the enthusiastic German reception of James Macpherson's invented Gaelic bard, Ossian. Scotland became associated with a new appreciation of primitive tribes and savage poetry, and hence, by extension, with a new understanding of the history of mankind.[10] I will return later to the ironical aspect of Ossian's role as a herald of the Scottish Enlightenment in Germany.

Scottish historians figured prominently in the Scottish–German intellectual link. Hume's *History of England* (1754–62) was translated and published as early as 1762, and twice at that, by two separate translators and publishers. William Robertson's *History of Charles V* (1769) also earned a

---

[7] Quoted by Waszek, *The Scottish Enlightenment*, 82.
[8] Quoted by Waszek, 'Bibliography', 238.
[9] *Mémoires de l'Académie Royale des Sciences et Belles-Lettres 1792–1793* (Berlin, 1798), 6.
[10] Howard Gaskill, 'German Ossianism: A Reappraisal?', *German Life and Letters*, 42 (1989), 5–26.

prompt German translation, subsequently annotated and revised. Both works met with considerable attention and praise.[11] This essay, however, focuses on the German reception of Ferguson, which was marked by a degree of eagerness and warmth unmatched by the reception of any other Scottish writer. Ferguson seems to have inspired in his German readers a particular sense of intellectual affinity, disrupted just occasionally by an awareness of cultural and political differences. He thus provides a special opportunity to test the extents and the limits of the German appreciation of Scottish historiography, and to touch on the attendant issues of historiographical method, cultural hypotheses, and political outlook.

II

Ferguson was born in 1723 in the village of Logierait in Perthshire, on the border between the Scottish lowlands and Highlands, as the son of a minister of the Church of Scotland.[12] Like other contributors to the Scottish Enlightenment, his thought was shaped by his Presbyterian background and classical education, but what made him an unusual Enlightenment thinker was his acquaintance with the Gaelic-speaking society of the Highlands. The first-hand and early encounter with both 'raw' clansmen and 'polished', Anglicized lowlanders was a formative experience in his life. At Edinburgh, where he studied divinity, Ferguson met Hugh Blair, John Home, and William Robertson, and later became acquainted with Hume and Smith, thus joining the core group of the Scottish Enlightenment. Unlike his friends, however, he proceeded from university to join the British army as a military chaplain to the Scottish regiment

---

[11] Günther Gawlick and Lothar Kreimendahl, *Hume in der deutschen Aufklärung: Umrisse eine Rezeptionsgeschichte* (Stuttgart, 1987); László Kontler, 'William Robertson's History of Manners in German, 1770–1795', *Journal of the History of Ideas*, 58 (1997), 125–44.

[12] The best recent account of Ferguson's life is Jane Bush Fagg, 'Biographical Introduction', in Vincenzo Merolle (ed.), *The Correspondence of Adam Ferguson* (London, 1995), i, pp. xix–cxvii.

known as the Black Watch, and took part in the Franco-British campaign in Flanders during the late phase of the War of the Austrian Succession. He then abandoned both army and ministry, and became a well-loved Edinburgh professor (first of physics, and later of moral philosophy) and man of letters.

Ferguson travelled widely in Europe, corresponded with d'Holbach, and met Voltaire. He was a politically active man, who campaigned for a Scottish militia, wrote political pamphlets, and travelled to America with the unsuccessful Carlisle commission sent by Parliament to negotiate a deal with the American rebels. Ferguson was a moderate Whig by political conviction, but a republican in sentiment and temperament: he chided the American rebels for taking a political gamble, but regarded the French Revolution and its military triumphs with open admiration. These aspects of his intellectual biography, however, were virtually unknown to his German readers and admirers, who seem to have known Ferguson only through his books.

The two history books authored by Ferguson were well received in Germany by a surprisingly varied audience. *An Essay on the History of Civil Society*, today clearly seen as his most original work, was published in English in 1767 and in German as early as 1768.[13] This book was read with great attention by some of the key figures of the German Enlightenment, among them the Swiss historian Isaak Iselin, Gotthold Ephraim Lessing, and Georg Friedrich Hegel. Ferguson's second historical work, the *History of the Progress and Termination of the Roman Republic*, which appeared in English in 1783 and in German during the following three years,[14] had a broad and not exclusively academic readership in Germany. It was read, for example, by Johann Georg Hamann on his deathbed. It is a 'nourishment to my soul', Hamann wrote.[15]

---

[13] *Versuch über die Geschichte der bürgerlichen Gesellschaft*, trans. anonymously by Christian Friedrich Jünger (Leipzig, 1768).
[14] *Geschichte des Fortgangs und Untergangs der Römischen Republik*, trans. and annotated C[hristian] D[aniel] B[eck]. (Leipzig, 1784–6).
[15] Johann Georg Hamann, *Briefwechsel*, ed. Walther Ziesemer and Arthur Henkel (Wiesbaden, 1956–79), vii. 33.

Most successful of all was Ferguson's philosophy textbook *Institutes of Moral Philosophy*, which in Christian Garve's brilliant translation caused a stir that carried on from the Enlightenment to the romantic period. This was the book which the poet Novalis read in the churchyard, sitting by the grave of his fiancée with a cup of milk at his elbow.[16] Let us, however, concentrate on Ferguson's two historical works. My first question concerns their appeal to German readers, and the second question touches on the limits of this appeal, the uneasiness and dissatisfaction that occasionally show through the approving book reviews and the scholarly references.

The problem faced by any study of Ferguson's German reception can be stated simply: how did the most republican-minded thinker of the Scottish Enlightenment end up being seen by most of his German-reading public as a preacher of spiritual perfectibility? Ferguson was a uniquely placed civic thinker and historian, being intimately acquainted not only with the writings of Montesquieu and Rousseau but also with the clan communities of the Scottish Highlands. In his *Essay* he famously located civic virtue not only in the classical polities but also in the political and martial communities of primitive nations. He had a clear political point to make— that modern Scots, and Britons in general, can retain or regain the role of citizen-soldiers and control the fate of their polity. Contrary to Rousseau, he claimed that primitive virtues were social, and that the basic social bonds were not irretrievably lost to modernity. Unlike his own contemporaries Hume and Smith, he argued that commercial society, based on the division of labour, should not encroach upon government and army. The blind fatality of history, the unintended consequences of technology and commerce, must be checked by a self-conscious, voluntary, non-professional, broadly based political citizenry.[17]

---

[16] Novalis [Friedrich, Freiherr von Hardenberg], *Schriften*, ed. Richard Samuel *et al.* (Stuttgart, 1975), iv. 37.

[17] See esp. David Kettler, *The Social and Political Thought of Adam Ferguson* (Columbus, Oh., 1965); Duncan Forbes, 'Introduction', in his edition of Ferguson, *An Essay on the History of Civil Society* (Edinburgh, 1966); more recently Oz-Salzberger, *Translating the Enlightenment*, ch. 4.

Guided by this political agenda, Ferguson wrote his large historical account of the Roman Republic, a book seen by several reviewers as a worthy companion to Gibbon's *Decline and Fall of the Roman Empire*, and praised with some warmth by Gibbon himself.[18] Unlike Gibbon, however, Ferguson's interest in ancient Rome focused squarely on the Republic, and his interest in the Republic was keenest when he discussed its downfall. He paid special attention to the question of the inevitability of this downfall, and continued the narrative through to Caligula, in whom he saw the death of the hope for republican revival. Both the *Essay* and the *Roman Republic* acknowledged a cyclical model of the rise and decline of nations, or, more precisely, the rise and decline of political institutions and national spirit. But this was pointedly a 'weak' cyclical model, offering an open-ended view of history and seeing voluntary agents as able to postpone republican downfall for as long as they cared. For Ferguson these voluntary agents were not leaders, legislators, or heroes but ordinary, politically active men.

When it came to modern Europe, Ferguson did not share Hume's view that absolute monarchies were a viable form of civilized modernity. He bluntly attacked the regimes of Spain, France, and Germany and their total loss of public spirit. Most European states of his day were 'merely a combination of departments, in which consideration, wealth, eminence, or power, are offered as the reward of service'.[19] All empires were graveyards of civic virtue. Contemporary Europe was a long way down the slippery slope from monarchy to despotism, particularly the Holy Roman Empire, where a dismantled national unity was further torn apart by rival aristocratic powers. Ferguson made one individual reference to a German prince, not by name, but with a footnote referring to Frederick the Great's *Memoirs of Brandenburg*. As Ferguson put it, Frederick had been 'pleased to ridicule' the English judicial system and the

---

[18] Gibbon's letter to Ferguson is reprinted in John Small, *Biographical Sketch of Adam Ferguson, LL.D., F.R.S.E., Professor of Moral Philosophy in the University of Edinburgh* (Edinburgh, 1864), 24.

[19] Adam Ferguson, *An Essay on the History of Civil Society*, ed. Fania Oz-Salzberger (Cambridge, 1995), 57–8.

broad civic base of the British polity: 'Men of superior genius sometimes seem to imagine that the vulgar have no title to act, or to think.'[20] There was no doubt left with regard to Ferguson's contempt for Europe's monarchies, or his appreciation of Europe's surviving republics.

Britain, however, was a case unto itself. Here was a polity uniquely endowed with legacy of political freedom, which could only be preserved by an ever-alert civic spirit. The best legal and constitutional arrangements, the habeas corpus and the trial by jury, enacted by the people or their representatives, could be constantly breached by arbitrary and oppressive courts: 'No wiser form was ever opposed to the abuses of power', Ferguson wrote, 'but it requires a fabric no less than the whole political constitution of Great Britain, a spirit no less than the refractory and turbulent zeal of this fortunate people, to secure its effects.'[21] By referring to 'Great Britain', Ferguson circumvented the separate constitutional legacy of his own country. Like other writers of the Scottish Enlightenment he was happy to see Scotland subscribe to the joys and responsibilities of English freedom. But Scotland was not merely an upstart junior partner to the English success: Ferguson made several allusions to the particular civic and military traditions associated with Scotland. In the *Essay* he did not mention his native land by name, but he made several significant references to the powerful civic life of primitive 'clans'. In the chapter on the history of literature Ferguson extolled the magnificent beauty and pureness of savage poetry, exemplified by the legendary bard Ossian, whom Ferguson never admitted to be a figment of James Macpherson's imagination.[22] Ferguson's own record as a leading proponent of a Scottish militia and an active sponsor of Macpherson's Ossianic epic was not emphasized in his books, but a Scottish agenda nevertheless shines through the pages of the *Essay*. With its living ancients, the Highlanders, Scotland was the home of

---

[20] Ferguson, *An Essay on the History of Civil Society*, 209.   [21] Ibid. 160.
[22] The reference to Ossian was inserted in the 2nd (1768) ed. of the *Essay*; cf. ibid. 166, editor's footnote. On Ferguson's Ossianic commitment see Fagg, 'Biographical Introduction', pp. lxviii–lxxii.

many men who still knew how to act as citizen-soldiers and could remind other modern Europeans how it was done. This was Ferguson's project.

It would not do, however, to present Ferguson's books as clear-cut statements on republican virtue, its capacity for survival, and its modern viability, because most of his German readers did not read them in this way. But many British and American readers did. David Hume, who disliked the idea of political virtue, politely and privately dissociated himself from Ferguson's moralizing fervour; the Yorkshire parliamentary reformers approached Ferguson asking for his support; and American publishers brought out numerous editions of his works, especially the *Roman Republic*, well into the nineteenth century.[23]

For Ferguson's German readers, on the other hand, his civic subtext mostly remained well beneath the text. Ferguson was well liked as a Scotsman, an empiricist, and a historian who combined ancient history with modern travel literature in a novel way and who wrote of society in a moral vein. When his republicanism did shine through, it was met with regret, unease, or open hostility. And these points of conflict were often acted out in historiographical discussions.

III

Rampant Anglophilia aside, any perusal of German book reviews and scholarly references to British works in this period reveals a growing self-confidence on the part of German academic historians. In Göttingen Johann Christoph Gatterer, who was hoping for a German Hume, was nevertheless quick to attack both bad British historians and petty German imitators of French and British writers.[24]

---

[23] See Richard B. Sher, *Church and University in the Scottish Enlightenment: The Moderate Literati of Edinburgh* (Edinburgh, 1985), 274–5; Kettler, *Ferguson's Social and Political Thought*, 86–8.
[24] J. C. Gatterer, 'Vorrede', *Allgemeine historische Bibliothek*, 1 (1767); Herbert Butterfield, 'The Rise of the German Historical School', in *Man on his Past. The Study of the History of Historical Scholarship* (Cambridge, 1955), 43.

The Leipzig professor Christian Daniel Beck, who translated Ferguson's *Roman Republic*, took the liberty of making substantial changes in the text (many of them unannounced), adding critical footnotes, checking and supplementing all references to primary sources, and providing a running critique of Ferguson's interpretation. This editorial project was applauded by every reviewer I have read. Beck was praised in the *Allgemeine Literatur-Zeitung* for avoiding 'slavish accuracy' in the translation and for abbreviating the book, which 'for Germany is too big and expensive'.[25] His editorial corrections were approved and expanded by learned reviewers, and there is a clear sense that both the translator and the reviewers were supplying Ferguson's opus with a new scaffolding of superior source criticism.

This goes some way towards explaining why Ferguson's politics were approached more easily by his German critics through the safe route of historiographical critique. This prism enabled Ferguson's German readers and mediators to cope with four problematic areas in his writings: his political use of history, his treatment of classical Greece and Rome, his 'Englishness' and, in a different way, his 'Scottishness'. An analysis of Ferguson's German reception should thus focus on each of these areas and bring out their interwoven significance.

The prompt translation of Ferguson's *Essay on the History of Civil Society*—fast even by the standards of that heyday of German Anglophilia—demonstrates the intellectual awareness and thirst of the German reading public, at least as interpreted by the actions of the German publishing houses, in this particular case the firm of Junius and Gleditsch of Leipzig. The book was taken to be part of the renewed and transformed genre of universal history, which Ferguson and then his fellow Scotsmen Robertson and Kames adopted from Voltaire and Rousseau. In Germany, where a strong indigenous tradition of universal history had existed since the sixteenth century, there were already works reflecting

---

[25] *Allgemeine Literatur-Zeitung* (Jan. 1785), pt. 1, 90–3 (continued Feb. 1786, pt. 1, 363–7; June 1787, 467–70).

the transformation of the genre in line with the philosophical tenor of the Enlightenment: Gatterer's *Universalhistorie* (1760), and Iselin's *Geschichte der Menschheit* (1764).[26] Ferguson's book thus fell conveniently into a genre which was both familiar and fashionable at the time.

'Philosophical history' was an eminently acceptable term in late eighteenth-century German discourse. There were no German echoes of the tension apparent in France between the rival historiographical traditions of the *érudits* and the *philosophes*—the former found guilty of stale antiquarianism, and the latter, especially Voltaire, of dashing shallowness. A number of German reviewers hailed Ferguson's two historical works as 'philosophical' in the most approving terms. This was understood as a bold attempt to subject history to what Moses Mendelssohn called a 'truly philosophical gaze'.[27] This approach was generally received with great approval in Germany and did not entail, as in France, suspicion of flippancy, contempt for detail, and inaccuracy.[28]

Yet Ferguson's philosophical history, unlike the works of Iselin before him and Lessing and Kant after him, was nevertheless conceived as an open challenge to contemporary political thought. Its critique of modernity, in a way comparable to Herder's, relied on a denial of linear moral progress. To readers versed in the recent attempts at universal history, to readers of Voltaire, Iselin, and of Ferguson's countrymen Hume and Robertson, the *Essay on the History of Civil Society* was a baffling book: a narrative of technological advance coupled with the ever present possibility of moral regression; a British philosophical history not averse to commerce and modernity, but hostile to the attendant discourse of politeness and sensibility; a writer whose best passages describe the unintended course of human affairs,

---

[26] Cf. Reinhart Koselleck *et al.*, 'Geschichte, Historie', in Otto Brunner, Werner Conze, and Reinhart Koselleck (eds.), *Geschichtliche Grundbegriffe*, ii (Stuttgart, 1975), 593–717.

[27] M. Mendelssohn, *Briefe die neueste Literatur betreffend* (Berlin, 1761), ix. 21.

[28] 'Erudition' and 'philosophy' became almost dichotomous in the French historiography of the 18th century, while no such opposition developed in Germany; this telling difference is discussed, from a French viewpoint, in the concluding section of Chantal Grell's *L'Histoire entre érudition et philosophie: Étude sur la connaissance historique à l'âge des lumières* (Paris, 1993).

but who nevertheless insists that informed, active individuals are the sole guarantors of a stable polity.

This agenda made Ferguson's 'universal history' pointedly less than universal. Thus the Göttingen philosopher Johann Georg Feder complained that Ferguson, just like Aristotle, bestowed false universality on military values:

> To make the belligerent spirit of a nation, as it seems to have occurred in several peoples, into a basic goal of the state, to maintain a standing army, to lay out fortresses, are ... rules, which already transcend the universal [principles of national security], but where they nevertheless apply, they may not be separated from those basic principles.[29]

Feder, like several other reviewers, was quite possibly making use of Ferguson's affection for warring nations to gibe discreetly at contemporary militarism nearer home, implying Frederick II of Prussia. Ferguson, with his very Scottish enthusiasm for a citizen militia, could probably not imagine what German readers would make of his classical republican belligerency.

Yet the central reference point remained historiographical: the verdict of the leading Göttingen historian August Ludwig Schlözer was that Ferguson was not a universal historian but a 'Specialgeschichtsschreiber'. This category, invented by Schlözer, in fact included all historians except Polybius and himself.[30] Ferguson's history of the Roman Republic nevertheless passed the Göttingen test, set by Gatterer and Schlözer, with flying colours. Referring to Ferguson's *Roman Republic* the classicist Christian Gottlob Heyne wrote:

> [T]he work deserves to be in the hands of all young readers. ... It is better than all [other] textbooks (*Handbücher*) on Roman History. ... [It] achieves fundamental knowledge of the Roman *Statistik* through facts, not from *Raisonnements* which are transferred from modern states to those totally different times; the author knew and really used the sources, but he used them with an enlightened philosophical spirit.[31]

---

[29] J. G. Feder, *Lehrbuch der praktischen Philosophie* (3rd expanded edn., 2 vols.; Hanau and Leipzig, 1775), ii. 217.

[30] A. L. Schlözer, *Vorstellung seiner Universal-Historie* (Göttingen, 1772), 22.

[31] *Göttingische Anzeigen von gelehrten Sachen* (1785), pt. 1, 629.

The approval was tellingly laced with contemporary fashionable terms: Ferguson's work was based on *Statistik*, the careful collection and arrangement of facts, rather than *raisonnements*, futile speculations with a suspiciously French aroma.

One reproach echoed through almost every book review of Ferguson's *Essay* and *Roman Republic*. Ferguson's open political approval of the Roman Republic was singled out as selective and biased reading of the sources, and emerged as a chief historiographical shortcoming. Thus, the most interesting footnotes added to Ferguson's history of the Roman Republic by his translator and editor Beck were those attempting to tone down his enthralment to the mores of republican Rome. Beck patiently commented that the citizens of Saguntum were not as heroic as Ferguson claimed in their stance against Hannibal, that the Romans, like citizens of other republics, were not magnanimous to the vanquished, and that Ferguson was far too naïve in his reading of the Roman writers when it came to their encomium of Roman virtues. As Heyne plainly put it in his book review, 'Herr F. is dazzled time and again by the beautiful side of the Romans' character.' Beck had done well to correct Ferguson's judgement here, Heyne added, 'because, basically, the Romans were nothing more than a rude people of barbarians, devastators of the globe to their own ruin'. And what can one expect, he added, again with Prussia possibly in mind, from a state ruled by the military?[32]

Heyne's colleague, the historian Christoph Meiners, a pioneer of racist historiography, accused Ferguson of misunderstanding the Romans from a different angle. Ferguson did not use enough primary sources, and made too much of the ancient historians and too little of other writers. His account of the republican constitution was too English, Meiners wrote, and not clear enough 'to readers who are not closely acquainted with the nature of free states'.[33]

A telling critique was launched by Isaak Iselin, who wrote a long and generally laudatory review of Ferguson's *Essay* in the Berlin journal *Allgemeine deutsche Bibliothek*. Iselin, whose own

---

[32] Ibid. 630.
[33] *Göttingische Anzeigen von gelehrten Sachen* (1784), pt. 2, 892–3.

history of mankind is the story of a linear ascent in morality and wisdom, was openly sarcastic about Ferguson's sociable savages and virtuous Spartans. 'Was the Spartan constitution in principle much more than a systematic barbarity?', he asked.[34] Republican spirit entailed dispute and conflict, and for Iselin this state of affairs went under the utterly pejorative label of 'disorder'. 'The way in which Ferguson expresses himself could mislead one into thinking that political divisions, factions, turmoils, are in his view the only convenient means to keep virtue going.' This was evidently what Ferguson thought, but Iselin hastened to defend his Scottish colleague from such a questionable reading:

but we believe that he only wants to say that, human opinions being by nature varied, each person should shamelessly express his [opinion] and fearlessly defend it. And he is right [in saying] that when this is no longer the case, then the state has been corrupted and freedom has vanished.[35]

The difficulty was explained away by claiming that it was freedom of expression, not political discord, that Ferguson advocated. Iselin thus turned Ferguson, as other German reviewers did, into a benign political Stoic who recommended good theoretical controversy rather than active civic strife.

And yet Ferguson's Roman insights were not completely lost in the translation. Friedrich Schiller read Ferguson with great excitement as a young man, and the Fergusonian fingerprints in his works are numerous. Unlike the academic historians, Schiller took Ferguson's republicanism at face value. One striking example should suffice here: concerning the Emperor Nerva Ferguson wrote that his rule would have brought perfect human happiness if only a people could be governed by a virtue other than their own. Schiller put the very same idea in similar words into the mouth of the Marquis of Posa in *Don Carlos*, his most republican play. The scope and depth of Ferguson's influence on Schiller's highly original philosophy are yet to be assessed.[36]

---

[34] *Allgemeine deutsche Bibliothek*, 11 (1770), pt. 1, 160.   [35] Ibid. 164.
[36] Two points of departure are Dushan Breski, 'Schiller's Debt to Montesquieu and Adam Ferguson', *Comparative Literature*, 13 (1961), 239–53; Oz-Salzberger, *Translating the Enlightenment*, ch. 12.

To his German critics Ferguson's 'Englishness' was the sum of all his historical judgements that were biased by his birth and breeding. His bias in favour of the ancient republics was explained in terms of English idiosyncrasy. Yet there was more to it than that. Ferguson's translator Christian Garve complained, in a very interesting commentary on Ferguson's *Institutes of Moral Philosophy*, that English terms such as 'public spirit' are simply not translatable into German:

> No virtue, no characteristic is in fact rarer among us [Germans], because it has two qualities, both of which are either less characteristic of the temperament of present-day Germans, or are obstructed by their circumstances: a great warmth and extension of the imagination; and a certain firmness and toughness of the mind. [We lack] the one, because we are stirred by nothing of which we cannot conceive. In order to be filled with concern for one's town, for one's fatherland, or for the human race, one must somehow carry their picture everywhere; this picture must be immutable and vivid if any prevailing inclination of the soul is to emerge from it. [We lack] the other because whenever we become very occupied with our own joys and sorrows, they always captivate our heart completely, and leave no room for alien feelings and more remote interests. The man of public spirit must forget his own self, and he must be able to put society in his stead.[37]

A sense of sad resignation *vis-à-vis* English political culture is apparent also in Jacobi's famous novel *Woldemar*, where young men and women discussing Ferguson's ideas are reduced to tears:

> thus, lacking feelings of fatherland and freedom, lacking all interests of the heart, lacking courage and lacking love—we know how to encourage contempt for death and injury by flogging—and to employ prisoners for our guard and protection; and to be happy and content, without virtue, without immortality, and without

---

[37] This passage makes an interesting forerunner to Benedict Anderson's recent definition of modern nations as 'imagined communities' (Benedict Anderson, *Imagined Communities: Reflections on the Origin and Spread of Nationalism*, London, 1991). Christian Garve, 'Anmerkungen', in *Fergusons Grundsätze der Moralphilosophie* (Leipzig, 1772), 330–2.

God.—So our eyes are wide open; the thousand-year Reich is near us, and we preach it with a new kind of enthusiasm, with the strange enthusiasm of materialism, with the rapture of cold blood.[38]

Other readers, however, felt neither inferior nor insecure. Especially among academic historians, and especially in Göttingen, Ferguson was proudly reproached for being too English. His presentation of the British judicial system in terms of 'natural law' caused special concern: 'The Englishman is accustomed from his youth to think so, and not otherwise. How easily he confuses this way of thinking, which is natural for *him*, with nature itself!'[39]

This tone intensified in the years following the French Revolution, when Ferguson's republican tendency was increasingly seen as flirting dangerously with the old notion of 'English freedom'. But the point was not merely political. In Göttingen, as Notker Hammerstein has shown, the legal history of the Reich was being developed into a new approach stressing the inner logic of German history.[40] The resentment was not against the English government as such. It was against the major Enlightenment theme laid out by Voltaire and Montesquieu and developed by Hume and Robertson, which put 'English freedom' forward not just in terms of a 'happy accident', but in terms of a cumulative constitutional project which could be taken as a model by other political societies. Comments on Ferguson show that German scholars were beginning to conceptualize a critique of this matrix in historiographical terms. They were ready to assert that German political culture cannot and need not emulate the English—just as in the 1790s the Göttingen historians would provide their own arguments to the effect that Germans cannot and need not emulate the French.

---

[38] F. H. Jacobi, 'Ein Stück Philosophie des Lebens und der Menschheit: Aus dem zweiten Bande von Woldemar', *Deutsches Museum* (1779), 394–5.

[39] 'Von Staatsgesetzen (Aus Adam Ferguson's Institutes of Moral Philosophy)', *Hannoverisches Magazin*, 93 (22 Nov. 1771), 1475–6, footnote *a*, emphasis in original.

[40] Notker Hammerstein, *Jus und Historie: Ein Beitrag zur Geschichte des historischen Denkens an deutschen Universitäten im späten 17. und im 18. Jahrhundert* (Göttingen, 1972).

If 'English freedom' was considered a bad terminus for universal history, Ferguson's Scottish identity worked in a different way. It has been noted by recent students of the Scottish Enlightenment that Ferguson made no mention of Scotland in his *Essay on the History of Civil Society*. Duncan Forbes has pointed out, however, that in Ferguson's lengthy description, the hilly landscape and robust social values of ancient Sparta deliberately resemble the Scottish Highlands of his day.[41] It is interesting to note that Iselin, the Basle town clerk, lawyer, and historian, recognized his Swiss homeland in the same physical and human landscape. Iselin had a keen sense of the Scottish–Swiss affinity—the long independent history, the role of the mountains, the native stubbornness and love of freedom. But like his German colleagues, he did not think that the 'freedom-loving Scot' was offering any viable republican alternative either to the Swiss oligarchies or to the German principalities.

What Ferguson did offer, and where he and his fellow Scotsmen supplied an important inspiration, was a model for a new kind of cultural politics. The Scottish thinkers were considered not just fresh and sharp philosophers, as Kant and Hegel would have them, but also as revivers of indigenous literary traditions and agents of restored national vigour. Ferguson, who read and spoke Gaelic, was one of the chief sponsors and mediators of Macpherson's Ossianic epic. The man who saw this most clearly was Herder, who, in his *Briefwechsel über Ossian*, begins a fantasy journey to England, which turns into an escape to Scotland, 'to become an ancient Caledonian for a while', to meet Macpherson and find the landscape of Ossian. This dream was significantly incorporated into Herder's own search for the authentic ancient roots of Germanic art and poetry in his epoch-making piece *Von deutscher Art und Kunst* (1773).[42] A great deal has been written of the German reception of Ossian, but little attention has been drawn to the impact of the Edinburgh literati who sponsored this project as role models for the German inventors of tradition.

---

[41] See Forbes's introduction to his edn. of Ferguson's *Essay* (Edinburgh, 1966), p. xxxix.

[42] Johann Gottfried Herder, *Werke in zwei Bänden*, ed. Karl Gustav Gerold (Munich, 1953), i. 838–9.

At the risk of overplaying the title of this essay, I have attempted to show that Ferguson, and Scottish historiography and political philosophy in general, had more than one 'reception history' in Germany. Political disagreements and cultural affinities, the former addressing the so-called Englishman in Ferguson, and the latter recognizing the Scotsman in him, often intersected in historiographical criticism. This device made it possible to avoid an open discussion of politics and cultural politics. Ferguson's republican models, ancient Sparta, Rome, and some crucial aspects of modern Britain, invoked in his German readers a whole range of responses, from Schiller's call to freedom to the scepticism of civilized monarchists and Jacobi's lament for the Holy Roman Empire. But the most effective way of dealing with Ferguson's civic zeal was the terse editorial footnote or the dry scholarly comment. Isaak Iselin handled Ferguson's primitivism particularly well in his review of the *Essay*. Our forefathers may have been 'proud, brave, rash, immoderate in love and hate', he wrote, 'but we thank heaven that the times of this admirable disorder are now long gone'.[43]

Ferguson's German reception suggests that the modern reworking of 'national uniqueness'—the attempt to define the indigenous linguistic and poetic genius of a modern nation *vis-à-vis* its neighbours—was double edged. As an 'Englishman', a philosopher of political liberty and advanced commercial society, Ferguson's claim to universality was consistently denied by his German critics. But as a 'Scotsman', setting out to construct a cultural identity for a nation which no longer enjoyed sovereignty, Ferguson was found by German readers to be relevant, exciting, and inspiring. Herder's imagined attempt 'to become an ancient Caledonian for a while' turned out to be an important leg of the great journey towards German cultural nationhood.

[43] *Allgemeine deutsche Bibliothek*, 11 (1770), pt. 1, 161.

4
Gibbon and German Historiography
Wilfried Nippel

More than two hundred years after its publication Gibbon's work is still well known among a general public, at least in the Anglo-American world, and is considered a challenge by professional historians. No other eighteenth-century historian has achieved such lasting success. Gibbon's work had an impact all over Europe, including Germany. However, the story of Gibbon's changing reputation in Germany illuminates the emergence of a peculiar self-image among German historians. They increasingly defined themselves primarily as scholars distinguished by their command of 'scientific' methods, and not as writers of history addressing a general public. This essay starts by outlining the mixed German reactions to Gibbon's work up to the end of the nineteenth century. A short comparison between Gibbon and Germany's leading ancient historians in the nineteenth century with regard to methodological standards follows. The conclusion reflects on the reasons for the ignorance of Gibbon among twentieth-century German historians. This essay therefore concentrates on the methodological aspects of German statements about Gibbon, rather than on how his substantive interpretations, such as his view of Constantine and Christianity, may have influenced later German historiography.

Gibbon's *History of the Decline and Fall of the Roman Empire*[1] (1776–88) evoked a considerable response among the German public. Translations were begun during the course

---

[1] Quotations are taken from E. Gibbon, *The History of the Decline and Fall of the Roman Empire*, ed. David Womersley, 3 vols. (London, 1994), hereafter cited as *DF*.

of its publication.[2] Some chapters were brought out in separate German editions.[3] A translation of chapter 44 on the development of Roman law was published in 1789 with comments by the distinguished Göttingen jurist Gustav Hugo.[4] Gibbon's controversy with Oxford dons over his interpretation of Christianity was documented and his *Vindication* translated.[5] The Göttingen popular philosopher Christoph Meiners published a book, *Geschichte des Verfalls der Sitten, Wissenschaften und Sprache der Römer in den ersten Jahrhunderten nach Christi Geburt* (1791), as a companion volume to a translation of Gibbon's *History*. The Kiel historian Dietrich Hermann Hegewisch dwelt upon Gibbon's picture of the Antonine age in his book *Über die für die Menschheit glücklichste Epoche der Römischen Geschichte* (1800). Intellectuals of all kinds—Schiller, Georg Forster, Hegel—discussed at least certain aspects of Gibbon's work. According to Herder, German Protestant theologians seemed prepared to discuss Gibbon's account of Christianity more freely than their Anglican counterparts.[6] Proudly stat-

[2] *Geschichte des Verfalls und Untergangs des Römischen Reiches: Aus dem Englischen übersetzt und mit einigen Anmerkungen begleitet von Friedrich August Wilhelm Wenck*, i (Leipzig, 1779); ii–viii and xiii–xv trans. Karl Gottfried Schreiter (Leipzig, 1788–93); complete edn. (continued by Christian Daniel Beck) in 19 vols. (Leipzig, 1805–6); *Geschichte der Abnahme und des Falls des Römischen Reichs: Aus dem Englischen . . . übersetzt von C. W. v. R[iemberg]*, i–vi (Magdeburg, 1788–90), vii–xiv (Vienna, 1790–2); *Geschichte des Verfalls und Untergangs des Römischen Reichs, abgekürzt in drei Bänden. Aus dem Englischen. Von Georg Karl Friedrich Seidel*, 3 vols. (Berlin, 1790).

[3] *Die Bekehrung des Kaisers Constantin* (Altona, 1784); *Leben des Attila, Königs der Hunnen* (Lüneburg, 1787); *Die Ausbreitung des Christentums aus natürlichen Ursachen* (Hamburg, 1788); all trans. by A. H. W. v. Walterstern.

[4] *Eduard Gibbons historische Übersicht des Römischen Rechts oder das 44. Kapitel der Geschichte des Verfalls des Römischen Reiches: Aus dem Englischen übersetzt und mit Anmerkungen begleitet von Prof. Hugo* (Göttingen, 1789); new edn. by O. Behrends (Göttingen, 1996). On Hugo see M. Diesselhorst, 'Gustav Hugo (1764–1844) oder: Was bedeutet es, wenn ein Jurist Philosoph wird?', in F. Loos (ed.), *Rechtswissenschaft in Göttingen. Göttinger Juristen aus 250 Jahren* (Göttingen, 1987), 146–65, and Behrends in the new edn. of Hugo's translation.

[5] C. W. F. Walch, 'Nachricht von der zwischen Eduard Gibbon und seinen Gegnern geführten Streitigkeit . . .', in id., *Der Zustand der neuesten Religionsgeschichte*, Pt. 8 (Lemgo, 1781), 91–172; *Verteidigung einiger Stellen im 15. und 16. Kapitel der Geschichte der Abnahme und des Falls des Römischen Reichs* (Vienna, 1792) (xiv of Riemberg's translation).

[6] See the references in J. Bernays, 'Edward Gibbon's Geschichtswerk. Ein Versuch zu seiner Würdigung', in id., *Gesammelte Abhandlungen*, ii, ed. H. Usener (Berlin, 1885), 206–54.

ing in his *Memoirs* that 'upon the whole the History of the Decline and Fall seems to have struck a root both at home and abroad, and may perhaps an hundred years hence, still continue to be abused', Gibbon added a footnote in which he quoted Johann Georg Meusel's opinion, expressed in his *Bibliotheca Historica*. Meusel, whom Gibbon called a 'learned and laborious German', praised the

> supremely organized arrangement of the work, the wise selection of subject-matter which can also show great subtlety, the language and style which is equally suitable for the historian and the philosopher and has not been surpassed by any English writer, Hume and Robertson not excepted. We congratulate our age on a history of this kind.[7]

This comment was originally written in Latin. If Gibbon had been able to read German, he would have seen that the reactions of German scholars were more mixed, as the reviews published in the journal *Göttingische Anzeigen von gelehrten Sachen* in particular demonstrated.[8] This was true especially of the review of volumes iv to vi of *Decline and Fall*, published in December 1788. Its author was in all probability the Göttingen historian Ludwig Timotheus Spittler.[9] The reviewer admired the literary qualities of Gibbon's work which were unmatched by German historiography, but while acknowledging Gibbon's erudition, he qualified it as somewhat dilettantish with respect to the treatment of the sources. He based this latter point only on some general remarks in Gibbon's account of church history, particularly those passages in which Gibbon could not borrow from Tillemont.[10] Of course, Gibbon relied on important previous

---

[7] Quoted from E. Gibbon, *Memoirs of my Life*, ed. B. Radice (Harmondsworth, 1984), 171, 186, 216.

[8] [A. v. Haller], review of *DF* i, *Göttingische Anzeigen von gelehrten Sachen* (1777), 20/17, 305–13; [M. Hißmann], review of *DF* ii, ibid. (1783), 1529–39. [L. T. Spittler], review of *DF* iii, ibid. (1783), 1698–704; [L. T. Spittler], review of *DF* iv–vi, ibid., (1788), 2049–56. The identification of the anonymous reviewers is taken from O. Fambach, *Die Mitarbeiter der Göttingischen gelehrten Anzeigen 1769–1836* (Tübingen, 1976).

[9] See above n. 8. On Spittler cf. P. H. Reill, 'Ludwig Timotheus Spittler', in H.-U. Wehler (ed.), *Deutsche Historiker*, ix (Göttingen, 1982), 42–60.

[10] S. Le Nain de Tillemont, *Mémoires pour servir à l'histoire ecclésiastique des six premiers siècles*, 10 vols. (Brussels, 1706); *Histoire des empereurs et des autres princes . . .*, 6 vols. (Brussels, 1732); cf. B. Neveu, *Un historien à l'École de Port Royal: Sébastien Le Nain*

work and repeatedly acknowledged, if with ironical overtones, his debt to such predecessors as 'the learned' Tillemont, 'whose bigotry is overbalanced by the merits of erudition, diligence, veracity and scrupulous minuteness'.[11] Apart from referring to one or two details Spittler did not elaborate on the inadequacy of Gibbon's scholarly standards. And one wonders which German historian of his time he could have named as capable of producing a better account of Byzantine ecclesiastical history, for example.[12] Spittler was obviously unable to appreciate Gibbon's synthesis of profane and ecclesiastical history as a scholarly as well as a literary achievement.

Spittler's review set the tone for the reaction of German ancient historians in the nineteenth century. On a number of occasions Niebuhr expressed his admiration for Gibbon's literary mastery. In the preface to his *Römische Geschichte* (1811) he announced that he intended to continue his work up to the time when Gibbon's *Decline and Fall* begins. A new history of the imperial age, Niebuhr suggested, was superfluous, while dissertations (*Abhandlungen*) on the constitution and administration of the Empire could compensate for the shortcomings of Gibbon's work.[13] Theodor Mommsen was well aware that continuing his *Römische Geschichte* (1852 ff.) into the imperial age would entail a literary competition with Gibbon. In 1856, when he had completed the third volume, Mommsen wrote to Wilhelm Henzen that a history of the imperial age demanded a method totally different from that employed by Gibbon:

---

de Tillemont, *1637–1698* (The Hague, 1966); M. P. R. McGuire, 'Louis-Sébastien Le Nain de Tillemont', *Catholic History Review*, 52 (1966), 186–200; D. P. Jordan, 'Le Nain de Tillemont: Gibbon's "sure-footed mule"', *Church History*, 39 (1970), 483–502; R. T. Ridley, 'On Knowing Sébastien le Nain de Tillemont: For the Tercentenary of his Histoire', *Ancient Society*, 23 (1993), 233–95.

[11] *DF* ch. 47 n. 79 (ed. Womersley, ii. 967).

[12] On Gibbon's Byzantine scholarship cf. J. Irmscher, 'Edward Gibbon und das deutsche Byzanzbild', *Klio*, 43–5 (1965), 537–59; D. J. Geanakoplos, 'Edward Gibbon and Byzantine Ecclesiastical History', *Church History*, 35 (1966), 170–85; S. Runciman, 'Gibbon and Byzantium', in G. W. Bowersock (ed.), *Edward Gibbon and the Decline and Fall of the Roman Empire* (Cambridge, Mass., 1977), 53–60.

[13] See also the preface to the 2nd edn. (Berlin, 1826) and Niebuhr's *Vorträge über römische Geschichte*, iii, ed. M. Isler (Berlin, 1848), 284.

But why are you so curious about the Imperial Age in particular? You have Moses and the prophets—I mean Gibbon who, after all, was quite a different historian from Mr Niebuhr, the cosmopolitan boy wonder. I do not dare to set myself up as a rival to Gibbon except by employing a totally different method.[14]

In 1883, when Wilamowitz urged Mommsen to continue his work, he literally exhorted him to write a new 'history of the fall and decline of the Roman Empire' (*sic*) and not to avoid a competition with Gibbon. In a second letter he added that Mommsen need not fear comparison with Gibbon.[15] But this was indeed the cause of Mommsen's reluctance. In 1885 he published only an account of the provinces of the Empire in the period from Caesar to Diocletian, which was presented as the fifth volume of his *Römische Geschichte*. In the introduction Mommsen explained that the work did not go beyond the time of Diocletian as that would have required an improved version of Gibbon's history.[16]

There may have been a number of reasons why he did not write the 'fourth volume' of the *Römische Geschichte*. But at least since 1992, when Alexander and Barbara Demandt published notes taken at Mommsen's Berlin University lectures,[17] one reason can be ruled out. It had previously been believed that he had little interest in the history of the Empire and especially in the rise of Christianity, but this assumption has now been demonstrated to have been wrong. In fact Mommsen dealt with the subject in a series of lectures which ran continuously from 1861 to 1887. If the listeners' notes reflect adequately what Mommsen said, it must be concluded that he was right to shrink from embarking on a competition with Gibbon. No outlines of a work

---

[14] 'Warum sind Sie denn aber gerade auf die Kaiserzeit so neugierig? Ihr habt ja Mosen und die Propheten—Gibbon meine ich, der denn doch ein ganz anderer Historiker war als Herr Niebuhr, das kosmopolitische Wunderkind, und mit dem ich mich nicht getraue anders zu rivalisieren als durch eine total verschiedene Methode.' Quotation from L. Wickert, *Theodor Mommsen: Eine Biographie*, iii: *Wanderjahre* (Frankfurt, 1969), 633.

[15] Quotations ibid. 661, 666.

[16] T. Mommsen, *Römische Geschichte: Vollständige Ausgabe in acht Bänden* (Munich, 1976), vi. 15.

[17] T. Mommsen, *Römische Kaisergeschichte: Nach den Vorlesungsmitschriften von Sebastian und Paul Hensel 1882/86*, ed. B. and A. Demandt (Munich, 1992).

based on a 'totally different method' are discernible. Mommsen vacillated between telling the stories of the individual emperors and a structural account without arriving at a convincing form. And he struggled to classify the Empire's constitutional system. The inconsistencies in this account betray his helplessness. His discussion of the role of Christianity is no more than a collection of platitudes. These lectures give the impression that, at least compared with Gibbon's work, characterized by elegance of composition and subtlety of historical judgement, a history of the Empire by Mommsen would have been a disaster.[18] Mommsen was invited to participate in a commemoration of the centenary of Gibbon's death to be held in London in 1894, or to write a piece on Gibbon which could be read at the meeting. Mommsen replied in English:

> As for the paper you want me to write, it is not easy for me to say No; but after long, and too long, consideration, I cannot say Yes. Acknowledging in the highest degree the mastery of an unequalled historian, speaking publicly for him I should be obliged to limit in a certain way my admiration of his work ... His researches are not equal to his great views; he has read up more than a historian should. A first rate writer, he is not a plodder.[19]

In 1918, when Wilamowitz commented upon Mommsen's reaction to Gibbon he wrote that strictly speaking Gibbon was 'not a man of historical science', 'not a (professional) historian'.[20]

A growing tendency among nineteenth-century German scholars to dismiss Gibbon's work as 'scientifically' irrelevant had already been noted in 1874 by the classicist Jacob Bernays in his dissertation on Gibbon's life and work. This manuscript remained fragmentary and was not published until Bernays's *Gesammelte Abhandlungen* were posthumously

---

[18] Compare W. Nippel, 'Review of Mommsen, *Römische Kaisergeschichte*', *Grazer Beiträge*, 20 (1994), 308–14.
[19] Quoted from B. Croke, 'Mommsen on Gibbon', *Quaderni di storia*, 32 (1990), 47–59, 56.
[20] 'Im eigentlichen Sinne kein Mann der Wissenschaft'; 'ein großer Geschichtsschreiber, aber kein Historiker.' U. v. Wilamowitz-Moellendorff, 'Theodor Mommsen: Warum hat er den vierten Band der Römischen Geschichte nicht geschrieben?', *Internationale Monatsschrift für Wissenschaft, Kunst und Technik*, 12 (1918), 206–19, 219; id., 'Geschichtschreibung', ibid. 353–76, 371.

edited in 1885. Bernays ascribed the growing ignorance of Gibbon in Germany to a trend towards specialization and professionalization which entailed neglecting works of historical synthesis. And, he suggested, the (German) general public would not be attracted by Gibbon's ironic detachment from the events he narrates.[21]

Bernays, however, was sure that nobody else would attempt to write a synthesis like that by Gibbon, whose work would therefore be indispensable for all time. Bernays mentioned some of the work's shortcomings with respect to the treatment of sources but his overall assessment of Gibbon's work was highly positive. This can be summed up in five major points. Gibbon's study was the very first modern work of any sort on ancient history; second, it recognized that the state of the evidence available meant that ancient history needed to be presented in a reflective style, and not just as a simple narration; third, Gibbon was the first to achieve a synthesis of the history of states, the church, and law; fourth, Gibbon's empiricism led him to exploit the older tradition of antiquarian works and to dissociate himself from the arrogant attitude of eighteenth-century *philosophes* towards *érudits*, which also implied that he did not exhibit the nineteenth-century love of speculation. And finally, Gibbon was the only historian who had completed a great work based on profound erudition in a sophisticated literary form.[22] Thus, Jacob Bernays had already made all

---

[21] Bernays, 'Edward Gibbon's Geschichtswerk', 210 f. 'Das jüngere Gelehrtengeschlecht, das durch mancherlei Ursachen zu verfrühten eigenen Hervorbringungen atomistischer Art angestachelt wird, hat meist die Neigung verloren, sich mit unbefangener Hingabe in die zeitraubende, zusammenhängende Lectüre umfänglicher Werke der Vergangenheit zu versenken.' (The younger generation of scholars which, for various reasons, is forced into prematurely producing its own atomistic works, has generally lost the facility simply to immerse itself in the time consuming reading, in context, of the voluminous works of the past.) '... für das große Lesepublicum der Gebildeten mag der leidenschaftslose, nie das Gemüth erwärmende Ton Gibbons nicht eben einladend sein.' (... for the great mass of the educated reading public, Gibbon's lack of passion, his tone that never involves the emotions, is not likely to be very attractive.) On Bernays cf. H. I. Bach, *Jacob Bernays: Ein Beitrag zur Emanzipationsgeschichte der Juden und zur Geschichte des deutschen Geistes im neunzehnten Jahrhundert* (Tübingen, 1974); A. D. Momigliano, 'Jacob Bernays', in id., *Quinto contributo alla storia degli studi classici e del mondo antico* (Rome, 1975), 127–58.

[22] Bernays, 'Edward Gibbon's Geschichtswerk', 247, 231, 246.

the points which were to provide the substance of Arnaldo Momigliano's famous account of Gibbon's originality.[23]

These points will provide the basis for a brief discussion of Gibbon's scholarly achievement in comparison with that of Germany's leading ancient historians in the nineteenth century, in particular, Niebuhr and Mommsen. It can seriously be asked whether Gibbon should be classified as 'the last of the ancient historians in the full sense, an eighteenth-century Tacitus *redivivus*, or rather as the first genuinely modern historian at least of the ancient world'.[24] Gibbon found himself on the side of the ancients in the *Querelle des Anciens et des Modernes*.[25] He was a great admirer of Tacitus, whom he praised as 'the first of historians who applied the science of philosophy to the study of facts'.[26] When Gibbon began his *Decline and Fall* in the Antonine age, he was obviously convinced that he neither could nor should treat a period that had already been covered by Tacitus. Instead, he decided to start with a time which lacked a comprehensive narrative by a great historian of Antiquity. After completing his work Gibbon noted that he should have begun with the Augustan age.[27] In his old age Gibbon no longer adhered to the principle of *historia continua*, whereas Niebuhr still did to a certain extent when he said that a new history of the Roman Empire besides Gibbon's was unnecessary.

Gibbon displayed a masterly command of all the relevant sources. He was able to integrate the diverse antiquarian traditions (Pliny, Solinus, Strabo, Pomponius Mela, and Vegetius), the fourth-century panegyrics, the spurious Historia Augusta biographies, and fragments of historiography into a single

---

[23] A. D. Momigliano, 'Gibbon's Contribution to Historical Method', in id., *Contributo alla storia degli studi classici* (Rome, 1955), 195–211; id., 'Eighteenth-Century Prelude to Mr. Gibbon', in id., *Sesto contributo alla storia degli studi classici e del mondo antico* (Rome, 1980), 249–63; id., 'After Gibbon's Decline and Fall', ibid. 265–84.

[24] P. Cartledge, 'The "Tacitism" of Edward Gibbon (Two Hundred Years on)', *Mediterranean Historical Review*, 4 (1989), 251–70, 252.

[25] Cf. J. M. Levine, 'Edward Gibbon and the Quarrel between the Ancients and the Moderns', *Eighteenth Century*, 26 (1985), 47–62.

[26] *DF* ch. 9 (ed. Womersley, i. 230).

[27] P. B. Craddock, 'Gibbon's Revision of the *Decline and Fall*', *Studies in Bibliography*, 21 (1968), 191–204, 200.

comprehensive narrative. He used footnotes—about 8,000, making up around a quarter of his text—to document his account, to discuss problems, and to refer comprehensively to the scholarly literature of the sixteenth to the eighteenth centuries.[28] However, there can be no doubt that his source criticism was pre-'scientific'. He operated with the methods used to examine a witness—common sense, the probability test, the internal coherence of a report, personal reputation—to identify one or two reliable accounts which, after their partiality had been eliminated, could be used as the basis for his own narrative. Thus he constantly used stereotypes to characterize the authors of sources: Dionysius of Halicarnassus, 'the rhetorician', Cassius Dio, 'the Roman senator', St John Chrysostomus, 'the Christian orator', and so on. He also applied this type of labelling to his secondary material, for example, 'the partial history by the Cardinal Baronius' versus the impartiality of the 'most learned and rational Mosheim'.[29]

Evidently Gibbon was not yet aware that the reliability of a later source depends primarily on the quality of the sources available to the author himself, and may thus change from passus to passus. By comparison with nineteenth-century German source criticism, his approach seems positively old-fashioned. But these methods of reconstructing the genesis of the historiographical texts of Antiquity were developed with respect to Livy and the annalistic tradition of the early centuries of Roman history. It was a long time before these criteria and methods were also applied to texts on other periods of ancient history. And Niebuhr's claim to be the first to have detected the unreliability of the annalistic tradition was based on his ignorance of important predecessors such as Perizonius, the participants in the early eighteenth-century debate within the Académie des Inscriptions, and

[28] Cf. G. W. Bowersock, 'The Art of the Footnote', *American Scholar*, 53 (1983–4), 54–62. The importance of Gibbon's footnotes had already been appreciated by the German literary historian Michael Bernays, the younger brother of Jacob Bernays; 'Zur Lehre von den Citaten und Noten', in id., *Schriften zur Kritik und Litteraturgeschichte*, iii, ed. G. Witkowski (Berlin, 1899), 302–22.

[29] For references see the 'Bibliographical Index' in Womersley's edition, and cf. J. D. Garrison, 'Lively and Laborious: Characterization in Gibbon's Metahistory', *Modern Philology*, 76 (1978–9), 163–78.

Beaufort.[30] Gibbon, however, was fully aware of the importance of those works, though as a young man he had dissociated himself from a position which to him had seemed to be a sort of historical Pyrrhonism (*Essai sur l'étude de la littérature*, 1761). In the flashbacks to early Roman history in *Decline and Fall*, Gibbon concentrated on the structural features of constitutional history and displayed sober judgement on the problematic nature of the sources. It is impossible to say how far he would have accepted Niebuhr's source criticism, but he surely would not have shared his optimism about the historian's ability to reconstruct a narrative history of a period for which there is no reliable ancient tradition.

Whatever the limits of Gibbon's source criticism, he was able to combine narrative and structural history, and to present the evidence for his account without detracting from its readability. This allowed him to deviate from strict chronological order without forfeiting his claim to be presenting 'authentic history'.[31] For example, he summarized the history of Christianity only when his narrative had already arrived at the age of Constantine. Niebuhr, by contrast, struggled constantly with the problem of combining narrative history with an account of his research in a readable form, and therefore did not get beyond the history of the early Republic. This led him to dream of a time when he would be able to write history in the manner of Livy again, without a scholarly apparatus at all. The time would come, he thought, when he would have definitively solved all the problems of Roman constitutional history.[32] In brief,

---

[30] It was only during the preparation of the 2nd edn. of his work that Niebuhr took account of this scholarly tradition; on Niebuhr's predecessors cf. A. D. Momigliano, 'Perizonius, Niebuhr and the Character of the Early Roman Tradition', in id., *Secondo contributo alla storia degli studi classici e del mondo antico* (Rome, 1964), 69–87; H. J. Erasmus, *The Origins of Rome in Historiography from Petrarch to Perizonius* (Assen, 1962); R. T. Ridley, 'Gibbon's Complement: Louis de Beaufort', *Memorie: Istituto Veneto di scienze, lettere ed arti*, 40/3 (1986); M. Raskolnikoff, *Histoire romaine et critique historique dans l'Europe des Lumières* (Paris, 1992).

[31] For Gibbon's claim to present 'fair and authentic history' see his 'Vindication', in *The English Essays of Edward Gibbon*, ed. P. B. Craddock (Oxford, 1972), 235.

[32] Niebuhr stated this several times in his letters; see *Die Briefe Barthold Georg Niebuhrs*, ii, ed. D. Gerhard and W. Norvin (Berlin, 1929), 177, 193 f., 223; *Barthold Georg Niebuhr. Briefe. Neue Folge 1816–1830*, iv, ed. E. Vischer (Berne, 1984), 117.

Niebuhr wanted to revive the strict distinction between the genres of 'antiquarianism' and 'history' which Gibbon had already overcome.

Mommsen, in fact, did separate the genres, as is shown by his *Römische Geschichte* on the one hand, and his *Römisches Staatsrecht* on the other. The young Mommsen had mocked Niebuhr's 'splendid phantasies'.[33] His *Römische Geschichte* radically discards the Roman tradition about the royal and early republican period. Mommsen therefore rejected narrative altogether in this context, offering only a structural account which involved writing about the Roman regal period without even mentioning the traditional names of the Roman kings.[34] For the early periods of Roman history Mommsen presented a reconstruction based on a combination of the recent insights of Indo-European comparative philology and the theory of the successive modes of subsistence.[35] But the reader was explicitly informed neither of Mommsen's fundamental preconceptions of societal evolution, nor of his critical evaluation of the ancient traditions. In the later parts of his work Mommsen continued to assume that there were a number of historical necessities of which the political actors should have been aware. Mommsen did not shrink from censuring the politicians of the past for their attempt to pursue these allegedly necessary aims, and he spelled out to his readers the lessons they should learn from history.[36] By comparison, Gibbon's ironic distance from the past, his playful treatment of ambiguous views, and the dialogue he entered into with the reader in his footnotes, which by their very existence qualify the self-sufficiency of the text, obviously had the advantage of making the

---

[33] T. Mommsen, *Die römischen Tribus in administrativer Beziehung* (Altona, 1844), p. vii. And cf. A. Heuß, 'Niebuhr und Mommsen: Zur wissenschaftsgeschichtlichen Stellung Theodor Mommsens', *Antike & Abendland*, 14 (1968), 1–18.

[34] Cf. A. Heuß, 'Theodor Mommsen als Geschichtsschreiber', in N. Hammerstein (ed.), *Deutsche Geschichtswissenschaft um 1900* (Stuttgart, 1988), 37–95, 48.

[35] Cf. W. Nippel, *Griechen, Barbaren und 'Wilde': Alte Geschichte und Sozialanthropologie* (Frankfurt, 1990), 86–90.

[36] Cf. C. Meier, 'Das Begreifen des Notwendigen: Zu Theodor Mommsens Römischer Geschichte', in R. Koselleck *et al.* (eds.), *Formen der Geschichtsschreibung* (Munich, 1982), 201–44.

reader more aware of the problems of objectivity and perspective.

Gibbon admittedly drew upon the theories of the social scientists of his time. There are passages in which he seems to operate with them as if they were historical laws, for example, the stages of subsistence in the ethnological digressions on Germans, Persians, and Huns. He employed these models in order to explain a complex development. Thus he made use of recent theories of the interconnection between private vices and public virtues to account for the positive repercussions of luxury in the City of Rome on industrial production in the provinces.[37] His interpretation of the role of Christianity provided an alternative to the traditional explanations of the decline of the Empire as having been caused by overextension and corruption by luxury. With the continuation of his work beyond the fall of the Empire in the West in AD 476 Gibbon finally took leave of the theme of a decline which had identifiable causes. The further his work progressed the more stress Gibbon laid on the tension between long-term developments and the contingency of historical events, 'the vicissitudes of human affairs', as he put it. And expressions such as 'real or imaginary', 'in truth or in opinion', 'by art and by accident', 'by chance and by merit' repeatedly draw the reader's attention to the tentative nature of any explanations a historian can offer.[38] From that perspective, it is surprising that Gibbon was not accepted as a man after the heart of German historians.

There is, of course, the famous exception of Gibbon's 'General Observations on the Decline and Fall of the Roman Empire in the West', an appendix to chapter 38 which concluded the narrative about the end of the Western Empire in AD 476. Here Gibbon elaborated on the traditional explanations of the decline, and did not shrink from giving an 'instruction for the present age', namely, that under the conditions of irreversible technical progress,

---

[37] Cf. W. Nippel, 'Gibbons "philosophische Geschichte" und die schottische Aufklärung', in W. Küttler *et al.* (eds.), *Geschichtsdiskurs*, ii: *Anfänge modernen historischen Denkens* (Frankfurt, 1994), 219–28.

[38] Cf. L. Braudy, *Narrative Form in History and Fiction: Hume, Fielding & Gibbon* (Princeton, 1970), 246.

the 'awful revolution' that had occurred in the Roman Empire could not be repeated. We now know that this text was written before the composition of *Decline and Fall*.[39] But since Gibbon decided to place it at the end of his third volume, at a time when he had not yet made up his mind whether he should continue his work, it cannot simply be dismissed. Yet any reader could have stated that the bulk of Gibbon's work was not just an illustration of this final chapter, otherwise Gibbon would not have needed to write his history at all.

All in all, the reactions of German ancient historians to Gibbon were dominated by a feeling of scholarly superiority which was only partly justified. They were not aware that their progress in source criticism was to some extent countered by their tendency to develop a new type of 'conjectural history'. They overrated the originality of their work by comparison with the learned products of the sixteenth to the eighteenth centuries.[40] But they were well aware that Gibbon still represented a challenge with respect to the composition of a great work of narrative history.

In contrast to the mixed reactions throughout the last century, German historians of the early twentieth century no longer seemed to take a serious interest in Gibbon. Of course, we find casual references to well-known quotations from the chapters on Christianity, the alleged praise of the Golden Age of the Antonines, or the 'General Observations'. But no substantial German assessment of Gibbon's importance for modern historiography exists. It is difficult to identify the causes of the growing neglect of Gibbon. First, it may be due to a tendency among German historians to concentrate on a type of scholarly production which is no longer addressed to a general public and therefore not judged by literary standards. Second, it may follow from an invention of tradition which canonized Niebuhr and

---

[39] See P. R. Ghosh, 'Gibbon's Dark Ages: Some Remarks on the Genesis of the *Decline and Fall*', *Journal of Roman Studies*, 73 (1983), 1–23; id., 'Gibbon Observed', ibid. 81 (1991), 132–56.

[40] This point had already been made in another splendid paper by Jacob Bernays, a review of Mommsen's *Staatsrecht* published in 1875. In id., *Gesammelte Abhandlungen*, ii. 256–75.

Ranke[41] as the founding fathers of true 'scientific' history. The more this self-image was taken for granted, the more Gibbon was likely to be labelled as a historian of the Enlightenment period, when true historical understanding allegedly did not play a large part.

In his *Einleitung in das Studium der Alten Geschichte* (1895), Kurt Wachsmuth provided a comprehensive account of research on Antiquity since the Renaissance. Whereas he devoted six pages to Niebuhr, Gibbon was dealt with on less than half a page and qualified as representing 'the spirit of Enlightenment philosophy' (20). In his *Entwicklung und Aufgaben der Alten Geschichte* (1910), Karl Johannes Neumann appreciated that Gibbon's was the first important modern work on ancient history, but he also stated that Niebuhr and not Gibbon was the originator of modern 'historical science' (37). Eduard Fueter in his *Geschichte der neueren Historiographie* (1911), Moriz Ritter in an article of 1914,[42] and Friedrich Meinecke in a paper of 1936 and a chapter of his well-known *Entstehung des Historismus*[43] all depicted Gibbon as a typical Enlightenment historian who was primarily interested in using historical material to illustrate preconceived ideas. Gibbon, who had always protested against Voltaire's nonchalant attitude towards historical facts, appears more or less as an epigone of Voltaire. The suspicion arises that the authors just quoted may have seriously studied only the chapters on Christianity and the 'General Observations'.

A revisionist approach of more recent times has attempted to rescue the historians of the German *Spätaufklärung*, that is, the Göttingen school of the late eighteenth century, from oblivion, and to stress their scholarly importance contrary to an established view that dates the emergence of 'scientific history' only to the nineteenth

---

[41] For Ranke's ambiguous assessment of Gibbon, see *Leopold von Ranke. Aus Werk und Nachlaß*, iv: *Vorlesungseinleitungen*, ed. V. Dotterweich and W. P. Fuchs (Munich, 1975), 226 f., 231, 359 f., 365.

[42] 'Studien über die Entwicklung der Geschichtswissenschaft IV: Das 18. Jahrhundert', *Historische Zeitschrift*, 112 (1914), 29–131, 118–24.

[43] 'Bemerkungen über Gibbon', in G. Albrecht (ed.), *Reine und angewandte Soziologie: Festgabe Ferdinand Tönnies* (Leipzig, 1936), 35–41; Friedrich Meinecke, *Die Entstehung des Historismus* (4th edn., Munich, 1965), 229–36.

century.[44] But its advocates seem to be so preoccupied with the German tradition that they do not realize that any debate on the beginnings of modern historiography must take account of Gibbon's achievements and shortcomings. There is still no substantial German contribution to the lively international debate on Gibbon which has produced many outstanding books and articles over the last two decades. Indeed, it has hardly been noticed by German scholars. For the German general public today, Gibbon is a relatively unknown author. The only translation available is an abridged version of some 600 pages which covers only parts of the first three volumes and omits the footnotes. The text is taken from the 1837 translation by Johannes Sporschil.[45] But perhaps its publication on the occasion of Gibbon's 250th birthday in 1987 may be taken as a positive omen of a new interest in Gibbon. Since the use and abuse of Gibbon continues even after more than two hundred years, it may not be too late for 'learned and laborious' German historians to present their own views of Gibbon.

[44] Cf. P. H. Reill, *The German Enlightenment and the Rise of Historicism* (Berkeley, and Los Angeles 1975); H. W. Blanke and J. Rüsen (eds.), *Von der Aufklärung zum Historismus: Zum Strukturwandel des historischen Denkens* (Paderborn, 1984); H. W. Blanke and D. Fleischer (eds.), *Theoretiker der deutschen Aufklärungshistorie* (Stuttgart, 1990); H. W. Blanke, *Historiographiegeschichte als Historik* (Stuttgart, 1991).

[45] *Verfall und Untergang des Römischen Reiches* (Nördlingen, 1987). The selection of chapters is based on *The Portable Gibbon*, ed. D. A. Saunders (New York, 1952). Sporschil published the last complete German translation (including the footnotes) of *DF: Geschichte des allmäligen Sinkens und endlichen Unterganges des römischen Weltreichs* (Leipzig, 1837, 12 vols.; 4th edn., 1862).

5

Niebuhr in England: History, Faith, and Order

NORMAN VANCE

In the earlier nineteenth century it was a surprisingly controversial undertaking to subject Roman history to critical scrutiny, an endeavour particularly associated with the German diplomat and pioneer Roman historian Barthold Georg Niebuhr (1776–1831) and his British disciple Thomas Arnold (1795–1842), Headmaster of Rugby School and a prominent liberal churchman. British commentators tended to feel that this revisionist historiography had a powerful if indirect bearing on contemporary political and religious issues. Conservatives, worried by any challenge to traditional authority, resorted to alarm and despondency, reminding themselves that nothing but trouble could come from German scholarship. (Had not Ovid long ago described 'Germania' as 'rebellatrix', *Tristia* 3. 12. 47 ?) But progressives such as Arnold and Niebuhr's English translators Hare and Thirlwall saw in Niebuhr encouragement for their own visions of a more generous and liberal social order and a more enlightened understanding of God, man, and nature.

In the normal course of things heavy consumption of the roast beef of Old England and the sturdy maintenance of traditional faith and order were the English antidotes to the crisis of authority stemming from revolutionary France. Clerical schoolmasters, though often mean about the roast beef, had their own ways of supporting the status quo and making sure that the teaching of history in particular was never in any danger of becoming somewhat too sensational. Modern history was often largely ignored in the schoolroom as too political; ancient history was preferred because it could be read, largely apolitically, as a safe repository of timeless moral example, not really very different from Holy Scripture. This view of the matter was not confined to conservative clerical schoolmasters. William Godwin, radical author of *Political Justice*, wrote to his new disciple Percy Bysshe Shelley in 1812 that

> it is universally agreed that, next to the history of our own country, the histories of Greece and Rome most deserve to be studied. Why? Because in them the achievements of the human species have been most admirable: in Rome, in high moral and social qualities; in Greece, both in them, and also in literature and art.[1]

But this view was becoming old-fashioned, at least in relation to Roman history, even before Niebuhr's influence was felt in England. It was already accepted that there was little that was admirable or exemplary at an individual level in Roman imperial history after the death of Augustus, and even less after the passing of the Antonines, and there was much for schoolmasters to skate over as quickly as possible. There was more interest, and more edification, in the earlier books of Livy dealing with the foundation of Rome and the achievements of early civic heroes such as Horatius on the bridge or the grimly impartial Lucius Junius Brutus. But even the history of republican Rome, periodically tumultuous, was tainted for some by French revolutionary appropriations of the land-reforming Gracchi and the oath-swearing Horatii celebrated by Jacques-Louis David and Roman *libertas* ruthlessly approximated to *liberté*, not to mention *égalité* and *fraternité*. This was so much the case that in 1808 the Anglo-Irish educational theorist Richard Lovell Edgeworth, father of the novelist Maria Edgeworth, was of the opinion that Roman history need not be taught in Irish charity schools in case it gave the pupils politically inconvenient ideas: 'to inculcate democracy and a foolish hankering after undefined liberty is not necessary in Ireland.'[2]

The challenges to established authority represented by

---

[1] Godwin to Shelley, 10 Dec. 1812, quoted in a note in *The Letters of Percy Bysshe Shelley*, ed. Frederick L. Jones, 2 vols. (Oxford, 1964), i. 340–1.

[2] Quoted in David Fitzpatrick, 'The Futility of History: A Failed Experiment in Irish Education', in Ciaran Brady (ed.), *Ideology and the Historians* (Historical Studies 17; Dublin, 1991), 170.

sceptical interrogations of already sometimes inflammatory history were bound to cause alarm to conservative critics looking for trouble. This had been happening since the seventeenth century. It is tempting to dismiss such criticism as hysterical, making unwarranted connections between purely historical and antiquarian matters and the sensitive political and religious issues of the day. But Niebuhr made the connections himself, reading ancient history as a north European liberal in politics (or so it seemed in Britain) and a liberal Protestant in religion. For him, political freedom had mattered throughout history. If popular enthusiasms were problematic in the aftermath of the French Revolution he made no secret of his interest in and enthusiasm for popular beliefs, perceptions, and traditions in the ancient world, perhaps more revealing, he claimed, than the views of the philosophers, and the basis of the largely mythic history of early Rome. Such democratic preferences did not always go down well in self-consciously counter-revolutionary Britain.

The son of a pioneering Arabian explorer, Carsten Niebuhr, Niebuhr belongs with nineteenth-century explorers, inventors, and scientists as much as with scholars. The pioneer geologist Charles Lyell quoted with approval his comment that 'he who calls what has vanished back into being, enjoys a bliss like that of creating'.[3] Niebuhr was a romantic adventurer embarked on a voyage of discovery, a quest for origins, with a courageous, perhaps reckless disregard for the dangers in store. The danger from hostile British critics was not immediately apparent. The first German edition of the *Römische Geschichte* (1811–12) was hardly noticed in Britain, partly because from the point of view of most Oxford and Cambridge ancient historians it was veiled in the decent obscurity of a learned language which they did not know or even want to know. There is no copy of this first edition in the Bodleian Library in Oxford. In July 1822 a reviewer of other books on early Roman history in the *Quarterly Review* commended Niebuhr in passing but gave it as his opinion that in Britain 'not half a dozen persons have

---

[3] Charles Lyell, *The Principles of Geology*, 2 vols. (London, 1830–3), i. 74, quoted in S. J. Gould, *Time's Arrow, Time's Cycle* (Harmondsworth, 1988), 155.

read him'.[4] It was not until 1827 that a slightly rugged English translation appeared, only to be rendered instantly obsolete by the substantially revised second edition of the German text (1827–32) which was rapidly translated into rather better English by Julius Hare and Connop Thirlwall, with a third volume by William Smith, between 1828 and 1842.

Both editions opened with a lengthy discussion of the ultimate, probably multiple origins of the Italian people, necessarily inconclusive because it engaged with doubtful matters of myth, legend, and prehistory. Perhaps comparisons would help. Even in the terser first edition Niebuhr risked some coat-trailing comparisons with the Old Testament, less startling in Germany than they would have been in England or even in Scotland, often more intellectually adventurous. In discussing conflicting accounts of the possible origins of the Oenotrians, who might or might not have been descended from one Oenotrius, he claims that 'no sober-minded man can treat these genealogies as historical narratives', explicitly compares them with genealogies offered in the tenth and eleventh chapters of Genesis, and says of the latter as of a matter beyond argument that 'they are palpably grounded upon very false assumptions'.[5]

Nobody in Britain seems to have worried about this, or even noticed, for seventeen years, but in the second edition, soon available in translation, the comparisons were more wide-ranging and detailed and this time they did not pass without comment. Many societies, Niebuhr insisted, preserved stories of ancient giants or monsters swept away by catastrophe to make room for their ancestors:

So the later Jews dreamt of giants before the deluge; so the Greeks of the Titans of Phlegra, and of those who perished in the flood of Deucalion or of Ogyges: so the savages of North America fable of the Mammoth, that the devastated world had invoked the lightnings of heaven, and not in vain, against the reason-gifted monster, the man of the primitive age. So Italy in its popular legends had the Campanian giants.[6]

[4] 'Early History of Rome', *Quarterly Review*, 27 (July 1822), 281.
[5] B. G. Niebuhr, *The Roman History*, trans. F. A. Walters, 2 vols. (London, 1827), i. 35 f.
[6] B. G. Niebuhr, *The History of Rome*, 3 vols., trans. J. C. Hare, C. Thirlwall, and (vol. iii) W. Smith (Cambridge, 1828, 1832; London, 1842), i. 145.

Noah and Deucalion, biblical and classical traditions, were old friends in the popular historical imagination but it was audacious if not positively naughty to bring in the Shawnee and Delaware Indians. It upset religiously conservative England. Between his first and second editions Niebuhr, who read everything, had been reading the work of the great French palaeontologist Georges Cuvier (1769–1832). In the preliminary section of his *Recherches sur les ossamens fossiles de quadrupèdes* (1812), separately translated as *Essay on the Theory of the Earth* (1813), Cuvier had written about mammoth remains in Siberia and the Americas, including the Mastodon or Mammoth Ohioticum found near the Ohio river, identified by the comparative anatomist J. F. Blumenbach (1752–1840). According to Cuvier the indigenous hunting tribes of North America knew about the mammoths and had 'invented a fabulous account of their destruction, alleging that they were all killed by the Great Spirit, to prevent them from extirpating the human race'.[7]

The *Essay on the Theory of the Earth* had run into problems with English conservatives because in some particulars it was at variance with the Genesis creation account. One George Bugg had retaliated with two indignant volumes entitled *Scriptural Geology* (1826–7). By using Cuvier's material Niebuhr left himself open to the same kind of attack. Even worse, he explicitly challenged literal readings of the story of Adam and Eve by suggesting that the creation of mankind might have taken place at different times for the different races of mankind and—worst of all—he maintained that such a view was not irreligious: 'That such a creation should have occurred only once, we are in no way forced to conclude . . . for God does not grow old, nor weary of creating, of preserving, of remoulding and training'.[8]

The most savage English attack on Niebuhr came from an unexpected quarter. John Barrow, second Secretary to the Admiralty, was supposed to be reviewing the Russian travels

---

[7] Georges Cuvier, *Essay on the Theory of the Earth* (1813; 4th edn., Edinburgh, 1822), 87. [8] Niebuhr, *The History of Rome*, i. 146.

of a half-pay naval surgeon, A. B. Granville, in the *Quarterly Review* for 1829. Granville had passed through Germany on his way to St Petersburg and praised the King of Prussia for refounding the University of Bonn where Niebuhr taught in his last years. Repeating more or less idle gossip, Granville mentioned the notorious sedition and turbulence of students at German universities and what he described as the 'incendiary' liberal political principles espoused by Niebuhr which he said some people thought might have contributed to that turbulence. Barrow entirely agreed. Niebuhr was clearly an intellectual troublemaker with no respect for tradition or authority, a 'pert, *dull* scoffer', his recently [re]published work 'pregnant with crude and dangerous speculations'. His distinguished English translators Julius Charles Hare and Connop Thirlwall were accused of wasting their talents on such material.[9] It was not at all clear that either Granville or Barrow had actually read Niebuhr or knew much about the man but this indiscriminate onslaught was almost enough on its own to make Niebuhr the darling of progressives and of liberal Anglicanism. More than thirty years later A. P. Stanley, pupil and biographer of Arnold of Rugby and himself a distinguished liberal churchman, saw this unprovoked attack and the 'burning indignation and withering scorn' with which Thirlwall and Hare responded as a significant episode in the development not so much of historical scholarship as of liberal theology.[10]

On more specifically Roman matters Niebuhr was equally heterodox. He was a rationalist demythologizer who made people wonder if nothing was sacred. To take just one example, he presented Livy's account of Romulus and Remus as originally a popular ballad or lay, a poetic fantasy which could be interpreted as a kind of allegory or fable of dual identity. Clearly the story offered two versions of the same name, a symbolic indication of the two different races, perhaps incoming Pelasgians and aborigines, who together

---

[9] [John Barrow], 'Dr Granville's Travels: Russia', *Quarterly Review*, 39 (Jan. 1829), 1–41, esp. 8 f.; see also Hare's reply, *A Vindication of Niebuhr's History of Rome from the Charges of the Quarterly Review* (Cambridge, 1829).

[10] A. P. Stanley, 'Essays and Reviews' (1861), reprinted in *Essays Chiefly on Questions of Church and State from 1850 to 1870* (1870; new edn., London, 1884).

made up the Roman people. The historic tensions between patricians and plebeians obviously represented a continuation of this prehistoric division, signalled by the binary Romulus/Remus.[11]

Niebuhr's self-confident but contentious historical revisionism needs to be set in context because it is even more intricately bound up with challenges to religious orthodoxy than at first appears. Questioning the authority of the received account of early Roman history was not new. It was as old as the Reformation and derived from the same kind of anti-traditionalist thinking. It had been tried in the early seventeenth century in the proudly Protestant Dutch Republic by Philip Cluvier or Cluverius, whose scepticism about Livy was embodied in his *Italiae Historia*, published in Leiden in 1623. Another seventeenth-century Dutch scholar, Jacobus Perizonius, not initially known to Niebuhr, had anticipated his theory of ballad origins lying behind Livy.[12] Other sceptics included the French Protestant Pierre Bayle and the Irish freethinker John Toland, sceptical about biblical as well as classical historical narrative. But such men were dangerous, their work intensely controversial. At least one of Toland's books had been publicly burnt.

There continued down into the nineteenth century an often unacknowledged sense that any critical probing of more or less exemplary ancient texts was playing with fire: the Bible was the supremely exemplary ancient text and if people started asking awkward questions about Livy or Homer there was no knowing where it might all end. Niebuhr's sceptical critique in fact had close connections with parallel movements in Homeric and biblical studies. The High Churchman Pusey, who knew enough about German critical methods to distrust them, took the line that 'the scepticism as to Homer ushered in the scepticism on the Old Testament', though J. G. Lockhart, the biographer of Scott, suggested in the *Quarterly Review* that it might have

---

[11] Niebuhr, *The History of Rome*, i. 251.
[12] Perizonius, *Animadversiones Historicae* (1685); see Arnaldo Momigliano, 'Perizonius, Niebuhr and the Early Roman Tradition', in *Essays in Ancient and Modern Historiography* (Oxford, 1977), 231–51.

been the other way round.[13] The question of priority was unimportant: the connection was indisputable.

One feature of very ancient texts that seemed to uphold their moral authority was the awe-inspiring, even providential fact of their survival apparently more or less intact even after so many centuries. This assurance of continuity and integrity was rudely shattered by Friedrich August Wolf's *Prolegomena ad Homerum* of 1795 which influentially suggested that many different strands of tradition had contributed to what were now known as the Homeric epics. The supposed integrity of the text of Homer could not withstand critical analysis: there were incoherences, repetitions and contradictions which indicated different classes of material brought together, probably at different periods, to form the texts now available to us. The real Homer, or at least the original and genuine shape ('prisca et genuina forma') of the Homeric poems, had been overlaid in the course of transmission but was perhaps recoverable by critical enquiry. Possibly anticipating hostile criticism, Wolf took the highest moral ground for his textual procedures, insisting that his entire project was historical, critical, and objective, concerned not with what one might like to find but with what actually happened ('non de optabili re, sed de re facta'). Aesthetic qualities were agreeable enough but the facts of history were sacrosanct ('Amandae sunt artes, at reverenda est historia').[14] Unfortunately this cut across other pieties: Wolf himself had called Homer 'the Bible of Greece' and the texts of the Judaeo-Christian Bible were clearly open to the same kinds of disconcertingly rigorous analysis where radical textual probing would be seen as tantamount to sacrilege.

This controversial moral imperative to pursue the truth at all costs, and the unflinching analytical method that went

---

[13] E. B. Pusey, *Collegiate and Professorial Teaching and Discipline in Answer to Professor Vaughan's Strictures* (Oxford, 1854), 62, quoted in F. M. Turner, *Contesting Cultural Authority* (Cambridge, 1993), 343 f. and n.; [J. G. Lockhart], 'Colonel Mure on the Literature of Ancient Greece', *Quarterly Review*, 87 (Sept. 1850), 434–68, esp. 436 f.

[14] Preface to Wolf's edn. of Homer, *Homeri et Homeridarum Opera et Reliquiae* (1795), quoted in Rudolph Pfeiffer, *History of Classical Scholarship from 1300 to 1850* (Oxford, 1970), 174.

with it, were taken up in succeeding generations by liberal biblical scholars as well as revisionist ancient historians such as Niebuhr. It was not surprising that George Eliot, English translator of David Strauss's controversially demythologizing *Life of Jesus* as well as realist chronicler of ordinary lives, tackled Wolf's *Prolegomena* just after completing the writing of *Middlemarch*. This may well have been because her friend the Oxford scholar Mark Pattison had been writing about Wolf.[15]

Pattison had also been one of the 'seven against Christ', a contributor to the once-notorious *Essays and Reviews* (1860). This volume, admired by liberals like A. P. Stanley, had challenged traditional literal-minded readings of the Bible by reporting some of the findings of recent scholarship and scientific enquiry, the kinds of demythologizing enquiry into origins which Niebuhr had taken in his stride more than thirty years earlier. Its essential continuity with the new classical historiography was confirmed by a hostile reviewer, Samuel Wilberforce, Bishop of Oxford, who claimed that this was a natural and alarming outcome of a remorseless historical criticism 'which with Niebuhr has tasted blood in the slaughter of Livy'.[16]

Up to a point he may have been right. Benjamin Jowett of Balliol College, another contributor to *Essays and Reviews*, had begun to lose faith in the detail of biblical narrative as a consequence of attending Robert Scott's undergraduate lectures relaying Niebuhr's sceptical Roman history: these 'first aroused in my mind doubts about the gospels'.[17] While Jowett was saved from complete scepticism by Plato and a Platonically idealist understanding of Scripture rising above textual detail, Pattison's scepticism, a matter of temperament as much as texts, perhaps, was reinforced by his researches in the history of thought and classical scholarship. He was the biographer of the great Renaissance *savant* Isaac Casaubon, which has led to speculation that he may

---

[15] Mark Pattison in *North British Review*, 42 (June 1865), 245–99; *The George Eliot Letters*, ed. G. S. Haight, 9 vols. (New Haven, 1954–78), v. 124 and n.
[16] [Samuel Wilberforce], 'Essays and Reviews', *Quarterly Review*, 109 (Jan. 1861), 293.
[17] Notebook entry dated 1876 quoted by Geoffrey Faber, *Jowett, a Portrait with Background* (1957; London, 1958), 134.

have suggested some details for the *Middlemarch* character Mr Casaubon, the ironically inadequate scholar of mythologies who fails to face up to moral realities. But the fictional Casaubon, toiling away in the 1830s, was unlike George Eliot and Mark Pattison in that he had not read the work of the appropriate German scholars, a limitation which would be accepted as disastrous by the time the novel was published in 1871–2 though it would not necessarily have appeared that way forty years earlier. The German authorities Casaubon had ignored would have included Wolf's disciple Karl Otfried Müller, author of *Prolegomena zu einer wissenschaftlichen Mythologie* (1825), who could have helped him (academically if not morally) to get closer to whatever truth could be established in his chosen field of study.

Niebuhr investigated early Rome, and indeed the early history of mankind, very much in the heroic spirit of Wolf and Müller.[18] He shared Müller's romantic sense that there were historical realities to be recovered through the study of myth and legend, and pursued them with Wolf's fearless concern for the truth. But it was not just Wolf's moral courage and analytical audacity that inspired Niebuhr and nineteenth-century classical scholarship: it was his broadly based, we would now say 'interdisciplinary', approach to classical Antiquity as a whole. Instead of concentrating narrowly on linguistic and textual scholarship, Wolf's practice as a scholar and brilliantly innovative teacher at the University of Halle was to engage with what he called *Altertumswissenschaft*, a 'science of Antiquity' which included history, archaeology, and religion as well as classical languages and literature. Although it took time to catch on in England, it was this broader approach, sustained by an increasingly scientific classical archaeology, which facilitated ever more detailed understanding of Roman life and customs. This in its turn made possible both a better-informed appreciation of Latin literature and the realistic nineteenth-century novels, plays, and paintings through

---

[18] Wolf's influence on Niebuhr, often asserted, is confirmed by the Finnish scholar Seppo Rytkönen in *Barthold Georg Niebuhr als Politiker und Historiker* (Helsinki, 1968), 194.

which the Romans came more or less convincingly to life in later Victorian Britain.

Niebuhr's boldness and self-confidence as a historian derived not just from his extensive reading in a wide range of disciplines but from his experience of public life. His career in the Prussian public service gave him a particular sensitivity to the nature and development of political institutions ancient and modern, and his intellectually (if not diplomatically) rewarding period as ambassador in Rome gave him easy access to primary sources. It was Niebuhr's sometimes misplaced confidence in his bold intuitions, rather than his argumentative cogency or narrative power, that imparted authority to his revisions of Roman history.

Niebuhr's own work, unlike that of his influential disciples Arnold and Michelet, was not so much a narrative history as a rather clogged series of specialist dissertations on particular points or theories. His most famous theory was that much of the early and clearly legendary history of Rome, including the Romulus and Remus story already mentioned, had been preserved in folk memory in the form of ballads or lays, now lost, traces of which survived in the heightened prose of Livy and other historians.

The non-classical inspirations of Niebuhr's theory were Herder and romantic theories of embodiments of popular consciousness and racial memory in the traditional lays of the common people or *Volk*. This romantic predilection was reinforced by Niebuhr's emotional attachment to the country people of the Dithmarschen in what is now north-west Germany, between the Eider estuary and the mouth of the Elbe. Niebuhr's family had moved to the area from Copenhagen when he was 2 years old. In the Middle Ages the Dithmarschen had been virtually an independent peasant republic, successfully resisting the attempted encroachments of the Schleswig-Holstein nobility in 1500. Even in the nineteenth century these country people had a form of provincial administration with popular representation and a degree of autonomy rare in Europe. Familiar with a community which had retained proud traditions of political independence, Niebuhr found it easy to believe in folk memory and popular ballads enshrining communal identity and exemplary republican ideals as the basis of the written versions of Roman history.[19]

But Niebuhr disconcertingly combined this romantic interest in popular tradition with a stern sense that popular tradition must not be confused with history. He read Livy as Strauss and Feuerbach were to read the New Testament, with an appearance of analytical rigour and scientific iconoclasm. The story of Rome under the kings was dismissed as 'altogether without foundation'. Conflicting evidence from Antiquity was mercilessly scrutinized. The heroic Regulus was deemed to have died from natural causes (probably) rather than under excruciating torture. The whole story of Coriolanus was summarily excluded from history. This severity did not pass without protest of an aesthetic rather than religious or political kind. Edward Fitzgerald, writing to his friend the historian W. B. Donne about Livy, complained robustly about 'old Niebuhr' and 'lumbering Germans': 'it is mean to attack old legends that can't defend themselves. And what does it signify in the least if they are true or not? Whoever *actively* believed that Romulus was suckled by a wolf?'[20]

But Niebuhr's severe and critical history was not as coldly impersonal and value-free as it seemed. It incorporated a kind of displaced liberal nationalism, which was one of the reasons why it appealed so strongly to English liberals such as Arnold and A. P. Stanley, patriotically committed to a Coleridgean vision of a national church and a sense of national harmony and collective purpose. The lost ballads or lays, largely untouched by Greek cultural influences, from which Niebuhr maintained Livy would have derived the more legendary parts of his history, somehow resembled the 'Lay of the Nibelungs' or *Nibelungenlied*, rediscovered only in the middle of the eighteenth century and an important

---

[19] See *Denmark*, Naval Intelligence Division Official Handbook (London, 1944), 109, 114; R. E. Dickinson, *Germany: A General and Regional Geography* (2nd edn., London, 1961), 605. See also F. Max Müller, 'On the Language and Poetry of Schleswig-Holstein' (1864), reprinted in *Chips from a German Workshop*, 4 vols. (London, 1870), iii. 133–7.

[20] Edward Fitzgerald to W. B. Donne [30 Dec. 1839], *Letters of Edward Fitzgerald*, ed. A. M. and A. B. Terhune, 4 vols. (Princeton, 1980), i. 240.

ingredient in Germanic resistance to French cultural hegemony. Niebuhr's historical method stemmed from a kind of cultural nationalism which invites comparison with that of Schiller. Like Schiller he admitted that he was influenced by the humiliation of his country under French occupation. When he started lecturing on Roman history in 1810 at the new University of Berlin he recorded that 'I went back to a nation, great, but long passed by, to strengthen my mind and that of my hearers. We felt like Tacitus.'[21] The sting of lost liberties which Tacitus had registered under the Empire and the dream of restored political freedom encouraged a libertarian reading of Roman constitutional history with parallels from the Whig version of English history, part of the reason for the controversial appeal of Niebuhr in Britain:

> Little as the Earl of Leicester forboded, when he summoned the deputies of the knights and commons to the parliament of the barons, that this was the beginning of an assembly which was at one time to be virtually possessed of the supreme authority in the kingdom; just as little did the plebeians on the Sacred Mount foresee, when they obtained the inviolability of their magistrates, that the tribunate would raise itself by degrees to a preponderating, and then to an unlimited power in the republic, and that the possession of it would be sufficient ... to lay the foundation of monarchal supremacy. Its sole purpose was to afford protection against any abuse of the consul's authority.[22]

It is not surprising that Niebuhr's concerns with checks and balances, authority and freedom, were of particular interest in the England of the 1830s when staunchly resisted popular pressure to broaden the parliamentary franchise had eventually led to a rather moderate Reform Bill in 1832. The first volume of Thomas Arnold's *History of Rome* was written at this period. Like Niebuhr, Arnold was interested in early Roman constitutional law and constitutional checks against the risk of governmental oppression. He felt that Livy's narrative was more likely to be trustworthy on such technical matters than on 'the mere poetical stories of Cincinnatus and Coriolanus', and tried with limited

---

[21] [H. H. Milman], 'Lieber's Reminiscences of Niebuhr', *Quarterly Review*, 55 (Dec. 1835), 234–50, esp. 240 f.   [22] Niebuhr, *History of Rome*, i. 542.

evidence to reconstruct constitutional changes *c*.450 BC possibly involving plebeian as well as patrician participation in an elected decemvirate or magistracy of ten. Unlike Niebuhr he had the good sense not to get bogged down in conjecture about the precise function and significance of the decemvirate which was in any case soon overthrown.[23] A much later period of constitutional reform which Arnold had written about some years earlier had encouraged him to develop a rather intricate parallel between popular enthusiasm alternating with popular apprehension associated with the contemporary British parliamentary campaign for Catholic emancipation, effectively admitting more citizens to full citizenship, and the controversial proposals of the tribune P. Sulpicius to make Roman citizenship available to all the inhabitants of Italy, a possible consequence of which might be leaving the newly enfranchised multitude at the mercy of a demagogue.[24]

Thomas Babington Macaulay did not worry about the constitutional details of the newly scientific Roman history and saw the newly established merely literary quality of Livy's narrative as a literary opportunity rather than a historiographical embarrassment. 'Horatius', the first and most famous of his *Lays of Ancient Rome* (1842), is represented as being composed in a less heroic and more acrimonious epoch about a hundred and twenty years after the events it describes, just long enough to permit the idealizing refrain 'In the brave days of old':

> For Romans in Rome's quarrel
> Spared neither land nor gold,
> Nor son nor wife, nor limb nor life,
> In the brave days of old.[25]

Livy's account of the battle of Lake Regillus, characterized as quasi-Homeric by Niebuhr and deemed to conclude the

---

[23] Thomas Arnold, *History of Rome* (1838–43; new edn., 3 vols., London, 1857), i. 243–6.

[24] Thomas Arnold, *History of the Later Roman Commonwealth*, 2 vols. (London, 1845), i. 179 and n. This work is a posthumous edition of Arnold's articles on Roman history contributed to the *Encyclopaedia Metropolitana* between 1823 and 1827.

[25] T. B. Macaulay, 'Horatius', stanza 31, *Lays of Ancient Rome* (1842), in *Essays and Lays of Ancient Rome*, Popular Edition (London, 1899), 854.

hypothetical original 'Lay of the Tarquins', supplied the basis for Macaulay's second 'Lay' which quite deliberately incorporates images and incidents from the *Iliad*.

The sheer verve and raciness of Macaulay's *Lays*, derided as 'pinchbeck' by that fastidious purist Matthew Arnold, probably helped to discredit Niebuhr's theory of ballad origins though this was certainly not the intention. The prose of Livy was far too prosaic to have derived directly from poetry like that. The scholar-politician Sir George Cornewall Lewis was sceptical in the tradition of Niebuhr to an extent that made him sceptical of Niebuhr himself. Where Arnold had commended Niebuhr's conjectures as 'almost like a divination' Lewis sternly disapproved of 'historical divination' as 'an attempt to solve a problem, for the solution of which no sufficient data exist'. He noted that there was not the slightest trace of metrical prose in those passages of Livy claimed to have ballad origins and felt that Macaulay of all people should have been wary of attributing vivid historical narrative (such as his own) to suppressed poetic originals.[26]

In the later part of the nineteenth century Niebuhr gradually ceased to matter very much in England. The historian J. R. Seeley followed Lewis in being sceptical even about Niebuhr in his critical commentary on the first book of Livy (1871), but this was a rather austere piece of technical scholarship superseding rather than celebrating Niebuhr's work. The conditions of public faith and order in which some had felt Niebuhr was a disturbing influence while others had praised him were changing. Darwin's *Origin of Species* (1859) gave the worried faithful a new range of things to worry about. Parliamentary reform, increasing prosperity, and comparative domestic stability from the 1850s onwards reduced interest in vexed questions of citizenship and the constitution in early Rome which Niebuhr had explored.

Roman history continued to appeal to a wide public, and German scholarship was increasingly admired, but with the growth of imperial sentiment, to which Seeley himself

---

[26] Sir G. C. Lewis, *An Inquiry into the Credibility of the Early Roman History*, 2 vols. (London, 1855), i. 12, 212 f.; Arnold, *History of Rome*, i. 245.

contributed with his Cambridge lectures on *The Expansion of England* (1883), attention tended to shift to Roman imperial history. Newer names than Niebuhr could be invoked in this connection, notably that of the great Theodor Mommsen. If heroes and exemplars were ever needed from the legendary early history of Rome they could easily be found in Macaulay: there was no need to go directly to Livy, let alone to Niebuhr. In a sense the epoch of Niebuhr was over, and the epoch of Mommsen had begun.

6

Stubbs, Maitland, and Constitutional History

JAMES CAMPBELL

In the nineteenth century historical study played a role which it had never played before. Consciousness of historic pasts, discovered or contrived, was intrinsic to nationalisms, creative or destructive. The era of nationalisms was also that in which university education of secular élites was new in scale and significance. Consideration of nineteenth-century academic history therefore has some special interest. The two great men with whom this essay is concerned dominated the study of English medieval history. William Stubbs was a founding father. Very many students of medieval England can trace their intellectual descent from him. He and his works were very important in the establishment of medieval history as a subject for study in British universities. His younger contemporary Frederic William Maitland was the outstanding historian of English law, and his work commanded, and still commands, the greatest admiration, not only for its learning but also for the lucidity of its brilliance. Both scholars owed much to German scholarship. Their debt was part of an Anglo-German intellectual relationship in which the study and understanding of history, not least of constitutional history, mattered a lot. The ways in which Stubbs and Maitland differed in their approaches to constitutional history are indices not only to generational change but also to contrasting intellectual traditions.

Stubbs (1829–1901)[1] produced all his major historical

---

[1] W. Stubbs, *The Constitutional History of England in its Origin and Development*, 3 vols. (Oxford, 1874–8). The final edn. was the 6th (1897). Reference is commonly made to the 'Library Edition' of 1880, and all references below are to this edn. Full bibliographies of his published works are in W. A. Shaw, *A Bibliography of the*

works before the age of 59, when he became a bishop. The major contribution from his years as Regius Professor at Oxford (1866–84) was his *Constitutional History of England in its Origin and Development* (1873–8). Maitland[2] was born in 1850 and died at the age of 56. The brilliant flow of his books began in 1884 and reached a climax in 1895–8, when he published three works of fundamental and lasting importance. Among these was *History of English Law before the Time of Edward I*, central to the theme of the present essay.[3] Also most germane is *A Constitutional History of England*, which is the text of lectures given at Cambridge in 1887 and 1888, not intended for publication, but published posthumously.[4]

What is, or was, meant by the term 'constitutional history'? The *Oxford English Dictionary* is misleading in quoting no instance of its use before 1841. Maitland was right in suggesting that the term may have been coined by Henry Hallam when he used it in the title of his *The Constitutional History of England from the Accession of Henry VII to the Death of George II*, published in 1827. Maitland commented that since Hallam there had been a 'steady tendency . . . to widen the scope of the term in one direction, to narrow it in another'.[5] What he meant is that it was widened in the sense of making

---

Historical Works of Dr. Creighton . . ., Dr. Stubbs . . . Dr. S. R. Gardiner and . . . Lord Acton (London, 1903), 15–23, and *Letters of William Stubbs, Bishop of Oxford*, ed. W. H. Hutton (London, 1904). For works on him, R. C. Richardson, *The Study of History: A Bibliographical Guide* (Manchester, 1988) and J. Campbell, 'William Stubbs', in H. Damico and J. B. Zavadil (eds.), *Medieval Scholarship: Biographical Studies on the Formation of a Discipline*, i (New York, 1995), 77–88. J. Vernon, 'Narrating the Constitution: The Discourse of "the Real" and the Fantasies of Nineteenth-Century Constitutional History', in id. (ed.), *Re-reading the Constitution: New Narratives in the Political History of England's Long Nineteenth Century* (Cambridge, 1996) provides a post-modernist account of Stubbs and of Maitland.

[2] A. L. Smith, *Frederic William Maitland: Two Lectures and a Bibliography* (Oxford, 1908) provides a bibliography. For later works on him see Richardson, *The Study of History*, C. M. S. Fifoot, *Frederic William Maitland: A Life* (Cambridge, Mass., 1971), R. Brentano, 'Frederick William Maitland', in Damico and Zavadil (eds.), *Medieval Scholarship*, i. 131–52, and J. Hudson (ed.), *The History of English Law: Centenary Essays on 'Pollock and Maitland'* (British Academy, Oxford, 1996). His most important articles etc. are collected in *The Collected Papers of F. W. Maitland*, ed. H. A. L. Fisher, 3 vols. (Cambridge, 1911).

[3] F. W. Maitland, *The History of English Law before the Time of Edward I*, 2 vols. (Cambridge, 1896; 2nd edn. 1898).

[4] F. W. Maitland, *The Constitutional History of England*, ed. H. A. L. Fisher (Cambridge, 1908). [5] Ibid. 536–7.

it an increasingly comprehensive account of institutions; but, on the other hand, narrowed by excluding from it any detailed account of the conflicts which had made the constitution. Hallam's own introduction indicates another potential ambiguity in the term. He said: 'The title which I have adopted appears to exclude all matters not referable to the state of government, or what is loosely denominated the constitution.'[6] Later, explaining his intention to deal with the established church, he said that this certainly has to do with 'the history of our constitution in the large sense of the word'.[7] He may have had in mind here constitution in the sense in which one might have spoken of an individual's constitution, meaning general make-up, determinative character. In this context 'constitutional history' could have a content and weight exceeding that of legal and institutional history. This potential duality in constitutional history contributed largely to its double intellectual significance in Victorian and earlier twentieth-century England. By 1900 modern history had become a subject of commanding importance in British universities. Thus at Oxford it had by the decade 1900 to 1909 become the most popular subject, taken by 23.4 per cent of undergraduates; and as late as 1948 the relevant figure was 26.6 per cent.[8] As history became a predominant subject in university education towards the end of the nineteenth century, constitutional history was treated as its backbone. When the Oxford History School was founded enormous emphasis was laid upon the absolute necessity of its including a large element of constitutional history. This was regarded as giving 'a strength and dignity to the School which it might otherwise lack'.[9] The reasons for

[6] Hallam, *Constitutional History*, i, p. v. (The 5th edn., 1846, has been used for this essay). [7] Ibid., p. vi.
[8] M. C. Curthoys, 'The Examination System', in M. G. Brock and M. C. Curthoys (eds.), *The History of the University of Oxford*, vi: *Nineteenth Century Oxford*, pt. 1 (Oxford, 1997), 372; J. B. Morrell, 'The Non-Medical Sciences', in Brian Harrison (ed.), *The History of the University of Oxford*, viii: *The Twentieth Century* (Oxford, 1994), 142.
[9] P. R. H. Slee, *Learning and a Liberal Education: The Study of Modern History in the Universities of Oxford, Cambridge and Manchester 1800–1914* (Manchester, 1986), 86–93. (The undergraduate study of modern (i.e. post-ancient) history at Oxford begins with the foundation of the School of History and Law in 1852. The independent School of Modern History was founded in 1870.)

this stress were significantly pedagogical. The subject was valued because it required the mastery of complicated data; it was protective against dissolution into mere loose discourse; and it had morally instructive force in providing training in judgement, honest judgement. Yet looked at more widely, constitutional history could be the subject or theme which focused, almost melded, many of the principal intellectual movements of the age. Undergraduate education in the later nineteenth century was seen much more in a context of social purpose and of moral improvement than is nowadays the case. Particularly in Oxford and Cambridge constitutional history was at the heart of a syllabus and a system consciously directed towards the mental and moral improvement of an élite.[10]

In both regards the central figure was Stubbs. The *Constitutional History* became the textbook of all textbooks. J. R. Tanner, writing at Cambridge in 1901, said, referring to a somewhat earlier period, that 'to read the first volume of Stubbs was necessary to salvation; to read the second was greatly to be desired; the third was reserved for the ambitious student who sought to accumulate merit by unnatural austerities—but between them they covered the whole ground'.[11] When G. M. Trevelyan was a schoolboy at Harrow (the earliest 'History specialist' there), he wrote out a full analysis of all three volumes of Stubbs as a counterbalance to 'brighter authors'.[12] Tanner himself, by publishing two volumes of constitutional documents on English sixteenth- and seventeenth-century history, played a large part in extending the reign of constitutional history in English universities far into the twentieth century.[13] Stubbs's *Select Charters and Other Illustrations of English Constitutional History* (1870) remained, in successive editions, a basis of English university courses for over a hundred years.

[10] R. N. Soffer, *Discipline and Power: The University, History and the Making of an English Elite, 1870–1930* (Stanford, Calif., 1994).
[11] F. W. Maitland *et al.*, *Essays on the Teaching of History* (Cambridge, 1901), 54.
[12] G. M. Trevelyan, *An Autobiography and Other Essays* (London, 1949), 14.
[13] J. R. Tanner, *Tudor Constitutional Documents* (Cambridge, 1922); id., *Constitutional Documents of the Reign of James I* (Cambridge, 1930). For the enduring strength of constitutional history in the syllabuses of British universities, B. [H.] Harrison, 'History at the Universities 1968: A Commentary', *History*, 53 (1968), 364.

That Stubbs intended the *Constitutional History* as a textbook is plain, not least in its presentation in a format in which each paragraph was numbered, thus facilitating reference. Yet it was far more than a textbook. His successor but one as Regius Professor, Frederick York Powell, a man of wide and fertile intellect, observed: 'I consider Adam Smith as perhaps the greatest scientific English historian before Darwin, and I see in Stubbs's *Constitutional History* not only an admirable legal textbook, but one of the finest examples of the process of evolution ever worked out.'[14] Powell was a little over-trenchant, as was his wont, but in his attitude he anticipated the long overdue modern recognition of Stubbs's work as 'one of the great books, in fact, of the nineteenth century'.[15]

While providing a detailed account of the institutional history of England from the fifth to the fifteenth centuries, Stubbs put forward an interpretation of English history which was always complex, frequently cautious, not infrequently cloudy, and, as a whole, a monument to the major significance of his place in the Victorian intellectual world.[16] He saw 'the great characteristic of the English constitutional system ... the principle of its growth, the secret of its construction' as 'the continuous development of representative institutions from the first elementary stage, in which they are employed for local purposes ... to that in which the national parliament appears'.[17] English history was interpreted in terms of a kind of manifest destiny, a product of 'the law of the progress in this world'.[18] A key concept for him was that of self-realization, that by which the growth of national consciousness gives the state a life which is real and characteristic. He recurrently used the image of a structure acquiring life, a progress, as he put it, from order to organization to organism.[19] Sometimes he saw the state as a human personality, better, for example, for castigation at a certain stage. Surprisingly often he deployed scientific metaphors,

---

[14] O. Elton, *Frederick York Powell: A Life and a Selection from his Letters and Occasional Writings*, 2 vols. (Oxford, 1906), ii. 85.
[15] J. W. Burrow, *A Liberal Descent: Victorian Historians and the English Past* (Cambridge, 1981), 129.   [16] Cf. Burrow's account, ibid. 97–151.
[17] *Constitutional History*, i. 611, para. 156.   [18] Ibid., iii. 661, para. 498.
[19] Burrow, *A Liberal Descent*, 146–8.

once that of 'natural selection'.[20] Not least, he saw constitutional history as essentially the story of moral struggle and one which had the highest moral dignity: 'the world's heroes are no heroes to it.'[21]

It is easier to catch the drift of Stubbs's general arguments than fully to understand them. They are of their age and in the spirit of historicism. Much of what Friedrich Meinecke said about this fits Stubbs well; for example, in Stubbs's emphasis on the importance of the individuality of the state, to be explained in terms of its own inner life and origins and not, or not simply, in terms of timeless reasons based on natural law. Stubbs saw the English state as individual, its personality and development deriving from particular vital forces, working out their necessary conclusion in ways no less mysterious than complicated. According to Meinecke, while most eighteenth-century historians dissected and differentiated, good nineteenth-century ones related and integrated. Stubbs's almost agonized efforts to work simultaneously in terms of the constitution and the nation, the machine and the spirit, fill the bill. Crucial in his interpretation were such concepts as that of the genius of a nation.[22] His ideas must, by one route or another, owe much to Burke and to Coleridge. Their precise origins and, in particular, their relationship to the theological thought of the day have not been established.

Maitland's intellectual stance was very different from that of Stubbs, though he had a high view of his achievement. His long obituary of Stubbs in the *English Historical Review* is full of praise,[23] though with some exceptions. And Maitland made remarks which, although on one level deeply appreciative, might nevertheless have tended to vex the Bishop. In describing his own relationship to the *Constitutional History* Maitland said that its 'battered and backless volumes told me of happy hours and heavy debts'. He described how he first met the great work: 'I picked it up in a London club and

---

[20] J. Campbell, *Stubbs and the English State* (Reading, 1989), 6.
[21] *Constitutional History*, i, p. v.
[22] F. Meinecke, *Historism: The Rise of a New Historical Outlook*, trans. J. E. Anderson (London, 1972), e.g. 178–82.
[23] *Collected Papers*, ii. 495–511.

found it interesting.'[24] The contrast between these observations and the first and last words of the *Constitutional History* is revealing. First: 'The History of Institutions cannot be mastered—can scarcely be approached—without an effort.'[25] Picking the book up in a London club hardly suggests effort. The last words of the *Constitutional History* are these: 'At the close of so long a book the author may be suffered to moralise. His end will have been gained if he has succeeded in helping to train the judgement of his readers to discern the balance of truth and reality . . . to rest content with nothing less than the obtainable maximum of truth, to base their arguments on nothing less sacred than that highest justice which is found in the deepest sympathy with erring and straying men.'[26] There is nothing here about 'happy hours'. Maitland was far too clever a man for such remarks as he made in his obituary of Stubbs to have lacked an element of mischief. Maitland wrote and lived with a light touch. It is difficult to imagine, *chez* Stubbs, a scene such as that in which Maitland was found with a monkey in his study, which had to be contained in a box, Madox's *Exchequer* forming the lid.[27]

Such differences between the two historians reflect those of background, career, and generation. Stubbs came from an impoverished though professional background. He gained a university education only as a servitor at Christ Church, as an undergraduate who paid his way by accepting lowly status and humble duties. When Stubbs was a country parson he married the village schoolmistress. He did very well in the end: Regius Professor, successively bishop of two sees, Chancellor of the Order of the Garter, preacher of Queen Victoria's memorial sermon at Windsor. But every penny he had, he earned. Maitland's circumstances were more fortunate. He came from a family of some means (and which had already included a distinguished historian), went to Eton, was a member of a golden intellectual circle at Cambridge, and married into a family comparable to his own. A more fundamental difference between Stubbs and Maitland lay in

[24] Ibid. 496, 503.
[25] *Constitutional History*, i, p. v.
[26] Ibid., iii. 668.
[27] Fifoot, *Frederic William Maitland*, 169.

their attitudes to religion. Stubbs's were those appropriate to a bishop of the established church. Maitland's approached those of an agnostic.[28] (But the contrast was not between Oxford and Cambridge. For strident religion preached from the professorial chair, Lord Acton, Regius Professor at Cambridge, would have been hard to beat. In his inaugural lecture he said of history that it aided one 'to see that the action of Christ, who is risen on mankind whom he redeemed fails not, but increases'. 'Our historical judgements have as much to do with our hopes of Heaven as public or private conduct.'[29])

The contrasts between the work of Stubbs and that of Maitland may be related to an apparent watershed in historiography in the late nineteenth century, which has been considerably discussed, for example by P. B. M. Blaas. Blaas sees a number of contrasts between the older and the younger generation, and it is interesting to consider the relationship between Maitland's and Stubbs's views of constitutional history in relation to these.[30] Blaas argues that the younger men paid far more attention to archival sources than did the older. True enough: Stubbs paid essentially no attention to unprinted sources in the Public Record Office, and had not grasped their scale.[31] For Maitland, on the other hand, his discovery of the enormous wealth of the legal records there was the key to the larger part of his work. According to Blaas another feature of the younger generation was an abandonment of 'the cult of Parliament' with an increased stress on the importance of administration.[32] Here

---

[28] Characterizing Maitland's religious stance is, unsurprisingly, difficult. His daughter Ermengard said that his 'position was that of a very Protestant agnostic, I might almost say of a Low Church agnostic', but this categorization is thought to be insufficiently nuanced, Fifoot, *Frederic William Maitland*, 180.

[29] J. E. E. D. Acton, *A Lecture on the Study of History* (London, 1896), 31, 20.

[30] P. B. M. Blaas, *Continuity and Anachronism: Parliamentary and Constitutional Development in Whig Historiography and in the Anti-Whig Reaction between 1890 and 1930* (The Hague, 1978).

[31] This is suggested by an observation which shows that he greatly underestimated the ease with which all medieval archives could be printed 'either in full or in ... abundant extracts'. He thought 'the time cannot be far off when this would have been accomplished'. W. Stubbs, *Seventeen Lectures on the Study of Medieval and Modern History and Kindred Subjects* (3rd edn., Oxford, 1900), 14.

[32] Blaas, *Continuity and Anachronism*, 23–34.

Maitland played a complicated role. His discovery in the Public Record Office and publication in 1893 of documents relating to the Parliament of 1305 was of key importance.[33] He showed that an early fourteenth-century Parliament was a largely judicial occasion, concerned with the settlement of difficult cases and the answering of petitions. This discovery has been taken by some later scholars, most recently the late Sir Geoffrey Elton, to demonstrate that Stubbs was wrong in attributing a major political role to the early medieval Parliament as a representative institution.[34] Maitland did not claim this, and would have been wrong so to do. While drawing attention to a neglected dimension of Parliament he did not seek to undermine the Stubbsian case for its political significance.

In Blaas's view, by the 1890s historians were tending to be essentially critical, destroyers rather than creators. Obviously by then keen research into medieval history had led to vigorous modification of some of Stubbs's views by, for example, Round,[35] but above all by Maitland, not only on Parliament, but also in relation to the status of the canon law of the medieval church in England. This was a constitutional subject on which Maitland differed decisively from Stubbs. He demonstrated that the medieval English church did not have any significant independence of Rome in the operation of the canon law.[36]

Certainly, a new force in English historiography was archival research by men who had received something like a technical training as historians, and who were much more exclusively concerned with the establishment of historical facts, above all in relation to administrative history, without anything of the wider and more religious or metaphysical concerns of their predecessors. This is true of Stubbs's two

[33] F. W. Maitland (ed.), *Records of the Parliament Holden at Westminster . . . (A.D. 1305) (Memoranda de Parliamento, 1305)* (Rolls Series, 1893).
[34] G. R. Elton, *The History of England* (Cambridge, 1984), esp. 17–18; discussed in Campbell, *Stubbs and the English State, passim.*
[35] Tanner emphasizes the extent to which controversy about some of Stubbs's conclusions had enlivened the subject by 1901, Maitland et al., *Essays on the Teaching of History*, 55.
[36] F. W. Maitland, *Roman Canon Law in the Church of England: Six Essays* (Cambridge, 1898), well discussed by Fifoot, *Frederic William Maitland*, 154–63.

most distinguished pupils, Tout and Round. By the next generation, that of, for example, V. H. Galbraith, any ideological content has completely disappeared. Galbraith had strong views on many subjects, but the idea of associating them with his history-writing was foreign to him.

Maitland's position was, however, an entirely different one and does not conform to the views of Blaas. It brought him closer, though only in the broadest terms, to Stubbs's general stance rather than to that of the modern 'professionals' of whom Tait and Tout were early examples. Maitland did not share all Stubbs's general or particular interpretation. But his work, like that of Stubbs, related to, and partly derived from, an ideological stance, as that of most 'professional' historians does not. Maitland was not trained as a historian; he said that he had hardly read a history book, other than histories of philosophy, until he had turned 30. His earliest, and strongest intellectual interests were philosophical. In this a most powerful and formative influence was that of the Cambridge philosopher Henry Sidgwick (1838–1900). Sidgwick was a marvellously influential teacher, with enlightened views, the highest connections, and a long white beard.[37] Sidgwick was, as Leslie Stephen put it, 'convinced of the necessity for the reconstruction of religious and social creeds in accordance with scientific methods'. Maitland's career demonstrated a relationship between history, philosophy, and law specific almost to his generation. Law, philosophy, and history were interrelated. Sidgwick had a strong interest in law and lectured on it for the Moral Sciences tripos. Maitland sought to become a Fellow in Philosophy of Trinity in 1875. One of his rivals in this was his friend William Cunningham, soon to become a most eminent economic historian and, later, Archdeacon of Ely.[38] Such a relationship between history and philosophy was not confined to Cambridge. In 1896 an American scholar applied simultaneously for the chairs of History and of

[37] Teaching: Fifoot, *Frederic William Maitland*, 35–6. High connections: below, p. 109. Beard: Trevelyan, *An Autobiography*, 16. For his intellectual importance and influence, J. B. Schneewind, *Sidgwick's Ethics and Victorian Moral Philosophy* (Oxford, 1977). For Maitland's view on him *Collected Papers*, iii. 531–40.

[38] Fifoot, *Frederic William Maitland*, 46.

Philosophy in the University of Glasgow.[39] The circle to which Maitland belonged was highly influential. His great friend at Eton was Gerald Balfour, whose brother Arthur not only became Prime Minister, but married one of Sidgwick's sisters. (Another sister married E. W. Benson, Archbishop of Canterbury 1883–96.) Arthur Balfour published an obituary note on Maitland.[40] His own writings on the margins of philosophy and history show how far he and Maitland came under the same intellectual influences.[41] Leslie Stephen, a major figure among the enlightened of the period, was part of the same nexus. His second wife was Maitland's wife's aunt; and Maitland's last work was a memoir of Stephen. H. A. L. Fisher, historian, cabinet minister, and Warden of New College, was Maitland's brother-in-law and Stephen's wife's nephew. He wrote a memoir of Maitland. Not the least remarkable of Maitland's contacts was Bertrand Russell (1872–1970). Like Maitland, Russell was a Trinity College undergraduate. He too was a member of the 'Apostles', a closed society of members of Cambridge University, including men of distinction and with some degree of influence on the development of political and moral attitudes. He too was influenced by Sidgwick and read the innovatory Moral Sciences tripos. Maitland and Russell were acquainted to the extent that in the winters of 1900 and 1901 the young Russells lived in Maitland's official house in Downing College while the Maitlands wintered abroad.[42] In many of their ideas, attitudes, and capacities Maitland and Russell were recognizably from the same school.

Maitland was a constitutional historian in senses which revealed a strongly philosophical interest in historical development. He saw the history of English law as one of complex intellectual development in which progress, the contribution

---

[39] The man concerned was the Revd John Martin Littlejohn, Fellow of Columbia College, New York. I owe this information to Professor Michael Moss of Glasgow University. [40] *Athenaeum* (1907), 47.

[41] e.g. A. J. Balfour, *Decadence* (Henry Sidgwick Memorial Lecture; Cambridge, 1908).

[42] See the 'Chronology' in B. Russell, *Toward the 'Principles of Mathematics' 1900–02*, ed. G. H. Moore (London, 1993). I am grateful to Richard Rempel for help here.

of successive generations and men, could be demonstrated. The history of that law was documented for seven centuries and more by an archive of unrivalled wealth, hundreds of thousands of cases, recorded one by one. To investigate the history of the law was to discover the movement and development of a kind of common mind in a way which was just about impossible to accomplish over the same long period elsewhere.

Maitland's style in the writing of his history was at a great distance from that of most other legal and constitutional historians. This is a reminder of the complexity of the influences on so clever a man at the centre of so kaleidoscopic an intellectual scene. He said, rather remarkably, that one of the duties of the legal historian was to recover the common thoughts of common men. His efforts to do this quite often took the form of producing a hypothetical vignette of medieval incidents. In this we see a strand in Maitland's thought which reveals a debt, direct or indirect, to Walter Scott and his capacity for revealing historical circumstances in the dialogues and predicaments of simple people. In an essay on 'Scott and the Historians', G. M. Young suggests that 'it is one of the most curious paradoxes of our literary history that the Middle Ages in England ceased to interest the educated intelligence just about the time when they began to lay hold on the educated fancy'. That is to say that as the learned tradition of such as Hickes and Madox petered out, the interest in 'Gothic' tales began. This interest was important for Scott. But when a revival in serious medieval scholarship came, 'the whole educated world was ... conditioned to read its documents as Scott might have read them, and so to see the medieval world, not as a pageant, but as a social structure where all, high and low, are linked together by the same customary law'. 'Not in a work of fiction now do we expect such vivid pictures of social relations as we find in historical treatises, in Maitland's *Domesday Book and Beyond*, in the prefaces to the successive volumes of the Selden Society.'[43] (The power of Scott could seem all but

---

[43] G. M. Young, *Last Essays* (London, 1950), 17–40, esp. 23; cf. in particular Trevelyan, *An Autobiography*, 200–5. Young's point is illustrated in valuable detail by D. H. Richter, 'From Medievalism to Historicism', in L. T. Workman (ed.), *Medievalism in England* (Studies in Medievalism 4; Cambridge, 1992), 79–104.

omnipresent. According to Acton, the initial impulse for Ranke's historical career came from his discovery that Scott's account of Louis XI was incompatible with that of Commynes.[44])

Very important to Maitland was his study of corporate or fictitious legal personalities. He was concerned by the way in which legal history illuminated the nature and importance, for example, of the emergence of legally recognized entities or associations intermediate between the state and the individual. He was not alone in these interests. They were paralleled, for example, by those of the economic and urban historian George Unwin working on urban guilds. These historians were concerned with the nature, importance, and development of what political theorists now term 'civil society'.[45] One definition of this would be that it encompasses the elements and organizations which, although partly regulated by legal rules emanating from the common mind of the state, are at an opposite pole from the subordinate organizations of a totalitarian state. They are not, predominantly or exclusively, components of the central government apparatus. Maitland's interest in municipal development was part of this focus on the relationship between the legal concept of a fictitious personality and the development of civil society. His interest in town history was strongly related to his concern with fictitious persons. In his *Township and Borough* he brought together this interest and one in the detailed topography of Cambridge and its fields.[46] Here Maitland brilliantly integrated, as only he could have done, two interests, one legal-philosophical, the other topographical.

Neither interest was shared by Stubbs. Stubbs had a general aversion to the approach of lawyers; his overt interest in topography was approximately nil (in which he differed much from his successor as Regius Professor, Freeman). For all that there is a kinship between Maitland's concern with fictitious persons and the intellectual stance of Stubbs, and also of the other great nineteenth-century historians near the

[44] Acton, *A Lecture on the Study of History*, 49–50.
[45] C. Parker, *The English Historical Tradition since 1850* (Edinburgh, 1990), 64–6.
[46] F. W. Maitland, *Township and Borough* (Cambridge, 1898).

centre of whose concerns was the reification of human collectivities: above all the state, the people, the nation. How far such entities can be given the attributes of a kind of personality by more than rough analogy is a fundamental question for historicism. The problem comes into sharp and special focus by relation to the lawyers' concept of *persona ficta*. It could seem that Maitland was adding, even by implication opposing, two concepts to the reification, personalization, or deification of the nation-state. These two concepts are as follows. One is that the law as an evolving and largely determinative historic entity has a life of its own, which represents a Burkean cumulative process by which each generation contributes to its successors, and which, although related to the development of the state, is separable from it. The second concept determinative for Maitland is that of the importance of associations lesser than the state whose independent life, though legally validated, was not necessarily created by the state power.

Maitland's positive concern with the importance of medieval urban organization had as its counterpart a negative concern with village organization. He seldom missed an opportunity to cast cold water on the significance of the early village community as a meaningful factor in the history of the development of free constitutions. Burrow has shown that the theme is not without its entertaining paradoxes.[47] Thus, Stubbs's willingness, guided by Waitz, to attribute constitutional significance to such communities put him into a broad European context somewhat more to the left than, as a sound Conservative, he may have wished.[48] Vinogradoff commented upon Maitland's concern to make the introduction of village institutions as late as possible, and to undermine any idea of common village property, in more than a restrictive sense, at a very early date. He praised Maitland's 'searching analysis', but added, 'in some cases people with a hopeful turn of mind may venture on reconstruction where

[47] J. W. Burrow, 'The "Village Community" and the Uses of History in Late Nineteenth-Century England', in N. McKendrick (ed.), *Historical Perspectives: Studies in English Thought and Society in Honour of J. H. Plumb* (London, 1974), 255–84.
[48] *The Letters of Frederic William Maitland*, ed. C. H. S. Fifoot (London, 1965), nos. 60, 62, pp. 57–8, 59–60.

his subtle scepticism has resolved and perhaps in the end we may get a better insight into historical peculiarities of thought and arrangement'.[49]

Vinogradoff expressed himself with thoughtful reserve; both Stubbs and Maitland were no less adroit. To seek to pin these historians down to clear general views is certainly risky. They are given to hedging their bets. But a broad general distinction between Stubbs's and Maitland's views of constitutional history seems to be as follows. The progressive development in constitutional freedom which Stubbs saw as determinative in English history had, for him, its ultimate origin in distant circumstances such as those described by Tacitus. The origins of English liberty lay in the forests of early Germany, and those origins and the transmission of the tradition of liberty had a great deal to do with race. The English were, he said, 'a people of German descent in the main constituents of blood, character, and language [and] in the possession of the elements of primitive German civilisation and the common germs of German institutions'.[50] The survival, in however fragmentary a form, of early institutions had for Stubbs a special interest because they took one back to determinative origins. He attached special importance to the antiquity of the village as a community of freemen whose assemblies emerge into the light of medieval documents as manorial courts.[51] Maitland did not attach anything like such importance to ultimate origins. An important element in his intellectual make-up was Liberal, almost radical. Stubbs believed in the preservation of ancient institutions. Maitland did not believe in the preservation of ancient laws, unless they served a demonstrably useful purpose. Rather, he stood for reform and rationalization. He emphasized the extent to which what was valuable in the development of the law was due to successive generations contributing their share of reason and sense to an increasingly sophisticated and rational system. Debts to a distant past and survivals from a distant past meant very much less to Maitland than they did to Stubbs.

---

[49] P. Vinogradoff, *The Growth of the Manor* (2nd edn., London, 1911), p. vi.
[50] e.g. *Constitutional History*, i. 2, para. 1.
[51] e.g. ibid., i. 93–6, para. 39, pp. 89–92, paras. 42, 43.

Blaas has contended that round about the turn of the nineteenth century history infused by doctrines was being superseded by technical history. Parker argues convincingly that there was a middle ground. In this he is surely right. Thus Maitland was not a 'pure scholar'. Such a person would, as a legal historian, be concerned, for example, to establish when, how, and why the Writ of Entry became established, or the Court of Chancery became so important, without attention to larger concerns in regard to the history of society and the possibilities of social progress. Running through Maitland's great learning was something other than an urge to dissect the past as though it were a dead frog. He was, in particular, concerned with the historical and theoretical justification of entities related to, but not by any means identical with, the nation-state: law, as particularly demonstrated by the marvellously evidenced law of England; associations within the state but not necessarily or intrinsically part of it. He was a constitutional historian, in both the broad and the narrow senses, as much as was Stubbs. Maitland's views or arguments reflect those of an intellectual generation and circle, largely from Cambridge. In general they are by implication contra-Stubbsian.

In all their work Stubbs and Maitland owed much to German scholars.[52] In general, their education and their intellectual ambience was open to Germany. Stubbs had been taught German at a minor school in his home town of Knaresborough.[53] German literature was a principal recreation for Maitland's father, whose reading extended as far as some of the work of Savigny.[54] In one of his last papers Maitland wrote: 'The German occupation of a considerable tract of English history has been a gradual process. The sphere of influence becomes a protectorate, and the protectorate becomes sovereignty.'[55] He was a little carried away by his metaphor, hot from the age of imperialism. The German

---

[52] For German influence on English 19th-century historiography in general see C. E. McClelland, *The German Historians and England* (Cambridge, 1971), and Burrow, *A Liberal Descent*, 119–25, 148, 252–3.
[53] *Letters of William Stubbs*, 7–8.
[54] Fifoot, *Frederic William Maitland*, 12.
[55] *Collected Papers*, iii. 447.

empire in English history had been well established for decades. The importance attached to German learning in the infant Modern History faculty at Oxford may be seen from the translation of Ranke's work having been undertaken as a joint venture there.[56] In the decades before the war of 1914 to 1918 aspiring young English historians might spend a period at German universities, as did other English scholars.[57] They could find an organized system of learning there hardly to be matched at home.

Germany was of special importance for Stubbs; he saw it as the distant home and source of English liberty and the foundations of much of his learning and many of his ideas were German. In particular he was strongly dependent on the work of Waitz, in his account of the early period. In the first chapter of the *Constitutional History* there are thirty-three references to Waitz, in addition to thirteen to Grimm, twelve to Maurer, and ten to Bethmann-Hollweg. The only British author with more than one was Kemble: he had six. Stubbs's learning related largely to the pre-1849 phase of German historiography. How little his historical judgement was affected by events in Germany in his own day (or how little he revised successive editions) may be seen in such a statement as: 'Bavaria, Saxony, Franconia, Suabia have their national policy ...' remaining in later editions as in the first.[58] Stubbs made no secret of to what an extent he regarded Germany as superior to France. The development of French history had been, he maintained, such as to lead to the establishment of 'actual despotism' which became 'systematic tyranny' 'and its logical result is the explosion which is called revolution'. The Franks had indeed brought the 'German system' to Gaul, but it had, unfortunately, been 'modified by its work of foreign conquest and deprived of home safeguards'.[59] Stubbs worked considerably on German

---

[56] L. von Ranke, *A History of England, Principally in the Seventeenth Century*, trans. C. W. Boase, W. W. Jackson, H. B. George, H. F. Pelham, M. Creighton, A. Watson, G. W. Kitchin, and A. Plummer, 6 vols. (Oxford, 1875).
[57] Stuart Wallace, *War and the Image of Germany: British Academics 1914–1918* (Edinburgh, 1988), 227–8. (I am grateful to J. Stevenson for this reference.)
[58] *Constitutional History*, i. 6, para. 4.
[59] Ibid., i. 4, para. 2.

history. Maitland expressed the wish that 'he had interpreted medieval Germany or even modern Germany, to Englishmen'.[60] Stubbs was one of the only two British historians (the other being Thomas Carlyle) awarded the Prussian order Pour le Mérite for distinction in the arts and sciences. The number of foreign members for this section of the order was limited to thirty.

Maitland's relationship to German scholarship appears time and time again, to the extent that in important areas his work almost depended on it. This is already evident in the earlier papers in which he first began to make his mark as a student of the history of law. He referred to Grimm,[61] Brunner,[62] Wilda,[63] Schmid,[64] Güterbock,[65] Hensler,[66] and Laband.[67] It would have been impossible to have studied early English law meaningfully without using German scholarship. All through Maitland's short, dazzling academic career he had German works beside him. But Tait very reasonably pointed out in his review of *Domesday Book and Beyond* that Maitland had been too far dependent on the German example in his emphasis on the military element in the origins of English towns.[68] The most important indication of Maitland's German involvement was his translation, at the suggestion of Sidgwick, of part of the third volume of Otto von Gierke's *Rechtsgeschichte der deutschen Genossenschaft*, published as *Political Theories of the Middle Ages* (1900). Its special interest for him lay in its legal/philosophical treatment of associations within the state and of their relations to the state.[69] Another more concrete example of the relation of German studies to the constitutional historiography of England was Charles Gross's *The Guild Merchant* (1890), which was based on a Göttingen thesis (*Gilda Mercatoria*, 1883).

The German contribution to English constitutional

---

[60] *Collected Papers*, iii. 501.
[61] 'The Law of Real Property', ibid., i. 178 (1879).   [62] Ibid. 174.
[63] 'The Laws of Wales: The Kindred and the Blood Feud', ibid. 226 (1881).
[64] 'The Criminal Liability of the Hundred', ibid. 244 (1881–2).
[65] 'The Seisin of Chattels', ibid. 344 (1895).   [66] Ibid. 345.
[67] Ibid. 352.   [68] *English Historical Review*, 12 (1897), 768–77.
[69] pp. 111–12, 114 above.

history took a more direct form in the work of Rudolf von Gneist. In the course of a long and distinguished career as an academic Roman lawyer, a judge, and a politician von Gneist studied and wrote extensively on English constitutional history (*Englische Verfassungsgeschichte*, 1882). He was a liberal and regarded English parliamentary government as in important respects a model for Prussia and for Germany. Furthermore, his work was much regarded in England. The English translations of his books on English parliamentary government and on the English constitution both reached their third editions.[70] For a time these works were outstanding as monographs, virtually textbooks, which took their subjects from the earliest beginnings to the most modern times. Gierke delivered and published a memorial address to von Gneist.[71] The relationship of such scholars to England and their contribution in different ways to the study and understanding of the history of English institutions, in the concrete or in the abstract, was part of a tradition at least two generations old. Gneist's work was valued in an intellectual climate in which the study of the history of English institutions, especially of medieval English institutions, was seen as relevant to the modern political concerns, not only of England, but also of Germany. A comparable conviction can be found in the somewhat later works of Sidney and Beatrice Webb. Their principal aims were political and contemporary; but their work has a most powerful dimension of enquiry into institutional history. And they particularly valued the work of von Gneist.[72]

A curious, and instructive, example of the Anglo-German relationship and of Stubbsian constitutional history in its broadest sense is F. M. Powicke's *Bismarck and the German*

---

[70] [H.] R. [H. F.] von Gneist, *History of the English Parliament, its Growth and Development through a Thousand Years: 800 to 1887* (3rd edn., London, 1889); id., *The History of the English Constitution* (3rd edn., London, 1891). Cf. G. W. Prothero, 'Gneist on the English Constitution', *English Historical Review*, 3 (1888), 1–33. For von Gneist's career see the account by Erich Angermann in *Neue deutsche Biographie*, vi (Berlin, 1971), 487–9.

[71] P. A. Ashworth, 'von Gneist', *Encyclopedia Britannica* (11th edn., Cambridge, 1910), xii. 151.

[72] S. and B. Webb, *English Local Government from the Revolution to the Municipal Corporations Act* (2nd edn., London, 1924), vii. 6–7.

Empire (1914).[73] Powicke (1879–1963) was very much a product of the school Stubbs founded. He was taught at Manchester by Stubbs's pupil Tout, and at Oxford by A. L. Smith, the pupil of Stubbs's pupils, and a great admirer of Maitland, on whom he published a book. Powicke was outstanding among the English medievalists of his day. Regius Professor at Oxford from 1928 to 1947, his works extended beyond Stubbs's range and were based on a professionalism and a lifelong commitment which Stubbs had not been in a position to match. He was not a 'constitutional historian' in a usual sense. But in much of his work, especially in *Henry III and the Lord Edward* (1947), his work is infused by a concern with constitutional development and, above all, with moral values in history which partly reflect his intellectual descent from Stubbs. This is evident from the dedication to his Festschrift. 'You have kept us to the study of men as they are beneath the destructiveness which scars the course of history, responding however faint-heartedly to the calls of friendship, practical idealism, and the love of God. . . . Under your guidance we have felt the deep influence of these lives which were the glory of their own time and still have power to invigorate us today.'[74] This affecting passage was published about fifty years ago, but in tone and message belongs much more to Stubbs's day than to the present.

The least known of Powicke's works is his *Bismarck and the German Empire* mentioned above, published, on internal evidence, before the outbreak of war. It was part of a series entitled 'The People's Books'. A slight work of ninety-one pages, it was in most respects inconsiderable, and certainly not much considered. In does not appear in lists of Powicke's works and the Bodleian Library did not contain a copy until fairly recently. What is interesting about it in relation to the concerns of the present essay is the extent to which its praise of Bismarck and of Germany is in terms which emphasize the importance of nationality and of the

---

[73] F. M. Powicke, *Bismarck and the German Empire* (London, 1914).
[74] R. W. Hunt, W. A. Pantin, and R. W. Southern (eds.), *Studies in Medieval History Presented to Frederick Maurice Powicke* (Oxford, 1948), p. v.

rights conferred on a nation-state by its very emergence and existence. 'The discovery of nationality has included the discovery of law and institutions no less than of national forces.'[75] 'If as we must believe, the right of nationality, based as it is upon a complicated series of physical and natural facts, does express a truth necessary for human progress, we may be sure time will avenge perverted assertions of it.'[76] He emphasized, without condemnation, the importance for Prussia of such doctrines as that 'healthy selfishness is the lawful motive of every organised state' and 'an organism is by its very nature self-supporting and has its own right to exist'.[77] In regard to the war of 1870 'the moral justification of Germany is to be found in the principles of the French empire'.[78] Moreover, German absolutism and subjection of unwilling provinces was more justifiable than French because it was 'rooted in the fibre of the nation'.[79] Yet there was to be a German democracy of the future 'founded upon the most enduring principles of German history and upon nothing that is casual or unreal'.[80] Bismarck was, in all this, 'the servant of a great people, which was slowly learning what it is to be a nation'.[81] These doctrines and the manner in which they are expressed much resemble some of the assumptions and contentions of Stubbs. One may reflect, in passing, how far Powicke's Bismarck resembled Stubbs's Edward I. Powicke seems to have got more from Stubbs than a knowledge of View of Frankpledge or the Assize of Clarendon. His half-buried little book is a reminder of how potent, indeed how dangerous, doctrines of constitutional history in its wider sense could be. There were elements in the Anglo-German study thereof which were not all sweetness and light.

In some of Powicke's words we have echoes of the thunderous and sinister doctrines and rodomontade of the nation-state. These were by no means always separable from true scholarship. Treitschke was a major scholar, as well as a bigoted, self-appointed prophet. It is undeniable that some of Stubbs's ideas and language further ideas of state and race

[75] Powicke, *Bismarck*, 23.   [76] Ibid. 24–5.   [77] Ibid. 35–6.
[78] Ibid. 83.   [79] Ibid. 83.   [80] Ibid. 91.   [81] Ibid. 68.

such that their later consequences would have been utter anathema to him. Here is one example among many: he chose to characterize the Britons attacked by the Saxons as 'sullen and treacherous' and, in describing the conquest of the last free Welsh, he said 'the day of account was come'.[82] The dual implication of the term 'constitutional history' half-signalled by Hallam in the work where the term seems first to appear[83] meant that for many decades the study of ancient institutions was bound up with theories, doctrines, and cults of state and race.

The long and intimate link between German and English historiography was smashed by the war of 1914–18. One can hear the breaking in works by H. W. C. Davis and Felix Liebermann. Both were major figures in the study of English constitutional history. Davis had studied history at Oxford while Stubbs was still Regius Professor. He edited the later editions of Stubbs's *Select Charters* and was himself to become Regius Professor. In 1914 (almost certainly after the outbreak of war) he published *The Political Thought of Heinrich von Treitschke*. This was a selection of von Treitschke's writings, in translation, with special attention to those of an anti-British complexion. On the title-page was a motto: *Fas est ab hoste doceri*. Liebermann was the most important student of Anglo-Saxon law there has ever been. His *Die Gesetze der Angelsachsen* is massive, durable, and indispensable. The serious student of Anglo-Saxon history would be lost without it. Liebermann knew England well. He had spent two years in Manchester as the representative of his family's textile firm. He was on good terms with Maitland. The terms of the dedication of the third and final volume of his great work, dated 20 July 1916, are the more arresting and sad. The initial dedication to Brunner and to Maitland is followed by a long text. This speaks first of the days when Germans concerned themselves with the life of the British state and its literature and British scholars unenviously smoothed the path for German research, including this contribution to the oldest history of their country. It goes on to express the hope that 'the storm

---

[82] Stubbs, *Constitutional History*, i. 69, para. 28 (cf. i. 10, para. 8), ii. 117, para. 179.
[83] p. 101 above.

of hate and sea of blood which are running high at the time of the conclusion of these pages will soon be understood as essentially having been caused by the historical necessity of a conflict between the reckless claims of an empire which was used, by its power, to commanding the passage of the seas and the trade of the world alone, and the justified decision of the united German people to struggle peacefully and calmly, freely and strongly, for the goods of this earth and to expand in line with their inherent vitality.'[84] Here we meet Treitschke again. It is a sad business that students of English institutions so eminent as Davis and (much more so) Liebermann should have been drawn into war in this way. Yet one can readily see how the tradition of constitutional historiography of which Stubbs was the leading English exponent contained, by the very nature of its historicist nationalism, implications which could be dangerous and destructive. This was by no means any less the case on the German side. The emphases and implications of Maitland as a constitutional historian were entirely different. They, and the Cambridge context from which they derive, stand in a long nineteenth-century liberal tradition which not infrequently tended towards pacifism. In his more nationalistic views Stubbs had no heirs except among popular historians. In searching for the continuation of the tradition to which Maitland belonged one might point to his brother-in-law. H. A. L. Fisher's biographer sees him as almost the last of the Gladstonian liberals, a man with a vision 'concerned with the

---

[84] The German text of the dedication is as follows: 'Dankbar gewidmet dem Andenken an Heinrich Brunner und Frederic William Maitland, die grössten zeitgenössischen Förderer der Rechtsgeschichte Englands im Mittelalter, ein Zeichen wehmütiger Erinnerung an die friedensgesegnete Entstehungszeit dieser Arbeit, da der Deutsche sich in Britanniens Staatsleben und Literatur bewundernd vertiefte, und der Brite Deutscher Forschung, darunter auch diesem Beitrage zur ältesten Geschichte seiner Nation, neidlos die Bahn ebnete, zugleich der innige Ausdruck vertrauender Hoffnung, dass der Sturm des Hasses und das Meer von Blut, die die Zeit des Abschlusses dieser Blätter umtosen, bald verstanden werden mögen als wesentlich verursacht durch die geschichtliche Notwendigkeit des Zusammenstosses zwischen dem rücksichtslosen Anspruche eines machtgewohnten Weltreiches, Seefahrt und Welthandel dauernd allein zu beherrschen, und dem berechtigten Entschlusse des geeinten Deutschen Volkes, um die Güter dieser Erde friedlich und besonnen, aber frei und stark mitzuringen und sich auszudehnen gemäss seiner eingeborenen Lebenskraft.'

working and progress of humanity', with 'the ordinary instincts of toleration, forbearance and good sense, and lastly on the common heritage of European culture, shared alike by France and Germany [on which] ... is imposed a solemn trusteeship for the civilisation of the world'.[85] This, admittedly rather heavy, rhetoric does convey something serious about the tradition to which Maitland belonged. His view of English constitutional history saw England as distinctly privileged by its archives, which enabled the progress of mankind to be traced through the law. Stubbs's *Constitutional History* is a tribute to the good fortune, maybe more than good fortune, which made the English privileged in political virtue, as he saw it.

[85] D. Ogg, *Herbert Fisher 1865–1940: A Short Biography* (London, 1947), 194.

7

'A place among the English classics'
Ranke's *History of the Popes* and its British Readers

PATRICK BAHNERS

Reviewing Michelet's *History of France* in the *Edinburgh Review* of January 1844, John Stuart Mill appealed to English historians to follow the lead set by their continental colleagues in order to achieve a 'renovation of historical studies'. Among German practitioners of the 'new school', Mill mentioned Niebuhr, Schlosser, and Ranke. 'One of Ranke's works has been twice translated: we would rather that two of them had been translated once.'[1] The main reason why Mill called for an increased supply of Ranke in English may have been utilitarian in a rather narrow sense. The first translation of the book in question, *Die römischen Päpste*, was by Sarah Austin, a friend of Mill's, the wife of John Austin, the Benthamite philosopher of jurisprudence.[2] 'Your German histories do well here, but not your German criticism,' Anna Jameson had reported to Ottilie von Goethe in 1838, informing her about Sarah Austin's assignment.[3] Published by John Murray in 1840, Mrs Austin's translation did indeed sell so well that a rival publisher

---

[1] 'Michelet's History of France', *The Collected Works of John Stuart Mill*, xx (Toronto, 1985), 4 f.

[2] *The Ecclesiastical and Political History of the Popes of Rome, during the Sixteenth and Seventeenth Centuries*, trans. Sarah Austin (4th edn., London, 1866). Though Mrs Austin was an experienced translator, she found mastering Ranke's prose an arduous task. See Lotte and Joseph Hamburger, *Troubled Lives: John and Sarah Austin* (Toronto, 1985), 130–5.

[3] *Letters of Anna Jameson to Ottilie von Goethe*, ed. G. H. Needler (Oxford, 1939), 106.

brought out his own version in 1842.[4] Nevertheless, Mrs Austin found it difficult to find a publisher willing to take his chances with another of Ranke's works.[5] While all of Ranke's national histories were eventually translated into English during the author's lifetime, none was so widely reviewed as the history of the popes. As early as 1843, Ranke was known in the Wordsworth circle as 'the Historian of the Popes';[6] this title of honour would remain with him all his life.[7] The fame of the author of the 'celebrated history of Popedom' spread from Paris salons to English country houses;[8] Ranke was invited to Embley, the home of Florence Nightingale, where he was to meet a former Foreign Secretary, a Baron of the Exchequer, a cardinal's nephew and the Speaker of the House of Commons.[9] In 1862, when Max Müller asked Charles Kingsley to dine with Ranke who was staying in Oxford, he described his guest as the man who had written 'The Popes'.[10] And one year later, when

---

[4] *The History of the Popes: Their Church and State in the Sixteenth and Seventeenth Centuries*, trans. W. K. Kelly (London, 1842). Walter Keating Kelly was a writer of popular history books such as a *History of the Year 1848* (London, 1849) and *The Life of Wellington for Boys* (London, 1853). He also translated Michelet, Louis Blanc, and Cervantes.

[5] Milman, advising Mrs Austin in 1841, believed that Ranke's name stood so well with the English public that a translation of his *Fürsten und Völker*, i.e. the volume on Spanish and Ottoman history which had preceded *Die römischen Päpste*, would succeed, 'as far as any book will at present which has no bearing on our modern controversies'. Arthur Milman, *Henry Hart Milman, D.D.: A Biographical Sketch* (London, 1900), 153. Mill tried in vain to persuade his publisher, John William Parker, to accept the *Deutsche Geschichte*. Mill to Sarah Austin, 28 Feb. 1843, *The Collected Works of John Stuart Mill*, xiii (Toronto, 1963), 571 f. Mrs Austin's version of the *History of the Reformation in Germany* was eventually published by Longmans (London, 1844); *Fürsten und Völker* was translated by her rival, Kelly, as *The Ottoman and Spanish Empires in the Sixteenth and Seventeenth Centuries* (London, 1843).

[6] Edward Quillinan to Henry Crabb Robinson, 1 Sept. 1843, *The Correspondence of Henry Crabb Robinson with the Wordsworth Circle (1808–1866)*, ed. Edith J. Morley, i (Oxford, 1927), 522.

[7] See the journal of George Henry Lewes, 13 June 1865, *The George Eliot Letters*, ed. Gordon S. Haight, iv (Oxford, 1955), 194; and the review of the English translation of the *Englische Geschichte*, 'Contemporary Literature', *Westminster Review*, 103 (1875), 547.

[8] Julius Mohl to Sir Graves Haughton, 8 June 1843, M. C. M. Simpson, *Letters and Recollections of Julius and Mary Mohl* (London, 1887), 33.

[9] Sir Edward Cook, *The Life of Florence Nightingale*, i (London, 1913), 36.

[10] *The Life and Letters of the Rt. Hon. Friedrich Max Müller*, ed. his wife, i (London, 1902), 266.

Ranke's *History of the Popes*

Stopford Brooke took up his duties as chaplain to the embassy in Berlin, he sent his father an account of his conversation with 'Professor Ranke—the Pope man'.[11]

What explains this singular success of a single work? While it did not, perhaps, supersede the most recent fashionable novel on the tables of young ladies, it was assigned to young ladies learning German.[12] Undeterred by Mill's version of Occam's razor—translations ought not to be multiplied without necessity—the invisible hand of the market brought forth two more, both appearing in 1846, by Mrs Elizabeth Foster[13] and David Dundas Scott,[14] respectively. In a letter to Mrs Austin, Mill ascribed the success of the *Popes* to the fact that there was a 'peculiarly English interest involved', namely 'the interest of Protestantism'.[15] Readers and reviewers of the *Popes* can be found in all religious parties. There was widespread agreement among them that Ranke's book did indeed mark a new era in historical studies. Where they differed was on whether this development should be regarded as promising or as dangerous. *The Times* welcomed Mrs Austin's translation by publishing an article in three parts, one for each volume.[16] The reviewer praised the *Popes* as 'a book extraordinary for its learning and impartiality'. This was the combination which was felt to be new: extensive archival research on the one hand, a just and dispassionate

---

[11] Lawrence Pearsall Jacks, *Life and Letters of Stopford Brooke*, i (London, 1917), 160.

[12] Meta, Elizabeth Gaskell's daughter, studied the book in Heidelberg in 1858. *The Letters of Mrs Gaskell*, ed. J. A. V. Chapple and Arthur Pollard (Manchester, 1966), 895.

[13] *The History of the Popes, their Church and State, and Especially of their Conflicts with Protestantism in the Sixteenth and Seventeenth Centuries*, trans. E. Foster (London, 1846). Published by Henry Bohn, this cheap edition, which was 'intended to come within the reach of all classes' ('Translator's Preface', pp. vii f.), was reprinted several times in Bohn's Standard Library of contemporary classics. Mark Twain used the 1876 edn. when preparing his *Life of Pope Leo XIII* (sold by Sotheby's, New York, 29 Oct. 1996: the Victor and Irene Murr Jacobs Collection, lot 208). Mrs Foster published *A Handbook of Modern European Literature* in 1849. She also translated Vasari's *Lives*.

[14] *A History of the Papacy, Political and Ecclesiastical, in the Sixteenth and Seventeenth Centuries* (Glasgow, 1846). In 1840, Scott had published an account of *The Suppression of the Reformation in France*.

[15] 22 May 1842, *The Collected Works of John Stuart Mill*, xiii. 522.

[16] 10 June, 11 and 18 Aug. 1840.

point of view on the other.[17] When the translation appeared, English Catholics had been enjoying equal rights only for a decade. After emancipation, the identity of the English church and state had to be redefined. The outcome was likely to be paradoxical. Equality for Catholics did not mean that the state had ceased to be Protestant. The memory of the glorious struggle against Catholicism needed to be expressed in a way that did not discriminate against living Catholics. In this situation, the historian of the popes was bound to find curious readers. Here was a Protestant who claimed that he could be just to Catholics and yet remain a good Protestant.

The Times recognized something peculiarly German about 'the philosophical benevolence' of Ranke's views. Too few English works, the reviewer said, displayed those qualities in which the German excelled: 'impartiality, gentleness, and research'. The first instalment of his review closed with the prediction that Ranke's information and the spirit in which it was treated would not 'fail of doing great benefit in a country where parties are so bitter as they are amongst us'. George Cornewall Lewis, the liberal politician and interpreter of German classical scholarship, shared this expectation.[18] He pointed out the article to Mrs Austin, encouraging her to translate another of Ranke's books. 'There is more probability of sweetening the bitter theological and sectarian spirit of this country by indirect than by direct means.'[19] The reviewer who, according to Lewis, had so justly appreciated the 'spirit' of Ranke's work was William Makepeace Thackeray. In a letter to his mother, Thackeray spoke of a 'great book', recommending it to those who did not understand how Protestants could talk about the 'beautiful Roman

---

[17] See e.g. the remarks on the *History of the Popes* in the review of Ranke's *History of the Reformation in Germany*, The Times, 27 Mar. 1845.

[18] He had translated the works of August Boeckh and Karl Otfried Müller. In 1855, when Chancellor of the Exchequer, he published an examination of Niebuhr's theories on the sources of early Roman history.

[19] *Letters of the Rt. Hon. Sir George Cornewall Lewis, Bart.*, ed. Sir Gilbert Frankland Lewis (London, 1870), 111. In 1843, Lewis was the host at the famous 'babel of a breakfast' described in Charles Greville's diary when Ranke and his reviewer Macaulay were unable to find a common language. *The Greville Memoirs*, ed. Lytton Strachey and Roger Fulford (London, 1938), v. 135.

Catholic church in whose bosom repose so many saints & sages'.[20] In this view, Ranke's work was part of that great romantic movement which discovered the Church of Rome as an object of aesthetic admiration. Some of those who were drawn to the beauty of holiness ended up as converts. One of them was Aubrey de Vere, the poet, who read Ranke's *Popes* in Rome. The initial idea of writing about the popes had indeed come to Ranke when he persuaded himself that there had been saints such as Pius V among the persecutors of Protestants.[21]

Some Catholics were grateful to Protestant scholars who showed that the popes had not been the monsters of legend. In 1838, the Catholic *Dublin Review* published a review of the German edition of the *Popes*. The author was Felix Papencordt, a German historian who had studied with Ranke before moving to Rome. Papencordt paid tribute to Ranke for making public his candid acknowledgement that the popes of those latter times had been in their private lives spotless and unblameable.[22] For other Catholics, this acknowledgement was not enough. Whatever concessions Protestant historians might make regarding the private morality of individual popes, the authority of the papacy as a divine institution could be accepted only on its own terms or rejected outright. In 1843, the *Dublin Review* printed another review of the *Popes* which retracted Papencordt's praises. The article by John Ennis, a parish priest, was entitled 'Is Ranke an Historian?' The answer was negative. Ennis acknowledged that the study of history had become a 'progressive movement', correcting prejudices by the study of original authorities. 'History is fast progressing towards perfection, by advancing towards simplicity of fact.'[23] Ranke, however, stood outside this movement. He was not interested in simple facts.

[20] *The Letters and Private Papers of William Makepeace Thackeray*, ed. Gordon N. Ray, i (Oxford, 1945), 461.
[21] Leopold Ranke to Heinrich Ranke, Feb. 1827, *Das Briefwerk*, ed. Walther Peter Fuchs (Hamburg, 1949), 105.
[22] [F. P. Papencordt], 'Ranke's History of the Popes', *Dublin Review*, 5 (1838), 14–51, at 50 f.
[23] [John Ennis], 'Is Ranke an Historian?', *Dublin Review*, 14 (1843), 321–79, at 321 f.

To Ennis it was evident that 'Ranke's mind' was 'system-loving and theoretic'.[24] The theory to which 'the whole work was adjusted' proclaimed the inevitable progress of knowledge. Ennis recognized the speculative groundwork which remained invisible to most readers who were dazzled by the splendid descriptions of colourful personalities and dramatic events.[25] He correctly identified Ranke's accounts of the Jansenist controversy and of the suppression of the Jesuit order as 'the great props of his system'.[26] In the course of the dispute with the Jansenists, Clement IX had to accept the autonomy of historical fact. While the pope had the right to declare a theological opinion heretical, he was not free to decide whether this opinion was in fact found in the works of a given theologian.[27] Clement XIV went even further. While the moderate Rospigliosi had acknowledged that matters of fact lay outside the papal jurisdiction, the even more moderate Ganganelli was prepared to submit to the verdict of history on matters of doctrine. Ranke interpreted the dissolution of the Jesuit order as an acknowledgement that the enthusiastic notions of absolute papal authority, which had been propagated by the Jesuits, had been overtaken by events. According to Ranke, Clement did not doubt that he was entitled to abolish what his predecessors had instituted.[28] In the hands of the learned and humble Clement, the freedom of decision which had formerly expressed the popes' claim to be exalted above history became an instrument for moving with the times.

Ennis pointed out that in Ranke's account 'the progress of events' led to the triumph of knowledge over superstition.[29] The popes were not persuaded by the grace of theological argument, but by the force of political circumstances. Truth works by indirect means. This had important consequences

---

[24] Ibid. 325. Two years later, Ennis repeated his criticism in a review of Sarah Austin's translation of the *Deutsche Geschichte*, 'German Reformation and its Times', *Dublin Review*, 18 (1845), 283–320.

[25] On the hidden philosophical premisses see Heinrich Lutz, 'Ranke e il papato', *Rivista di storia della chiesa in Italia*, 16 (1962), 443 f.

[26] [Ennis], 'Is Ranke an Historian?', 378.

[27] Leopold von Ranke, *Die römischen Päpste in den letzten vier Jahrhunderten* (*Sämmtliche Werke*, xxxvii–xxxix; Leipzig, 1874), iii. 101 f.

[28] Ibid. 141.

[29] [Ennis], 'Is Ranke an Historian?', 378.

for the historian. He himself had to employ indirect means. The pattern of causality was more complex than the simple scheme of cause and effect, intention and act. Ennis reproached Ranke with the 'cardinal error' of abandoning 'obvious data' in favour of 'latent or supposititious causes'.[30] This remark indicates what was seen as provocative in Ranke's method. The historian of the popes indeed proceeded in the counter-intuitive manner described by Ennis. He regularly rejected the obvious interpretation of a given event, namely the interpretation suggested by the participants in what they themselves said about their motives. Ranke's art of contextual explanation had implications which were not lost upon his Catholic readers. To them it was obvious to take at face value the religious reasons which the popes themselves had given for their actions. Ranke frequently substituted a political explanation for the religious justification. Ennis censured Ranke for tracing all events 'to the interference of the successive pontiffs with politics and states'.[31] According to Papencordt, this secular interpretation misrepresented the spiritual character of the papal office. While acknowledging Ranke's good faith, Papencordt anticipated Ennis's criticism that Ranke had adopted a 'system' which made him distort the facts. Papencordt compared this 'theory' to the rationalist method of biblical hermeneutics.[32] Just as the rationalist advanced a natural explanation for a miracle, Ranke accounted in terms of earthly politics for the papacy's claim to represent the hierarchy of heaven.

The fear that Ranke's method resulted in a dangerous secularization of historical understanding was not limited to Catholic readers. The Swiss Protestant historian J. H. Merle D'Aubigné contributed a lengthy 'introductory essay' to Scott's translation, correcting what he perceived as the author's excessive impartiality. The effect of Ranke's method of treating the popes in the same way as he would treat the kings of France or England was apologetic. 'As the pope openly professes being the representative of the Son of God

[30] Ibid. 326.   [31] Ibid. 369.
[32] [Papencordt], 'Ranke's History of the Popes', 37 f.

on earth, one must either cast himself at his feet, or reject him as a usurper and a blasphemer; I avow that here I do not see how there can be any compromise (*juste milieu*).'[33] The anonymous Protestant who reviewed the *Popes* in *Fraser's Magazine* was equally unhappy with Ranke's *via media*. He found the book tainted by 'a false philosophy', namely 'the modern leprosy of "liberalism" '.[34] The reviewer criticized Ranke for giving only 'temporary causes' for Catholicism's failure to reconquer the world.[35] Relying on diplomatic records which necessarily present a worldly view of things, Ranke ignored the prime sources of papal history, the prophetic books of the Bible. The reviewer regarded it as significant that the book had been translated by Mrs Austin, a notorious unbeliever. He offered the interesting reflection that professional scholarship involved a kind of structural atheism. 'Men like Professor Ranke, who are too much occupied with their learned researches to pay much attention to the Word of God, necessarily get into a mode of speech which differs little from that of the atheist.'[36] The reviewer rejected Thackeray's argument that Ranke's point of view was vindicated by the fact that it was attacked from both sides: 'are the Romanists and Protestants, then, two parties who are equally in the wrong; and does the truth lie between the two?'[37] This criticism of the indifferentism of the professional historian anticipated later charges of relativism against what came to be known as historicism.

It was not uncommon for readers of the *Popes* to remark that they did not know where the author stood. J. W. Worthington, vicar of Holy Trinity, Gray's Inn Road, wrote in the *Foreign Quarterly Review*: 'In various passages we are led to think the writer inclines to the Romanist, in others to the Protestant persuasion.'[38] In 1856, Thackeray introduced his

[33] 'Introductory Essay: Original Sources of the Popedom', p. xiii. On the popularity of Merle D'Aubigné's *History of the Great Reformation in the Sixteenth Century* among Scottish Calvinists see A. G. Dickens and John M. Tonkin, *The Reformation in Historical Thought* (Oxford, 1985), 189 f.
[34] 'Ranke's History of the Popes of the Sixteenth and Seventeenth Centuries', *Fraser's Magazine*, 22 (1840), 127–42, at 129. [35] Ibid. 131.
[36] Ibid. 134. [37] Ibid. 129.
[38] [J. W. Worthington], 'Ranke's *History of the Popes of Rome*', *Foreign Quarterly Review*, 26 (1840), 1–28, at 1.

daughter Anne to Ranke 'as a young lady who had read his history of the Popes, and didn't know if he were Catholic or Protestant'.[39] Ennis regarded 'inconsistency' as 'the pervading error' of the whole work: 'praise and condemnation alternate on identical subjects.' He charged Ranke with intellectual cowardice. As a Prussian professor who had travelled in Italy 'at the treasury expense', Ranke had been careful not to offend his royal master by openly applauding the Catholic Church. Ennis hinted, however, at a more subtle explanation by suggesting that the pattern of inconsistency might well be 'the covert design' of the whole work.[40] 'The very subject of his eulogy in one chapter becomes the theme of censure in another; and the preponderance of papal power which here we find instrumental in every good, is there the spring and sole cause of every discomfiture in the same march of intellectual and moral progress.'[41] This is an exact description of the literary and philosophical strategy which sets Ranke apart from the dogmatic interpretation of history defended by Ennis. In Ranke's view, an institution which fulfilled a useful function in one epoch might have lost it in the next. The living spirit of one day became the dead letter of another. It was the cardinal error of the Church of Rome that it claimed eternal validity for a system of rules which could be of only temporary use.

This error itself, however, could be recognized only in the fullness of time. The hidden plot of Ranke's *Popes* is the triumph of the invisible church of true believers over a visible church which has confounded heaven and earth, time and eternity. Seeing itself as the product of history, the invisible church does, however, acknowledge that the ceremonies of the visible church were once essential, and may be useful still. The papacy fulfilled its mission in the Middle Ages, when Latin Europe formed a kind of universal state. Without medieval unity there would not have been modern pluralism. In such reflections, Ranke sought to capture 'Momente

---

[39] *Letters of Anne Thackeray Ritchie*, ed. Hester Ritchie (London, 1924), 91.
[40] [Ennis], 'Is Ranke an Historian?', 334.
[41] Ibid. 357.

der Erziehung des Menschengeschlechtes'.[42] He had a place in the tradition of a speculative philosophy of history going back to Lessing,[43] and elaborated by Schelling.[44] Ranke counted Schelling among the members of the 'invisible church of conviction and thought' whom he saw as the ideal readers of his *History of the Popes*.[45] Drawing on a heterodox theory of progressive revelation, Lessing had presented history as a never ending process in which truth gradually unfolded, the divine spirit adjusting itself to men's limited powers of understanding and developing these powers at the same time. Thus it was possible both to understand each epoch on its own terms, and to view it as a step in the march of progress. The historical process developed its own rhythm, each action provoking a reaction. A number of oppositions kept history moving.[46] The *History of the Popes* is organized around 'the repeated dualities between spirit and flesh, morality and interests, religion and politics, world and nations'.[47] The most important opposition may be the dialectics of the ideal and the real. In Ranke's hands, it became the principle of a sociology of institutions. The Society of Jesus abandoned the ideas of its founder in the very act of putting them into practice.[48] The perspective of

[42] *Die römischen Päpste*, i. 22. Cf. Patrick Bahners, 'Generatio praeterit, et generatio advenit: Zeit und Wahrheit in Rankes Papstgeschichte', in Heinrich Pfusterschmid-Hartenstein (ed.), *Zeit und Wahrheit* (Vienna, 1995), 278 ff.

[43] On Lessing's *Erziehung des Menschengeschlechtes* as a classic text of historicist philosophy see Gerrit Walther, *Niebuhrs Forschung* (Stuttgart, 1993), 66 ff. For Lessing's influence on Ranke, mediated through Friedrich Schlegel, see Carl Hinrichs, *Ranke und die Geschichtstheologie der Goethezeit* (Göttingen, 1954), 169.

[44] On Schelling's influence on the writing of church history see Gustav Adolf Benrath, 'Evangelische und katholische Kirchenhistorie im Zeichen der Aufklärung und der Romantik', *Zeitschrift für Kirchengeschichte*, 82 (1971), 210 ff.

[45] 'unsichtbare Kirche der Gesinnung und des Gedankens', Ranke to Friedrich von Thiersch, 25 Feb. 1837, *Briefwerk*, 283.

[46] *Die römischen Päpste*, i. 47, 190; ii. 328.

[47] Leonard Krieger, *Ranke: The Meaning of History* (Chicago, 1977), 153.

[48] Cf. Worthington, 'Ranke's *History of the Popes of Rome*', 8 f.: 'possibly no founder ever formed an order that more varied from himself than the Jesuits did from Loyola. He was all emotion—an entire emotionist—if we may be allowed the term; but the Jesuits were keen calculators of the effects of a crafty policy.' Thackeray was fascinated by Ranke's version of Jesuit history; he quoted extensively from the character sketch of Ignatius. He thought the narrative of the later development of the order 'a very curious and instructive one' (*The Times*, 18 Aug. 1840).

the historian is ironic.[49] He knows that the unexpected outcome has to be expected.[50]

This knowledge all but destroyed the traditional moral function of history, its office of passing judgement on the past and giving guidance for the future. Among the 'laws' in Ranke's 'theoretic code', Ennis named the maxim that 'moral effects' may be produced by 'immoral causes'.[51] The fundamental law of Ranke's code might be called the sovereignty of history, the exclusion of all external interference. God, as Max Weber observed, was turned into a constitutional monarch who ruled but did not govern.[52] Human actors, conversely, were not allowed to step outside the historical process in order to control it as a whole. In Ranke's view, it was not possible to make history. Were the historian to pronounce moral judgements on abstract grounds, ignoring the complex texture of conditions, he would himself violate the immanence of history. Ranke's ethics of historical interpretation implied a hermeneutics of social life. Its categorical imperative said: Contextualize! Modern history has produced an order of autonomous yet intersecting contexts of social organization. Ranke acknowledged two institutional guarantors of moral and religious pluralism: the separation of church and state on the one hand, and the system of great powers on the other. The subject of the *Popes* is the education of the popes. Ranke told the story of how they came to accept the rules of the game. The papacy owed the restoration of its temporal dominions to the very Protestant powers it had once tried to destroy.[53] The survival of the popes now depended on the

---

[49] Julian Schmidt analysed Ranke's account of the Jesuits as a brilliant example of his technique of indirect judgement by way of ironic presentation. 'He never becomes passionate, but for any educated person his account offers a more decisive justification for condemning the whole order than any one of the well-known pamphlets', *Geschichte der deutschen Literatur im neunzehnten Jahrhundert*, iii (3rd edn., Leipzig, 1856), 396.
[50] *Die römischen Päpste*, i. 37, 53, 205; ii. 119, 186, 341.
[51] [Ennis], 'Is Ranke an Historian?', 325 f.
[52] Max Weber, 'Roscher und Knies und die logischen Probleme der historischen Nationalökonomie', in *Gesammelte Aufsätze zur Wissenschaftslehre*, ed. Johannes Winckelmann (3rd edn., Tübingen, 1968), 21.
[53] *Die römischen Päpste*, iii. 155.

same balance of power that had ended the religious wars and secured the autonomy of politics.

It might be thought that Ranke's idealist premisses and irenic intentions would have been sympathetically received by the liberal Anglican historians studied by Duncan Forbes. Thomas Arnold and his friends transformed the theological doctrine of accommodation, of the adjustment of the teaching of the church to the minds of the listeners, into a philosophy of history which acknowledged both the individuality of each epoch and the unity of the historical process. Arnold himself had his pupils at Rugby read Ranke's *Popes*.[54] Significantly, the book had been introduced to the English public by Henry Hart Milman, the historian of the Jews, who later became Regius Professor of Ecclesiastical History at Oxford and Dean of St Paul's. His detailed summary of Ranke's narrative appeared in two parts in the *Quarterly Review* of 1836 and 1837. According to Milman, the English historian envied 'the dispassionate and philosophical serenity' of his German colleague.[55] Apart from 'profound research' and 'great fairness', it was 'a constant reference to the genius and spirit of each successive age' which to Milman seemed characteristic of the German school of historians.[56] Ranke and Milman both wanted to calm the confessional conflict by demonstrating that what appeared to be universal and eternal differences had arisen out of local and temporal conditions. If history could be shown to be in a state of permanent flux, religious parties would acknowledge the need to move on. Both Catholics and Protestants had painted the papacy as unchanging. From Ranke the reader was to learn that, in Milman's words, 'the annals of few kingdoms' are 'more strongly modified by the genius of successive ages, or are more influenced by the personal character of the reigning sovereign'.[57]

---

[54] Duncan Forbes, *The Liberal Anglican Idea of History* (Cambridge, 1952), 114.
[55] Henry Hart Milman, 'The Popes of the Sixteenth and Seventeenth Centuries', in id., *Savonarola, Erasmus and Other Essays* (London, 1870), 149–243, at 149.
[56] Ibid. 152.
[57] Ibid. 149 f. Cf. Ranke, *The Ecclesiastical and Political History of the Popes*, trans. Sarah Austin, i, p. xxiii: 'The papal power was not so unchangeable as is commonly supposed.' German original: *Die römischen Päpste*, i, p. xiii.

It was Ranke's aim to historicize the papacy. His first strategy was the biographical perspective, very well understood by Milman. Ranke showed the popes to have been human beings. He removed both 'the dazzling halo' of Catholic panegyric and 'the thick darkness' of Protestant polemic, allowing 'the peculiar and distinctive lineaments of the Gregories, and Innocents, and Alexanders' to appear.[58] However, after giving the popes their individuality, Ranke took it away again. He demonstrated that the personality of even the most powerful man was irrelevant when compared with the larger forces of political interest and public opinion. In the end, Peter's successors had to bow to the only authority on earth from which no appeal was possible: the course of things ('der Gang der Dinge'), history itself.[59] This ultimate contextualization was Ranke's second, more radical strategy of historicization. Milman remained closer to the pragmatic tradition of historical writing. He deplored the fact that the later fifteenth-century popes had 'voluntarily descended' from their 'lofty position' as arbiters of Europe.[60] Ranke stressed that their involvement in Italy's dynastic politics accorded with the spirit of the age.[61] Milman castigated Paul III for pursuing a 'double and dissembling policy' in the interests of his family.[62] Ranke saw Paul's schemes as justified by tradition and honour. He suggested, however, that the temper of the times was slowly making these dynastic politics unacceptable.[63] Milman did not seem happy with these indirect paths of moral progress. The liberal Anglican historians saw themselves as moral teachers of their nation. The success of their teaching depended on their pupils being able to rise above circumstance and listen to moral argument.

[58] Milman, 'The Popes of the Sixteenth and Seventeenth Centuries', 150.
[59] Ranke, *The Ecclesiastical and Political History of the Popes*, trans. Sarah Austin, i. 22: 'It seems as though all human designs and actions were subject to the silent and often imperceptible, but mighty and resistless march of events. The previous state of the world had been favourable to the papal domination; that of the moment we are considering was directly hostile to it.' German original: *Die römischen Päpste*, i. 22–3.
[60] Milman, 'The Popes of the Sixteenth and Seventeenth Centuries', 156.
[61] *Die römischen Päpste*, i. 29.
[62] Milman, 'The Popes of the Sixteenth and Seventeenth Centuries', 172.
[63] *Die römischen Päpste*, i. 169.

The more brutal yet also more subtle lessons which Ranke's popes had to learn concerned the separation of religion and politics. Only occasionally did Milman stress this conflict between the commands of Caesar and the will of God. In Ranke's view the community of scholars was preparing to take over from the Protestant denominations the role of an invisible church freely enquiring after the truth. Scholarship was one of the autonomous spheres characteristic of the modern world, like politics, religion, and art.[64] The ideal of the liberal Anglicans, on the contrary, was a national church which would unite religion and politics through the moral example of an enlightened clergy.[65] The implications of Ranke's analysis for the future of established religion were noticed by Philip Harwood, a unitarian minister, who reviewed Mrs Austin's translation in the *Westminster Review*, the organ of philosophical radicals. Once, Harwood argued, the community of believers had represented the unity of the nation. The 'complexity and freedom of our newer civilization' have made this form of social unity anachronistic. The church has to share 'the power that once centred in clerical or priestly hands' with literature, art, philosophy, and the institutions of politics.[66] Of all the reviewers of the *Popes*, Harwood followed Ranke's reasoning most closely. Interestingly, he treated him as a 'philosophic historian' in the tradition of Gibbon, a dispassionate observer drawing general conclusions from the history of civilization.[67] Henry Crabb Robinson was another reader who delighted in the 'general views' and 'philosophic thoughts on questions of social importance' suggested by Ranke's 'most exciting and

---

[64] The autonomy of modern art is the subject of Ranke's study of Italian painting, a fragment of that comprehensive history of Italy which shrank or rather grew into the *History of the Popes*. By following the law of form, artists emancipated themselves from the dictates of the church. Cf. Notker Hammerstein, 'Leopold von Ranke und die Renaissance', in August Buck and Cesare Vasoli (eds.), *Die Renaissance im neunzehnten Jahrhundert in Italien und Deutschland* (Berlin, 1989), 59 ff.

[65] When Bunsen, the friend of the liberal Anglicans, published his plan for a church of the future, his 'identification of the church with the state' failed to convince Ranke. 'The essence of the church is that it is not identical with the state', *Tagebücher* (*Aus Werk und Nachlass*, i), ed. Walther Peter Fuchs (Munich, 1964), 130 f.

[66] [Philip Harwood], 'Ranke's History of the Popes', *Westminster Review*, 34 (1840), 405–33, at 431.   [67] Ibid. 405.

instructive book'.[68] Harwood recognized the firm subordination of individual agency in Ranke's scheme of things.[69] It is true that the 'personal characters' of reforming popes such as Paul IV and Pius V gave force to the idea of moral regeneration. 'Yet the elevation of these men was chiefly important as being the effect of a general cause, the expression of an altered state of feeling and opinion throughout the church.'[70]

In 1843 Leopold Ranke married Clara Graves, the daughter of a barrister who had been chief police magistrate of Dublin. Two of Ranke's brothers-in-law were clergymen who represented the Anglican tradition of gentlemanly scholarship, combining literary and scientific interests. The Revd Charles Graves was Erasmus Smith Professor of Mathematics at Trinity College, Dublin, and served as secretary to the Commission for the Publication of the Ancient Laws and Institutes of Ireland. He became Bishop of Limerick in 1866, one of the last bishops appointed before the disestablishment of the Church of Ireland. The Revd Robert Perceval Graves, curate in charge of Windermere from 1835 to 1853, was a friend of Wordsworth.[71] He wrote the life of Sir William Hamilton, the mathematician and Royal Astronomer of Ireland. Ranke's personal contacts with English intellectuals ranged across the whole spectrum of religious parties. He knew Richard William Jelf, the High Church principal of King's College, London, from the time when the latter had been tutor to Ranke's pupil, Prince George of Cumberland.[72] James Martineau, the prominent unitarian,

---

[68] Henry Crabb Robinson, *Books and their Writers*, ed. Edith J. Morley, ii (London, 1938), 638 f.

[69] Cf. Ulrich Muhlack, 'Leopold von Ranke', in Notker Hammerstein (ed.), *Deutsche Geschichtswissenschaft um 1900* (Stuttgart, 1988), 35: 'Above all, Ranke neglects to derive the course of historical events from the will of individuals. Rather, he sees new circumstances as constantly thwarting and modifying the decisions of individuals.'

[70] [Harwood], 'Ranke's History of the Popes', 421.

[71] See *The Letters of Dorothy and William Wordsworth*, ed. Ernest De Selincourt, vii (2nd edn., Oxford, 1988), 917.

[72] Richard William Jelf to Leopold Ranke, 19 Oct. 1852 (Berlin, Staatsbibliothek Preußischer Kulturbesitz, Nachlass Ranke Ergänzung). On Ranke's lectures on modern history for the blind Prince George (King of Hanover, 1851–66) see Leopold Ranke to Heinrich Ranke, 26 Nov. 1835, *Briefwerk*, 272.

who as a student had attended Ranke's lectures, met him in 1848 in Berlin.[73] When Crabb Robinson visited Clara Ranke in 1851, she praised Martineau's sermons, being herself 'in religious matters very liberal'.[74] Ranke may well have felt closest to liberal Anglicans, but the different confessional situations of England and Germany probably gave rise to reservations and misunderstandings.

Some English visitors were offended by Ranke's 'air of wonderful self-conceit'.[75] Mrs Austin, meeting him in 1842 at Schelling's house, thought 'his manner not pleasant nor gentlemanlike'.[76] When Arthur Stanley visited Berlin in 1844, he 'talked to Ranke a little about the Hussites and the Reformation, and got a little, but not much, out of him'.[77] Returning in the following year, he found Ranke 'altogether more agreeable'. Ranke spoke favourably of the *Deutschkatholiken*, the liberal Catholics who had broken away from the Roman Church, showing Stanley a map upon which he had marked the progress of the new denomination, and comparing relations between Protestants and Catholics in England and Germany.[78] English interest in the historian of the popes continued to concern matters of church and state. There was even an article in an English newspaper reporting that Ranke was a follower of Ronge, the founder of the *Deutschkatholiken*.[79] Although Ranke dined at the deanery of St Paul's when visiting London,[80] no continuing dialogue with Milman and his friends evolved. It seems fair to say that his influence on liberal Anglican thinking

---

[73] James Drummond and C. B. Upton, *The Life and Letters of James Martineau* (London, 1902), i. 185 f.; ii. 329 f.

[74] *Diary, Reminiscences, and Correspondence of Henry Crabb Robinson*, ed. Thomas Sadler, iii (2nd edn., London, 1869), 383.

[75] *Life and Letters of Stopford Brooke*, i. 160.

[76] Janet Ross, *Three Generations of English Women: Memoirs and Correspondence of Susannah Taylor, Sarah Austin and Lady Duff Gordon* (London, 1893), 185 f.

[77] Rowland E. Prothero, *The Life and Correspondence of Arthur Penrhyn Stanley*, i (London, 1893), 331.

[78] *Letters and Verses of Arthur Penrhyn Stanley, D.D., between the Years 1829 and 1881*, ed. Rowland E. Prothero (London, 1895), 89 f.

[79] Theodor Fontane to Bernhard von Lepel, 25 May 1857, *Ein Freundschafts-Briefwechsel*, ed. Julius Petersen, ii (Munich, 1940), 180.

[80] Leopold von Ranke, *Neue Briefe*, ed. Hans Herzfeld (Hamburg, 1949), 378; Lord Acton and Ignaz von Döllinger, *Briefwechsel 1850–1890*, ed. Victor Conzemius, i (Munich, 1963), 412.

cannot be compared to that of Niebuhr or even of Bunsen.[81] An exception is Julius Hare's *Vindication of Luther*. Hare, who with Connop Thirlwall had translated Niebuhr's *Römische Geschichte*, praised Ranke for giving a portrait of Luther which was psychologically plausible, historically specific, and theologically resonant. He contrasted Ranke's insight into the sixteenth-century mind with unhistorical judgements on Luther by both Catholic and Protestant writers such as Newman and Hallam.[82] The synthesis of humanism and Lutheranism in the *Deutsche Geschichte* came very close to liberal Anglican ideals of salvation through learning.

To a reader of the *Popes* it must have been less apparent that Ranke might be won as an ally in the quest for the reconciliation of reason and faith. Thanking Mrs Austin for her translation, Ranke informed her of something she may not have taken as a compliment. At first he had set himself the task of reading the whole work in English, but he did not carry out his intention. This, however, was not because he did not think the translation adequate, but precisely because it was so good that it had caused him the 'illusion' that he had written it himself. 'It has been said with truth that it is *my English self*; and who cares to study himself, when the world for so many centuries offers so much that is infinitely greater?'[83] Ranke's wish to extinguish his self, which he expressed in aphorisms scattered throughout his collected works, was not only a methodological precept, but also the expression of a spiritual longing for communion with God and the universe.[84] While popes such as Urban VIII suffered from an exalted 'Selbstgefühl' (self-confidence) which made

---

[81] Cf. Ernst Bammel, 'Niebuhr und England', in Gerhard Wirth (ed.), *Barthold Georg Niebuhr: Historiker und Staatsmann* (Bonn, 1984), 131–75; Klaus D. Gross, *Die deutsch-englischen Beziehungen im Wirken Christian Carl Josias von Bunsens (1791–1860)* (Ph.D. thesis, University of Würzburg, 1965), 58–72.

[82] Julius Charles Hare, *Vindication of Luther against his Recent English Assailants* (2nd edn., London, 1855), 22–9, 39–42, 90 f., 282 ff.

[83] Ranke to Sarah Austin, Apr. 1841, Ross, *Three Generations of English Women*, 164.

[84] Cf. Lothar Gall, 'Ranke und das Objektivitätsproblem', in Norbert Finzsch and Hermann Wellenreuther (eds.), *Liberalitas: Festschrift für Erich Angermann zum 65. Geburtstag* (Stuttgart, 1992), 37–44.

them disdain the voice of the past,[85] the historian sought personal fulfilment by erasing his personality and letting history speak for itself. This *amor intellectualis dei* was, however, easily misinterpreted as a love of the things of this world. Though the *History of the Popes* took the popes to task for neglecting their spiritual office, it could be read as a celebration of worldly politics. The eloquent silences of German metaphysics might be lost even on those English readers who had studied their Schleiermacher. Perhaps Ranke covered his traces rather too well.

In his *History of Latin Christianity*, Milman cites Ranke as an expert on the constitution of the Holy Roman Empire.[86] 'The progress of the human intellect' which overthrew 'the Hierarchical system' is sketched without much reference to that autonomous political realm in which, in Ranke's eyes, modern pluralism had replaced medieval subordination.[87] In his introductory lectures on ecclesiastical history,[88] and again in his study of 'the subtle genius of the institution of the Papacy',[89] Stanley quotes Macaulay's review of the *Popes*, not the book itself.[90] The issues Ranke had dealt with in the *Popes* became ever more topical as the Catholic hierarchy was restored in England, and the temporal power of the pope was again put on the international political agenda. There was probably no shortage of subjects for conversation when Ranke met the editor of *The Times* at the Foreign Secretary's dinner-table in 1857.[91] However, it seems unlikely that Ranke

---

[85] 'An objection drawn from the old papal constitutions was once made to some argument of his; he replied, "that the judgment of a living pope was worth more than the maxims of a hundred dead ones" ', Ranke, *The Ecclesiastical and Political History of the Popes*, trans. Sarah Austin, ii. 381–2. German original: *Die römischen Päpste*, ii. 354 f.

[86] Henry Hart Milman, *History of Latin Christianity Including that of the Popes to the Pontificate of Nicolas V*, ix (3rd edn., London, 1864), 43 f.

[87] Ibid. 343, 350.

[88] Arthur Penrhyn Stanley, *Lectures on the History of the Eastern Church with an Introduction on the Study of Ecclesiastical History* (London, 1861), p. lxxviii.

[89] Id., *Christian Institutions: Essays on Ecclesiastical Subjects* (London, 1881), 232.

[90] Ibid. 201.

[91] Arthur Irwin Dasent, *John Thaddeus Delane, Editor of 'The Times'. His Life and Correspondence*, i (London, 1908), 253. Lord Clarendon's other guests on 24 April included Macaulay, the Duke of Argyll, Lionel Rothschild, Sir George Cornewall Lewis, and Henry Reeve.

had any noticeable impact on the English debate about ecclesiastical establishments at home and abroad, although English historians played a considerable part in it. When Lord Palmerston met Ranke in 1844, he 'addressed to him some compliments on his history of the popes, with which he was acquainted in the English translation'; their 'long conversation', however, dealt with 'eastern affairs'.[92] Gladstone read the *Popes* twice, once when Mrs Austin's translation appeared, and once in 1866, in Rome.[93] Like Ranke, Gladstone wished to relieve the papacy 'of its obsession about temporal power' so that it might renew its association with the progress of the human mind; like the historian, he was disillusioned when Pius IX refused to listen to 'history and reason'.[94] Alas, I have found no reference to Ranke's book in Gladstone's writings on the Roman question. In 1857, Ranke met Gladstone 'at a breakfast of his' and was 'very much struck by his turn of mind'.[95] In personal conversation, Ranke usually evaded religious topics,[96] and English visitors were unlikely to receive clear answers from him in this field.[97] When Frederick William Farrar brought together Ranke and Heinrich Ewald, the biblical scholar and

---

[92] John Ward, *Experiences of a Diplomatist, being Recollections of Germany, Founded on Diaries Kept during the Years 1840–1870* (London, 1872), 47 f. I owe this reference to Rudolf Muhs.
[93] *The Gladstone Diaries*, ed. M. R. D. Foot and H. C. G. Matthew (Oxford, 1968–94), iii. 45–8 (14–22 July 1840); vi. 477 (29 Oct. 1866). Gladstone also read the *Deutsche Geschichte*, iv. 421 (18 Apr. 1852), the study of Ferdinand I and Maximilian II in the *Historisch-politische Zeitschrift*, translated in 1853, iv. 494 (3 Feb. 1853), the *Briefwechsel Friedrich Wilhelms IV. mit Bunsen*, viii. 525 (13–14 Sept. 1874), and the *Englische Geschichte*, xi. 188 (14 Aug. 1884).
[94] Richard Shannon, 'Gladstone, the Roman Church, and Italy', in Michael Bentley (ed.), *Public and Private Doctrine. Essays in British History Presented to Maurice Cowling* (Cambridge, 1993), 118 f.
[95] *Neue Briefe*, 381.
[96] See Herman Wichmann, 'Leopold von Ranke unter Freunden', in id., *Gesammelte Aufsätze*, ii (Leipzig, 1887), 203.
[97] Or, indeed, in any other field. Sarah Ross remembered Ranke at the home of her parents, Sir Alexander and Lady Duff Gordon, walking up and down the drawing-room and 'talking vehemently in a kind of *olla podrida* of English, French, German, Italian and Spanish. Now and then a Latin quotation would come in. It was almost impossible to understand him as he talked fast, and mixed up all his languages into a compound of his own' (*Three Generations of English Women*, 446). Carlyle remarked: 'Conversation with Ranke is like talking to a rookery.' Thomas Wemyss Reid, *The Life of Richard Monckton Milnes, First Lord Houghton*, i (London, 1890), 435.

one of the *Göttinger Sieben* (Göttingen Seven),[98] and invited Stanley and Max Müller to dine with them, Ranke would talk of nothing but 'the probable danger to be apprehended in reference to European politics from Serbia and Bulgaria'.[99]

Similarly, the voice of the author of the *Popes* became harder to understand as time went by. When the first German edition appeared, the author could count on Protestant readers sympathetic to Catholicism on grounds of liberal theology, conservative politics, or romantic aesthetics. The lessons the book contained were only hinted at. History itself, such was the author's hope, would bring peace between the denominations, without needing directions from the historian. This hope was disappointed. The Pope disavowed every intention of falling in with modern times. The teleology which held together the narrative of the *Popes* quite suddenly lost its *telos*. The confrontation between the Catholic Church and the Prussian state which culminated in the deposition and arrest of the Archbishop of Cologne shattered Ranke's optimism.[100] In later German editions, he toned down his hopeful remarks on a future reconciliation of the churches; in 1874 he added an account of the Vatican Council. Tacitly admitting that his philosophical enthusiasm had been disappointed, he destroyed the magnificent symmetry which in the first edition had symbolized the unity of the spirit. When Crabb Robinson met Ranke in 1843, he was surprised to find the irenic historian an alarmist on the subject of papal power.[101] By the time Mrs Austin's translation came out in 1840, the forces of the Counter-Reformation were widely seen to be marching again. Indeed, events in Prussia were quoted against Ranke by his Catholic as well as by his Protestant critics. Both sides ridiculed what

---

[98] The Göttingen Seven was a group of professors who protested against the abolition of the constitution of Hanover in 1837.
[99] *The Life and Letters of the Rt. Hon. Friedrich Max Müller*, 267.
[100] The influence of the *Kölner Ereignis* on the writing of the *Deutsche Geschichte* is demonstrated by Heinrich Lutz, 'Ursprung der Spaltung in der Nation. Bemerkungen zu einem Kapitel aus Rankes Reformationsgeschichte', in id., *Politik, Kultur und Religion im Werdeprozeß der frühen Neuzeit* (Klagenfurt, 1982), 211–24.
[101] *The Correspondence of Henry Crabb Robinson with the Wordsworth Circle*, i. 519.

they saw as the naïvety of the preface in which he had declared that Protestants felt secure from Catholic ambition.[102] When Mrs Foster published her translation in 1846, she offered it as a contribution to the Protestant cause, calling upon the reader to recognize the Jesuit strategies described by Ranke in the devious doings of Newman and his followers.[103] The Scottish church historian David Dundas Scott, bringing out his version in the same year, even apologized for the 'extreme moderation' of the author which might offend orthodox readers.[104] In 1866, Sarah Austin asked Dean Milman to write a preface for a new edition of the *Popes*, as the publisher wanted 'a little éclat'.[105] Milman duly supplied the preface. He limited himself to summarizing the main points of his original review, written thirty years earlier. Not with one word did he allude to the changed situation in Europe; Murray, the publisher, had to do without his *éclat*.

The new edition did, however, call forth a review by Richard William Church, a High Churchman who later became Milman's successor as Dean of St Paul's. Church treated the book as a contemporary classic ripe for re-examination.[106] While repeating the obligatory praise for Ranke's 'industry' and 'power of doing justice',[107] Church had harsh words to say about the book as a work of historical art. 'His book is not properly so much a history of the Popes, as a series of philosophical comments on the connection of their policy and history with the progress of European history.

[102] 'Ranke's History of the Popes of the Sixteenth and Seventeenth Centuries', 132; [Ennis], 'Is Ranke an Historian?', 379.
[103] 'Translator's Preface', p. vi. Presenting her work to the author six years later when travelling through Berlin, Mrs Foster hinted that the original translator's lack of orthodoxy had made a new version necessary. Given 'the character of the present times', namely the 'efforts' of the 'Catholic Hierarchy', clarity was called for, especially in the interest of 'our large and varied middle class' which Bohn's edn. was meant to reach. [Mrs Foster] to Ranke, 20 Aug. [1852?], Nachlass Ranke Ergänzung.
[104] 'Prefatory Notices by the Translator', p. iii.
[105] Arthur Milman, *Henry Hart Milman*, 205.
[106] Church had drawn on Ranke's work twenty years earlier when reviewing Audin's ultramontane *Histoire de Léon* X. Richard William Church, 'Audin's Leo X', in id., *Essays and Reviews* (London, 1854), 282, 293, 333.
[107] R. W. Church, 'Ranke's "History of the Popes"', in id., *Occasional Papers*, i (London, 1897), 143–54, at 145. The original review appeared in the *Saturday Review*, 15 Dec. 1866.

This is perhaps more convenient for the writer than for the reader.'[108] Church criticized Ranke for sometimes distorting the chronological order of events. Critics such as Ennis had commented before on Ranke's violation of the conventions of historical narrative. 'His mind is too elastic to be controlled by everyday occurrences, it springs out of the track of all his predecessors in the career of history.'[109] While Milman had regretted that the *Popes* did not contain 'more of the life and circumstance of history', he had left no doubt that this conciseness was the result of artistic intention.[110] Church, however, presented Ranke as the professional scholar who took no interest in the aesthetics of historical writing.[111] Acton in 1867 similarly explained the gaps in the narrative by Ranke's intention to base his work on original sources.[112] It may, however, be argued that it made sense to tell the story of the fragmentation of Christendom in a fragmentary manner. Descriptive and narrative passages alternate; the 'polyphony' of the

[108] Church, 'Ranke's "History of the Popes"', 147. Reviewing the *Deutsche Geschichte*, W. B. Donne similarly remarked that the author appeared 'to aim at a sort of fragmentary conciseness, which gives his work in many places rather the air of historical notes or illustrations than of a connected narrative'. 'Histories of the Reformation: Ranke and D'Aubigné', *British and Foreign Review*, 15 (1843), 101. According to E. H. Thompson, the *Französische Geschichte*, 'though calling itself a "history"', partakes 'rather of the character of an historical essay', as Ranke 'scarcely touches upon any facts but such as illustrate his leading idea'. 'English and Foreign Historians: The Massacre of St Bartholomew', *Rambler*, 13 (1854), 168. The *Englische Geschichte* seemed to W. M. W. Call a 'philosophical treatise rather than a historical narrative'. 'Contemporary Literature', *Westminster Review*, 75 (1861), 277.

[109] [Ennis], 'Is Ranke an Historian?', 357. Papencordt thought it strange that Luther, the 'author' of the Reformation, 'is spoken of only once or twice, as if by accident' ('Ranke's History of the Popes', 38).

[110] Milman, 'The Popes of the Sixteenth and Seventeenth Centuries', 152.

[111] Similarly, Henry Reeve had attributed the 'fragmentary character' of Ranke's books to his tendency 'to dilate with extreme minuteness on a particular transaction' which could be illustrated from hitherto unknown documents. 'Ranke's *House of Brandenburg*', *Quarterly Review*, 86 (1850), 338. Reeve was Mrs Austin's nephew; in 1836, travelling in Germany, he had approached Ranke on behalf of his aunt. John Knox Laughton, *Memoirs of the Life and Correspondence of Henry Reeve*, i (London, 1898), 68. The translation of the *Neun Bücher preussischer Geschichte* which Reeve reviewed was by Sir Alexander and Lady Duff Gordon, Mrs Austin's daughter and son-in-law. *Memoirs of the House of Brandenburg, and History of Prussia, during the Seventeenth and Eighteenth Centuries* (London, 1849).

[112] Lord Acton, 'Ranke', in J. Rufus Fears (ed.), *Essays in the Study and Writing of History* (Indianapolis, 1985), 166.

European states 'could neither be described as a static system nor as a homogeneous development. It was a precarious blend of both.'[113] The fact that the story, as Church complained, moves 'not continuously, but by a series of jerks',[114] shows that order in history depends on selection by the historian. The narrator deliberately downplays many highly visible events;[115] unlike the popes, the historian is not deluded by appearances.

As the idea of the work was no longer understood, the form appeared strange. John Addington Symonds expressed his astonishment in 1884: 'What a badly composed book Ranke's *Popes* is!'[116] While readers noticed the author's philosophical ambition, they were not sure what his philosophy was. It seemed fortunate that the book had attracted the attention of a writer who knew how to express himself clearly. Thomas Babington Macaulay had, in Church's words, 'gathered up its lessons'[117] in his review article which appeared in the *Edinburgh Review* of October 1840. Macaulay read the original German edition in 1838 on his voyage from India and 'was exceedingly interested and struck by it'.[118] He was also acquainted with the French translation by J. B. Haiber which Ranke criticized for its Catholicizing tendency.[119] Visiting Rome in the winter of 1838, Macaulay recommended 'Von Ranke's history of the Papacy since the Reformation' in a letter to Lord Lansdowne: 'I have owed much of my pleasure here to what I learned from him of the nature of the Ecclesiastical state, of the characters of the

---

[113] Ernst Schulin, 'Universal History and National History, Mainly in the Lectures of Leopold von Ranke', in Georg G. Iggers and James M. Powell (eds.), *Leopold von Ranke and the Shaping of the Historical Discipline* (Syracuse, NY, 1990), 74.

[114] Church, 'Ranke's "History of the Popes"', 146.

[115] On *Die römischen Päpste* as a modern 'masterpiece of literary concentration' in the manner of Stendhal, preferring allusion to description, see Gerrit Walther, 'Der "gedrungene" Stil: Zum Wandel der historiographischen Sprache zwischen Aufklärung und Historismus', in Otto Gerhard Oexle and Jörn Rüsen (eds.), *Historismus in den Kulturwissenschaften* (Cologne, 1996), 110 f.

[116] *The Letters of John Addington Symonds*, ed. Herbert M. Schueller and Robert L. Peters, ii (Detroit, 1968), 951.

[117] Church, 'Ranke's "History of the Popes"', 144.

[118] *The Letters of Thomas Babington Macaulay*, ed. Thomas Pinney, iii (Cambridge, 1976), 268.

[119] See Ranke's letter to Mrs Austin, quoted in her 'Translator's Preface', p. xi.

different Popes, and of the progress of those great families which were founded by the nepotism of the sixteenth and seventeenth centuries.'[120] After his return from Italy, he reread the work in order to brush up his German.[121]

There was no doubt about Macaulay's enthusiasm. But were the lessons he drew from it really the lessons of Ranke's book? Reviewing Macaulay's collected essays in 1841, Edgar Allan Poe joked that the article on Ranke was called a review 'as *lucus* is *lucus a non lucendo*'.[122] The review's most striking passage became 'a proverb' which was 'repeated daily by men who never heard of Macaulay, much less of Von Ranke'.[123] This passage recounted a vision of a New Zealander who would one day be found 'on a broken arch of London Bridge' sketching 'the ruins of St Paul's'.[124] After the decline and fall of the British Empire, the Church of Rome would still stand. Macaulay was captivated by an institution which seemed immune to historical change. Catholic readers such as Cardinal Manning recognized 'outlines of truths and ghosts of great principles' in what could be read as a celebration of the unchanging presence of the Catholic Church.[125] In Munich, the Catholic philosopher Ernst von Lasaulx found in Macaulay corroboration for his belief in the eternity of Rome.[126] Macaulay's position was, however,

---

[120] *Letters*, iii. 268. As the result of what seems to have been a curious misreading of the title-page, Macaulay regularly called the author of *Die römischen Päpste* 'Von Ranke', thus anticipating Ranke's ennoblement by twenty-seven years.

[121] Macaulay's diary, 9 Feb. 1839 (Cambridge, Trinity College Library): 'Read some of Von Ranke. My German is a good deal out of order, but I find that I recover it fast'; 11 Feb.: 'I am going on slowly with Von Ranke'; 6 Mar.: 'I go on reading Von Ranke before breakfast at the rate of 10 or 12 pages a day which keeps up my German.' See also Macaulay's letter to Mrs Austin, *Letters*, iii. 325 f.

[122] *The Complete Works of Edgar Allan Poe*, ed. James A. Harrison, x (New York, 1902), 158. Acton's opinion was that the essay demonstrated Macaulay's 'incompetence'. *Letters of Lord Acton to Mary Gladstone*, ed. Herbert Paul (London, 1904), 285.

[123] Frederic Harrison, *Studies in Early Victorian Literature* (London, 1895), 75. In Germany, Macaulay's Antipodean visitor was so well known that he became an object of satirical allusion. See Theodor Fontane, 'Nante Strump als Erzieher', *Sämtliche Werke*, xxi, pt. 1, ed. Kurt Schreinert (Munich, 1963), 484.

[124] 'Von Ranke', *The Works of Lord Macaulay* (London, 1898), ix. 286–334, at 288. Cf. Michael Bright, 'Macaulay's New Zealander', *Arnoldian*, 10 (1982), 8–27.

[125] Shane Leslie, *Henry Edward Manning: His Life and Labours* (London, 1921), 333.

[126] Siegbert Peetz, *Die Wiederkehr im Unterschied. Ernst von Lasaulx* (Munich, 1989), 307 ff.

the exact reverse of the lesson Ranke had intended to convey. Ranke warned the reader not to be deceived by the appearance of continuity. There had been a Pius in the second century, and there was a Pius in the nineteenth century; 'but we must not suffer ourselves to be misled by this appearance, since in truth the popes of different ages are distinguished from each other by differences nearly as essential as the dynasties of a kingdom.'[127] Macaulay was willing to be misled. Attending Mass at St Peter's on Christmas Eve 1838, he had reflected on 'the immense antiquity of the Papal dignity which can certainly boast of a far longer clear, known, and uninterrupted succession than any dignity in the world, and which links together the two great ages of human civilization'.[128] He remained fascinated by the idea that 'the proudest royal houses are but of yesterday, when compared with the line of the Supreme Pontiffs'. To his eye, there was but one 'august dynasty', an 'unbroken series', stretching 'from the Pope who crowned Napoleon in the nineteenth century to the Pope who crowned Pepin in the eighth', and far beyond.[129] Ranke wanted to historicize the power which claimed to stand above history. The new historical scholarship could set itself no aim more ambitious. In Ranke's philosophy, the only timeless element in history was the invisible spirit, represented in the present by the free and rational method of Protestant scholarship. In Macaulay's reversal of the classical image which he shared with Ranke, it was the forces of unreason which turned out to be visibly eternal.

Macaulay had once before painted a vision of the ruins of St Paul's. In the peroration to his review of William Mitford's

---

[127] Ranke, *The Ecclesiastical and Political History of the Popes of Rome, during the Sixteenth and Seventeenth Centuries*, trans. Sarah Austin, i, p. xxiii. German original: Ranke, *Die römischen Päpste*, i, pp. xii f.

[128] Macaulay, Diary, 25 Dec. 1838.

[129] Id., 'Von Ranke', 287. Harwood took up Ranke's lesson: 'The papal dynasty may be nominally one; but the unity that reaches through seventeen centuries, from Clement I, the friend and associate of St Paul, to Clement XIV, the suppressor of the Company of Jesus, is of a somewhat shadowy description, and only adds the vividness of contrast to the interest of the vast moral and social revolutions that intervene between the times and men thus strangely brought into fellowship' ('Ranke's History of the Popes', 405).

History of Greece, written when he was still a student at Trinity College, Cambridge, he had evoked a time 'when the sceptre shall have passed away from England; when, perhaps, travellers from distant regions shall in vain labour to decipher on some mouldering pedestal the name of our proudest chief; shall hear savage hymns chaunted to some misshapen idol over the ruined dome of our proudest temple'. In 1824, it was the 'intellectual empire' of Athenian philosophy which was held to be immune to the vanity of earthly things, 'exempt from mutability and decay'.[130] In 1840, Athens had given way to Rome. According to Mrs Austin, the 'chief interest' of Ranke's book 'lies in the solution it affords of the greatest problem of modern history'.[131] This problem was the fact that the Catholic Church had not only stood its ground against the Protestant attack, but had even succeeded in reconquering considerable strips of territory. To a Benthamite observer, this spectacle might suggest the depressing reflection that progress was not irreversible and that rational argument might be powerless against the forces of passion and interest. In Macaulay's hands, Ranke's material demonstrated the limits of enlightenment. G. H. Lewes reproached Macaulay with underestimating the power of the 'great principle' of Protestantism, 'liberty of thought'.[132] In 1868 Theodor Fontane, writing a fictitious letter from London to the arch-conservative Berlin *Kreuzzeitung*, extracted a lesson in anthropological pessimism from the essay on Ranke: 'The lack of influence of so-called "progress" on humanity's power to believe, even on the forms of belief.'[133] To liberal Anglican politicians, the struggle for Catholic emancipation had symbolized 'an optimistic view of national destiny'. Ireland was to be regenerated spiritually 'by allowing the superior truths of Protestantism to be received without prejudice by the Catholic population'.[134] When Macaulay wrote his review, it

---

[130] 'On Mitford's History of Greece', in *The Works of Lord Macaulay*, xi. 392 f.
[131] 'Translator's Preface', p. xii.
[132] [George Henry Lewes], 'T. B. Macaulay', *British Quarterly Review*, 9 (1849), 28.
[133] 'Die Einflusslosigkeit des sogenannten "Fortschritts" auf die Glaubenskraft des Menschen, selbst auf die Glaubensform.' [Theodor Fontane], 'Die Grenzen des "Fortschritts"', in Heide Streiter-Buscher (ed.), *Unechte Korrespondenzen*, ii (Berlin, 1996), 841.
[134] Jonathan Parry, *The Rise and Fall of Liberal Government in Victorian Britain* (New Haven, 1993), 52.

was obvious that no large-scale conversion had come to pass in Ireland.

Behind the political issue there was a philosophical problem, the suspicion that the senses which were attracted by spectacles such as Catholic ceremonies would in the end be stronger than cool, clear-headed reason. Macaulay himself had experienced the power of Catholic ritual during his Italian trip. The review of the *Popes* was his attempt to come to terms with his own fascination with 'the wonderful skill with which the system of the Catholic Church is framed'.[135] There was something miraculous about the fabrication of miracles. 'The stronger our conviction that reason and Scripture were decidedly on the side of Protestantism, the greater is the reluctant admiration with which we regard that system of tactics against which reason and Scripture were employed in vain.'[136] The fortress of fanaticism seemed impregnable because the defenders had taught themselves to use the weapons of the attackers. This ability to learn, but to withstand persuasion, was the sinister art of the Jesuits; they made a mockery of enlightenment by putting rational means at the service of irrational ends. The critique of superstition had an honoured place in Whig political philosophy.[137] Whigs were usually found on the side of Ghibellines and Erastians; they admired sceptical statesmen who made the anti-social passion of believers serve the interests of society. Macaulay revealed that the most skilful manipulators of religious feeling were to be found among the shepherds of the Catholic flock. The 'profound policy' with which the Catholic Church 'used the fanaticism of such persons as St Ignatius and St Theresa' was to Macaulay an object of reluctant admiration.[138] Macaulay transformed the enlightened distrust of priestcraft into a sociology of power which accepted that illusions were necessary for social cohesion. 'It is impossible to deny that the polity of the Church of Rome

---

[135] Diary, 4 Nov. 1838. See also the essay on Machiavelli, *The Works of Lord Macaulay*, vii. 69. [136] 'Von Ranke', 316 f.
[137] Cf. John W. Burrow, *Whigs and Liberals: Continuity and Change in English Political Thought* (Oxford, 1988), 64 ff.
[138] Macaulay, 'Von Ranke', 321.

is the very masterpiece of human wisdom.'[139] The anti-intellectual empire of Rome has revoked the promise of Athens. The world wants to be deceived.

The danger posed by the Jesuits lay in what Macaulay saw as a separation of rationality and morality. Milman similarly remarked that the Jesuits' 'exclusive devotion' to the pope 'did not trammel the free development of all their intellectual faculties'. Their order was 'founded by enthusiasm which bordered on insanity, but regulated by wisdom which approached to craft'.[140] The Gibbonian echo in this antithesis is unmistakable. In 1838, Milman had produced an annotated edition of the *Decline and Fall*. To Ranke, the struggle between Catholic and Protestant powers was also a contest between two types of modern rationality. He contrasted the mechanical method of Jesuit instruction with the free spirit of Protestant scholarship.[141] A reading of Milman, however, reveals an uncanny resemblance between the Jesuits, 'learned, subtle, pliant',[142] who assumed 'the education of the people as their peculiar province',[143] and the liberal Anglicans who were willing to relax doctrinal standards in the name of inclusiveness. In reforming the liturgy, the Jesuits practised 'a skilful accommodation to the state of the public mind at that period'; they respected 'the more advanced state of Christian knowledge'.[144] Had the Jesuits anticipated the liberal Anglican philosophy of accommodation? In reflecting on the Society of Jesus, 'inclined to the latitude of the milder and more moderate opinions',[145] the latitudinarian historian was confronted with the spectre of a relativism which lurked inside his own liberalism.

Macaulay accorded Ranke's *Popes* 'a place among the English classics',[146] and it may be the fate of all classics that the reputation of the work survives while the intention of the author is forgotten. The *Popes*, written for a particular moment which had passed very quickly, came to be seen as

---

[139] Macaulay, 'Von Ranke', 316.
[140] Milman, 'The Popes of the Sixteenth and Seventeenth Centuries', 205.
[141] *Die römischen Päpste*, ii. 17.
[142] Milman, 'The Popes of the Sixteenth and Seventeenth Centuries', 224.
[143] Ibid. 205.   [144] Ibid. 212.   [145] Ibid. 224.
[146] Macaulay, 'Von Ranke', 286.

the timeless model of a new timeless scholarship which did not engage with the questions of the day.[147] The impartiality which had caused a sensation when the book first appeared now limited its appeal. To Max Müller, it illustrated the dangers of detachment. 'Ranke's "History of the Popes" may be very accurate, but for thousands who read Macaulay and Froude is there one who reads Ranke, except the historian by profession?'[148] There were British historians who were proud to write only for historians. Despising the complacency of Whiggish story-telling, they hailed Ranke as 'the accepted and revered head of contemporary historical science'.[149] To Church, Ranke's aesthetic failure had a redeeming feature. 'The example of an historian who is ready to sacrifice convenience, symmetry, the look of consistency, to the paramount claim of evidence to which he will not shut his eyes, even though he cannot adjust it to his view, is invaluable.'[150] Keeping their eyes open for every scrap of evidence, Ranke's admirers in the historical schools of Oxford and Cambridge overlooked 'the philosophical assumptions that supported the edifice of Rankean history'.[151] In his obituary of Ranke, Samuel Rawson Gardiner asserted that 'the unattractive nature of German politics in the years after the overthrow of Napoleon' had made Ranke lead the way 'in the divorce of history from modern politics'. Gardiner deplored the fact that Ranke, though aware of 'the influence upon individuals of great waves of feeling and opinion', had not sought 'for the law of human progress which underlies them', neither rejoicing in progress nor regretting decline.[152] Objectivity, which in the

[147] See e.g. George Peabody Gooch, *History and Historians in the Nineteenth Century* (London, 1913), 86.
[148] F. Max Müller, *Auld Lang Syne* (London, 1898), 86.
[149] [Robert Laing], 'The First Stewart in England: Von Ranke, Pattison, Spedding, Gardiner', *Quarterly Review*, 139 (1875), 2.
[150] Church, 'Ranke's "History of the Popes" ', 152 f.
[151] Doris S. Goldstein, 'History at Oxford and Cambridge: Professionalization and the Influence of Ranke', in Iggers and Powell (eds.), *Leopold von Ranke and the Shaping of the Historical Discipline*, 144, speaking of Stubbs. It may well be that Goldstein, in her turn, underestimates Stubbs's own sophistication. For a view of Stubbs as 'one of the most philosophical of British historians', see James Campbell, *Stubbs and the English State* (Reading, 1989), 6.
[152] *Academy*, 29 May 1886.

case of the *Popes* had had complicated philosophical premisses, was reinterpreted as indifference to all political issues and moral values.

This interpretation was made canonical by Lord Acton. Visiting Ranke in 1861, Acton had discussed with him the future of the papacy.[153] After the Pope had been declared infallible, Acton was deeply disappointed that professional historians did not protest more loudly against what he condemned as a falsification of the historical record. His pronouncements on the moral duties of the historian expounded a radical criticism of the relativist tendencies of German historical scholarship.[154] At the same time, perplexing his listeners and interpreters, Acton emphatically called Ranke his master. The anathema he pronounced upon amoral professional history may have been an unconscious attempt to exorcize the nihilistic shadow of the 'intellectual agnosticism' he found himself moving into.[155] Reviewing Mandell Creighton's *History of the Papacy during the Period of the Reformation* in 1887, Acton accused the author of having learnt from Ranke 'to be so dispassionate and inattentive to everything but the chain of uncoloured fact'.[156] Gone were the days when readers of the *Popes* had complained about too much theory and too few facts. What was memorable about the book was that it had long been 'the only modern history from Mss.'[157] In his inaugural lecture in 1895 Acton

---

[153] Acton and Döllinger, *Briefwechsel*, i. 229.

[154] Cf. Lothar Kettenacker, 'Lord Acton: Wegbereiter der deutschen historischen Schule und Kritiker des Historismus', in Adolf M. Birke and Kurt Kluxen (eds.), *Kirche, Staat und Gesellschaft im neunzehnten Jahrhundert: Ein deutsch-englischer Vergleich* (Munich, 1984), 99–120.

[155] Owen Chadwick, *Acton, Döllinger and History* (The 1986 Annual Lecture of the German Historical Institute London; London, 1987), 18.

[156] *Essays in the Study and Writing of History*, 365. In 1873 the Oxford History School decided to produce a translation of Ranke's *Englische Geschichte*, and Creighton undertook to translate one volume. The real work was done by his wife, who found it 'an unsatisfactory piece of work from the literary point of view as old Ranke wished it to be very literal'. Louise Creighton, *Memoir of a Victorian Woman*, ed. James Thayne Covert (Bloomington, Ind., 1994), 54. Creighton later reviewed several volumes of Ranke's *Weltgeschichte* in the *Contemporary Review*, 46 (1884), 144 f.; 47 (1885), 597.

[157] Quoted from Herbert Butterfield, *Man on his Past. The Study of the History of Historical Scholarship* (Cambridge, 1955), 90.

declared that there was not one of Ranke's 'seventy volumes' which had 'not been overtaken'.[158] Indeed, *pace* Macaulay, the *History of the Popes* could not 'be a classic for this age as it was for the last'.[159] If manuscripts were all that mattered, historical science did not produce classic texts.

One historian who did notice that Ranke had written a philosophical history of the modern world which might not so soon become obsolete was Henry Thomas Buckle. As Buckle's most recent biographer has pointed out, the German edition of the *Popes* was one of the books which the author of the *History of Civilization in England* quoted most frequently.[160] With astonishing perspicacity, Buckle selected those often unobtrusive asides in which the 'great historian'[161] developed his theory of the separation of church and state as the foundation of modern pluralism. While Ranke's *Französische Geschichte*, studied by Buckle in the English translation,[162] furnished the system-building positivist with bricks of hard fact,[163] the *Popes* gave him an idea of the structure of the modern world. Ranke's 'eloquent remarks'[164] on the emergence of the sovereign state in modern Europe were made to illustrate the progress of a secular art of politics. Henry IV[165] and Richelieu[166] were the chief characters in this story. Buckle recognized that in Ranke's eyes landmarks of diplomatic history were also events of intellectual history.

---

[158] Lord Acton, 'The Study of History', in id., *Essays in the Study and Writing of History*, 512. In 1862 Acton had already announced to Döllinger: 'Eine Menge dem Ranke unbekannte Dinge, über Julius II., Clemens VII., Paul IV., Sixtus V. etc., die Licht verbreiten auf die Natur der Sache, und zur Physiologie der weltlichen Gewalt der Kirche dienen, habe ich auch bereit' (I also have available many things of which Ranke is unaware, about Julius II, Clemens VII, Paul IV, Sixtus V, etc., and which cast light on the nature of the matter, and serve the physiology of the secular power of the Church.) (*Briefwechsel*, i. 258 f.).

[159] Acton, 'Ranke', 165.

[160] Eckhardt Fuchs, *Henry Thomas Buckle: Geschichtsschreibung und Positivismus in England und Deutschland* (Leipzig, 1994), 235.

[161] Henry Thomas Buckle, *History of Civilization in England*, i (London, 1857), 482.

[162] *Civil Wars and Monarchy in France in the Sixteenth and Seventeenth Centuries*, trans. M. A. Garvey (London, 1852).

[163] *History of Civilization in England*, i. 470, 516, 772.   [164] Ibid. 713.

[165] *Die römischen Päpste*, ii. 157, 162, quoted in *History of Civilization in England*, i. 471.

[166] *Die römischen Päpste*, ii. 331, quoted in *History of Civilization in England*, i. 492.

The peace treaties of 1648[167] and 1659[168] ratified the victory of a new mentality which separated religious and political concerns. The historian of the autonomy of modern politics was himself no narrow political historian. He was interested in the demographic strength of social groups;[169] 'M. Ranke's important work on the *History of the Popes*' could even be read as an account of the changing social position of the Catholic clergy.[170] Buckle's posthumous notebooks reveal Ranke's works, especially the *Popes*, as a mine of sociological information on topics such as the condition of women, the influence of the aristocracy, the spirit of chivalry, the rise of the towns, the nature of modern civilization, the supply of precious metals from America, the theatre, the fine arts, education, polite behaviour, taxes, monks, European knowledge of Sanscrit, and popular legends.[171] Even in these scattered notes, however, Buckle time and again returned to Ranke's main theme: the secularization of politics in the modern system of states.[172]

More limited and more typical was the use Symonds made of the *Popes*. In his series on the Renaissance, Symonds took specific facts, not general ideas, from what he had called that badly composed book.[173] To Symonds it was obvious that 'the campaign of the Counter-Reformation' had been a 'reactionary movement' against 'the spirit of the modern world'.[174] Anticipating more recent notions of a 'Catholic reformation', Ranke had identified a genuine reforming

---

[167] 'The religious element is become powerless; political considerations rule the world', Ranke, *The Ecclesiastical and Political History of the Popes*, trans. by Sarah Austin, ii. 404. See also Buckle's commonplace book, *Miscellaneous and Posthumous Works*, ed. Helen Taylor (London, 1872), ii. 642.

[168] Buckle quotes Ranke's remarks on the exclusion of the Pope from the negotiations which ended in the conclusion of the treaty of the Pyrenees (*Die römischen Päpste*, iii. 105): 'The consequences and the meaning of all this are well noticed by M. Ranke' (*History of Civilization in England*, i. 549).

[169] *History of Civilization in England*, i. 500.

[170] Ibid. 464. Cf. Buckle, *Miscellaneous and Posthumous Works*, i. 108.

[171] *Miscellaneous and Posthumous Works*, i. 184, 380, 392, 442, 443, 465, 466, 488, 512, 541, 548; ii. 248, 573, 642; iii. 555.   [172] Ibid., i. 165, 504, 540; iii. 643 f.

[173] John Addington Symonds, *Renaissance in Italy*, vi–vii: *The Catholic Reaction* (London, 1886), vi. 33 (Contarini), 145 (papal elections), 167 (finances), 169 (nepotism), 248 (the Jesuits). Symonds used Mrs Foster's translation in Bohn's Standard Library.   [174] Ibid., vii. 425, 423, 414.

impulse at the heart of the Catholic revival.[175] To Harwood, no part of Ranke's work was 'more interesting than that in which he traces the relations of this spirit to the Lutheran movement'.[176] Provocatively, Ranke recognized something of the spirit of the modern world in the dogmatic, aggressive, and uniform features of Tridentine Catholicism which were offensive to civilized Protestant taste.[177] Far from preserving every medieval tradition, the triumphant Church destroyed the visible testimonials of its own past. Sixtus V erased what remained of the old palace of the Lateran, erecting in its place 'one of the first specimens of the uniform regularity of modern architecture'.[178] At the Council of Trent, the Church of Rome defined its own identity. Every definition is a limitation; in a sense, the Catholic Church acknowledged that it was no longer catholic.[179] The popes left behind the medieval cosmos of half-understood ritual and unquestioned custom. They entered the modern world of objective observation and explicit description.

As a young man, Ranke had been roused by Fichte who taught that self-assertion and self-recognition belonged together. Though the papal bid for universal dominion had to be opposed for the sake of liberty, it was a characteristically modern move, built as it was on an ambitious plan for conquering the future, a programme not unlike secular philosophies of history.[180] The *Griff nach der Weltmacht* had failed; 'the confidence inspired by a politico-religious position

---

[175] On Ranke's place in the history of scholarship cf., at some length, Ferdinand Hennerbichler, *Untersuchungen über Leopold von Rankes terminologische Konzeption des Begriffs Gegenreformation und ihre Aufnahme bis ins beginnende zwanzigste Jahrhundert* (Ph.D. thesis, University of Vienna, 1971).
[176] [Harwood], 'Ranke's History of the Popes', 411.
[177] *Die römischen Päpste*, i. 324.
[178] Ranke, *The Ecclesiastical and Political History of the Popes*, trans. Sarah Austin, i. 332. German original: *Die römischen Päpste*, i. 315. Cf. iii. 48 on Alexander VII. Milman, 'The Popes of the Sixteenth and Seventeenth Centuries', 211 f. found Counter-Reformation ecclesiastical architecture lacking 'that traceable progressive development of the art, the silent encroachment of a new taste upon old established models'; the baroque churches of southern Germany 'are seemingly all of the same date'. The spirit of Christian art was not to be found in an artificial stylistic unity imposed from above, but in the fine shades of liberal Anglican gradualism.
[179] *Die römischen Päpste*, i. 227.   [180] Ibid., ii. 120.

restrained by no rival or superior, must vanish.'[181] The Pope came to understand that his autonomy as a player in international politics presupposed the autonomy of everybody else. The realism of great-power politics turns out to be founded on the idealist ethics of *Anerkennung*. Though no orthodox Protestant himself, Ranke acknowledged the utility of dogmatic definitions. Without clarity about one's own point of view, there could be no recognition of differences. Ranke dismissed the romantic complaint that the process of confessionalization had damaged the cause of religion. In modern, confessional Europe, Christians had to argue about their view of the world; religion had become a matter of rational choice.[182] The confessional states had played a part in the history of modern individualism.[183]

Symonds, writing as a man of letters unsure about his own place in society, took the artist as his model of the free agent.[184] Seen in the light of this aesthetic conception of individuality, the consolidation of political and ecclesiastical authority in the confessional age had retarded the emancipation of modern man. Deploring 'the tyranny of priests and princes',[185] Symonds limited himself to 'the barest generalizations' in discussing 'the political implications and the theological complexities of the Reformation'.[186] In drawing philosophical lessons from the history of the Catholic reaction, Symonds chose as his antagonist not Ranke, but Ranke's reviewer. The melancholy reflections which the spectacle of 'the marvellous vitality and longevity of the Roman Catholic Church' had suggested to Macaulay were based on a false premiss. The march of mind had not stopped when the progress of Protestantism was arrested at the end of the sixteenth century. The 'enlightened thinkers' of later ages moved straight from dogmatic Christianity to

---

[181] Ranke, *The Ecclesiastical and Political History of the Popes*, trans. Sarah Austin, iii. 134. German original: *Die römischen Päpste*, iii. 128.
[182] *Die römischen Päpste*, ii. 376.   [183] Ibid. 377.
[184] Cf. J. B. Bullen, *The Myth of the Renaissance in Nineteenth-Century Writing* (Oxford, 1994), 251–5, 302–6.
[185] Symonds, *Renaissance in Italy*, vii. 432.
[186] Richard Titlebaum, *Three Victorian Views of the Italian Renaissance* (New York, 1987), 168.

'what may variously be described as free thought or science or rationalism'.[187]

Did freethinkers have no use for Ranke's discreet irony and veiled philosophy? At the end of the nineteenth century one reading list placed Ranke's *History of the Popes* in its natural company of modern classics of historical speculation on church and state: Milman's *History of the Jews*, Stanley's *Jewish Church*, Renan's *Vie de Jésus*, Lecky's *History of Rationalism*, and Buckle's *History of Civilization*. The conditions under which this canon was to be studied were, however, the very antithesis of the situation in which disinterested and well-to-do scholars reaffirmed an established tradition by benevolent criticism. The original of the reading list is in the files of the Home Office. It is the list of books requested by Oscar Wilde when he was an inmate of Reading Gaol.[188] Some titles were crossed out by the prison governor.[189] Ranke was not one of them. Thus, finally, it was officially confirmed that reading the *History of the Popes* posed no danger to the spiritual health of a reformed sinner.

---

[187] Symonds, *Renaissance in Italy*, vii. 427 ff.
[188] *The Letters of Oscar Wilde*, ed. Rupert Hart-Davis (London, 1962), 405 f.
[189] Among them Stanley, Buckle, and Lecky. Renan was permitted only in French.

8
Lord Acton and German Historiography

HUGH TULLOCH

In his writings Lord Acton recounted the anecdote that, in the nineteenth century, France held dominion over the land, Britain over the sea, and Germany over the air. This commonplace observation referred to the tradition of French continental conquest exemplified by Louis XIV and Napoleon, to Britain's naval supremacy which held its vast global empire together, and to Germany's supremacy in the sphere of scientific scholarship and abstract metaphysics. It was in the early years of the nineteenth century that German scholarship acquired its unparalleled reputation for dedicated and disinterested research especially in the field of historical science, when the Göttingen scholar would lament the fact that its libraries were open for only thirteen hours a day, and when the researcher from Bonn would gain admiration and respect for dedicating thirty years of his life to writing the definitive work on Homer. Acton was himself unreserved in his praise of this national supremacy. 'The great growth in intellectual life is in Germany, and nearly all that has been done in France or in England for science is inspired by the Germans.'[1]

Though born in Naples in 1834 and descended from an ancient family of Shropshire gentry, Acton's temperament and intellect were shaped predominantly by a Catholic and German inheritance. His mother, Marie Pelline de Dalberg, was heiress of one of the most illustrious families of the Holy Roman Empire who brought as her dowry the castle of Herrnsheim and large hereditary estates on the Rhineland.

---

[1] John E. E. D. Acton, *Selected Writings of Lord Acton*, ed. J. Rufus Fears, 3 vols. (Indianapolis, 1985–8), iii. 597.

The historian's father, Sir Richard, died prematurely in Paris in 1837, three years after the birth of his only son, and in 1840 his widowed mother married Lord Leverson Gower, later the second Earl Granville, a leading Whig aristocrat. But his mother's insistence that her son should be brought up in the Catholic faith and her dying wish that he should marry a Bavarian cousin, Countess Marie von Arco-Valley, served to strengthen further his close links with southern Germany and with Catholicism. Most importantly, in 1850, having been refused admission to Cambridge on religious grounds, he gained permission from his stepfather to travel instead to Munich to study privately under the famous theologian and historian Ignaz von Döllinger, who was then at the centre of a revival of Catholic learning in Bavaria. Intellectually, this decision was to be the most formative in his life and was decisively to mould his thinking thereafter.

Lord Acton's immense contemporary prestige was owing, in part, to the fact that his planned magnum opus on *The History of Freedom* remained unwritten. As the years passed the growing silence of the historian became almost palpable, and encouraged the belief that the immense weight of erudition crushed Acton under an avalanche of accumulated knowledge and esoteric learning. But more relevantly, Acton's stock remained high because he had early imbibed German historical methodology in Munich, and introduced its more stringent and forensic methods into Britain. In acknowledgement of his unique understanding, Mandell Creighton, the editor of the *English Historical Review*, urged Acton to contribute his synoptic 'German Schools of History' to its first number in 1886. In 1890 Acton contributed further articles on 'Döllinger's Historical Work' and 'Wilhelm von Giesebrecht' to the same scholarly journal.[2]

In his 'German Schools of History' Acton discerned three main strands which, together, characterized the schools' innovative thinking. The first, pioneered by Niebuhr in his

---

[2] Reprinted in John E. E. D. Acton, *The History of Freedom and Other Essays*, ed. John Neville Figgis and Reginald Vere Laurence (London, 1907), 375–435, and John E. E. D. Acton, *Historical Essays and Studies*, ed. John Neville Figgis and Reginald Vere Laurence (London, 1907), 344–92 and 496–502.

study of Roman history, was the rigorous critical investigation of sources derived from both biblical and classical scholarship. This investigative weighing of sources was taken up and formalized in Ranke's famous research seminars at the new University of Berlin after 1825, and in the critical apparatus which appeared as appendices to his historical works. With the opening of state archives from the 1830s onwards, the scientific historian's task was carefully to sift through this plethora of new, primary material, assessing its testimony and evaluating its authority and veracity. The forensic process had to be pursued, as Michelet put it, with all the *désintéressement des morts*, and the historian himself and his secondary writings had, likewise, to be cross-examined to establish their authenticity and objectivity.

The second strand derived from Hegel's philosophical dialectic which was firmly rooted in historical evolution, and whose impact was acknowledged by Acton in a letter written to his close friend and fellow Catholic Richard Simpson in 1864. 'His philosophy is, in many shapes, the subtlest pervading influence of the present day' and 'the greatest force ever applied to the theory of history'. Here history became the shaper of world destiny and of the *Zeitgeist*, and the scientific aim of the historian was to discern the underlying pattern and purpose of history, to charge history with meaning and so reveal the cunning of reason operating through time. For Acton Hegel, for the first time, 'displayed all history by the light of scientific unity, as the manifestation of a single force, whose works are all wise, and whose latest work is best'. Here, significantly, Acton stressed the conservative implications of the Hegelian dialectic, but his metaphysic was so notoriously accommodating that it could form the starting point of Marx's revolutionary material dialectic as well as German National Socialism and Acton's own historical understanding. From this capacious philosophy Acton drew upon the Hegelian stress on historical self-consciousness and the ever-widening growth of individual conscience as a prerequisite for personal freedom. As Schiller had written: 'The History of the world is the world's court of justice.'[3] For the historical

3 Acton, *Selected Writings*, iii. 647, 640. Id., *Historical Essays and Studies*, 360–1.

profession as a whole, the consequences of Hegelianism were both tremendous and paradoxical, for 'the restoration of history coincided with the euthanasia of metaphysics'. In Hegel's philosophy, self-knowledge and self-revelation could only be attained in and through history. The study of philosophy was transformed into the history of philosophy; the study of jurisprudence, in the hands of Savigny in Germany or Sir Henry Sumner Maine in England, became the study of ancient law and of legal development; economics became the material history of mankind as interpreted by Marx or by Buckle. In his 'German Schools' Acton wrote of 'the process of emancipation by which the servant of many rose to be a master over them, and having become a law to itself imposed it on others'; and in his notes, 'history went on invading other provinces, dissolving systems into process, and getting the better of philosophy'. In essence Hegel had discarded the eighteenth-century search for 'the discovered law' in favour of the nineteenth-century quest for 'the law of discovery'.[4]

This transformation owed much to the third and last intellectual current which characterized the German schools— the emergence of romanticism following upon the humiliation suffered at the hands of Napoleon's conquering armies. These conquerors had carried with them and attempted to impose the cosmopolitan and universalist claims of the eighteenth-century Enlightenment enterprise. The French *philosophes* had asserted the principles of eternal justice, the infallible conscience, the reign of reason, and universal laws. They had, in the culminating event of 1789, abolished history and the unregenerate past entirely, and with it 'the system of administration, the physical divisions of the country, the classes of society, the corporations, the weights and measures, the calendar'. They and 'their followers renounced acquaintance with [history], and were ready to destroy its records, and to abolish its inoffensive professors'.[5] Together Jefferson and Sieyès had applied their desiccated reasoning in order to nullify the past and assert the

---

[4] *Historical Essays and Studies*, 344, 389. Herbert Butterfield, *Man on his Past: The Study of the History of Historical Scholarship* (Cambridge, 1955), 98.

[5] Acton, *History of Freedom*, 278. Id., *Essays on Freedom and Power*, ed. Gertrude Himmelfarb (London, 1956), 38.

sovereignty of the present, a process which culminated in the perilous denouement of the French Revolution. As a consequence, 'the romantic reaction which began with the invasion of 1794 was the revolt of outraged history', and 'History issues from the Romantic School. Piecing together what the Rev[olution] snapped.'

In place of dissecting and sceptical intellect, Fichte and Herder and the German romantics affirmed continuous and organic being and growth. They asserted the uniqueness and primacy of language, laws, custom, tradition, myth, habit, race, and a mystic, potent, yet indefinable *Volksgeist*. A state and its people could not be constructed by decree or manufactured like a pen or a button. Rather, like an apple or feather, the state, held together by tenuous but powerful threads, had its own natural laws of being, and that sense of being and of belonging was rooted, inextricably, in a shared past. The romantic school, with its insistence upon the search for roots, legitimacy, seeds, and genetic continuities, gave an immense fillip to historical research, not least in the field of the Middle Ages, the nineteenth-century rediscovery of which, Acton held, equalled the Renaissance's intellectual rediscovery of the classical world. 'This renaissance of the Christian Ages, this discovery of a palimpsest, this renewal of an interrupted continuity, is the great work of the nineteenth century.'[6] The school emphasized, too, the weight the past exerted upon the present, the way in which it shaped and moulded. By the same token, the school's heightened awareness of historical perspective, its imaginative recreation of past ages, led to a fuller recognition that the past was very different from the present and that things were done differently there. That is to say, the school contributed both to a belief in historical continuity and to historical relativism.

Among the German schools Acton was most influenced, indirectly, by Ranke, its acknowledged leader, and directly by his own mentor, Döllinger, but his attitude towards both was ambivalent and could be critical. Ranke was 'the real

---

[6] Acton, *Historical Essays and Studies*, 346. Butterfield, *Man on his Past*, 70, 212.

originator of the heroic study of records', and he taught fellow historians 'to be critical, to be colourless, and to be new'. He was the first to make full use of newly opened state archives; his writings were concerned with statecraft, the delicate balance of the great powers, and an interpretation of history as seen through the diplomatic eyes of Venetian ambassadors. Even after their intellectual estrangement in the late 1870s, Döllinger was Acton's closest contact among German historians. Together they hoped for and encouraged a liberal revival of Catholic learning both in Bavaria and Britain; together they explored the Roman archives in 1854, and Döllinger's pioneering work on *Papstfabeln des Mittelalters* (1871) encouraged Acton's own obsession with historical myths, forgeries, and false decretals. This joint fascination was to lead, finally, to Döllinger's excommunication in 1871, and take Acton himself to the very brink four years later. Acton admired the strict impartiality of Ranke and Döllinger, but came increasingly to question the non-judgemental nature of their historical writings, from both an ethical and a historical point of view. Acton came to believe that they did not, could not, judge because they had not sufficiently penetrated private archives or probed deeply enough into the psychology of interior motivation. Of Ranke he wrote: 'The cup is not drained; part of the story is left untold, and the world is much better and very much worse than he chooses to say.' And of Döllinger: 'He was never in contact with the sinister side of things.'[7] But equally influential was the Christian teleology which underlay the historical writings of both the Protestant Ranke and the Catholic Döllinger, which was deeply to infuse Acton's own writing. For Ranke, history clearly revealed the work of God. 'It stands there like a holy hieroglyph ... May we, for our part, decipher this holy hieroglyph. Even so we do serve God. Even so we are priests. Even so we are teachers.' For Döllinger, in turn, history constituted 'the narrative of the conquest of the world by Christ' and 'the uninterrupted

---

[7] Acton, *Essays on Freedom and Power*, 31, 42. Id., *Historical Essays and Studies*, 353. Id., *History of Freedom*, 411.

employment of the powers committed by Christ for the salvation of man'.[8]

In the middle years of the nineteenth century Acton was appalled by the backwardness and insularity of historical writing in Britain. Its practitioners tended either to indulge in bland national celebration or to write loose, unscientific narrative devoid of any philosophical basis. History was something one wrote rather than thought about. The theoretical resolve of pragmatic and unspeculative British writing stopped short at two questions: 'What is mind? No matter. What is matter? Never mind.' More especially, Acton contrasted British partiality with German academics' scientific impartiality. 'We have little experience of that abstract love of knowledge for its own sake, of that self-denying and disinterested indifference to consequences, and of that faith in the consistency and harmony of all truths, which inspire the energy of the laborious German.'[9] But then Acton discerned a change of direction: once again historical events intruded into the academic study. In retrospect he believed the change came in 1848 with the failure of the liberal intelligentsia at the Frankfurt parliament. Until then German scholars had held fast to the Baconian dictum that knowledge was power. The events of 1848 proved deeply disillusioning and thereafter there was a marked tendency for historians to abandon the realm of abstract thought and objective science for the more tangible aims of national destiny and support for the martial successes of the big battalions. The scientific impulse was not entirely abandoned; it was simply directed to more secular, nationalist ends. 'Consistency in the powers that direct the world is the supreme acquisition of all German thought. It is not partiality, but renunciation of party feeling and personal preference, to hold that the world works well, that what lives permanently in the light and strife of civilisation lives rightfully, that whatever perishes has earned its fate.'

[8] Peter Novick, *That Noble Dream: The Objectivity Question and the American Historical Profession* (Cambridge, 1988), 27. Acton, *History of Freedom*, 383, 384.
[9] Acton, *History of Freedom*, 51. Id., *Essays on Church and State*, ed. Douglas Woodruff (London, 1952), 375.

Increasingly the German schools, especially those historians in Berlin, grew anti-Austrian, supported Hohenzollern Prussia, and urged German unification. Acton appreciated only too well that 'history has been one of the chief forces making Germany'; that Droysen, for example, in his Prussian history of 1870, had anachronistically made Prussia the predominant state in eighteenth-century Germany; that Sybel was 'the first classic of imperialism [who] helped to form that garrison of distinguished historians that prepared the Prussian supremacy with their own, and now hold Berlin like a fortress'.[10] Here it is not only the military metaphors that are significant: it is the complicity and collaboration of the historian that is emphasized. By 1886, the date of his 'German Schools of History', and in the light of the Franco-Prussian War, Acton recognized that Germany had reversed the humiliations suffered following the French Revolution. Both militarily and in the realm of thought Jena had been avenged at Sedan, and German scholars no longer felt the need to defer, or waste their powder on salutes. By 1871 the eighteenth-century French laws of nature had been decisively replaced by nineteenth-century German laws of nationalism.

Since his early influential essay on 'Nationality' (1862) Acton had pitted himself with all the intellectual force at his command against the rise of nationalism. At first his attack was prompted by a conservative, Catholic apologetics: the new secular force of nationalism conflicted with the Pope's temporal powers in Italy and the universalist claims of his church. But increasingly, Acton came to see the full emergence of the nation-state as the chief nineteenth-century enemy of liberty. Hegel had insisted that positive freedom could only be achieved by the individual merging into the collective will of the state, that 'the State is the march of God through the world'.[11] Nationalism led not only to a dangerous concentration of powers and the ultimate submission of the church to secular authority—as exemplified by Bismarck's policy of *Kulturkampf*—but also to the dominion

---

[10] Acton, *Historical Essays and Studies*, 382–3, 378. Id., *Selected Writings*, iii. 597.
[11] Karl Popper, *The Open Society and its Enemies*, 2 vols. (1950; London, 1992), ii. 31.

of a majoritarian tyranny, for 'it is worse to be oppressed by a majority. For there is a reserve of latent power in the masses which, if it is called into play, the minority can seldom resist. But from the absolute will of an entire people there is no appeal, no redemption, no refuge but treason.' Thus, among a list Acton made of the enemies of liberty he included Hegel along with Comte, Fichte, and Mommsen. Nationalism became the chief obstacle to individual freedom. 'The process of civilisation depends on transcending Nationality', he wrote, 'for patriotism cannot absolve a man from his duty to mankind'; and again, 'the nations aim at power, and the world at freedom'. Acton devoutly believed that just as God had ordained a dualism within each state, of a visible church to neutralize and offset the secular power, so, within each individual, God had planted conscience to offset the profane claims of Caesar, and granted to each and everyone the free will to choose between good and evil. That freedom to choose was the prerequisite of liberty, the source of God's grace working in the world, and centred the gravity of history not in the state but in the moral drama of individual motive and action. History could not be other than 'a narrative told of ourselves, the record of a life which is our own, of efforts not yet abandoned to repose, of problems that still entangle the feet and vex the hearts of man'.[12] Because all men were equal in the sight of God, and because the past exerted its pressure specifically on each and every one of us (history made and history making were conjoined), history had to be universal and not national.

For Acton ideas were the mainspring of history, not institutions, constitutions, borders, battles, dates of reigns; and fresh, innovative ideas by definition transcended and crossed borders. 'If we are to account mind not matter, ideas not force, the spiritual property which gives dignity and grace and intellectual value to history, and its action on the ascending life of man, then we shall not be prone to explain the universal by the national, and civilisation by custom.' Spinoza, for example, took up where Descartes left off,

---

[12] Acton, *History of Freedom*, 11. Gertrude Himmelfarb, *Lord Acton: A Study in Conscience and Politics* (London, 1952), 183. Acton, *Essays on Freedom and Power*, 32.

Lockean ideas were further developed by Condillac, and Hume's scepticism was refuted by Kant. Acton's history, rooted in the fallible individual conscience and the primacy of ideas, was universal history. 'By universal history', Acton said in his letter to the syndics of Cambridge University Press in 1896, 'I understand that which is distinct from the combined history of all countries, which is not a rope of sand but a continuous development, and is not a burden on the memory, but an illumination of the soul . . . These things are extraterritorial, having their home in the sky, and no more confined to race and frontier than a rainbow or a storm.'[13]

Acton's fears concerning the close collaboration between nationalism and historicism were expressed in his 'German Schools of History', where he argued that the contribution of German historians to a national myth helped forge the Bismarckian state. 'Probably', he wrote, 'there is no considerable group less in harmony with our sentiments in approaching the study of history.' This deep concern was powerfully reinforced by his own personal history. Acton's liberal struggle against ultramontanism, culminating in the promulgation of papal infallibility at the Vatican Council of 1869–70, is well known. Acton had, at first, been thrilled by Newman's novel application of historical method to church history in his *Essay on the Development of Christian Doctrine* of 1845. Then he began to have doubts. For just as Newman's essay led, inexorably, to the deification of the current theological dispensation within the church, so ultramontane historians rummaged through, rewrote, and falsified Catholic history to justify the infallibility of Pius IX. Instead of impartial pursuit of objective truth, 'a crust of designing fiction' and 'a vast tradition of conventional mendacity' was fabricated in furtherance of a current cause. This was the dethronement not the reign of history, for as the ultramontane Cardinal Manning starkly stated at the Vatican Council, 'Authority must conquer History'.[14]

[13] Acton, *Selected Writings*, iii. 682–3.
[14] Acton, *Historical Essays and Studies*, 382; Damian McElrath, *Lord Acton: The Decisive Decade 1864–1874* (Louvain, 1970), 140; Hugh McDougall, *Lord Acton on Papal Power* (London, 1973), 115.

While Acton struggled against infallibilism and inopportunism in Rome and failed, and against Prussian historicism in Berlin, so in London, as a liberal Gladstonian, he was deeply implicated in the battle against imperialism and authoritarianism. Here the Prussian school's complicity was reflected in the milder but equally insidious writings of Maine, Froude, Seeley, and Carlyle ('the most detestable of historians'), all of whom found good reasons for adopting government policies. Yet even the liberal school of British historians, most notably A. E. Freeman, Goldwin Smith, and James Bryce, was infected by a German historicism which stressed sluggish organic continuities and racial destinies, institutions and forms whose seeds grew from the Teutonic forests. Thus Freeman stressed the continuity of Anglo-Saxon custom which underlay and absorbed the Norman Conquest of 1066, and Bryce interpreted the American Revolution as essentially the innocuous enlargement of ordered English liberties by fellow Englishmen in the colonies. Acton unequivocally rejected what he called this organic materialism and, by implication, the theoretical underpinnings of the German schools' attempt to enforce uninterrupted historical growth. Pointing to Columbus, Machiavelli, Erasmus, Luther, and Copernicus, Acton insisted:

> The modern age did not proceed from mediaeval by normal succession, with outward tokens of legitimate descent. Unheralded, it founded a new order of things, under a law of innovation, sapping the ancient reign of continuity ... It was an awakening of new life; the world revolved in a different orbit, determined by influences unknown before.

Likewise he undercut the prevalent myth of primitive, embryonic institutional freedoms which sustained the concept of historical continuity: 'the footsteps of a silent yet prophetic people who dwelt by the Dead Sea, and perished in the fall of Jerusalem, come nearer to our lives than the ancestral wisdom of barbarians who fed their swine on the Hercynian acorns.'[15]

---

[15] Acton, *Essays on Freedom and Power*, 28, 27.

In this remaking of national history, the hero—Frederick the Great of Prussia, Napoleon in France—was exempt from judgement or blame; untrammelled by mere laws or morality, he was the agent who embodied and unfolded the *Zeitgeist*. Acton was acutely aware of the dazzling appeal the decisive actor on the historical stage held for timid, contemplative academics and how, in Britain, historians such as Carlyle, Kingsley, Gardiner, and Firth clustered like moths around the flame of Cromwell. More insidious still was what Acton took to be the Hegelian stress on predetermination, and absence of contingency, choice, and chance, in nineteenth-century historical narrative. If Ranke invoked 'the goddess Necessity, fixed fate, and unrelenting force', it was because, before him, Hegel had subjected 'all things to the government of intelligible law, and to prefer the simplicity of resistless cause to the confused conflict of free will'.[16] Such belief in history's scientific, inexorable laws led to a history of victors over victims and the ignoring of causes which had gone down in defeat: it looked to the past, essentially, to trace and to confirm the triumphalism of the present. Acton would have none of this because he believed most passionately in free will and the moral duty of each individual to extract good from the implacable forces of evil.

Acton's attempt to undermine the philosophical presuppositions of the German school can be seen most clearly in his inaugural lecture on 'The Study of History', where he distanced himself from its conservative implications in favour of the French school's emphasis on revolutionary discontinuities. Just as the individual struggled with his God-given conscience and strove to reject the Whiggish politics of compromise and concession in pursuit of the liberal ideal, so, collectively, societies sought irrevocable change to overthrow the injustices of the existing order and inaugurate an ideal social community; to consummate 'the advent of the reign of general ideas which we call the Revolution'. In a historiographical appendix to his *Lectures on the French Revolution* he wrote again of the historian's complicity with history, but here the historian assists in effecting revolution-

---

[16] Butterfield, *Man on his Past*, 229. Acton, *Historical Essays and Studies*, 360.

ary change to bring about a juster society. 'History is resurrection . . . History is also restitution . . . the revolution is the advent of justice and the central fact in the experience of mankind.'[17]

Like Marx, Acton adopted the revolutionary implications of Hegelianism and insisted that history was iconoclastic, not a teacher of wisdom. But he combined this with the providential history of his masters, Ranke and Döllinger. He sought, uniquely, to combine the sound scientific methods of the German schools with his own distinct brand of a science of historical judgement based on ethics, not metaphysics. The metaphysics of the German schools had culminated in the worship of a nationalist mythology and abject submission to the temporal order. In one sense Acton sought to return to the absolute, universalist principles of the Enlightenment which had been undermined and destabilized by nineteenth-century historical relativism. But in place of profane eighteenth-century reason Acton wanted to return the divine spark of providence to the historical centre; to employ the Christian ethic of the New Testament as a yardstick by which to provide a timeless and absolute moral imperative and impose it upon the flux of relative historical values. He wrote of conscientious rather than apologetic history, of imposing judgement on history rather than deriving judgement from it. Once having, with the aid of scientific method, fully reconstructed a historical event, the final seal of science lay precisely in judgement. As he wrote in 'German Schools of History': 'the marrow of civilised history is ethical not metaphysical, and the deep underlying cause of action passes through the shape of right and wrong.' And again, in his inaugural address: 'Opinions alter, manners change, creeds rise and fall, but the moral law is written on the tablets of eternity.' History was divine revelation and the 'full exposition of truth is the great object for which the existence of mankind is prolonged on earth'.[18] Acton's final synthesis was to link a divine providence

[17] Acton, *Essays on Freedom and Power*, 28. Id., *Lectures on the French Revolution*, ed. John Neville Figgis and Reginald Vere Laurence (London, 1910), 351.
[18] Acton, *Historical Essays and Studies*, 362. Id., *Essays on Freedom and Power*, 51. Id., *Essays on Church and State*, 38.

governing the world which was to be reflected upon earth in spiritual and secular progress. This was to be the central theme of his unwritten *History of Freedom*. Acton had travelled a long way from his early conservative, Catholic polemic to reach a theological doctrine close to the Protestant Vinet's writing on the sovereign conscience and Michelet's history of universal revolution. Reaction against the implications of the German schools had played a major part in his emancipation.

9

Views and Reviews

Mutual Perceptions of British and German Historians in the Late Nineteenth Century

PETER WENDE

In most Western European countries the evolution of historical science in the nineteenth century was a twofold process. On the one hand there were strong links with the rise of modern nationalism, as most historians focused on national histories. On the other hand, the European *res publica litterarum*, dating from the Renaissance and reinvigorated during the Enlightenment, was still functioning even in those fields which provided the soil for the plants which were to bear the fruits of nationalism. This holds true for the long-lived art of historiography as well as for the evolution of modern historical science. Everywhere, both were repeatedly boosted by exchanges and transfers, by attempts to imitate or at least to draw on models created by foreign achievements.

The starting point in this process of intellectual interaction was, of course, mutual perceptions. This essay will therefore attempt an overview of mutual perceptions of British and German historians, mainly during the last half of the nineteenth century, by concentrating on the principal organs of scholarly discourse: learned periodicals and journals in which reviewers might occasionally disclose the general views they held of each other. The main source

---

On this topic see also Peter Wende, 'Perzeption und Transfers: Zur gegenseitigen Wahrnehmung deutscher und britischer Geschichtswissenschaft im 19. Jahrhundert', in Gerhard A. Ritter and Peter Wende (eds.), *Rivalität und Partnerschaft: Studien zu den deutsch-britischen Beziehungen im 19. und 20. Jahrhundert. Festschrift für Anthony J. Nicholls,* Publications of the German Historical Institute London, 46 (Paderborn, 1999), 13–28.

material for such a survey is provided by the *Historische Zeitschrift* (*HZ*) on the German side, founded by Heinrich von Sybel in 1859, and the *English Historical Review* (*EHR*), launched in 1886, and which Acton tried to model on the *HZ*. This gap of twenty-seven years points to a time-lag between the professionalization of the two historical academes, but another factor was that numerous literary magazines had been established in England during the nineteenth century, and their reviews had already absorbed much of the market for historical writing. Thus the gap between the first publication of the *HZ* and the *EHR* might adequately be bridged by looking at the *Edinburgh Review* and the *Westminster Review*—both periodicals which paid special attention to the field of historiography.

To concentrate on the main periodicals also implies that no comprehensive quantifying approach is intended, because in this field quality of insight does not relate to quantity of sources inspected. Therefore no attempt has been made to register all books or even articles by German historians which were noticed or reviewed by their British colleagues, or vice versa. A few samples suffice to convey an idea of the extent of mutual perceptions between these two historical academes up to the First World War. A brief glance at the first volumes of the main sources for this essay, the *HZ* and the *EHR*, is informative. Each journal demonstrated a strong regard for the other country's historiography. In 1859 the first volume of the *HZ* carried an article of more than fifty pages in length by an eminent liberal historian from the south-west of Germany, Ludwig Häusser, on Macaulay's 'Frederick the Great'.[1] And in the same issue, thirty-six books of English origin were either reviewed, such as James Anthony Froude's *History of England*, or at least mentioned, such as four volumes of the *Calendar of English State Papers*. And the first volume of the *EHR* contained not only Acton's famous article on 'German Schools of History', which opened the new periodical, but also substantial reviews of books by Dahlmann, Waitz, Mommsen, and Treitschke.

---

[1] Ludwig Häusser, 'Macaulay's Friedrich der Große. Mit einem Nachtrag über Carlyle', *HZ* 1 (1859), 43–107.

These first impressions of intense mutual perceptions are partly qualified and partly confirmed by the few quantifying samples on which this essay draws. Volumes 16 to 18 in the new series of the *Westminster Review* of the years 1859 and 1860, the years in which the *HZ* was launched in Germany, displayed no marked interest in German history. Out of a total of ninety books reviewed in the section *History and Biography*, only ten were by Germans, as against twenty-two by French historians. Just over fifteen years later, out of 253 reviews in volumes 49 to 52, published in 1876–7, forty-eight dealt with the works of German historians and only one was on a French publication. This marks a rise from 11 to 19 per cent.

Similar proportions can be noticed for the year in which the first volume of the *EHR* was published, with ten books by German historians and nine by French scholars reviewed out of a total of seventy-four titles. Ten years later the figures were twenty-seven German and fourteen French titles out of 156, and in 1909 (volume 24), forty-one German and fifty French titles were reviewed or mentioned out of a total of 391 (13.5, 13.6, and 10.4 per cent respectively). Thus it can be concluded that in England more attention was usually paid to the works and achievements of German historians than to those of their French colleagues, whereas the *HZ* paid more attention to French than to British authors. In a survey of historical literature published in 1861, featured in volume 8 (1862) of the *HZ*, thirty pages were dedicated to the history of England, and forty-five to the history of France; three years later fifty pages were devoted to England, and ninety-eight to France etc.[2] These samples suggest a marked reciprocal interest between German and British historians, slightly more marked on the British side, and reaching a peak on both sides during the 1870s and 1880s.

The decisive rupture in this mutual relationship came with the outbreak of the First World War. This was especially evident on the British side. The volume of the *EHR*

---

[2] M. F. Stieg, *The Origin and Development of Scholarly Historical Periodicals* (Tuscaloosa, Ala., 1986), who states that only '2 out of [a total of] 104 [books reviewed] in 1869 and 6 out of 214 in 1879' were written in English (p. 31), is rather misleading.

published in 1914 contained reviews of thirty-six German titles, but after this there was a complete halt: not a single book in German was reviewed in subsequent years, with the exception of volume 7 of the Swiss historian Alfred Stern's *Geschichte Europas* which, as the reviewer wrote, 'has grown towards completion on a free and neutral soil'.[3] After the war attention returned only gradually, and from then on German books were reviewed on a smaller scale: one in 1919, five in 1920, and twelve in the following year.

The break was less abrupt on the German side, where editors went on commissioning reviews of British books, though obviously on a reduced scale (on average, five titles per volume). But the political undertones which had occasionally been heard in some reviews before 1914 now became overtones or even dominant themes.[4] And when Maitland was highly praised in a review of his *Collected Papers*,[5] it was because the author welcomed the introduction of the *Bürgerliches Gesetzbuch* (Civil Code) in Germany as an achievement which could set an example to Great Britain. On the whole, reviewers such as Justus Hashagen were generally on the warpath when they took note of something from the enemy side.[6]

The potential productiveness of this kind of quantifying approach should not be overrated. Even if a comprehensive index of historical reviews were to be compiled, it would not reveal the dispensation of the *Weltgeist*, but the contingencies of personal constellations. Thus the perceptions of British historians by the *HZ* most often turned out to be the perceptions of British historians by their eminent German colleague Reinhold Pauli, who seemed to have enjoyed a lifelong monopoly on reviewing English books. And the same applied in reverse to his British colleague A. Ward, a great authority on Anglo-Hanoverian relations and Master of Peterhouse, who was more or less responsible for the reviews of German books in the *EHR*. Therefore care must be taken

---

[3] *EHR* 33 (1918), 126.
[4] Cf. *HZ* 113 (1914), 158 ff. A. O. Meyers's review of Carlos Lumsden, *The Dawn of Modern England* (London, 1910).   [5] *HZ* 114 (1915), 321–34.
[6] *HZ* 116 (1916), 364; *HZ* 118 (1917), 367: 'notieren wir von feindlicher Seite' (we note from the enemy side).

not to interpret as the mutual perceptions of national academes what is the result of personal idiosyncrasies.

To look at German reviews of the work of British historians and vice versa means to look at business as usual in a significant sector of the great *res publica litterarum*. It was the *Internationale* of historical science as Stubbs, for example, described it in his inaugural lecture of 1867: 'a great republic of workers able and willing to assist one another; not working for party purposes, unfettered by political prejudices ... anxious above all to find the truth, and to purify the cause that each loves best from the taint of falsehood, every inclination to calumny or concealement.'[7] In the spirit of this kind of international co-operation, not only important general works such as Lamprecht's *Deutsche Geschichte* or Freeman's *History of the Norman Conquest* were noticed and reviewed in the context of the latest achievements in the field, but also specialist studies on national history, such as Paul Joachimsen's dissertation on *Gregor von Heimburg*.

But there were a few significant exceptions to this rule, and to concentrate on them sheds some light on general perceptions of national differences, and on the pathways and directions of academic transfer. German reviewers in particular tended to digress in favour of more general reflections on mutual relations. Viewed as a whole, of course, the usual expressions of national sensibilities appear in a twofold manner. There was the complaint about insufficient or even non-existent understanding and awareness of the achievements of the reviewer's own national historical science. Reinhold Pauli sometimes pointed out that leading British historians such as Froude and Freeman, for example, had obviously not studied Giesebrecht, Kluckhohn, or Lappenberg, and that Froude was not even familiar with the works of Ranke.[8] And on the British side, especially towards the turn of the century, historians, now proud of their own achievements, pointed to the shortcomings of German textbooks on British history and historians. Thus Gustav Wolf's *Einführung in das Studium der neueren Geschichte* 'gives less

---

[7] W. Stubbs, *Seventeen Lectures* (Oxford, 1900), 13 f.
[8] *HZ* 6 (1861), 447; *HZ* 22 (1869), 220; *HZ* 37 (1877), 210.

than the necessary minimum of information about such institutions as . . . the British Museum, the Public Record Office and the Historical Manuscript Commission. In regard to English historians and archives he is exceptionally weak.' And Powicke expressed his hope that for the second edition the authors of the *Quellenkunde zur Weltgeschichte* 'will put themselves under the guidance of some British scholars before they reissue the British section of their work'. After all, they had divided Sir George Trevelyan into two authors in the index.[9]

Observations like these, which occurred throughout the century but can be found more frequently towards the eve of the First World War, were often regarded as matters of national pride to be defended by reviewers increasingly sensitive to misrepresentation. Ward, while praising Treitschke as the German Macaulay, whose achievements in many respects surpassed even those of the English Macaulay, was 'not ashamed to confess some solicitude as to the treatment which . . . [this] country's name and fame may receive at the hands of a writer of real eminence'.[10] Similarly, twenty-five years earlier Häusser had accused Macaulay of wrongfully belittling Frederick the Great of Prussia.[11] But on the whole, especially before the turn of the century, national irritation was far outweighed by mutual acknowledgement, admiration, and respect. A book such as Gardiner's *The Thirty Years' War*, for example, was valued as 'an encouraging sign of the close relations between German and English intellectual life',[12] and on the publication of Heinrich Brunner's *Forschungen zur Geschichte des deutschen und französischen Rechts*, Maitland wrote: 'Dr Brunner has thrown a noble and stable bridge over the high seas, and we hope that English students will cross it.'[13]

Mutual perceptions and transfers were occasionally seen and valued as having grown and developed on common ground, as the expressions of a common Germanic

---

[9] *EHR* 25 (1910), 807; *EHR* 26 (1911), 543.　　[10] *EHR* 1 (1886), 810.
[11] *HZ* 1 (1859), 45 ff.
[12] 'ein erfreuliches Zeichen des innigen Verkehrs Deutschen und Englischen Geisteslebens', *HZ* 34 (1875), 212.　　[13] *EHR* 9 (1894), 594.

heritage.[14] 'The works which have been produced on both sides of the German sea reveal their intellectual propinquity as much as the two peoples and their languages. The differences between them are such as are found between siblings, and make understanding possible. To achieve this it is necessary to remember that the divergent living conditions and destinies of the English and German people have occasionally sent the development of their respective historiographies down different paths.'[15] And on the British side Stubbs echoed this view when he called on his English colleagues to take an interest in German history because 'the history of Germany is bound up with our national and natural identity'.[16]

The English perception of and interest in German historical science was greatly stimulated by the fact that so many eminent German scholars had a strong interest in the field of British history.[17] In addition to Ranke, Lappenberg, Pauli, and Gneist there were others like Dahlmann, Raumer, Redlich, and Marx who approached the subject on a more or less grand scale, while numerous nineteenth-century scholars studied specific problems or edited sources, especially in the field of English medieval history. This interest, of course, to a large extent sprang from contemporary political conditions and aims. England was seen as being in the vanguard of historical progress, moving towards political freedom and an industrial economy. For German scholars,

[14] Cf. Pauli's review of Stubbs's *Constitutional History of England*, in which the author's affinity with German medieval scholarship, and the fact that he draws upon it, are explained as the consequence of 'a clear recognition of the Germanic basis of the characteristics of his nation', *HZ* 33 (1875), 128.

[15] 'Die Werke, welche diesseits und jenseits des deutschen Meeres hervorgebracht worden sind, verläugnen ihre geistige Verwandtschaft so wenig wie die beiden Völker und deren Sprachen. Ihre Verschiedenheit ist eine solche, wie sie unter Geschwistern zu sein pflegt, und läßt der Verständigung Raum. Um zu einer solchen zu gelangen, ist es notwendig zu erwägen, daß die abweichenden Lebensbedingungen und Schicksale des englischen und deutschen Volkes der Entwicklung der Historiographie hier und dort eine andere Bahn gewiesen haben.' Review of Freeman's *Historical Essays*, *HZ* 30 (1873), 151.

[16] W. Stubbs, 'On the Present State and Prospect of Historical Study' (1876), in id., *Seventeen Lectures*, 60. And Pauli, reviewing Stubbs, notes the 'comprehensive use of German literature'. See note 14 above.

[17] Cf. Charles McClelland, *The German Historians and England* (Cambridge, 1971).

studying the history of England was like opening a window onto their own country's future. This strong German interest in English history also sprang from that peculiar perception of a universal mission or supranational disposition so characteristic especially of early nineteenth-century German historiography. The Germans argued that this allowed them to overcome the prejudices and restricted views of the national historians of other countries. They also claimed that it qualified German historians to take a bird's-eye view, unfolding a European perspective, and thus to put English national history into the context of international relations.[18]

The strong interest in the history of England on the part of German historians was, on the whole, appreciated by British historians. Even a 'pamphlet of 78 pages' (Fueter's *Religion und Kirche in England im 15. Jahrhundert*, 1904) was regarded as 'a very important contribution to English church history'.[19] And on the publication of Reinhold Pauli's *Lebenserinnerungen*, G. W. Prothero praised his 'labours . . . in the cause of English history' which, he regretted, 'though fully recognized by English historians, have not met with the acknowledgement they deserve at the hands of the general public'.[20] And again, Stubbs delivered the highest praise of German historical scholarship, which explored every nook and cranny of ancient and medieval English history. He did 'not believe that they want to take from us anything . . . or that they want to engross to themselves by conquest the whole domain of historical knowledge. But I am sure that they have a great object—to increase human knowledge . . ., to perfect the instruments of historic study.'[21] At the same time he deplored and criticized the insularity of British scholars who focused on national history instead of taking an equal interest in German history. And he called upon them not merely to study 'the works of Waitz, Sohm, Brunner, and the Maurers, but the . . . evidence on which those writers have based their conclusions'.[22]

[18] Cf. e.g. K. v. Noorden's review of Ranke's *Englische Geschichte*, HZ 17 (1867), 89, 106 f., 108.   [19] EHR 19 (1904), 349.
[20] EHR 12 (1897), 385.   [21] Stubbs, 'On the Present State', 69, 71.
[22] Ibid. 71.

Thus, on the whole, the aims and achievements of German studies of English history were noticed and appreciated by British historians. And not only their learned colleagues, but also the reviewers in the popular periodicals like the *Athenaeum*, the *Westminster Review*, and the *British Quarterly Review*, stressed the merits of German historians dealing with British history. They, too, appreciated the attention paid to international relations as a valuable contribution to traditional British historiography, and esteemed 'the judgement of a wise and unbiased outsider', of 'the intelligent foreigner' as the representative of 'impartial posterity', who stood aloof from British party strife which usually affects historical judgement.[23] Here German criticism of specific deficiencies of British historiography and English praise of the merits of their German colleagues often confirmed each other. In his review of Green's *Short History of the English People* (1875), Pauli pointed out that 'the relations between English and foreign policy are inadequately explained, as is the case in most English works'. And in the same year the *Westminster Review* praised Onno Klopp's *Der Fall des Hauses Stuart* for demonstrating 'the connexion between the English policy and European complications'.[24]

But the relationship between German and English historians was regarded on both sides of the Channel as that between a master and his pupil. Aware of their undisputed achievements in the field of historical method in general and source criticism in particular, German reviewers set their own standards self-confidently and often rather condescendingly. Thus Freeman, for example, who was generally highly praised because his meticulous scholarship was closely akin to German historical workmanship,[25] was nevertheless severely criticized as soon as he dared to stray from the narrow path Droysen prescribed, especially when he did not

---

[23] Cf. *Athenaeum* (1875), 285 where Ranke's *Englische Geschichte* is aptly labelled as 'An essay on the foreign relations of England'; *British Quarterly Review*, 61 (1875); *Westminster Review*, NS 50 (1876), 270 f.
[24] 'Die Beziehungen der englischen zur auswärtigen Politik werden überhaupt mangelhaft ergründet, wie in den meisten englischen Werken' *HZ* 34 (1875), 209; *Westminster Review*, NS 48 (1875), 526.
[25] Cf. R. Pauli on Freeman's *History of the Norman Conquest*, *HZ* 29 (1873), 2.

give preference to what Droysen termed the *Überreste* ('unintentional' sources) over the *Traditionsquellen* ('intentional' sources) when judging the value of sources.[26] German reviewers had no doubt that they set the standards for modern historical scholarship, and monitored them.

To a certain extent this German claim to academic supremacy was echoed and accepted by the British side. 'As a rule good books are in German,' claimed John Robert Seeley. And in his obituary for Paul Ewald he observed that 'in the organisation of research, we may for the present safely follow the example of Germany'.[27] Not only Acton was impressed by 'the ways in which they [the German historians] break new ground and add to the work and notion of history', as he wrote in the final sentence of his famous article on 'German Schools of History'.[28] When Stubbs proclaimed that the History School at Oxford aimed to 'take its stand beside the historical schools of Paris, or Bonn, or Göttingen, or Munich, or Vienna', he pointed among other things to German historical dissertations and German historical reviews as possibly providing guidelines for the practice of English historians.[29] And he even tried to introduce German words such as *Geschichtsquellen* (historical sources) or *Kritik der Quellen* (source criticism) as technical terms into the language of the British historian.[30] It was not only the eminent representatives of the profession such as Ranke, Gneist, or Mommsen who inspired the idea of German historical scholarship as a model. Even in a review of Paul Joachimsen's *Gregor von Heimburg*, a dissertation by a young scholar, we read: 'This is one of that class of German publications which always causes a sigh for the study of history in England.'[31]

The pupil's respect on the one side corresponded to the master's criticism and censure on the other. For example, James Anthony Froude's extremely popular *History of*

---

[26] *HZ* 59 (1888), 116: 'Droysen's outline, which is so much shorter, here offers a great deal much more.'
[27] J. R. Seeley, *Lectures and Essays* (London, 1870), 235; *EHR* 3 (1888), 298.
[28] *EHR* 1 (1886), 42.
[29] Stubbs, 'On the Present State', 43, 45, 60.   [30] Ibid. 87, 90.
[31] *EHR* 7 (1892), 561.

England from the Fall of Wolsey to the Death of Elizabeth was relentlessly and repeatedly critized on the publication of each new volume. 'A book of this sort is not history, and the author is not a historian', the reviewer concluded in the first issue of the *HZ*. In volume 20, Maurenbrecher claimed: 'Yet Froude has still not achieved a reliable and real critical method', and three years later Pauli observed 'that he certainly lacks the seriousness of a true historian'.[32] This was severe and to a certain extent unfair criticism of one of Ranke's most ardent followers among British historians, of a scholar who had toiled relentlessly in the Spanish archives of Simancas, and had also consulted the dispatches kept in Vienna, Paris, and Brussels. But such comments, bordering on condescension or arrogance, were often mixed with appreciation or even praise, expressed in the reviewers' knowledge of their own shortcomings. Though Froude may have been careless in handling his sources, his narrative powers and his style were highly appreciated.[33] German historians were conscious of their scholarship, their erudition, and their mastery of the sources, but at the same time they were aware that most of them could not attract a wide readership. Here their British colleagues were the unrivalled champions. 'Gibbon started it, and from then on until far into our own century the Continent has satisfied its need for readable history books by turning to England.'[34] That is why the rare books by British historians on subjects drawn from German history, such as Seeley's *Life and Times of Stein*, were judged to be 'popular in the best sense of the word'. And it was pointed out that 'we lack such books in Germany. Our authors either aspire to the highest, with greater or lesser success, or they are themselves rather limited thinkers and superficial workers with at most a certain formal skill in writing. Thus those who find Droysen and Treitschke too

---

[32] 'Ein solches Buch ist keine Geschichte und der Schreiber kein Historiker.' *HZ* 1 (1859), 563; 'Doch ist Froude immer noch nicht zu einer sicheren, eigentlich kritischen Methode gelangt.' *HZ* 20 (1868), 220; 'daß er den Ernst des wahren Historikers gar nicht besitzt.' *HZ* 25 (1871), 193.

[33] Pauli in *HZ* 3 (1860), 98.

[34] 'Gibbon eröffnet den Reigen, und von da ab hat der Continent bis tief in unser Jahrhundert seinen Bedarf an lesbaren Geschichtsbüchern aus England bezogen.' *HZ* 30 (1873), 152.

demanding have to be satisfied with Beitzke and Eberty. The result is that for years, the most widespread biography of Goethe in Germany has been that by the Englishman Lewes. And similarly popular here are Carlyle's biography of Frederick the Great, Sime's biography of Lessing, and now Seeley's biography of Stein. The value of these books is very different, and even if it varies in inverse proportion to their popularity, this phenomenon reflects the main qualities of the two nationalities, English common sense and the German rather doctrinaire idealism.'[35]

Critical insights like this into specific national deficiencies, not so much of German historical science but German historiography, were echoed by British observations, usually taking the form of ironic comments on 'the familiar type of the German scholar ... who complained that the public library allowed him only 13 hours a day to read, the man who spent 30 years on one volume'.[36] Thus the reviewer of Ranke's English translation of his *English History* recommended to the reader that 'the best way to parry the terrifying effect produced by 6 volumes of closely packed type' was to concentrate on certain chapters only.[37]

But the same reviewer raised a point which sprang from a more fundamental difference between German and English historiography, one which was duly registered on both sides. Ranke was accused of advancing a general misconception of the seventeenth-century English Revolution, with the result that 'the England of our historian is singularly unlike the

---

[35] 'im besten Sinne des Wortes populär.' 'Solche Bücher fehlen uns in Deutschland. Unsere Autoren streben entweder mit mehr oder weniger Erfolg nach dem Höchsten, oder es sind selbst beschränkte Köpfe und oberflächliche Arbeiter, höchstens mit einem gewissen formalen Schreibtalent. So kommt es, daß man den, dem Droysen und Treitschke zu hoch sind, bei Beitzke und Eberty belassen muß. Das Resultat ist, daß in Deutschland lange Jahre hindurch die verbreitetste Biographie Goethes diejenige von dem Engländer Lewes war, und ihr schließen sich an: Friedrich der Große von Carlyle, Lessing von Sime und jetzt Stein von Seeley. Ist der Wert dieser Bücher auch ein sehr verschiedener und steht derselbe auch vielleicht in umgekehrtem Verhältnis zu ihrer Verbreitung, so ist die Erscheinung doch ein Reflex hervorragender Eigenschaften beider Nationalitäten, des englischen common sense und des deutschen etwas doktrinären Idealismus.' *HZ* 43 (1880), 329, 331.
[36] Lord Acton, 'German Schools of History', *EHR* 1 (1886), 14.
[37] *Athenaeum* (1875), 285.

England with which we fancy we are acquainted. The Parliament he has before his eyes never sat at Westminster.'[38] Of course, the reviewer's anger about 'so contemptible a narrative' was provoked by Ranke's calm and detached judgements on seventeenth-century party strife in general, and on the royalist position in particular.[39] But it was also the result of an attitude which allowed the reviewer to assert the importance of specific characteristics of English historiography.

Although English historians acknowledged the leading position of German historical science in the field of methodology, techniques, and the organization of historical research, this does not imply that they also accepted the tenets and principles of German historiography. The attitudes of Stubbs and Freeman illustrate this difference. Whereas Stubbs, as already shown, was prepared to follow the German example in establishing a scientific community of the historians of all nations, Freeman vehemently defended the traditional practice of English historiography against any guidelines prescribed by the German model. In a well-known passage in his *Methods of Historical Study*, he turned against

> the fashionable idolatry of the last German book. One has sometimes heard the question 'Have you read the last German book?' ... the only grievance is that one has to read from one end to the other to find out what the points are ... I only demand the right to keep our independence, and to believe that on many matters of historical learning an Englishman ... is better fitted to judge than a German. A Swiss or Norwegian may judge of the workings of free constitutions in old Greece, in Italy, in any other land, because he, like the Englishman, has a daily experience of their working in his own land. But these things are mysteries to German professors, because they are mysteries to German statesmen also. The German scholar simply reads in a book of things which we are always looking at and acting in. He therefore utterly fails to understand many things at Athens or Rome ... which come to us like our ABC.

---

[38] Ibid.
[39] Cf. *HZ* 17 (1867), 106: 'Ranke demonstrated that the majority of Tories in the seventeenth century, although so roundly denounced ... were as good parliamentarians, and as loyal to the constitution, as Stanley and Disraeli are today.'

This applied even to Mommsen, 'the greatest scholar of our times', who also lacked 'the moral insight which is born with a man, the political insight which is gained only by living in communities of freemen ... That the weak can have any rights against the strong never enters the mind of one who has had in his own person some experience of the rule of blood and iron.'[40]

The German reviewer Walther Schultze, who, apart from some criticism of Freeman's methodological expositions, praised 'the book which is, on the whole, excellent', registered these fundamental assertions with irritation and lack of comprehension. 'Should one be surprised or annoyed by the assertion, born of true English arrogance, that German historians will never be able to appreciate the free states of Greece and Italy properly, in the same way as English, Swiss, or Norwegian scholars, because they lack practical political experience of what they write about? What can we say?'[41]

Others, like Heinrich Nissen in his review of Freeman's *Historical Essays*, knew what to say. They recognized this difference as the result of different political cultures defining the political role of historical science. Nissen pointed to the indisputable fact that the 'divergent living conditions and destinies of the English and German people have occasionally sent the development of their respective historiographies down different paths'.[42] In England, where a powerful state based on a free constitution allowed a national political historiography to flourish, the truth of Matthew Arnold's dictum could be observed 'that the history of Greece and Rome is not an idle inquiry about remote ages and forgotten institutions, but a living picture of things present, fitted not so much for the curiosity of the

---

[40] E. A. Freeman, *The Methods of Historical Study* (London, 1886), 288–92.

[41] 'das im ganzen treffliche Buch.' 'Soll man sich wundern oder ärgern über die von echtem englischen Hochmut zeugende Behauptung, daß der deutsche Historiker die Freistaaten in Griechenland und Italien nie in gleicher Weise werde richtig würdigen können, wie der englische, schweizerische, norwegische, weil ihm die praktische politische Erfahrung letzterer abgehe? Was soll man dazu sagen?' *HZ* 59 (1888), 118 f.

[42] 'daß die abweichenden Lebensbedingungen und Schicksale des englischen und deutschen Volkes der Entwicklung der Historiographie hier und dort eine andere Bahn gewiesen haben.' *HZ* 30 (1873), 151.

scholar, as the instruction of the statesman and citizen'. And the reviewer added: 'We recognize that this point of view, which dominated England's classical studies in the past, and still does so today, is fully justified. With us it retreats into the background.'[43] Though German historians were convinced that 'the utilitarian trend ... in England ... prevents research from attaining the extent and level achieved on the Continent',[44] many felt and lamented the lack of this kind of popular national historiography in their own country, especially during the period before the foundation of the German Empire.

In conclusion, this essay returns to the obvious interest of German academics in English historical writing, and the way in which Macaulay's achievement impressed them. In addition to Häusser's essay in the first volume of the *HZ* there were articles by Rudolf Haym in the *Preussische Jahrbücher* in 1860 and by von Noorden 1867 in the *HZ*, this time to mark the publication of the final volumes of Ranke's *Englische Geschichte*.

This interest was to a considerable extent the historians' reaction to Macaulay's immense popularity in Germany, where soon every politician felt obliged to quote him.[45] Harsh criticism, especially after Macaulay had dared frivolously to tarnish the shining image of Frederick the Great, was often mixed with admiration for the historian who could reach and impress a huge audience. Accomplishing this mission, which German historians so far had not been able to fulfil, was seen as an essential part of the public role of the politically minded historian writing national history. At least this was the position of Rudolf Haym when he set German profundity against British pragmatism by contrasting Wilhelm von Humboldt's famous essay on the task of the

---

[43] 'Wir erkennen die volle Berechtigung dieses Standpunktes an, der die classischen Studien Englands beherrscht hat und beherrscht. Bei uns tritt derselbe in den Hintergrund.' Ibid. 157.
[44] 'die utilitarische Tendenz ... in England ... es der Forschung verwehrt, sich zu dem Umfang und der Höhe zu erheben, welche dem Festland eignet.' Ibid. 155.
[45] R. Haym, *Preußische Jahrbücher*, 6 (1860), 353: 'it was not long before the influences of British historiographical and stylistic methods were noticeable in our own literature; not long before a superfluity of quotations from Macaulay was to be found everywhere, in parliamentary speeches, and in historical and political works.'

historian with Macaulay's article on the theory of historiography, written in 1828.

While Humboldt's theory is more profound and more correct, Macaulay's theory surpasses it in terms of technical utility.... As the most human of the sciences, history is there for everyone. It shares this quality with the Bible and the law. Above all, at present historiography has the task of continuing the human and national education which our classical writers began. And for this purpose Macaulay is not a bad leader... There is much to be learned from him. Our historiography will, with even greater justification, be able to pride itself on its intellectual content and its deeper insights into the essence of the historical process drawn from German philosophy when, orientating itself by the Englishman's healthy understanding, it has purged the tendency, which has the same source, to construct and arrange—in a word, its unhealthy idealism.

But an important qualification must be added: 'Of course, this will only be fully possible when we have our own history, whose result in the form of a state fills us with as much satisfaction and justified pride as the British feel in their constitution, which is the result of a development the foundation for which was laid by the hero of Macaulay's history.'[46] Ten years later the German nation-state had been established and soon Treitschke would play the role of the German

---

[46] 'Um soviel die Humboldt'sche Theorie tiefsinniger und richtiger ist, um soviel wird sie an technischer Brauchbarkeit von der des Engländers übertroffen ... Geschichte ist gerade diejenige Wissenschaft, die, als die menschlichste Wissenschaft, am meisten für Alle ist. Das hat sie mit der Bibel und der Gesetzgebung gemein. Die Geschichtsschreibung vor allem ist berufen, gegenwärtig das Werk humaner und nationaler Bildung unter uns fortzusetzen, das unsere klassischen Dichter begonnen haben. Und zu diesen Zweck ist Macaulay kein übler Führer ... es gibt sehr viel, was wir von ihm lernen können. Unsere Geschichtsschreibung wird sich mit noch größerem Recht ihres geistigen Gehalts, ihrer aus der deutschen Philosophie stammenden tieferen Einsicht in das Wesen des historischen Prozesses rühmen dürfen, wenn sie ihre, gleichfalls von dort her stammende Neigung zum Konstruieren und Arrangieren, ihren ungesunden Idealismus, mit einem Worte, an dem gesunden Verstande des Engländers läutert.' 'Mit vollem Erfolg freilich wird dies erst dann möglich sein, wenn wir selbst eine Geschichte haben werden, deren staatliches Ergebnis uns mit ebenso viel Befriedigung und mit ebenso gerechtem Stolze erfüllt, wie den Briten seine Verfassung, das Ergebnis der Entwicklung, zu welcher der Held der Macaulay'schen Geschichte den bedeutsamen Grund gelegt hat.' Ibid. 385, 396.

Macaulay,[47] doing to English history even more of what Macaulay had done to the history of Frederick of Prussia. But this takes us back to the birth of national historiography in Germany, and thus to a story which has already been told by the second essay in this volume. In some respects, it could be illustrated by taking a closer look at the views of the reviewers.

[47] Ward on Treitschke's *Deutsche Geschichte*, iii. in *EHR* I (1886), 813: 'The historian of modern Germany having ... more in him of the training of the Zunftprofessor than was accessible to his English prototype and having issued forth from a school of historians the secret of whose triumph he rightly himself finds in their complete command of their material, in my opinion surpasses Macaulay where Macaulay is strongest.'

10
Historicism and the 'Noble Science of Politics' in Nineteenth-Century Germany

GANGOLF HÜBINGER

For Britain, Stefan Collini, Donald Winch, and John Burrow have written a fascinating study which borrows from Macaulay the title *That Noble Science of Politics*, demonstrating how political thinking became institutionalized as a discipline from the end of the eighteenth century.[1] No comparable study exists for Germany. The impression there is that the science of politics was an invention of the twentieth century, dating from the establishment of the *Hochschule für Politik* in Berlin after the First World War, or the setting up of university chairs in the subject after the Second World War. If a book were to be written about the genesis of political science in Germany, its focus would not be on political economy, as is the case for Britain, but on history. This essay is about the great significance of historicism for the 'scientific' analysis of political action and political systems. The most precise definition of 'historicism' was given by Ernst Troeltsch, theologian and cultural philosopher and a close friend of Max Weber's, in his great work *Der Historismus und seine Probleme*. The term 'historicism' is to be understood as a 'fundamental historicization of all our thinking about mankind, its culture, and values'.[2] The two most important categories of this thinking are 'individuality' and 'development'. 'History to some extent excuses deeply rooted evils by

Trans. Angela Davies, GHIL.

[1] Stefan Collini, Donald Winch, and John Burrow, *That Noble Science of Politics: A Study in Nineteenth-Century Intellectual History* (Cambridge, 1983).
[2] Ernst Troeltsch, *Der Historismus und seine Probleme* (*Gesammelte Schriften*, iii; reprinted Aalen, 1977), 102.

referring to their origins: their cure can be borrowed only from the provisions of the science of politics, which has come into being in our times.'[3]

In what form and to what extent did historicism lead to an institutionalization of the study of politics and ideas of political order? In the age of historicism, how did the content of what Leopold Ranke in his Berlin inaugural lecture of 1836 called the new science of politics, 'which has come into being in our times', differ from the theories of the political wisdom of the state in the eighteenth century? The subject of this essay, therefore, is not the ideological interpenetration of history and politics, which Ranke criticized adequately in his inaugural lecture, and to which Georg Iggers devoted central aspects of his study *The German Conception of History* of 1968.[4] Nor does this essay present the one-dimensional, proverbial apotheosis of the state that Johann Gustav Droysen put into practice, and which provoked Wolfgang J. Mommsen in 1971 to call for a 'historiography beyond historicism'.[5]

The theory and practice of historicism are concerned with the wider question of the adequate attributions of cultural development and political form. This means, for example, that Germany's cultural development is quite different from that of France. The political results of the French Revolution cannot, by any means, be applied to Germany. Germany's 'natural form', most historians argued, remained the monarchy. For them, states were independent 'individuals'. Two rival methods of doing this were tested and defined in theoretical terms during the nineteenth century. The 'individualizing' method shielded national cultural identity from positivist generalizations. Recent scholarship sees it, along with Droysen's famous criticism of Buckle's *History of*

[3] L. Ranke, 'Über die Verwandtschaft und den Unterschied der Historie und der Politik: Eine Rede zum Antritt der ordentlichen Professur an der Universität zu Berlin im Jahre 1836', in *Sämmtliche Werke* (Leipzig, 1867–90), xxiv. 280–93, quotation on 282.

[4] G. G. Iggers, *The German Conception of History: The National Tradition of Historical Thought from Herder to the Present* (Middletown, Conn., 1968; German edn. 1971).

[5] W. J. Mommsen, *Die Geschichtswissenschaft jenseits des Historismus* (Düsseldorf, 1971).

Civilisation in England, as an exemplary method of defining historicism as such.[6] But comparative, generalizing methods which tried to find laws and argued by analogy were also highly influential in the nineteenth century. They are more important than the history of historiography has so far assumed.[7] The older scholarship refers to these methods here and there. Thus Walter Bußmann's verdict on Wilhelm Roscher's linkage of history, economics, and politics is that 'the unique is less sought after than the recurring; the incalculable and the coincidental aspects of history are less attractive than those governed by laws and analogy.' He obviously considers Roscher a good example of a historicist,[8] whereas at present he is regarded as belonging merely to a 'sidestream of historicism'.[9] The tensions and contradictions between individualizing and generalizing historicism are especially clearly expressed in Roscher's theories of economics and politics relating to his own times. Roscher also represents the end of an impressive tradition of political lectures on historicism, and will therefore be dealt with in greater detail at the end of this essay.

1. Interdisciplinary Problems and Configurations

Nineteenth-century historians, more even than political economists, saw political science as having a firm place in research and academic teaching. Heinrich Luden (1778–1847), Friedrich Christoph Dahlmann (1785–1860), Georg Gottfried Gervinus (1805–71), Johann Gustav Droysen (1808–86), Heinrich von Sybel (1817–95), Georg Waitz (1813–86), Heinrich von Treitschke (1834–96), Wilhelm Roscher (1817–94), and Otto Hintze (1861–1940) are the most prominent examples. This somewhat puzzling cluster has

---

[6] This is the interpretation put forward by F. Jaeger and J. Rüsen, *Geschichte des Historismus* (Munich, 1992), 141.

[7] Cf. the first systematic collection of evidence in E. Fuchs, *Henry Thomas Buckle: Geschichtsschreibung und Positivismus in England und Deutschland* (Leipzig, 1994).

[8] Roscher's generalizing method is emphasized by W. Bußmann, *Treitschke: Sein Welt- und Geschichtsbild* (2nd edn., Göttingen, 1981; 1st edn. 1952), 194; still important is G. Eisermann, *Die Grundlagen des Historismus in der deutschen Nationalökonomie* (Stuttgart, 1956), esp. 132 f.

[9] Jaeger and Rüsen, *Geschichte des Historismus*, 122.

never been systematically investigated. On the contrary, present-day political science sees the history of its own discipline in the nineteenth century as the story of loss and decline by comparison with the political philosophy of the seventeenth and eighteenth centuries. Hans Maier was particularly clear in this respect. In 1985 he succinctly restated the argument he first put in his great study of German political and constitutional science. With the advent of 'historicism and positivism', he said, political science 'forfeited its character as a fundamental discipline' and became 'a mere component of positivist subjects'. And 'as these subjects became more and more independent, political science increasingly disappeared'. 'The lack of social-ethical points of view' caused this disintegration, 'because sociological research without an image of the "social body" threatens increasingly to lose itself in the *l'art pour l'art* of formal academic activity'.[10] In his entry under 'Politics' in the *Historisches Wörterbuch der Philosophie* Ernst Vollrath puts this argument even more strongly. 'Old political science', he writes, as a practical science, had been unjustifiably criticized by the philosophy of German idealism.[11] Vollrath and Maier mention only in passing that the tradition of integrated politics lectures survived in the professionalized subject of history. They put down this development, 'deriving from Kant',[12] merely as intellectual impoverishment. They do not, however, see it as a creative reformulation of problems in response to the far-reaching changes caused by the industrial and political revolutions in

---

[10] H. Maier, *Politik und Staatswissenschaft an den deutschen Universitäten* (Passau, 1985), 3, 31, 34. Reprinted in id., *Politische Wissenschaft in Deutschland: Lehre und Wirkung* (Munich, 1985); as a basis cf. id., *Die ältere deutsche Staats- und Verwaltungslehre* (Neuwied, 1966; reprinted Munich, 1986).

[11] Joachim Ritter and Karlfried Gründer (eds.), *Historisches Wörterbuch der Philosophie* (Darmstadt, 1989), vii. 1061.

[12] Cf. H. Maier, 'Akademische Politik- und Staatswissenschaft in Heidelberg: Von den Anfängen bis zu Max Weber', in *Die Geschichte der Universität Heidelberg: Vorträge im Wintersemester 1985/86* (Heidelberg, 1986), 129–56, here 132: 'After all, the trio of ethics-economic-politics was a fixed component of academic teaching for four hundred years; it was not until the upheaval in the teaching of philosophy that, originating with Kant, took place at the turn of the eighteenth to the nineteenth century, that the Aristotelian tradition was finally banished from the German universities.'

England and France, which also produced a new order within political knowledge, and changed the relations of academic disciplines to each other.

If we take an interdisciplinary instead of a purely disciplinary perspective, it quickly becomes clear that the period of historicism was not one in which there was a neat, sterile distinction between ethics, political economy, political science, and history. Historicism, as defined by Ernst Troeltsch and quoted above, as a 'fundamental historicization of all our thinking about mankind, its culture, and values',[13] by no means reduced 'the presentation of political science' to a mere component. After all, the point of historicism was that it offered an 'interpretative framework for historical research as an ethic of political action' on the basis of verified sources, cutting across all ideological camps.[14] A long tradition was built up from August Ludwig Schlözer (1735–1809), Professor of History and Political Science at the University of Göttingen in the late Enlightenment, to Otto Hintze, Professor of Constitutional, Administrative, and Economic History and Politics at the University of Berlin. The titles of these chairs were not merely names; they described an interdisciplinary programme whose influence increased throughout the nineteenth century. Historians, economists, and political scientists all saw their task as comparative research on an empirical basis using the 'historical method', giving economics its due place, and confirming that politics held the key to the system of the human sciences. At the beginning of his *Grundriß zu Vorlesungen über die Staatswirthschaft*, Wilhelm Roscher explicitly made this connection: 'Political economy is not . . . the art of becoming rich, but it is a political science which rests upon judging and ruling people. Our aim is to describe what peoples thought in economic terms, what they wanted and felt, what they aspired to and achieved, and why. Such an account is possible only in the closest co-operation with the other disciplines which relate to the lives of peoples—in particular

---

[13] Troeltsch, *Historismus*, 102.
[14] J. Rüsen, *Konfigurationen des Historismus: Studien zur deutschen Wissenschaftskultur* (Frankfurt am Main, 1993), 160.

legal history, the history of the state, and cultural history.'[15] The following essay concentrates on three aspects of the age-old question addressed by political science, namely, how people rule and how they are ruled. First, the conclusions to be drawn from the revolutions of 1789 and 1830 are examined. Secondly, experiments in the 'bourgeois laboratory' (Pierangelo Schiera) between 1840 and 1871 are discussed. And finally, the type of historicism that Wilhelm Roscher created by combining the disciplines of history, economics, and politics is examined by way of a conclusion.

2. *The Impact of Revolutions: Politics on a Historical Basis 1800–1840*

A contemporary moral precept of 1789, 'historians, be worthy of your times',[16] assumes that historians are intellectually capable of diagnosing their own times. Historians as political analysts should be able to place breaks with tradition into a new relationship with a commitment to tradition, to explain changes in the legitimacy of political rule, and to see new social groups such as the people and the bourgeoisie as political actors.[17] August Ludwig Schlözer and Heinrich Luden, each in his own way, achieved considerable public success in Germany. Schlözer's attempt to systematize political knowledge is entitled *Statsgelahrtheit* (1793 and 1804).[18] The published key to his lectures can be regarded as a landmark in the history of the discipline. With their tripartite division of the concept of politics, Schlözer and his colleague

---

[15] W. Roscher, *Grundriß zu Vorlesungen über die Staatswirthschaft: Nach geschichtlicher Methode* (Göttingen, 1843), p. iv.

[16] Cf. E. Schulin, ' "Historiker, seid der Epoche würdig!": Zur Geschichtsschreibung im Zeitalter der Französischen Revolution—zwischen Aufklärung und Historismus', *Tel Aviver Jahrbuch für deutsche Geschichte*, 18 (1989), 1–28. For the quotation by the journalist Duval see n. 1 of Schulin.

[17] Ibid. 6; for the boost given to scholarship by the 1789 revolution cf. also U. Muhlack, *Geschichtswissenschaft im Humanismus und in der Aufklärung: Die Vorgeschichte des Historismus* (Munich, 1991), 416–18.

[18] A. L. von Schlözer, *StatsGelahrtheit nach ihren HauptTheilen im Auszug und Zusammenhang*, pt. 1: *Einleitung, Encyklopädie, Metapolitik, Statsrecht und von RegirungsFormen. Allg. StatsRecht u. StatsVerfassungsLere* (Göttingen, 1793); pt. 2: *Allgemeine Statistik. Theorie der Statistik. Nebst Ideen über das Studium der Politik überhaupt* (Göttingen, 1804).

at Göttingen, Ludwig Timotheus Spittler,[19] provided the framework for a redefinition of the subject in the nineteenth century. According to their scheme, 'metapolitics' explains the anthropological foundations of 'societas civilis sine imperio' and demands that 'civil society and the state must be investigated separately from each other'. 'Politics as the doctrine of state intelligence against other states' relates to the historical-empirical dynamic of the European system of states.[20] And finally, 'true politics', as the 'science of the best institutions of the state', relates to the level of civilization and education of its citizens. This tripartite division into political anthropology, international relations, and the theory of constitutions and systems of government has, in principle, been maintained to the present day in the designations of university chairs and their subjects. With reference to Aristotle, Schlözer suggested that political knowledge could defuse political conflicts: 'Political knowledge is a tried and true protection against an obsession with projects and revolution. It transforms malcontents into peaceful, willing, and grateful citizens.'[21]

Heinrich Luden, celebrated Jena historian of the Napoleonic wars and student fraternities, took up this thread in his *Handbuch der Staatsweisheit oder der Politik* of 1811. In a complicated paragraph he summed up why historians were destined to be teachers of politics:

Politics as a discipline ... therefore has the following task: to investigate what the ruler in a given state should do in order to guarantee the independence and security of the whole state without the citizens thereby giving up the reasons for which they entered the state in the first place. Further, once the security of the whole is ensured, politics must investigate how conditions within the state can be balanced with the individual aspirations of people, which change according to the level of culture, in such a way that these aspirations do not make the dissolution of the said conditions

---

[19] Cf. also M. Behnen, 'Statistik, Politik und Staatengeschichte von Spittler bis Heeren', in H. Boockmann and H. Wellenreuther (eds.), *Geschichtswissenschaft in Göttingen* (Göttingen, 1987), 76–101.

[20] Spittler emphasizes this more strongly than Schlözer. L. T. Spittler, *Vorlesungen über Politik*, ed. K. Wächter (Stuttgart, 1828), lectures given at the University of Göttingen in the summer semester of 1796, pt. 1: *Begriff der Politik*, 1–7.

[21] Schlözer, *StatsGelahrtheit*, pt. 1, 4.

necessary, or what can be done to make it possible for everyone freely to live life to the full.[22]

Schlözer was reacting to the events of 1789. That is why his writings are permeated by the concerns of an enlightened citizen of the world, as well as by an anti-revolutionary appeal for reconciliation between prince and people for the sake of the common good: 'Princes will remain princes and all Germans will become free.'[23] His student Luden was reacting to the events of 1806 and the defeat by Napoleon. That is why he emphasized national independence as opposed to Napoleonic rule, yet not without criticizing the absolutist regime of the Prussian kings. Yet Schlözer and Luden shared an early historicist methodology based on the conviction that the type of constitution appropriate to each nation could be deduced from a comparative study of the history of states and cultural history (which in Schlözer's case explicitly included economic and social history). This sort of political science was intended historically to reduce the universalism of the French Revolution. It also provided the basic theme of what was to be the central demand for political reform in the *Vormärz*: national unity, conditional upon gaining civil liberties. More stringently than Luden, Schlözer's *Politik* aimed for the professionalization of the civil service. In the old cameralist tradition, Schlözer advocated an élitist bureaucratic constitutionalism of the sort that was to dominate the constitutional thinking of most liberals until the revolution of 1848.

Political science in Germany received its most important boost in 1830, the year of European revolutions. The *Staatslexikon* by Karl von Rotteck and Karl Theodor Welcker (1834),[24] Friedrich Christoph Dahlmann's *Politik* (1835),[25]

---

[22] H. Luden, *Handbuch der Staatsweisheit oder der Politik: Ein wissenschaftlicher Versuch* (Jena, 1811), here para. 16, 37 f.
[23] *StatsAnzeigen*, 16 (1791), 96. Quoted from C. Dipper, *Deutsche Geschichte 1648–1789* (Frankfurt am Main, 1991), 314.
[24] *Das Staats-Lexikon: Encyklopädie der sämmtlichen Staatswissenschaften für alle Stände. In Verbindung mit vielen der angesehensten Publicisten Deutschlands herausgegeben von Carl von Rotteck und Carl Welcker*, 15 vols. (Altona, 1834–43), 4 supplementary vols. (1846–8).
[25] F. C. Dahlmann, *Die Politik, auf den Grund und das Maß der gegebenen Zustände zurückgeführt* (Göttingen, 1835). Quotations taken from the new edn., introd. Manfred Riedel (Frankfurt am Main, 1968).

Georg Gottfried Gervinus's review article arguing for systematic 'politics' (1836),[26] and Ranke's inaugural lecture (1836), mentioned above, were all linked in a direct and stimulating nexus. Liberal historians valued the *Staatslexikon* as a political code for citizens, but decisively rejected the claim that it fulfilled the functions of a 'legal or political science'. For Rotteck, 'ideal politics' were derived directly from the law of reason, not from 'historically justified conditions'.[27] This would have conflicted too strongly with the methodological awareness which was also developing among liberals. Even Dahlmann's *Politik, auf den Grund und das Maß der gegebenen Zustände zurückgeführt*, whose title claims to offer a genetic explanation, is still caught between the Enlightenment and historicism. In some respects, he adheres more strictly to Aristotelian thinking about the state than Schlözer, his predecessor at Göttingen. Dahlmann starts his book by claiming that the state is a manifestation of 'original order', 'an invention neither of art nor necessity; it is not a limited company, a machine, or the result of a contract arising out of a state of nature which has been freely given up.'[28] Manfred Riedel, the only scholar to have investigated, in his classic essay of 1963, the context of historiography as the institutional seat of political science,[29] sees the 'pre-revolutionary' resort to Aristotle as responsible for Dahlmann's inadequate treatment of contemporary political phenomena. Riedel's criticism is

---

[26] G. G. Gervinus, 'Über Dahlmann's Politik', in *Blätter für literarische Unterhaltung* (Leipzig, 1836), here quoted from the reprint in id., *Gesammelte kleine historische Schriften* (Karlsruhe, 1838), 593–618.

[27] 'Philosophical jurisprudence was the true bride of my youth. I heartily devoted myself to history as her noble friend, but she never jealously demanded that I should be unfaithful to the bride of my youth.' Karl von Rotteck, 'Über den Streit natürlicher Rechtsprinzipien oder idealer Politik mit historisch begründeten Verhältnissen: Eine öffentliche Antrittsrede, gehalten bei Uebernahme des akademischen Lehramts des Vernunftrechts und der Staatswissenschaften (1818)', in id., *Sammlung kleinerer Schriften, meist historischen oder politischen Inhalts*, ii (Stuttgart, 1829), 42–70, quotation on 43.

[28] Dahlmann, *Politik*, 37.

[29] M. Riedel, 'Der Staatsbegriff der deutschen Geschichtsschreibung des 19. Jahrhunderts in seinem Verhältnis zur klassisch-politischen Philosophie', *Der Staat*, 2 (1963), 41–63.

partly correct. Yet it takes too little account of the fact that the Aristotelian classification of constitutional change could be used in a highly flexible way, and could be combined with revolutionary experience. Thus Dahlmann did not ignore growing industrialization and pauperism. Rather, in a way that was critical of contemporary issues he continued, as he put it, to cultivate the soil of politics made arable by Aristotle. Methodologically, Dahlmann's work was developing into a comparative constitutional theory. In practical terms, it gave the Prussian reformers a justification for holding up England as a model. Everywhere in Europe, where an 'increasingly uniform middle class provided the core of the population' and 'was replacing the aristocracy as the focal point of the state', a 'good' constitution, he suggested, was a mixed constitution, providing for a hereditary monarchy and a bicameral parliament. Dahlmann's history lesson on England was provocative for the German Confederation, although on a crucial point it accepted the German state tradition of a welfare bureaucracy—because for Dahlmann, a 'good' constitution largely meant good administration.[30] It did not mean free, co-operative self-government, which Rudolf von Gneist and Otto von Gierke later elevated into a constitutional principle opposed to that of monarchical rule.

Georg Gottfried Gervinus, a protégé of Dahlmann's who was appointed to the chair of History and Literature at the University of Göttingen in 1835, became a fierce theoretical critic of this concept. 'Über Dahlmann's Politik' is less a review than a programme with which Gervinus intended to follow the tradition of the Göttingen lectures in politics, but also to break with it to some extent.[31] For him, the task of the new discipline of politics, building on a universal historical foundation, was to 'pick the laws and the general out of the immense sum of fleeting historical phenomena, to explain the state in terms of the states, to set up a political system

---

[30] For Ranke, too, 'political science, whether an art or a science, was state administration'; see Ranke, 'Über die Verwandtschaft', 285.

[31] On this complex see R. von Thadden, 'Georg Gottfried Gervinus und Friedrich Christoph Dahlmann', in Boockmann and Wellenreuther (eds.), *Geschichtswissenschaft in Göttingen*, 186–203.

that will be tantamount to a history of the state, and provide the necessary foundation for a philosophy of history.'[32] Thus instead of individualized understanding, he advocated generalized explanation; he sought the laws of history by drawing analogies, a method which 'classical' historicism rejected. In theoretical terms, and later in practice, with his evolutionary *Einleitung in die Geschichte des 19. Jahrhunderts*, Gervinus was closer to Henry Thomas Buckle than to Droysen.[33] In it, Gervinus surveyed all the stages of rule in the history of European-American civilization. It therefore comes as no surprise that Droysen noted critically that Gervinus had written no more than an 'encyclopaedia of political studies'.[34] Gervinus, in turn, railed against Hegelian idealism, and embedded political theory in an alternative tradition: 'For the laws of the main side of history, the state-based, political side ... Aristotle and Machiavelli, whom both Vico and Hegel failed to consult, are still the only useful guides.'[35]

Dahlmann and Gervinus developed their political theories in the context of a structural historical comparison which took account of the forces driving the European revolutions of 1789 and 1830 in order to increase the political activity of German society.[36] Ranke, by contrast, in his inaugural lecture in Berlin, insisted that there was a logical difference between perceiving the world (*Welterkenntnis*) and actively trying to change it. He distanced himself from the new discipline's insistence that it could 'improve the states, or cast them into new forms'. In his view, the claims of the

[32] Gervinus, 'Über Dahlmann's Politik', 595. The methods of comparing, of identifying typical constant structures, of systematizing, and generalizing were so important to Gervinus that he repeated this passage almost literally in his autobiography. See *G. G. Gervinus Leben: Von ihm selbst. 1860*, ed. J. Keller (Leipzig, 1893), 298. In distinction to Droysen's 'forschendem Verstehen', therefore, Gervinus's method could be described as 'forschendes Erklären'.
[33] This is explained in greater detail in G. Hübinger, *Georg Gottfried Gervinus: Historisches Urteil und politische Kritik* (Göttingen, 1984).
[34] J. G. Droysen, *Historik*, ed. Peter Leyh (Stuttgart, 1977), 278.
[35] *G. G. Gervinus Leben*, 281.
[36] The final chapter of Dahlmann's 'Vorlesung über Geschichte der Politik', lectures held in the winter semester of 1851/2, discusses the 'struggle of representative constitutions with theories of revolution and absolutism'. Notes taken by Alfred von Gutschmid, in private ownership.

new discipline of politics to be a science were limited by the freedom of action which statesmen needed.[37]

3. *Power, Freedom,* Bürgerlichkeit: *Builders of Political Modernity 1840–1871*

At no time was the science of politics on which historians were working limited by the academic restraint called for by Ranke. Nor was it exploited, as he feared it would be, by the party-political camps which were separating out from each other more and more strongly in the 1840s. On the contrary, conceptual innovations and ideological impregnations entered a complex reciprocal relationship which is clearly illustrated by Gervinus. In Heidelberg, in the academic year 1846/7, he gave a series of lectures about politics on a historical foundation to a mixed audience of students as well as non-academics. His lectures were much more empirical and practical than his criticism of Dahlmann had led his listeners to expect.

Gervinus gave a broad account of classical political theory in Aristotle and Machiavelli. This was followed by a detailed analysis of changes in the political system in recent Prussian history, couched in the relevant Aristotelian terms relating to constitutional change and Machiavellian categories relating to the politics of a constitutional-monarchical order based on power. He analysed a series of changes from the bureaucratic, interventionist welfare state in the final years of Frederick II's reign, to the oligarchic decadence that was unleashed by his death and the legislation of the Prussian reformers, which was 'circumspect' by comparison with the French revolutionary system, to the 'absolutism, aristocracy, and orthodoxy' of the Metternich era, right up to the *juste milieu* of his present. From all this Gervinus concluded that Prussian politics were more likely to turn back to absolutism than to develop into constitutionalism.[38]

---

[37] Ranke, 'Über die Verwandtschaft', 280, cf. also 288 f.: 'Thus it is the task of history to extract the essence of the state from a number of earlier examples of it, and to explain it, whereas the task of politics is to develop the state further and complete it, after it has been understood and knowledge of it gathered.'

[38] 'Politik auf geschichtlicher Grundlage', notes taken by Ludwig Benz (University Library Heidelberg, HHs 1405, Bl. 55).

In a more structural way than comparable contemporary historians and political theorists, Gervinus in his politics lectures combined constitutional questions, power structures, industrialization, state economic policy, and the mobilization of the political public into a modernization theory *avant la lettre*. This made him the preferred academic interlocutor of the Rhenish business bourgeoisie around David Hansemann.[39] Gervinus summed up the relevant passages of his politics lectures in a memorandum about the Prussian constitution for their political reforms at the first unified Prussian *Landtag* early in 1847.[40] In it he outlined the expectations of the moderate, liberal, bourgeois opposition— increased industrialization, and the expansion of political participation into a representative constitution—without calling for a national *Sonderweg*: 'The truth is that all the states formed in recent times were not exclusively German or French, but common European ones.'[41]

In the year of European revolutions, 1848, liberal-historicist political theory had the effect of limiting revolution. Its leading exponents were Dahlmann, Droysen, and Gervinus, who were academic analysts, political theorists, and public moralists. Theoretical reflections on a harmonious balance between past and present practically demanded a political 'agreement' between prince and people, and a privileged position for monarchical-constitutional models of order as opposed to legitimistic or democratic ones. The revolution then took a different direction from that suggested by historians.

Johann Gustav Droysen planned his course of lectures on politics during the *Vormärz*, but did not actually give them in Jena until the summer of 1850. He saw them as incorporating the lessons learned during the 'very serious course in practical politics'—the failed revolution—in which he had himself just participated.[42] The essence of his course is a discursive

---

[39] Cf. R. Boch, *Grenzenloses Wachstum? Das rheinische Wirtschaftsbürgertum und seine Industrialisierungsdebatte 1814–1857* (Göttingen, 1991), esp. 220 ff.
[40] G. G. Gervinus, *Die preußische Verfassung und das Patent vom 3. Februar 1847* (Mannheim, 1847). Cf. also Hübinger, *Gervinus*, 126 ff.
[41] Gervinus, *Patent*, 79.
[42] R. Hübner, 'Joh. Gust. Droysens Vorlesungen über Politik', *Zeitschrift für Politik*, 10 (1917), 325–76, here 339.

dissection of the concept of power as a definition of politics. Politics is the 'science of the means of power available to the state and of their disintegration, of changes in power and power relations'.[43] This was not intended as pragmatic conformity with what contemporaries called *Realpolitik*. On the contrary, it conceals a grandiose, idealistic revision in which national identity, civil rights, and the history of individual liberty are conceived of as a single entity and described by the relevant cognitive rules in his *Historik*. 'The study of history, not of law, is the foundation for a political and administrative training.'[44] This is the basic tenet of the *Historik*, and while theoretically quite logical, it was not realized in the training of Prussian officials.

Gervinus worked with comparative historical categories. In particular, he used this method, of which classical historicism strongly disapproved, in his most famous work, *Einleitung in die Geschichte des neunzehnten Jahrhunderts*. In it, Gervinus ardently supported the principle of a federal state and a democratic society. No longer England, but America now provided his model for political reform. Gervinus saw world history as a political history of freedom: 'From the despotic Oriental states to the aristocratic states of Antiquity and the Middle Ages, based upon slavery and serfdom, and from there to the new states which are still in the process of being built, steady progress is to be maintained from the intellectual and civil liberty of the individual to that of the many and the majority.'[45] This introduction was followed by eight sizeable volumes which made Gervinus an outsider among German historians, both politically and methodologically. His central theme was the history of the impact of the French Revolution in

---

[43] Quoted from ibid. 354.

[44] Droysen, *Historik*, 449, 269. The discipline of politics, however, is not limited to studying the state. A thorough study of 'moral forces'—the family, work, and religion—is considered a prerequisite: 'The system of our historical disciplines, as the second part of our *Historik* must show, is quite clearly preparatory instruction in politics' (ibid. 278). For foundations in cultural anthropology cf. also F. Jaeger, *Bürgerliche Modernisierungskrise und historische Sinnbildung: Kulturgeschichte bei Droysen, Burckhardt und Max Weber* (Göttingen, 1994), 40 ff.

[45] Georg Gottfried Gervinus, *Einleitung in die Geschichte des neunzehnten Jahrhunderts* (Leipzig, 1853), 13.

Europe and South America. These volumes looked at Europe's stagnation as a result of the Congress of Vienna and the Metternich system, the Greek revolt against Ottoman rule, the export of the French Revolution to a number of South American states and its impact from there back on the Iberian Pensinsula, and, finally, the causes of the European revolutions of 1830. His *Geschichte des neunzehnten Jahrhunderts* is a comparative European contemporary history unprecedented for the times.[46] For Droysen, by contrast, 'what is now generally known as political science' must 'sharpen a state's sense of itself as an *individual* entity', and enhance its ability to pursue foreign policy in the awareness of power. 'There is nothing more absurd than trying, for example, to introduce an English-style constitution in France.'[47] Droysen saw Prussia's hegemonic policy as having an ethical quality. He regarded it as Prussia's historical mission. Droysen's historicist *Politik* gave the Protestant middle classes of the period when the Reich was founded a national identity of which their religion was a constituent part. The historical rebirth of Germany out of Prussia's moral strength provided for bureaucratic domination to increase at the expense of parliamentary rule in the internal political order. At this point Droysen's *Historik* becomes polemical. The constitutional right to put one's oar in, he said, must make way for the administration as the bearer of the idea of the state. 'It is one of the unhappiest of ideas, which is, of course, highly fashionable at the

[46] Id., *Geschichte des neunzehnten Jahrhunderts seit den Wiener Verträgen*, 8 vols. (Leipzig, 1855–66).

[47] All quotations from Droysen, *Historik*, 273; on the foreign policy implications of Droysen's teleology of the state see Wolfgang Hardtwig, 'Von Preußens Aufgabe in Deutschland zu Deutschlands Aufgabe in der Welt: Liberalismus und borussianisches Geschichtsbild zwischen Revolution und Imperialismus', in id., *Geschichtskultur und Wissenschaft* (Munich, 1990), 103–60, quotation on 125. In his theory of historical stages Gervinus, by contrast, comes to the conclusion that under industrialization, political systems will tend to merge: 'German history since the Reformation has followed the same regular course as that of England and France, except that it has proceeded more slowly. It has taken us through religious freedom (Reformation) and intellectual freedom (literary period in the previous century) to the brink of state freedom. It holds out the hope that we will achieve this too, in a way that justifies the thoroughness of the preparations.' *Einleitung in die Geschichte des neunzehnten Jahrhunderts* (Leipzig, 1st edn., 1853; 4th revised edn. 1864), 179.

moment, that freedom has suffered to the extent that the organization of power has grown.'[48]

Heinrich von Treitschke was still working in this tradition at the end of the nineteenth century. His influence on historical thinking in the German Reich was unequalled. He was part of the immediate discourse on the discipline of political science using the 'historical method' developed at the universities of Göttingen, Heidelberg, Leipzig, and Berlin. Treitschke considered himself a student of Droysen, although he had studied with Dahlmann in Bonn and Wilhelm Roscher in Leipzig. The politics lectures he gave in Freiburg and Heidelberg, and regularly in Berlin, aim beyond the epistemological goals of his predecessors, and define politics as having a threefold task: 'First, by observing the real world of states, it should attempt to recognize the basic principles of the state; then it should look historically at what people have wanted from political life, what they have created and achieved, and why; and this will allow it, thirdly, to find historical laws and to establish moral imperatives.'[49] Treitschke, however, levelled out Droysen's philosophical reflections as well as Roscher's comparative perspective on political economics. The historical law and moral imperative which he found was that, essentially, 'the state in itself is a moral power', which is why its citizens 'have to take the blame for all the mistakes that the state makes'.[50] Such reductions in Treitschke's *Politik* mark the switch from the reforming nationalism of the period when the *Reich* was founded to integral nationalism as a state cult at the turn of the century.

4. Wilhelm Roscher and the Crisis of Historicism

In 1892, at the age of 75, Wilhelm Roscher published his 700-page study, *Politik*, the labour of his old age. During the era

---

[48] Droysen, *Historik*, 358.

[49] H. von Treitschke, *Politik*, i, ed. Max Cornicelius (5th edn., Leipzig, 1922), 2 (1st edn. 1897–8, on the basis of his lecture notes). A detailed recent work on Treitschke is U. Langer, *Heinrich von Treitschke: Politische Biographie eines deutschen Nationalisten* (Düsseldorf, 1998).

[50] Ibid., chapter on 'Das Verhältnis des Staates zum Sittengesetz', 112; cf. also 11, 105.

of neo-Kantianism and at the time when the foundations of the empirical social sciences were being laid, this publication attracted a great deal of interest. As late as 1908 it went into a third edition and sold 1,200 copies. Roscher had studied mainly with Gervinus and Ranke. After completing his *Habilitation* at the University of Göttingen, he became Professor of Political Economics and in 1848 was appointed to Leipzig.

Roscher's *Politik: Geschichtliche Naturlehre der Monarchie, Aristokratie und Demokratie* counts as a masterpiece of historicist historiography.[51] It provides a universal empirical model of constitutional forms (*Naturlehre*), which are located within a developmental sequence (*Stufenlehren*). Given the instability of the industrial social order, Roscher advocated a moral-political option, the harmonizing power of the monarchical principle. Thus those features of the historicist conception of science which had been formed more by Göttingen political science than by the philosophical tradition of Humboldt and Hegel cluster in Roscher's *Politik*. We can therefore also reconstruct the boundaries which led his critics such as Georg Jellinek, Otto Hintze, and Max Weber pragmatically to redefine political science in Wilhelmine Germany.

As a 'geschichtliche Naturlehre', Roscher's *Politik* firmly renounces all constructions of 'a best state',[52] applying instead what his *Grundriß zu Vorlesungen über die Staatswirtschaft* of 1843 had already defined as 'historical method' in the political sciences: 'To study human political drives, which can be investigated only by comparing all known national groups. To extrapolate developmental laws out of what is similar in the various ways in which different national groups have developed. The work of the historian resembles that of the natural scientist.'[53] Roscher had taken this method of arguing by analogy from Gervinus and developed it further. Now he passed it on to a young student in Leipzig, Karl Lamprecht, and it entered Lamprecht's evolu-

---

[51] W. Roscher, *Politik: Geschichtliche Naturlehre der Monarchie, Aristokratie und Demokratie* (Stuttgart, 1892; 2nd edn. 1892–3; 3rd edn. 1908); record of print-runs in the Deutsches Literaturarchiv Marbach, Cotta-Archiv.
[52] Ibid. 3.   [53] Roscher, *Grundriß*, 2.

tionary and causal-genetic understanding of cultural history.[54]

Roscher, one of the founding fathers of the famous Historical School of Political Economy, turned the *economic* factor into the pivot of his analysis of the historical-political process. His works are part of the philosophy upon which the Association for Social Policy (Verein für Sozialpolitik), the most important political advisory body on economic affairs in the Kaiserreich, was founded in 1872.[55] Even Roscher's Aristotelian *Politik* integrates economic explanatory models. He saw a disintegration of civil institutions leading to the political system of Caesarism, and as a conservative, Roscher interpreted this process as a conflict, not directed by the state, between capitalist plutocracy and proletarian lack of property.[56]

In the historicism of this provenance, the old individual political sciences continued to be closely connected by the anthropological approach to 'politics'. Roscher prefaced his political *Grundriß* with a similar system of 'political sciences', and Karl Knies, like Roscher one of the founders of the Historical School of Political Economy, also retained this perspective which had been accepted by scholars from Aristotle to de Tocqueville.[57] The historicism embodied by Roscher thus rests directly on the unity of ethics, economics, and politics. Max Weber, for example, was the first to use Roscher's concept of *Wissenschaft* to draw a methodological distinction between *Sein* and *Sollen*. In the subsequent debate on value judgements, however, Weber remained in the intellectual minority. The powerful Gustav von Schmoller and his circle launched an offensive in the old

---

[54] See Hübinger, *Gervinus*, 99 ff.; on Roscher and Lamprecht see now R. Chickering, *Karl Lamprecht: A German Academic Life (1856–1915)* (Atlantic Highlands, NJ, 1993), 48 ff.

[55] See Schmoller's letter to Roscher, 15 July 1872, in *Briefwechsel zwischen Wilhelm Roscher und Gustav Schmoller*, ed. Eduard Biermann (Greifswald, 1922). In a European context see P. Wagner, *Sozialwissenschaften und Staat: Frankreich, Italien, Deutschland 1870–1980* (Frankfurt, 1990).

[56] Roscher, *Politik*, 473 ff.

[57] Roscher, *Grundriß*, 4 f. The character of political economy as a 'political science' in this sense is justifiably emphasized by W. Hennis, *Max Webers Fragestellung* (Tübingen, 1987), esp. 130.

tradition on behalf of the normative claim asserted by the historical social sciences.

Roscher's historical *Politik* served the new generation of interdisciplinary political scientists as a starting point for some fundamental criticism. Georg Jellinek, Professor of Public Law, International Law, and Politics at the University of Heidelberg, and Otto Hintze, Professor of Constitutional, Administrative, and Economic History and Politics at Berlin, reviewed Roscher's *Politik* with new programmatic expectations. They considered that the appropriate levels at which to compare states were 'social structure and legal institutions'.[58] The 'political urge to power' is the 'motor' driving us to 'come to terms with the whole complex of human relationships' in the modern system of great national powers which, by now, has encircled the globe.[59] This marks the transition from the historicist theory of politics to the historical-sociological political theories of the early twentieth century, such as those developed by Jellinek, Hintze, and in particular Max Weber.[60]

---

[58] G. Jellinek, 'Eine Naturlehre des Staates (1893)', in id., *Ausgewählte Schriften und Reden* (Berlin, 1911; reprint Aalen, 1970), ii. 320–9, quotation on 322.

[59] O. Hintze, 'Roschers politische Entwicklungstheorie (1897)', in id., *Gesammelte Abhandlungen*, ed. Gerhard Oestreich, ii: *Soziologie und Geschichte* (2nd edn., Göttingen, 1964), 3–45, quotation on 5.

[60] See G. Hübinger, 'Staatstheorie und Politik als Wissenschaft im Kaiserreich: Georg Jellinek, Otto Hintze, Max Weber', in Hans Maier, Ulrich Matz, Kurt Sontheimer, and Paul-Ludwig Weinacht (eds.), *Politik, Philosophie, Praxis: Festschrift für Wilhelm Hennis zum 65. Geburtstag* (Stuttgart, 1988), 143–61; S. Breuer, *Max Webers Herrschaftssoziologie* (Frankfurt am Main, 1991).

11

The Historicization of Political Economy?

KEITH TRIBE

During the last quarter of the nineteenth century Political Economy as conceived by Adam Smith, and perpetuated by Malthus, Ricardo, and the Mills, began to give way to a new economics, whose most prominent English champion was Alfred Marshall. Classical Economics, as the older Political Economy soon came to be known, had turned upon a theory of value for which input costs and the organization of production dictated the formation of prices, the distribution of incomes, and patterns of consumption. A limited set of principles and their consequences were expressed as a finite deductive system, a style of argumentation well adapted to the demands of the men of affairs who made up the reading public for political economy. Hence it was quite possible, and plausible, for J. S. Mill to announce in 1848 that there remained 'nothing in the laws of Value which remains for the present or any future writer to clear up; the theory of the subject is complete'.[1] An understanding of political economy was accepted as a necessary part of the intellectual armoury of the educated citizen, but its principles could for most purposes be satisfactorily mastered by reading one or two books.

The new economics, which slowly developed into the neoclassical orthodoxy which dominates academic economics today, did not immediately displace Classical Economics. The reason for this was quite straightforward: the new

---

The Japanese version of this essay appeared in K. Sumiya and K. Yagi (eds.), *Rekishi Gakuha No Sekai*, Nihon Keizai Hyoron Sha (Tokyo, 1998), 171–92.

[1] J. S. Mill, *Principles of Political Economy*, vol. ii of *Collected Works of John Stuart Mill* (in two parts) (London, 1965), 456.

doctrine was less directly relevant to those issues of trade, commerce, and employment to which the principles of political economy were so readily applicable. 'Marginalist' economics turned upon consumer preferences and subjective utilities. The spheres of distribution and production were linked together in a consistent manner: incomes were received according to the marginal productivity of labour or of capital, and the expenditure of these incomes by consumers maximizing their subjective utilities determined the structure and volume of production.[2] Hence the marginalist principle linked the spheres of production and of distribution, assured their optimal arrangement, lent itself to mathematical formalization, and generally facilitated a more abstract style of analysis. But it was precisely these qualities that rendered the new doctrine more academic than practical in character, and in the absence of widespread specialized teaching its impact was for some time strictly circumscribed.

This turning point in the development of economic doctrine has become known as the Marginal Revolution. Three key works in the three leading world languages of the time overturned the existing system: Jevons's *Theory of Political Economy* (1871), Carl Menger's *Grundsätze der Volkswirthschaftslehre* (1871), and Leon Walras's *Élements d'économie pure* (1874). All wrote in ignorance of the work of the others, and strictly speaking their interests diverged. In Britain it was Marshall's *Principles of Economics* (1890) that was instrumental in leading the breakthrough; in Austria the writings of Menger's students von Wieser and Böhm-Bawerk; while the implications of Walras's system were first properly understood and expounded by Vilfredo Pareto.[3]

Germany remained for the time being largely resistant to this 'modernizing' trend—the respective positions symbolized of course by the controversy over method between Schmoller and Menger,[4] in which Schmoller upheld the

[2] This stylization of course reflects theoretical developments that were not complete until the mid-20th century at the earliest, quite apart from the diffusion of a general understanding of their implications.
[3] See J. Schumpeter, *History of Economic Analysis* (London, 1954), 828–9.
[4] See my *Strategies of Economic Order* (Cambridge, 1995), 66–79 for a critical outline of the *Methodenstreit*.

The Historicization of Political Economy?

principles of historical economics in the face of the new subjectivist doctrine. As international interest in political economy grew, the Historical School became in the later nineteenth century perhaps the most widely recognized European brand of economic study. The existing eminence of German historical, philosophical, and philological scholarship made the work of historical economists more accessible to overseas readers, while foreign students were attracted to seminars in Berlin, Heidelberg, Halle, and Breslau. In Britain, as elsewhere, this trend prompted a new historical approach to economic affairs, denying the universal applicability of the immutable principles of a deductive system and arguing instead for the relation of economic analysis to historical circumstance.

Thus a third element was introduced into the transition inaugurated by the Marginal Revolution, for the rise of neoclassical economics was in Britain consistently challenged by historical economists such as Ashley and Cunningham who were critical both of the 'old' and of the 'new' economics. Ashley had himself studied briefly in Göttingen,[5] and Cunningham's own approach to economics was compared by John Neville Keynes to those of 'the more extreme members of the German historical school'.[6] How influential, then, was German historicism for critics such as Ashley and Cunningham? More precisely, how important to them was the work of German historical economists? Why were they ultimately unsuccessful in recasting the study of economics as a historical, rather than an analytical, enterprise, contributing instead to the formation of economic history as a substantial subdiscipline of historical, rather than economic, studies?

The intellectual and institutional careers of Ashley and Cunningham were very different. William Cunningham was a Scot, an arts student of Edinburgh University.[7] Graduating

---

[5] Ashley visited Germany in 1880, 1883, and 1884, but he was more directly influenced by the lectures of Arnold Toynbee and the essays of Cliffe Leslie—see A. Ashley, *William James Ashley. A Life* (London, 1932), 22–3.
[6] J. N. Keynes, *The Scope and Method of Political Economy* (London, 1891), 167 n. 1.
[7] These details are taken from W. R. Scott, 'William Cunningham 1849–1919', *Proceedings of the British Academy*, 9 (1919–20), 465–74.

in 1868, he first went to Tübingen to study German, an experience which not only left upon him a powerful impression of the German state, but also resulted, on his return, in his joining the Church of England. In 1869 he began his lifelong association with Cambridge by entering Caius College, reading for the Moral Sciences tripos; in 1872 he moved to Trinity College, consequent upon his election to a Moral Science scholarship, and in the same year was bracketed top in the tripos together with Maitland. There followed several years as an extension teacher, during which he lived for three years in Liverpool, before returning to Cambridge in 1878, shortly afterwards taking on the lectures in economic history required by the History tripos and examining alongside Keynes and Sidgwick on the Moral Sciences tripos. For want of a suitable textbook to use in his teaching he wrote *The Growth of English Industry and Commerce* (1882), which quickly became the standard account of English economic development. During the 1890s he was a trenchant and persistent critic of Marshall's plans for the development of economics and its systematic teaching in Cambridge. Marshall's Cambridge campaign, detaching the responsibility for the teaching of political economy from both History and Moral Sciences triposes, culminated successfully in the establishment of the Economics tripos in 1903. One consequence of this was that the teaching of political economy in the History tripos, which had lent Cunningham a platform for many years, was curtailed; and this also in effect terminated Cunningham's crusade against the new economics.[8]

Ashley was both a Londoner and an Oxford history graduate. In contrast to Cunningham, he maintained cordial relations with Marshall—both Marshall and Cunningham were referees for his appointment as Professor of Commerce and Public Finance at Birmingham in 1901, but as the Principal of the university wrote to Marshall, this was 'chiefly owing to the testimony of yourself on the economic side, and of Dr. Cunningham on the personal side'.[9] He was also among the candidates for Marshall's chair in 1908, and if

---

[8] See A. Kadish, *Historians, Economists, and Economic History* (London, 1989), 214–18.   [9] Ashley, *William James Ashley*, 94.

successful would have had to direct the development of Marshall's new tripos. Ashley was a student of Arnold Toynbee's and, from 1885, Fellow of Lincoln College, Oxford. In 1888 he was appointed to the chair of Political Science at Toronto, where he immediately arranged for the chair to be renamed 'Political Economy and Constitutional History'. His inaugural lecture announced that his chief attention in Toronto would be directed to political economy.[10] The subject, he explained at some length, had fallen into disrepute in recent years,[11] but the historicist criticisms levelled by Ingram, Toynbee, and Cliffe Leslie presented a means for the reinvention of the subject. We will see below quite what this might have meant, but already five years later in his Harvard inaugural, he speaks of these original hopes being largely unrealized:

They [members of the Younger Historical School] looked for a complete and rapid transformation of economic science; and it needs only a glance at the most widely used textbooks of to-day to see that no such complete transformation has taken place.[12]

This was in part explained, he went on, by the fact that the historical economists had fallen back on the deductive principles of classical economics; but despite this, he suggested that the 'Historicist moment' had altered the nature of economics—it had led to the general acceptance of the relationship between economic conclusions and given conditions, and of the fact that economic considerations were not the only ones of which account should be taken in judging social phenomena.[13]

When in 1907 Ashley was President of Section F of the

[10] W. J. Ashley, *What is Political Science* (Toronto, 1888), 10.
[11] 'Ten or fifteen years ago Political Economy occupied, in English-speaking countries, no very dignified or useful position. In England it was represented by two very able men, Cairnes and Jevons. Neither of these, however, had any considerable influence upon the educated public; and the professorial teaching at Oxford and Cambridge was of but small scientific importance. In University and College instruction, Political Economy was the convenient stopgap.' Ibid. 10.
[12] W. J. Ashley, 'On the Study of Economic History', originally published in *Quarterly Journal of Economics*, 7 (1893), 115–36; here cited as reprinted in his *Surveys Historic and Economic* (London, 1900), 2. Ashley was the first holder of the Harvard chair of Economic History.
[13] Ashley, 'On the Study of Economic History', 3–4.

British Association, he used the opportunity to reflect once more upon the development of economics in the latter part of the nineteenth century, unequivocally declaring classical economics a 'closed chapter in intellectual history'.[14] The abstract, deductive Ricardian system had quickly won dominance, thanks to the coincidence of its conclusions with manufacturing interests; and John Stuart Mill's essay on method from 1833 was further evidence of its totally unhistorical character.[15] Mill's 1848 textbook, according to Ashley, prolonged the life of the classical system for a further twenty years, and subsequently Fawcett's *Manual of Political Economy* (1863) remained the textbook for passmen into the 1880s.[16] This system remained impervious to foreign influences, although, suggests Ashley, 'I suppose the victories of 1870 did more to make us learn German than any spontaneous enlargement of interests'.[17] A number of factors combined in the 1870s to seal the fate of classical economics, among them the publication of Jevons's *Principles*, Cliffe Leslie's essay on the German Historical School, and in 1881–2 Arnold Toynbee's Oxford lectures.

It has already been suggested that Jevons's general influence was limited, and in fact Ashley's citation of Leslie's essay on the German Historical School is misleading, since that essay is nothing more than a partial summary of the structure of Roscher's *Geschichte der National-Oekonomik in Deutschland* (1874).[18] More relevant is Cliffe Leslie's determinedly historicist treatment of political and economic

---

[14] W. J. Ashley, 'The Present Position of Political Economy', *Economic Journal*, 17 (1907), 467. The article was republished with slight alternations the following year in Schmoller's Festschrift as 'The Present Position of Political Economy in England', in *Die Entwicklung der deutschen Volkswirtschaftslehre im neunzehnten Jahrhundert*, i (Leipzig, 1908), pp. xv, 1–26.

[15] J. S. Mill, 'On the Definition of Political Economy; and on the Method of Philosophical Investigation in that Science', drafted in 1831, revised in 1833, and published in 1836; see *Collected Works of John Stuart Mill*, iv (London, 1967), 309–39.

[16] On Fawcett see P. Deane, 'Henry Fawcett: The Plain Man's Political Economist', in L. Goldman (ed.), *The Blind Victorian: Henry Fawcett and British Liberalism* (Cambridge, 1989), 93–110.

[17] Ashley, 'The Present Position of Political Economy', 474.

[18] Leslie's essay 'The History of German Political Economy' was first published in the *Fortnightly Review* in 1875 and republished in T. E. C. Leslie, *Essays in Political and Moral Philosophy* (Dublin, 1879), 167–78.

phenomena and his opposition to Natural Law conceptions. His more substantial essay on the work of Adam Smith displays the potential of historicism as a form of criticism, distinguishing between the historical, inductive framework deployed in *Wealth of Nations* and the Natural Law basis of the principle of natural liberty—concluding that 'the philosophy of Adam Smith, though combining an inductive investigation of the real order of things, is pervaded throughout by this theory of Nature, in a form given to it by theology, by political history, and by the cast of his own mind'.[19]

In fact Cliffe Leslie's historicist project had little to do with his reading of Roscher, but was based on the work of his teacher, Henry Maine, whose own historicism derived principally from the work of Savigny and the German Historical School of Law.[20] Thus Cliffe Leslie states in his preface that

the conception ... is followed throughout that every branch of philosophy of society, morals and political economy not excepted, needs investigation and development by historical induction; and that not only the moral and economic condition of society, but its moral and economic theories and ideas, are the results of the course of national history and the state of national culture.[21]

This is, therefore, a historicism which emphasizes the interdependence of culture and ideas within a given national context. Though in some respects compatible with Savigny's historicism, it is emphatically not congruent with that of Roscher, for the latter's project was to identify common developmental laws through the study of the diversity of historical development—Roscher's invocation of Savigny in 1843 is more cosmetic than anything else.[22] Historicism was for Roscher a means of identifying general developmental laws, and not simply a form of relativism to be deployed against Natural Law doctrine.

Ashley's suggestion that Leslie in some way 'introduced' English readers to the German Historical School of

---

[19] Leslie, 'The Political Economy of Adam Smith', *Essays*, 152.
[20] See for a discussion of Maine's early influences J. Burrow, *Evolution and Society* (Cambridge, 1966), 142–5.   [21] Leslie, *Essays*, p. v.
[22] W. Roscher, *Grundriß zu Vorlesungen über die Staatswirthschaft: Nach geschichtlicher Methode* (Göttingen, 1843), 2. See for a general discussion of the problems of Roscher's historicism my *Strategies of Economic Order*, 68–71.

Economics is deceptive; it would be more defensible to suggest that Leslie translated Maine's comparative jurisprudence into a comparative economics, which is of course analogous to the claims with respect to the German Historical School of Law made by Roscher in 1843. His statement that it was Toynbee's lectures of 1881–2 which showed 'how the historical method could be applied to the interpretation of actual conditions'[23] also requires qualification. These lectures, to Indian Civil Service candidates and Balliol history students,[24] sought to provide a survey of English economic history since 1760 by linking three distinct epochs to the work of their most representative economist. Hence Smith is used to characterize England on the eve of the Industrial Revolution, Malthus for the period of the revolution, and Ricardo for the post-Napoleonic period. In this way, argued Toynbee, he would demonstrate that 'economic laws and precepts are relative'.[25] This did not however mean that he rejected classical economics and its deductive method. Indeed, in his first lecture he drew freely upon Mill's essay on method, the very same source that Ashley condemned in 1907 for 'its totally unhistorical character'.[26] Furthermore, in commending the historical approach to his listeners Toynbee suggested that

> in studying the past, we could always bear in mind the problems of the present, and go to that past to seek large views of what is of lasting importance to the human race . . . You must pursue facts for their own sake, but penetrate with a vivid sense of the problems of your own time.[27]

As Alon Kadish points out, this idea becomes more marked in his later lectures, as Toynbee sought to fit his preoccupation with current problems into the narrative.[28]

---

[23] Ashley, 'The Present Position of Political Economy', 475.
[24] Ashley attended the lectures and his notes, together with those of Bolton King, formed the basis for their published form as *Lectures on the Industrial Revolution of the Eighteenth Century in England* (London, 1884).
[25] Ibid. 5.
[26] Ashley, 'The Present Position of Political Economy', 472.
[27] Toynbee, *Lectures*, 5–6.
[28] A. Kadish, *Apostle Arnold: The Life and Death of Arnold Toynbee, 1852–1883* (Durham, NC, 1986), 125, 128, 147 f.

Little consistency of argument or method can be detected in Toynbee's writing. He was certainly indebted to contemporary historians such as Seeley and Freeman, who were in turn of course influenced by German historical research.[29] Toynbee's, and by extension Ashley's, intellectual debt to German historicism originated in the relationship that prevailed in the 1870s and 1880s between the study of history, politics, and political economy. As Cunningham was later to observe, German historical economics played very little part in the development of English economics.[30] This was not because its English adepts failed as proselytizers; it was, primarily, because there were no adepts.[31] Toynbee's relationship to the writings of classical economics was even more of a muddle; at once a proponent of *laissez-faire* and a land reformer, his treatment of Smith, for example, lacked the rigour that Cliffe Leslie demonstrates.

It is perhaps unsurprising then that Ashley noted that such work had not brought about a 'substantial reconstruction among English-speaking economists on *historical* lines', and that by the early 1900s the new Marginalist economics was in the ascendant. Ashley certainly grasped the main principles of the new economics—not something one could say with confidence about Cunningham—but his reaction was to distance himself from the enterprise. It was all true, he conceded, 'so far as it goes'; but

instead of leading us to the very heart of the problem, the doctrine of marginal value seems to me to remain entirely on the surface: it is not much more than a verbal description of the superficial facts at a particular point in time. The intensity of demand varies inversely, more or less rapidly, with the extent to

---

[29] See J. Burrow, *A Liberal Descent: Victorian Historians and the English Past* (Cambridge, 1981), 119 ff.

[30] W. Cunningham, 'Why Had Roscher so Little Influence in England?', *Annals of the American Academy of Political and Social Science*, 5 (Nov. 1894), 317–34; characteristically Cunningham fails to answer his rhetorical question. Ashley published a translation of the 'Preface' and 'Introduction' in the *Quarterly Journal of Economics*, 8 (1894), reprinted in his *Surveys Historic and Economic*, 31–7.

[31] This contrasts, for example, with the reception of Austrian economics in Britain: William Smart, first Lecturer then Professor of Political Economy at Glasgow from 1892 to 1915, both translated and wrote outlines of their work: see for example his 'The New Theory of Interest', *Economic Journal*, 1 (1891), 675–87. James Bonar and Edgeworth were also active in reviewing Austrian work.

which it is satisfied; for different commodities there are different scales of intensity; under certain conditions one demand will be substituted for another. True, doubtless. But *why* do people demand just those things? On what does the rapidity of satiation depend? Have their desires always been the same; or the possibilities of production in order to meet them? How are desires related to one another? What are they likely to become? What are the limits to demand set by the economic situation of the demanders? These are the things we really want to know. The problem is, in a wide sense of the term, an *historical* one; or, if you prefer the phrase, a *sociological* one, both 'static' and 'dynamic'.[32]

This is a curiously detached view of the contemporary development of economic science, given that a few months later Ashley was to put himself forward as a candidate for Marshall's chair in Cambridge. But this passage from his British Association presidential address serves to demonstrate the gap that had, by the early 1900s, opened up between historians and economists. The historian was simply interested in a different set of questions from those of the economist; this was mutually recognized and so the way was open for the development of economic history as a related, but independent, university discipline. Historical economics became, in Britain, economic history because it addressed a different domain of problems from those being marked out for economic analysis.

It has been noted in passing above that Cunningham, in publishing the first concise textbook of English economic history, played an important part in the formation of this new discipline. At the time that the book appeared no hard and fast division had yet been established between economic history and economic science. Such a division became more evident during the 1890s, as teaching in universities became more specialized, and of course consequent upon the formation of the British Economic Association together with its *raison d'être*, the *Economic Journal*—both projects initiated and promoted by Marshall. Cunningham remained undeterred by the implications of these developments. He continued to pronounce confidently upon economic history and econom-

---

[32] Ashley, 'The Present Position of Political Economy', 476–7.

ics alike. During the 1890s he tirelessly proclaimed the limitations of economics,[33] in 1892 delivering an especially provocative address to the Royal Historical Society which rehearsed the inadequacies of Marshall as an economic historian on the evidence of the first edition of his *Principles*.[34] His forays into economic theory were idiosyncratic, to say the least; and it is evident that he saw the development of an analytical apparatus as significant merely as a means to the creation of a classification of all possible economic activity, present and future:

> We require an exhaustive analysis of all possible forms of exchange: we might thus discriminate the different kinds of bargains that can possibly take place, so that we might at once recognise any type when we come across it . . . If it were worked out as to give us a complete analysis of the process of exchange in all its various forms, it would be a boon of the greatest possible advantage to the historian. He would have at once a means of naming and discussing phenomena which are no longer actual in the present day, and which are therefore very unfamiliar, but which may have been the prevailing type in some bygone age. The complete analysis of the process of exchange in all its possible forms would furnish him with an organon of the first importance as an instrument of study and with a most convenient terminology for his investigations.[35]

Furthermore, this account of the process of exchange was to be developed from the standpoint of the seller, an approach which, as John Maloney has demonstrated, results in an incoherent account of price formation. By leaving the consumer's demand schedule out of the account entirely, Cunningham is forced into a series of contortions in seeking to account for the emergence of a stable level of prices, in

---

[33] His inaugural lecture as Tooke Professor of Economic Science and Statistics, King's College, London, damned contemporary economics with faint praise: 'Economics may help us to see the extent and nature of the difficulties involved in some particular scheme of improvement.' W. Cunningham, 'The Relativity of Economic Doctrine', *Economic Journal*, 2 (1892), 15.

[34] W. Cunningham, 'The Perversion of Economic History', *Economic Journal*, 2 (1892), 491–506.

[35] W. Cunningham, 'A Plea for Pure Theory', *Economic Review*, 2 (1892), 28, 29. It is not clear whether his use of *organon* in this context, a term that Marshall used to describe the instrumentaria of the trained economist, is meant ironically.

which it is the seller alone who determines the final level of prices.[36]

This is an economic theory of sorts, however, even if an untenable one; and it already characterizes the framework within which Cunningham's *Growth of English Industry and Commerce* is written. Book I consists of three chapters, on property, collective industry, and exchange. The economic system is introduced from the first as an organism, rather than a machine, for

> a machine only produces, but each part of an organism needs to be constantly nourished, and the means by which the various parts are sustained is a most important part of animal economy. ... A great nation is not a mere machine for producing the greatest amount of wealth with the greatest amount of speed, it is an organism which cannot be healthy unless the conditions of distribution are satisfactory as well as those of production. Indeed, when the distribution of wealth is thoroughly unsatisfactory there can neither be really good production nor true national progress.[37]

The nature of this interdependence is then elaborated metaphorically through the following pages, but the interdependence envisaged is constantly one between production and distribution, the latter treated as a means for the continuation of production; consumption, the third pillar of the classical system as first outlined by Say, plays no part here.

As far as the history of economic systems themselves goes, the shift from 'ancient' to 'modern' is conceptualized by Cunningham via the emergence of competition as the principal agent of change, a concept which has a key role in Cunningham's treatment of modernity. The degree of equality and fairness inhering in the 'modern' system is related to the number of agents engaging in economic activity; although when dealing with the medieval idea of the 'just' price Cunningham writes of the number of buyers, not of

---

[36] J. Maloney, *Marshall, Orthodoxy and the Professionalisation of Economics* (Cambridge, 1985), 93–4.

[37] W. Cunningham, *The Growth of English Industry and Commerce* (London, 1882), 3.

sellers, as being decisive.[38] Furthermore, by dealing with 'modern times' as ruled by the principle of competition Cunningham denies that modern economic theory has any analytical purchase upon older economic forms.[39] The history of industry and commerce, Cunningham states, 'is only the story of the various ways in which these human *resources* have been applied so as to satisfy constantly developing human wants'.[40] Wants, Cunningham implies, develop autonomously, they are not primarily historically given; the objective of historical understanding is the changing character of the resources embodied in the spheres of production and distribution.

On this point Cunningham was perfectly consistent: in his critique of free trade he argued that

> the Free Trader insists that he looks at economic life from the point of view of the consumer ... He argues that by Free Trade and the competition of nation with nation, every country will receive from the total of the world's stock an equivalent for the contribution which that nation has made to the world's stock ... This is an inadequate view of economic life. Consumption is certainly the object in view in manufacturing or transporting goods, and it is a necessary phase in utilising them at all. As we have seen, the question as to what persons shall have a claim to share in consuming is of supreme importance; but apart from this, consumption does not call for much consideration: after all, it is a form of destruction, and can be left to take care of itself.[41]

But, argues Cunningham, the future of national prosperity cannot be left to itself with such equanimity: this must be the object of constant vigilance, with the government formulating national aims based upon forecasts of future conditions: 'The maintenance of prosperity depends on calling forth the active principles of energy and enterprise which

---

[38] Ibid. 244–7. Although Cunningham does discuss the issue of consumers' utilities here in the formation of prices, he also refers to *sellers'* utilities. The treatment of exchange and the price mechanism is extremely confused, and gets no better in later work.

[39] 'Unless the free competition which they take for granted existed to some considerable extent, modern economic principles only confuse our study of the actual industrial development of any period of the past.' Ibid. 8.

[40] Ibid. 12.

[41] W. Cunningham, *The Case against Free Trade* (London, 1911), 42–3.

shape the materials furnished by nature, so that they may serve human purposes to better advantage.'[42]

Historical economics is rendered, therefore, as supply-side economics, pointing up its lack of congruity with the new economics for which resources are made scarce and allocated according to the subjective utilities, wants, and needs of consumers. Hence also Marshall's frustration with Cunningham's criticisms: far from subscribing to the view that the same motives have been at work through the ages, producing similar results and hence demonstrating the constancy of economic laws, Marshall described his *Principles* as follows: 'The whole volume is indeed occupied mainly in showing how similar causes acting on people under dissimilar conditions produce more or less divergent effects. The leading motive of its argument is the opposite of that which Dr. Cunningham ascribes to it.'[43]

Cunningham's history, in its first edition, ended its account in the late eighteenth century, as the production and distribution of wealth become part of an autonomous sphere, and thus susceptible to analysis 'as though they were almost isolated from other social phenomena'.[44] History ceases here, and modern political economy takes over—the entire nineteenth century is an undifferentiated present not susceptible to historicizing interpretation.[45] Here there was indeed some complementarity with Marshall, whose new Cambridge curriculum gave an important role to economic history, where the 'student of economics is invited to give his main attention to recent history, that is chiefly the history of the nineteenth century, with some reference to earlier times'.[46]

As has already been noted, the first edition of Marshall's *Principles* had begun with a lengthy treatment of the growth both of industry and commerce on the one hand, and economic science on the other. From the opening passage of

---

[42] Cunningham, *The Case against Free Trade*, 43.
[43] A. Marshall, 'A Reply', *Economic Journal*, 2 (1892), 508.
[44] Cunningham, *Growth*, 387.
[45] This was modified in later editions, but only through the extension of the period of study into the early 19th century. The 3rd edn., published in three sections between 1896 and 1907, brings the account up to the 1840s in its later pages.
[46] A. Marshall, *The New Cambridge Curriculum in Economics* (London, 1903), 27.

the first chapter, however, there is a clarity of purpose quite absent from Cunningham's accounts of the nature and purpose of economics:

§1. POLITICAL ECONOMY, or ECONOMICS, is a study of man's actions in the ordinary business of life; it inquires how he gets his income and how he uses it. Thus it is on the one side a study of wealth and on the other, a more important side, a part of the study of man.[47]

The history which Marshall unfolds from this starting point is one of dynamic development, formed in the conflict between human interests, with the Darwinian principle of natural selection playing a major role. Hence industry and enterprise are part of an evolutionary system; a system, that is, undergoing progressive adaptation and change.

These were the conditions under which the modern industrial life of England was developed: the desire for material comforts tends towards a ceaseless straining to extract from every week the greatest amount of work that can be got out if it. The firm resolution to submit every action to the deliberate judgement of the reason tends to make every one constantly ask himself whether he could not improve his position by changing his business, or by changing his method of doing it. And, lastly, complete political freedom and security enables every one to adjust his conduct as he has decided that it is his interest to do, and fearlessly to commit his person and his property to new and distant undertakings.[48]

None the less, Marshall did not harness this evolutionary history to an unalloyed belief in progress. Already in the first chapter of *Principles* the hope had been expressed that poverty might be eradicated, while the wretchedness of those millions living in near-poverty was also recognized.[49] Although this might be a worthy ethical aim, evolutionary change would not automatically rectify the plight of the poor. Marshall recognized that the Darwinian principle of 'natural selection' (his quotation marks) stated that those organisms tended to survive which were best fitted to benefit from the environment for their own purposes—not those which most benefited the environment.[50] In an after-dinner

---

[47] A. Marshall, *Principles of Economics*, i (London, 1890), 1.
[48] Ibid. 36–7. [49] Ibid. 3–4. [50] Ibid. 302.

speech to the Royal Economic Society in 1907 he extended this thought to include the importance of urban planning for the welfare of future generations, and thence reversed the customary meaning of *laissez-faire* to 'let the State be up and doing'.[51] It was, of course, Pigou, Marshall's successor, who developed these thoughts into a welfare economics circumscribing the role and functions of the state, in which government activity at most facilitated and directed those forces already at work in the economy.

The role of government is here analytically circumscribed in a way not to be found in Cunningham, for whom the state played a pre-eminent role. This was certainly influenced by the political and economic preconceptions of German historicists, although only serving further to underline the differences between Cunningham's and Marshall's understanding of economics. First of all, Marshall conceived economic analysis as a science of human action, more generally as a science of man. The historical projects of the German economists—among them, for example, Conrad, Brentano, and Schmoller—emphasized not this moulding of human life, but rather the creation of differing modes of political and economic organization. Secondly, there was in this no evolutionary development in the sense envisaged by Marshall. Schmoller's conception of state formation was relentlessly teleological, turning on the imperatives called forth by the creation of a new imperial Germany in 1871.[52] Darwinism was itself very popular in Germany in the same period, but closely associated with the idea of progress, representing a scientific, secular demonstration that outmoded institutions would in time give way to more modern, democratic ones. A belief in evolution and the power of natural selection was more often than not a scientistic inflection of a political liberalism baulked by the events of 1848.[53] The idea that evolutionary development might

[51] A. Marshall, 'The Social Possibilities of Economic Chivalry', *Economic Journal*, 17 (1907), 19.

[52] I have argued this at length elsewhere. See my 'Mercantilism and the Economics of State Formation', in Lars Magnusson (ed.), *Mercantilism* (Boston, 1993), 175–86.

[53] A. Kelly, *The Descent of Darwin: The Popularization of Darwin in Germany, 1860–1914* (Chapel Hill, NC, 1981), 22.

turn out badly for the future of a particular group of society is not part of this perspective; that 'natural selection' could turn out beings fitted to a given environment, but unfitted to promote the general welfare of society as a whole, is not envisaged.

As we have seen above, Ashley approached economic phenomena with a set of questions different from those of Marshall and his like-minded peers. Ultimately the economic histories which Ashley and Cunningham produced were indebted to the principles of the very classical economics which they are so often thought to have supplanted. This in turn undermined their position when disputing the authority of the newly emergent marginalist economics. Cunningham understood its principles poorly, and his forays into economic analysis are confused and contradictory. He did nevertheless provide a substantial basis for the teaching of economic history in his *Growth of English Industry and Commerce*. Ashley understood these principles rather better, but found them uninspiring; he was, shortly before his death, instrumental in the formation of the Economic History Society which secured the institutional place of economic history in much the same way that the foundation of the British Economic Association had inaugurated that for economics.[54] Each of these writers had embraced historical economics at a time when political economy required no licence for its practice. By the early 1900s this was no longer so—economics had become embedded in the curricula of a modernizing university system and its practitioners were increasingly specialized academics. In Britain, historical economics did not survive this transition as a form of economics; it became instead economic history.

The high standing of German historicism at this time has led many to assume that it must have somehow exerted an influence during this brief period in which historical economics appeared to offer a viable alternative to the new economics. There is some truth in this, but the influence is indirect—German writing on history and law had some

[54] T. C. Barker, 'The Beginnings of the Economic History Society', *Economic History Review*, 2nd Series, 30 (1977), 5.

impact on British historians, and they in turn upon writers such as Ashley and Cunningham; but the German Historical School of Economics remained in Britain for the most part a brief list of names that was then, and has been since, rarely extended beyond the canonical invocation of Roscher, Hildebrand, and Knies (the Older School), or Schmoller and Wagner (the Younger School).[55]

[55] As evidenced even by Ashley's own account, 'Historical School of Economists', in *Palgrave's Dictionary of Political Economy*, ed. H. Higgs (London, 1926), ii. 310–14.

12

English Positivism and German Historicism

The Reception of 'Scientific History' in Germany

ECKHARDT FUCHS

Historians of historiography have recently taken a new interest in developments in international historiography since the end of the nineteenth century. They are paying increasing attention to international comparisons between specific national processes that took place when history was professionalized and institutionalized as an academic discipline. German historians of historiography have tended to concentrate on the emergence of 'new history' or 'nouvelle histoire' around the turn of the century, that is, on developments in the USA and France after the discipline was established on an international basis. As a result, they have taken little notice of the theoretical and methodological discussions that took place during this process and influenced it decisively.[1] It is imperative to look at these discussions, however, and not merely from the point of view of the history of the discipline. An analysis of these debates can show what theoretical views of history coexisted with the main thrust of the discipline's development. And it can also make clear at what price the dominant scientific paradigm

---

Trans. Angela Davies, GHIL.

[1] The most recent attempts to investigate historiographical movements other than historicism are Stefan Haas, *Historische Kulturforschung in Deutschland 1880–1930: Geschichtswissenschaft zwischen Synthese und Pluralität* (Cologne, 1994); and Eckhardt Fuchs and Steffen Sammler (eds.), *Geschichtswissenschaft neben dem Historismus, Comparativ*, 5/3 (1995).

rejected alternative concepts as the subject became professionalized.

This essay concentrates on positivist 'scientific history', which developed in England in the middle of the nineteenth century and gave rise to a theoretical and methodological debate there as well as in Germany. It starts by briefly introducing the positivist concept of history, which goes back to the work of Auguste Comte. Secondly, it discusses the development of a positivist 'scientific history' in England. Thirdly, the German discussion is analysed. In conclusion, the attitudes of German and English historians to this view of science are compared and located within the history of historiography.

I

The general scientific *Zeitgeist* of the mid-nineteenth century produced the conditions that allowed the positivist scientific ideal to be created and widely disseminated. In the broadest sense it can be traced back to the revolutionary upheavals in the natural sciences, whose discoveries had overturned the traditional view of the world. The impact of this *Zeitgeist* on historiography, however, was often filtered through a mixture of theories and views of science that overlapped in contemporary theoretical discussions. In addition to the philosophical positivism of Auguste Comte, there were many other philosophical influences on the scientific discourse. These included Enlightenment ideas, idealism in its post-Kantian or Hegelian guise, romantic natural philosophy, and English utilitarianism. From the 1860s, evolutionist ideas such as those of Charles Darwin and the theories of Herbert Spencer also gained increasing influence among historians. Apart from the theoretical and methodological views of history put forward by Auguste Comte in his *Cours de philosophie positive*, published between 1832 and 1840, and John Stuart Mill's *System of Logic* (1843), no actual historical theory of positivism was developed, although historians such as Henry Thomas Buckle and Frederic Harrison explicitly explained their theoretical and methodological premises in their writings. For the most part, however, theoretical concepts and methods remained implicit in the works of positivist historians, and they varied widely.

Given the different attempts to produce theories, and the numerous and differing concepts of positivism, it does not seem appropriate to speak of 'positivism' as a specific scientific concept. Instead I propose 'positivistic scientism' as a general term to encompass all the movements that originated in a nomothetic understanding of science, that is, the assumption that all phenomena in nature and society are based on general laws, which have to be revealed by scientists. Thus, the term positivism as it is used in this essay refers to a view of science that, consciously or unconsciously deriving from Auguste Comte's system, attempted to formulate a new 'theory of science' by replacing the metaphysical universal science of philosophy by the epistemological achievements of positivist individual branches of science, or at least to set up criteria governing research in these individual sciences. For historiography, influenced by the flourishing natural sciences, this initially meant pursuing the universal scientific ideal of discovering historical laws. Rejecting metaphysical speculation, this positivist nomothetic scientific ideal aimed to elevate historiography into the ranks of the exact sciences by generalizing on the basis of historical facts derived from empirical research. This scientism, orientated by the natural sciences, aimed less to adopt specific scientific methods than to use the most recent findings from all areas of the natural sciences in order to explain historical processes. The history of humanity was thus not only thought of as forming part of natural history; as a specific 'natural organism' humanity was also related to natural conditions. The purpose of this evolutionary and secularized historiography was to explain future social developments, and its potential to do this derived from the regular, unitary, and universally progressive process of history.

II

In England there was a broad response to Comte's ideas on the theory of science, his empiricism, and his social theory.

They fitted in with an unlimited and optimistic belief in progress and a faith in science which were both based on remarkable developments in the natural sciences.[2] As late as the 1830s natural scientists such as Charles Wheatstone and David Brewster were introducing scholars to positive philosophy.[3] Later, Mill's *System of Logic* and the work of George Henry Lewes, a historian of philosophy, popularized positivism beyond the natural sciences.[4] The circle around Mill rejected Comte's late work, seeing it as an authoritarian plan for a reformed social order marked by religious altruism and Catholic ritual. From the 1850s this work was the subject of controversial debate among different groups.[5]

However, Comte's religious system is of less interest for the subject of this essay than his nomothetic concept of science. In both England and Germany the crucial link between Comte's positivist philosophy and historiography was provided by Henry Thomas Buckle's *History of Civilization in England*, published in two volumes in 1857 and 1861.[6] Buckle's theoretical and methodological principles included a rejection of traditional historiography, which consisted largely of an assemblage of facts, a recounting of political events, and description. Instead, he advocated a theoretically based history-writing that aimed to discover laws in the historical process by using the methods of natural science, such as statistics, on an interdisciplinary basis. Thus, he claimed, it would be possible to present a teleological

---

[2] See S. S. Schweber, 'Scientists as Intellectuals: The Early Victorians', in James Paradis and Thomas Postlewait (eds.), *Victorian Science and Victorian Values: Literary Perspectives* (New Brunswick, NJ, 1985), 1–37.

[3] See *Edinburgh Review*, 67 (1838), 271–308.

[4] John Stuart Mill, *System of Logic, Ratiocinative and Inductive; Being a Connected View of the Principles of Evidence and the Methods of Scientific Investigation* (3rd edn., London, 1851). George H. Lewes, *A Biographical History of Philosophy*, iv (London, 1846), 245. The 3rd and subsequent edns. published from 1867 appeared under the title *The History of Philosophy from Thales to Comte*.

[5] For a detailed account of English positivism see Eckhardt Fuchs, 'Wissenschaft, Positivismus und Geschichtsschreibung in England Mitte des 19. Jahrhunderts', *Zeitschrift für Geschichtswissenschaft*, 42 (1994), 7–26.

[6] 2 vols. (London, 1857, 1861). The German edn. was prepared by Arnold Ruge and was published as *Geschichte der Civilisation in England* (Leipzig, 1860). For details of Buckle's theoretical and methodological views, see Eckhardt Fuchs, *Henry Thomas Buckle: Geschichtsschreibung und Positivismus in England und Deutschland* (Leipzig, 1994).

account of history as a unified, universal, and progressive process. History was to be made 'scientific' on the model of the natural sciences, which had been revolutionized in the nineteenth century. And the knowledge of the present and the future that this sort of historiography made possible would allow it to have an impact on shaping society. Starting with natural factors such as climate, soil, food, and natural phenomena in general, Buckle drew up specific laws that were intended to demonstrate that the intellectual development of mankind was the crucial factor in historical development, and that historical progress took place as a result of the specific climatic conditions found in Europe, and principally in England. His main methods were causal explanation and historical comparison. Buckle's attempt to give history a theoretical basis as a nomothetic science and to translate this into practice triggered a discussion among historians in the 1860s. It was to last, with interruptions, until the end of the century, and made a substantial contribution to institutionalizing historiography as a separate academic discipline in England.

After Buckle's first volume appeared, his English critics linked him with Comte and positivism. After all, Buckle repeatedly quoted Comte and left his readers in little doubt as to the extent of his agreement with John Stuart Mill on theoretical issues. From the start, the young Acton, Richard Simpson, Charles Kingsley, James A. Froude, and Goldwin Smith firmly opposed this deterministic view of history. As Simpson put it, the fact that 'history is a generalised account of the personal actions of men', while 'science is the combination of a great mass of similar facts into the unity of a generalisation' that allows certain events to be predicted takes the notion of a 'science of history' *ad absurdum*. At the same time, he argued, free will as a driving force in human actions precludes inductive generalization.[7]

According to Acton, the main task of the historian was to apply strict methods to the use and criticism of historical sources, quite separate from any philosophical speculation

---

[7] [Richard Simpson], 'Mr Buckle's Thesis and Method', in John E. E. D. Acton, *Historical Essays and Studies* (London, 1907), 305, 309, 321.

and generalization. In 'German Schools of History', his inaugural contribution to the *English Historical Review*, first published in 1886, he condemned Buckle's theory of history. He regarded German historicism as a model for English historiography, and rejected the use of both philosophy and the natural sciences as aids to historical research. What made history a science in Acton's view was not the formulation of general laws, but the application of a scientific objectivity whose value judgements were based on firm moral principles.[8] Froude, a follower of Carlyle, had endorsed the same views in his lecture to the Royal Institution in 1864.[9]

In his inaugural lecture of 1860 Charles Kingsley had also rejected the idea of adopting methods taken from the natural sciences. For him, the 'science of history' belonged 'rather to the moral sciences, than to that "positive science"'. In his view moral and not statistical laws determined the course of history. None the less Kingsley approved of attempts to find specific laws in history, and saw the limited application of statistics as an acceptable method for historical research.[10] Goldwin Smith, Kingsley's Oxford counterpart, discussed Buckle's and Comte's ideas in his inaugural lecture, although he did not mention them by name. He rejected positivism as a threat to free will and theological morality and by insisting that necessary laws direct history, he claimed that a 'new physical science of history' would deny the real driving force behind history, free human action and its motives.[11]

Buckle had died in 1861 and could not take part in the debate, but he was supported by a group of amateur 'scientific historians' who defended his nomothetic view of history. This group consisted of students and tutors who had founded the Positivist Brotherhood at Wadham College,

---

[8] John E. E. D. Acton, *Die neuere deutsche Geschichtswissenschaft* (Berlin, 1887), 51; id., 'Mr Buckle's Philosophy of History', in id., *Historical Essays and Studies*, 340.

[9] James Anthony Froude, 'The Science of History', in id., *Short Studies on Great Subjects*, i (London, 1891), 12, 21, 27, 33 ff.

[10] Charles Kingsley, 'The Limits of Exact Science as Applied to History', in id., *The Roman and the Teuton: A Series of Lectures Delivered before the University of Cambridge* (London, 1891), 320, 331, 334 f.

[11] Goldwin Smith, *Lectures on Modern History, Delivered in Oxford, 1859–61* (New York, 1972), i. 11 f., 15; ii. 45 f., 51.

Oxford, early in the 1850s. Its members included Edward Spencer Beesly, later to become Professor of History at University College London, and the journalist and historian Frederic Harrison. These 'Comtists' had translated into English the entire *Cours* as well as Comte's second main work, the *Système de politique positive*. Despite their different views of Comte's philosophy, John Stuart Mill, John Morley, and the young W. E. H. Lecky must also be counted as supporters of 'scientific history'.[12] For Harrison, Morley, and Beesly, the epistemological aim of historiography was to discover historical laws. In their view the basis of such laws was the application of methods borrowed from the natural sciences and the selection of subjects that had nothing to do with an individualizing view of history.[13] As early as 1844 Mill had called for a 'scientific history' that was to assume that 'all history is conceived as a progressive chain of causes and effects' that happened in accordance with 'some law'. In Mill's view the aim of this 'historical philosophy' was to find the principles that, deriving from human nature and the laws of nature, determine every social and intellectual stage.[14]

However, the debate about 'scientific history' and the positivist concept of science it used soon moved away both from Comte's original definition and from Buckle's work. As this concept related to science in general without reference to its nomothetic character, it was emptied of its content relating to the theory of history and transformed into a positivism of facts. But the triumph of Darwinism,[15] new, anthropologically

---

[12] Edward S. Beesly, 'Mr. Kingsley on the Study of History', *Westminster Review*, 19 (1861), 305 ff.; Frederic Harrison, 'Mr. Goldwin Smith on the Study of History', *Westminster Review*, 20 (1861), 293 ff.; John Morley, 'Mr. Froude on the Science of History', *Fortnightly Review*, 2 (1867), 226 ff.

[13] Morley, 'Mr. Froude', 234; Harrison, 'Mr. Goldwin Smith', 333. See also James F. Stephen, 'The Study of History', *Cornhill Magazine*, 3 (1861), 666–80, reprinted in *History and Theory*, 1 (1961), 186–201.

[14] John Stuart Mill, *Dissertations and Discussions*, ii (London, 1867), 124–9.

[15] In retrospect, Stephen judged that Buckle 'went wrong just from not having the Darwinian clue'. Cf. Leslie Stephen to C. F. Adams, 2 June 1899, in Frederic William Maitland, *The Life and Letters of Leslie Stephen* (London, 1906), 452. See also Peter Bowler, *The Invention of Progress: The Victorians and the Past* (Oxford, 1989), pt. 2; and Jürgen Osterhammel, 'Nation und Zivilisation in der britischen Historiographie von Hume bis Macaulay', *Historische Zeitschrift*, 254 (1992), 339.

based concepts of evolution, and the narrowing down of Comte's intentions to a sectarian 'positivistic society' were not the only factors leading to a decline in positivism, rendering Buckle's theory of history less attractive in the process. More important was the fact that, from the 1870s, history began to establish itself as an academic discipline at English universities. University historians attained a public status that increasingly overshadowed that of amateur historians.[16]

III

In general, the emergence of positivism in Germany is dated to the second half of the nineteenth century. But the journalist and historian Friedrich Buchholz had published parts of Comte's writings in Germany as early as the 1820s.[17] This early reception, however, seems to have had little public impact and was soon forgotten. Yet repeated references in the *Augsburger Allgemeine Zeitung* and other newspapers suggest that by the 1850s Comte's work was more widely known in Germany than has hitherto been assumed.[18] The

---

[16] There is general agreement that William Stubbs's appointment to a professorship in Modern History at Oxford in 1866 and John R. Seeley's appointment at Cambridge in 1869 marked the beginning of history becoming established as an academic discipline. On the history of historiography in England see, among others, Christopher Parker, *The English Historical Tradition since 1850* (Edinburgh, 1990); Doris S. Goldstein, 'The Professionalization of History in Britain in the Late Nineteenth and Early Twentieth Centuries', *Storia della storiografia*, 3 (1983), 3–27; Rosemary Jann, *The Art and Science of Victorian History* (Columbus, Oh., 1985); John Kenyon, *The History Men: The Historical Profession in England since the Renaissance* (London, 1983); Jürgen Osterhammel, 'Epochen der britischen Geschichtsschreibung', in Wolfgang Küttler, Jörn Rüsen, and Ernst Schulin (eds.), *Geschichtsdiskurs*, i: *Grundlagen und Methoden der Historiographiegeschichte* (Frankfurt am Main, 1993), 157–88.

[17] *Monatsschrift für Deutschland*, 14 (1824), 314–51, 439–76, and 15 (1825), 52–84. This corresponds to Comte's 'Entwurf der wissenschaftlichen Arbeiten, welche für eine Reorganisation der Gesellschaft erforderlich sind' (1822). *Monatsschrift für Deutschland*, 19 (1826), 87–106, 193–222, 312–39, and 429–57, and 20 (1826), 60–82, and 176–201. Cf. Rütger Schäfer, *Friedrich Buchholz: Ein vergessener Vorläufer der Soziologie*, i (Marburg, 1971), 118 ff. and 167 ff.

[18] See, among other pieces, [Adolph Helfferich], 'Comte und der Positivismus' and [Hermann Orges], 'August Comte', *Augsburger Allgemeine Zeitung*, 351 (17 Dec. 1857), 5605, and 356 (22 Dec. 1857), 5685–6; Hermann Orges, 'Auguste Comte', *Deutsches Museum*, 9 (1859), 89–96.

co-editors of the journal *Zeitschrift für Philosophie und philosophische Kritik*, Hermann Ulrici and Jürgen Bona Meyer, in particular, ensured that their readers were familiar with contemporary French and English literature by publishing reviews and bibliographies. The philosopher Franz Vorländer wrote the first comprehensive study of the *Cours* as early as 1853.[19] The correspondence of Johann Gustav Droysen, the fiercest opponent of positivist thinking at the time, also shows that the term 'positivism' was widespread and in common use even before the publication of Buckle's work.[20] While appreciating the 'physical method' in the natural sciences, Droysen considered that positivism posed a threat not only to the theoretical and methodological foundations of German historiography, but also to the traditional social relations that he tried to defend in his polemic against positivism.[21]

As in England, the real impact of scientific positivism in Germany was achieved less as a direct result of Comte's writings than by mediation through Mill. The first German translation of Mill's *System of Logic* was published in 1849.[22] The historian Theodor Gomperz became one of his first admirers. Gomperz had read Mill's *Logic* as a student in Leipzig in 1853 and had immediately started to translate it. He corresponded with Mill and met him in 1856. Gomperz was also in personal touch with the French positivist Émile Littré. Through them he became familiar with Comte's

[19] Franz Vorländer, 'Die Grundlage der Wissenschaft der Gesellschaft (Sociologie) von Aug. Comte', *Allgemeine Monatsschrift für Wissenschaft und Kultur* (1853), 937–58.
[20] Thus Droysen wrote as early as 1852: 'Unfortunately, crass positivism is finding a great deal of support in the German sciences. The other disciplines have tried, with the greatest success, to emulate the brilliant results which the justifiably materialistic physical method, using the scales and the microscope, has achieved in the appropriate areas.' See Johann Gustav Droysen, *Briefwechsel*, ed. Rudolf Hübner, ii (Berlin, 1929), 48. [21] Ibid. 120.
[22] This translation by Schiel, published as *Die inductive Logik: Eine Darlegung der philosophischen Principien wissenschaftlicher Forschung, insbesondere der Naturforschung*, was not of the entire work. The first complete translation of Mill was published under the title *System der deductiven und inductiven Logik: Eine Darlegung der Principien wissenschaftlicher Forschung, insbesondere der Naturforschung*, trans. J. Schiel (Brunswick, 1862–3).

work.[23] Both Gomperz and Droysen diagnosed positivism as a low point in the German scientific and academic landscape, and they expressed their dissatisfaction with this state of affairs. Yet they recommended different treatments. Whereas Gomperz saw English and French positivism as a way out, Droysen wanted to overcome the positivist approach in his course of lectures on 'Methodologie und Enzyklopädie der historischen Wissenschaften'.[24]

In 1859 Karl Twesten anonymously published an article, 'Lehre und Schriften August Comte's', in the *Preußische Jahrbücher*.[25] The subsequent debate that took place between Twesten and the editor Rudolf Haym in the pages of the same journal[26] marked the beginning of the process by which German scholars came to terms with positivism. With respect to historiography, the first climax was the discussion of Buckle's work. A crucial factor in this controversy was the fact that in Germany, unlike in England, discussion of the scientific character of history was not based on Buckle's work. English historiography had only started to become scientific since the middle of the century, under the influence of the debate, prompted by Buckle, about the relationship between natural science and historiography. In Germany, by contrast, there was already an academic historiography with an established methodology going back to Humboldt, Niebuhr, and Ranke. The scientific understanding of history, whose ideal was objectivity and whose main aim was to develop a strictly defined methodology, was fully developed in early historicism. In Germany around the middle of the century it seemed at first to be protected

---

[23] Cf. Theodor Gomperz, 'Zur Erinnerung an John Stuart Mill (1806–1873)', in id., *Essays und Erinnerungen*, ed. Franz von Lenbach (Stuttgart, 1905), 87 ff. On Gomperz see Robert A. Kann (ed.), *Theodor Gomperz: Ein Gelehrtenleben im Bürgertum der Franz-Josef-Zeit* (Vienna, 1974); Adelaide Weinberg, *Theodor Gomperz and John Stuart Mill* (Geneva, 1963). [24] Droysen, *Briefwechsel*, 54 f.

[25] *Preußische Jahrbücher*, 4 (1859), 279–307.

[26] Twesten had become familiar with the work of Comte during a stay in Paris in 1851. Accepting Comte's basic views, he had since then been working on a 'philosophy of history based on highly specialized studies in cultural history' with the aim of discovering the laws governing historical phenomena. Cf. Twesten to Haym, 28 June 1859, 8 Apr. 1859, in Julius Heyderhoff, Rudolf Haym, and Karl Twesten, 'Ein Briefwechsel über positive Philosophie und Fortschrittspolitik 1859–1863', *Preußische Jahrbücher*, 161 (1915), 248, 237.

against the challenge of the natural sciences. However, from the 1850s their influence, especially in the form of positivism, and dissatisfaction even amongst academic historians,[27] led to a theoretical and methodological shift in emphasis towards early historicism.

Advocates of historicism at its height, such as Johann Gustav Droysen and Heinrich von Sybel, were members of the generation of historians who had to articulate their theoretical and methodological views on the scientific nature of history and how it was to be implemented in the face of competition from scientific epistemology and its procedures.[28] In Germany, as in his home country, Buckle was linked with Comte and positivism.[29] But Comte was not regarded as a threat to German historiography and sociology. Positivism was seen less as a philosophical-historical system than as a branch of the empirical and materialistic natural sciences,[30] which, after the rejection of philosophy and the Enlightenment tradition,[31] were seen as the adversary posing a real challenge.

Sybel, for example, who was strongly influenced by the

[27] The following account is indebted to Johann Gustav Droysen, *Historik: Vorlesungen über Enzyklopädie und Methodolgie der Geschichte*, ed. Rudolf Hübner (Munich, 1937); id., 'Die Erhebung der Geschichte in den Rang einer Wissenschaft', ibid. 386–405, first published in *Historische Zeitschrift*, 9 (1863), 1–22; and Heinrich von Sybel, 'Ueber den Stand der neueren deutschen Geschichtsschreibung' (1856), in id., *Kleine historische Schriften*, i (Munich, 1863), 345–59; as well as the lecture he gave in Bonn in 1864, 'Über die Gesetze des historischen Wissens', in id., *Vorträge und Aufsätze* (3rd edn., Berlin, 1885), 3–20.

[28] Sybel, too, consciously reflected this. See Sybel, 'Stand', 345; id., 'Gesetze', 3.

[29] See the impact of 'philosophical radicalism' in the English literature, in *Augsburger Allgemeine Zeitung*, 316–17 (12/13 Nov. 1861), 5153–5, 5169–71; Franz Vorländer, 'Englische Geschichtsphilosophie', *Preußische Jahrbücher*, 9 (1862), 501, 515; Jürgen Bona Meyer, 'Neue Versuche einer Philosophie der Geschichte', *Historische Zeitschrift*, 25 (1871), 316–65.

[30] Weber described Buckle as the most important representative of the 'materialistic-statistical' direction, in Georg Weber, 'Gedanken über Geschichte und Geschichtsschreibung', *Grenzboten*, 45 (1886), 302 f.

[31] For an example within historiography see the controversy about Schlosser's view of history. Georg Gottfried Gervinus, *Friedrich Christoph Schlosser: Ein Nekrolog* (Leipzig, 1861); Wilhelm Loebell, *Briefe über den Nekrolog Friedrich Christoph Schlossers von G. G. Gervinus* (Chemnitz, 1862); Ottokar Lorenz, 'Friedrich Christoph Schlosser und über einige Aufgaben und Principien der Geschichtsschreibung', *Sitzungsberichte der Akademie der Wissenschaften in Wien*, Philosophisch-Historische Klasse, 88 (1877), 131–219; Karl Hillebrandt, 'G. G. Gervinus', *Preußische Jahrbücher*, 32 (1873), 379–428.

optimistic belief of natural scientists about what they could find out and know, and their claim to objectivity, saw history as a uniform and progressive 'continuum developing along channels governed by laws'.[32] As 'we are all human beings and determined by the same rules of human nature', he concluded that historiography was capable of 'pushing forward to achieve absolutely exact knowledge'. The 'reliability of the knowledge' achieved depended entirely on the 'absolute regularity of development'. In Sybel's view, however, the scientific nature of history depended not only on the laws to be discerned in the process of history, but equally on a method based on 'regular laws'. Whereas the natural sciences deal with sensory perceptions, he pointed out, historians rarely gained knowledge of historical events from their own observations. Therefore, they could not use the 'means of exact control' available to natural scientists, but had to approach history through 'intellectual understanding'.[33] In the process of gaining knowledge the historian had a number of options in addition to the hermeneutic method, argued Sybel. He could work inductively or, in order to investigate incompletely understood details, he could deduce them from already established contexts.[34] Like Buckle, Sybel attempted to define 'real' historiography as a 'combination of methodological research, philosophical understanding, and artistic reproduction'.[35]

This 'middle position between idealistic tradition and positivist theory'[36] taken by Sybel was abandoned by Droysen in a review of Buckle's work published in 1863, in which he clearly rejected a nomothetic understanding of science. Droysen's criticism of early historicism for threatening a 'loss of history' overlapped with the danger that the positivist

[32] Volker Dotterweich, *Heinrich von Sybel: Geschichtswissenschaft in politischer Absicht (1817–1861)* (Göttingen, 1978), 127.
[33] Sybel, 'Gesetze', 11, 19, 5.
[34] Ibid. 9, 11 f. See also Heinrich von Sybel, 'Gedächtnisrede auf Leopold v. Ranke', in id., *Vorträge und Abhandlungen* (Munich, 1897), 310 f.
[35] Sybel, 'Gedächtnisrede', 303.
[36] Dotterweich, *Heinrich von Sybel*, 275, 379. See also Joachim Wach, *Das Verstehen: Grundzüge einer Geschichte der hermeneutischen Theorie im 19. Jahrhundert*, iii (Tübingen, 1933), 189.

approach would fill the gap left by this 'loss of history' with theoretical and methodological views modelled on the natural sciences. Droysen's methodology and theory of history thus grew out of his battles on two fronts.[37] Droysen regarded it as the achievement of Buckle and the natural sciences to have placed the problem of defining history as an academic discipline on the agenda, for in his view historical studies so far had defined historiography neither theoretically nor systematically.[38] According to Droysen this sort of definition could not, as Buckle believed, be achieved by the application of the scientific method. This would not elevate historiography into a science, he argued, but simply place it within the 'ambit of the natural sciences'. To adopt the scientific method, he objected justifiably, would relieve the historian of the need to investigate and define the terms and methods of historiography.

Droysen criticized Buckle's unclear definitions of terms such as 'civilization', 'history', 'progress', 'freedom', and 'law'. In his view these and Buckle's contradictory logical-methodological assertions revealed this shortcoming, and emphasized that his demand was justified. Droysen contrasted the 'explanations' provided by the natural sciences with the 'specific type of knowledge' and the 'specific area of knowledge' typical of historiography—the hermeneutic method and the 'moral world'. A plurality of sciences each devoted to a different subject demanded different methods, all of which would serve to ensure objective results. Thus to this extent Droysen fully accepted the methodology of the natural sciences and the fact that in addition to methods specific to particular disciplines, there were also methods that were more generally applicable.[39]

[37] According to Droysen history still had to justify its theory and method, and could not deny the problems which this threw up 'without running the risk of tasks being set, methods being prescribed, and definitions of the concept of science being imposed on it from outside, which it cannot comply with without giving itself up.' See Droysen, 'Erhebung', 389.

[38] 'Work such as that by Buckle is most appropriate to remind us to what extent the foundations of our discipline are unclear, controversial, and exposed to arbitrary opinions.' See ibid.

[39] Ibid. 391 f., 396 ff. Droysen mentioned statistics as an example. He called Comte's system an 'attractive "Philosophie positive" '. See ibid. 387.

Droysen defined the method specific to the historian as a 'questioning understanding' and regarded it as a result of the moral mediation between man and the world that constitutes history. Using Humboldt's terms, he described this method as 'an intuitive conclusion drawn by someone with understanding, deriving the existence of a "central power" of the manifestor from manifestations of human life'.[40] Reduced to the formula $A = a + x$, where 'A' is the sum of human actions, 'a' external circumstances, and 'x' the individual will, for Droysen this 'x', however small, represented the only value from the human and moral point of view.[41] Because of man's dual nature, that is, his outer and his inner intellectual-sensory actions, it was possible, he claimed, by using understanding to recognize the meaning of an event from the empirically accessible phenomena even without sensory observation. Droysen's criticism of positivism's one-sided orientation by the scientific method was undoubtedly justified. At the same time, however, he elevated the specific historical method, that is, the hermeneutic method, into an absolute for historiography. And his rejection of nomothetic explanation as a methodology not only contributed to a polarization between rational and hermeneutic sciences, but also initiated the 'hermeneutic turn' that became characteristic of German academic historiography.[42]

However, this change was not immediate, and it did not take place without further theoretical and methodological reflection. This is demonstrated by the reaction of historians over the next twenty years to the threat posed by the nomothetic understanding of science in the form of a sociological social history, naturalistic philology and literary history, cultural history, and ethno-psychology. An article on the philosophical foundations of historiography by Paul

---

[40] Droysen, *Historik*, 22.   [41] Droysen, 'Erhebung', 397 f.
[42] Jörn Rüsen, 'Johann Gustav Droysen', in Hans-Ulrich Wehler (ed.), *Deutsche Historiker*, ii (Göttingen, 1971), 19. Riedel regards the 'false opposition between metaphysics and science', which was first manifested in the debate between Twesten and Haym, as the origin of the question of an alternative to this opposition, which was the fundamental problem for the subsequent dispute between positivism and historicism. Starting with Droysen, this controversy then led into the direction of hermeneutics. Manfred Riedel, *Verstehen oder Erklären? Zur Theorie und Geschichte der hermeneutischen Wissenschaften* (Stuttgart, 1978), 118, 122 ff.

Hinneberg, a philosopher of history, published in the *Historische Zeitschrift* in 1889 illustrates this. Hinneberg complained that there was no generally accepted historiographical direction in Germany and blamed the backwardness of the humanities as compared with the natural sciences on the 'lack of a well developed method'.[43] For Hinneberg, Droysen's *Historik* represented the 'best formal methodology', although he regarded it critically since it did not do justice to the demands of modern science, especially after the publication of Darwin's theory of the origin of species. In his view, these included the separation of nature and history, space, and time, which, like Dilthey, he replaced by a classification into natural sciences and humanities, with historiography being assigned to the latter. According to Hinneberg the history of the intellect and the relationship between body and spirit were both proper subjects for historiography.[44]

The reciprocal relationship between freedom of the will and necessity was a central issue in Hinneberg's argument. 'Thus historiography no longer asks whether determination is a factor in history in addition to free action. Instead it asks how these two factors relate to each other.'[45] This is where Hinneberg's main criticism of Droysen's formula $A = a + x$ began. Whereas he recognized the 'individual moral worth' of individuals in history as something that is 'independent' and thus not susceptible to scholarly assessment, he saw the task of historiography as extending its subject beyond the area of individual actions. In an 'evolutionary view', 'a' and 'x' were variables. For the historian, it was not just the 'x' values symbolizing the lives of great princes and leaders that were valuable sources of knowledge.[46] For Hinneberg—and this is where he went beyond Droysen—the second and crucial object in the pursuit of knowledge was the variable 'a'. This alone could lead to a recognition of regularities,

---

[43] Paul Hinneberg, 'Die philosophischen Grundlagen der Geschichtswissenschaft', *Historische Zeitschrift*, 63 (1889), 19. Hinneberg (1862–1934) had studied political science and philosophy in Berlin, gaining his doctorate from the University of Halle in 1888 for a thesis on the philosophical foundations of historiography. From 1885 he worked with Ranke, and edited vol. vii of his *Weltgeschichte*.

[44] Ibid. 22 ff.   [45] Ibid. 29, 31 f.   [46] Ibid. 35 ff.

that is, 'to the recognition of the main causes in history'. As the scientific nature of the humanities consisted in 'finding laws and subsuming them under ever higher laws in a step-by-step progression',[47] the question arose as to a suitable method. As the small 'x' modified the laws in various unpredictable ways, these deviations must be eliminated. This was possible by the application of the statistical method.

Thus, Hinneberg saw the synthesis of both subject areas of history as the basis of 'scientific historiography'. By placing 'research into regularities' next to 'questioning understanding' he tried to adapt historiography to the 'nomothetic age' without giving up Droysen's theory and methodology of history. Undoubtedly, the intention, method, and aim of his undertaking broadly resembled those of Buckle's project thirty years before.

IV

In attempting a comparison between the two countries, we initially see a certain parallelism in the reception of Comte's philosophy. It started at different intensities in the 1830s, with Germany lagging behind a little, and grew in strength during the 1840s. As in England, the first people to be interested in Comte's work were natural scientists—physicists and mathematicians—followed by philosophers. In England, Mill was the main mediator of Comte's work. In Germany, Comte's works were first mentioned in literary and philosophical journals, and there was little mediation through the writings of other positivists or through translations. The publication of Comte's works in German had not begun until the 1880s. In England, the first phase of reception was marked by strong theological reservations about the alleged atheism of Comte's philosophy, whereas in Germany the accusation of atheism was much less important. There, the liberal social views of the 'positivist' Buckle were the main cause of offence.

Apart from the temporarily influential religious Positivist

[47] Ibid. 51.

Society, positivism first found an institutional base in England in the intellectual circle around John Stuart Mill, and later in specialist journals such as the *Fortnightly Review* and the *Positivist Review*. It did not seem to have this sort of institutional base in Germany. There, however, references to it continued to appear in literary journals until the end of the century, and it was discussed in academic circles, such as the *Selbstmörderklub* in Berlin and the *Positivistenkränzchen* in Leipzig.[48]

At the beginning of the 1860s Buckle's work was the catalyst that extended discussion of the scientific nature of knowledge in the natural sciences and the humanities to include historiography in both countries at the same time. The process by which historiography came to be seen as a science, however, did not proceed at the same pace in both countries. In England, this process of scientification can be seen as advancing the discipline; in Germany, it posed a challenge to the discipline. English historiography was confronted with positivism at a time when it was beginning to establish itself as an academic discipline, that is, during the first phase of the process of professionalization. Although it was criticized and condemned by the first academic historians, there was no radical rejection of the nomothetic programme. The discussion between professional and 'scientific' historians was therefore moderate in tone; the methodological dispute flared up from time to time until the turn of the century. Thus, at this point no break can be discerned in the history of the discipline. In the 1860s, especially, the non-academic 'scientific historians' were a powerful movement, and Comte long remained popular in the public discourse. Among natural scientists, philosophers, and historians in particular, the discussion about science was

[48] In Berlin, for example, an intellectual circle known as the *Selbstmörderklub* (suicide club) met weekly during the 1860s. Its members included young scholars such as Julian Schmidt, Wilhelm Scherer, Bernhard Erdmannsdörffer, Wilhelm Dilthey, and Alfred Boretius, and they discussed political and scholarly problems in a relaxed setting. See Bernhard Erdmannsdörffer, 'Alfred Boretius', *Preußische Jahrbücher*, 104 (1901), 5 ff.; id., *Kleine historische Schriften*, ed. Heinrich Lilienfein, i (Berlin, 1911), p. viii. See also Erich Rothacker, *Einleitung in die Geisteswissenschaften* (Tübingen, 1930), 137 f. For Leipzig see Roger Chickering, 'Der "Leipziger Positivismus"', *Comparativ*, 5/3 (1995), 20–31.

largely a debate about Comte's positivism, Buckle's scientific historiography, Spencer's sociology, and Darwin's theory of evolution.

The polemic against Buckle took place against the complex background of a decline in religion and a movement for secularization which had a profound impact on English social and intellectual life in the middle of the century. The emergence of new social classes, the development of the natural sciences, and criticism of inscriptions and religious education even within the orthodox Church of England produced a growing mistrust of church doctrine.[49] Scientific knowledge and its practical application accelerated economic expansion, which held out the promise of an improved life in this world. Science and reason, not theological doctrine, seemed to hold the key to solving social problems. Darwin's book, the scientists' 'Bible', was published two years after Buckle's work, and the quarrel between religion and science reached a first climax in Huxley's defence of Darwin against Bishop Wilberforce in 1860. In this crisis of the Church of England, Buckle was the first historian who wanted not only to provide scientific and historical demonstrations of the negative role and decline of Christianity, but also to question its future existence as a moral institution in its existing form on the basis of growing scientific knowledge.[50] His suppression of belief in God and predestination distinguished Buckle from the Anglican historians around Thomas Arnold, as well as from the highly influential Thomas Carlyle. And James A. Froude, William Stubbs, and John R. Seeley and later on Edward A. Freeman and John R. Green worked in the universities under the

---

[49] See Susan Budd, 'The Loss of Faith: Reasons for Unbelief among Members of the Secular Movement in England, 1850–1950', *Past and Present*, 36 (1967), 106 ff.

[50] The 'crisis' of religion and loss of Christian faith by no means, however, implied a rejection of religion. The aim was to reform church institutions and to achieve religious freedom. A study dating from 1874 shows that 70% of professional scientists, including William Whewell and Michael Faraday, were Christians. See Francis Galton, *English Men of Science: Their Nature and Nurture* (London, 1874), 95 ff. For these 'men of science', science and religion could coexist so long as they were kept separate, a view that accorded with Buckle's view of religion. See W. H. Brock and R. M. MacLeod, 'The Scientists' Declaration: Reflections on Science and Belief in the Wake of Essays and Reviews, 1864–65', *British Journal for the History of Science*, 9 (1976), 39 ff.

slogan 'God educating man',[51] attacking the secularization of historical thinking.[52]

The polemics against Buckle and the positivist 'scientific historians' were linked with the general decline of 'men of letters' as a species. The development of the various scientific disciplines had created a new public that was no longer interested in moral instruction, but expected exact scientific findings. 'Professional scientists' and academic historians became critics of, and rivals for, the claim to 'cultural leadership', which had previously been the preserve of 'men of letters'. This was associated with the devaluation of the amateur status of many 'men of letters' who pursued science as a hobby, and was reflected in the way in which professionals attacked them for the shallowness and incorrectness, biased nature, and didactic purpose of their work. The professionalization of history and the establishment of the 'research ideal' was tied, by the professional historians, to objective and systemized knowledge, or in other words, factual knowledge. This expert knowledge could be verified, mastered, and extended only by specialists who had acquired the requisite theoretical and methodological standards by a thorough education. History as a science now brought together primary research and source criticism with a division of labour between the various historical disciplines. Such a general scientific concept of history based largely on methodology was also acceptable to the former opponents of 'scientific history'. Thus, in a lecture, Froude declared that historical knowledge, like every other sort of knowledge, could be achieved only by the application of 'scientific methods'. 'History itself depends on exact knowledge, on the minute, impartial, discriminating observation and analysis of particulars which is equally the

[51] Kingsley, 'The Limits of Exact Science', 338.
[52] See ibid. 337; William R. Stephens (ed.), *The Life and Letters of Edward A. Freeman*, ii (London, 1895), 312. As a rule, orthodox opponents reacted even more sharply. The correspondence between Acton and Simpson, both editors of the influential Catholic *Rambler* from 1858, reflects the extent to which the 'un-Christian' philosopher Buckle was perceived as a threat. See Josef Lewis Altholz and Damian McElrath (eds.), *The Correspondence of Lord Acton and Richard Simpson*, i (Cambridge, 1971), 34.

basis of science.'[53] And in 1877 Stubbs declared that he was firmly convinced 'that in the reasonable and intelligible sense of the word there is such a science' as history, but that it is a science not bound to generalizations.[54]

During the 1870s the professionalization and institutionalization of history as an academic discipline began to accelerate, and this meant that the theoretical and methodological definition of history as a science could hardly be left to an amateur like Buckle. Moreover, it should be noted that many English historians had come into greater contact with German historiography since that time. They saw its methodologically strictly defined ideographic and hermeneutic concept of historiography, which ignored ideological implications, as realizing their own anti-philosophical attitudes and their aim of finding an alternative to the natural science model for making history scientific. Thus only when the meaning of the term 'scientific' changed among historians during the last quarter of the century did the positivist but not the 'scientific' influence in general wane.

In Germany the process of professionalization, producing an academic caste that defined its subject in methodological terms, was complete by the middle of the nineteenth century. This explains why the profession showed so little interest in finding out about new concepts of science, let alone integrating them into its views. Positivism and Buckle's definition of science were therefore immediately rejected. None the less, for contemporaries Droysen's pronouncement of 1863 neither answered the question of the scientific character of history and the other social sciences, nor solved the theoretical problem of historical laws. Outside the academic history profession there was widespread interest in the views of the amateur Buckle on issues relating to the theory of science—in particular, among social scientists and

---

[53] James A. Froude, 'Scientific Method applied to History', in id., *Short Studies*, ii. 566.

[54] William Stubbs, 'Methods of Historical Study (May 18, 1877)', in id., *Seventeen Lectures on the Study of Medieval and Modern History and Kindred Subjects* (1866; New York, 1967), 97; id., 'On the Purposes and Methods of Historical Study (May 15, 1877)', ibid. 89 ff.

amateur scholars. Scientific ideas, many of which did not come directly from positivism but were the expression of an intellectual consensus about a concept of science based on inductive reasoning and empirical observation, were quickly accepted in historical and theoretical studies. The general lack of interest shown by leading historicists in the development of thinking in the natural sciences and in scientific research, and their ignorance of serious attempts to test new methods, contrasted with the high level of historical awareness revealed by natural scientists in these debates. Moreover, an important debate took place within other social sciences that went considerably further than academic historiography in relating to the natural sciences.

On the whole, Buckle's scientific view of history should not be seen as a contradiction to mid-century historicism. Buckle himself did not regard them as being in opposition. The nomothetic model of a positivist historical science provided theoretical and methodological approaches that went beyond the historicist paradigm, or supplemented it. Similarly, historicism raised issues that positivism did not deal with. The impact of positivism on historiography was largely the result of a theoretical and methodological attempt to define a nomothetically based 'science of history'. Its achievement lay in having stimulated this historiographical development. Positivism as a basis for defining the discipline, however, was not an alternative that was acceptable to the academic profession in either England or Germany. In England this would have been impossible anyway as the positivist experiment took place before the subject had defined itself. Indeed, the discipline began to define itself in response to the positivist model.

Not until after the middle of the century, when historicism began to decline as a result of 'a temporary renunciation of philosophical and theoretical definition' and a 'noticeable trend towards absolutizing individual elements',[55] did historicists begin to separate historicism theoretically and methodologically from positivism, and

---

[55] Karl-Georg Faber, 'Ausprägungen des Historismus', *Historische Zeitschrift*, 228 (1979), 11.

reject positivist thinking. Justified criticism of one-sided interpretations of positivism and its scientific determinism, of the nomothetic concept of science, and of knowledge of laws disguised the fact that in terms of the aims and functions which they assigned to historiography, their overall concept of history, and the metaphysical frame of reference they used, the two views did not materially differ. For as Otto Gerhard Oexle and Wolfgang Hardtwig have pointed out in relation to positivism, 'scientific' concepts had a number of things in common with historicism—namely, objectivism, a religious view of history in the search for a universal meaning (secularized in positivism), and a normative and teleological view of history.[56] The main difference, however, was probably to be found in the nomothetic character of positivist concepts, which differed from historicism mainly in methodology and in the way it defined the subjects of historiography. Its radical rejection of the innovative potential of positivism certainly made historicism more one-sided. And a concentration on the individualization of the historical process and on political history, the elevation of hermeneutics and its ideographic method into an absolute value, as well as a self-imposed limitation to editorial work based on textual criticism, ultimately favoured an atheoretical positivism (positivism of facts).[57]

[56] Oexle distinguishes the following as the main features of positivism: the formulation of laws of history or nature on the basis of facts; the acknowledgement of science as the highest form of knowledge; the didactic function and role of the natural sciences as the most important of the disciplines. See Otto Gerhard Oexle, ' "Wissenschaft" und "Leben": Historische Reflexionen über Tragweite und Grenzen der modernen Wissenschaft', *Geschichte in Wissenschaft und Unterricht*, 41 (1990), 145–61; Wolfgang Hardtwig, 'Geschichtsreligion—Wissenschaft als Arbeit—Objektivität. Der Historismus in neuer Sicht', *Historische Zeitschrift*, 252 (1991), 1–32.

[57] See Gerhard Oestreich, 'Die Fachhistorie und die Anfänge der sozialgeschichtlichen Forschung in Deutschland', *Historische Zeitschrift*, 208 (1969), 322.

13
Historicism and Social Evolution
John Burrow

To speak of historicism and of social evolution is to speak of something typically if not exclusively German, and of something typically if not quite exclusively British. It is therefore to remind oneself of a good deal of the respective intellectual and historiographical traditions of the two countries, which has led us often to reaffirm their distinctiveness, sometimes to recognize affinities and, of course, influences. To speak specifically of historicism and social evolution as ways of conceiving the past, however, may accentuate the differences to their greatest extent, and may seem in doing so to preclude any possibility of important affinities or influences. This essay contends that this is not entirely true, though to attempt to establish them may certainly seem a rather unpromising enterprise.

The term 'Historicism' has acquired, more perhaps in English than in German, a troublesome semantic ambiguity. It is freely applied, that is, both to notions of universal history derived chiefly from Herder or from Hegel, and also, epistemologically, to the conception, whose most influential philosophical expositor, though hardly its originator, was Wilhelm Dilthey, of historical understanding as a unique mode of knowledge, entirely distinct from the comparative, inductively based, abstract kind of knowledge we have of scientific laws. In this essay I propose largely to leave aside the question of the penetration of versions of universal history by historicist ideas. It is true that a contrast of, say, Hegel's philosophy of history with, say, Herbert Spencer's social evolutionism presents a neat kind of symmetry, but it would perhaps be too obvious to be challenging and in any case it would leave too much unsaid about the actual practice of historiography, albeit seen in terms of the metaphysical assumptions which may underlie it, which I want to make the chief object of attention.

The feature of historicist ideas—the central one, I am inclined to say—I want to focus on therefore is the concept, derived ultimately it seems from Herder, of an animating Individuality, or rather of Individualities, as the protagonists of history: unique historical configurations in each of which is embodied an underlying unique Idea, of which they are the manifestation, and which it is the peculiar business of the historian to grasp. The contrast here is with the concept proclaimed by the phrase 'social evolution' in Britain and France in particular: the comparative study of social structures and their supposedly parallel sequences of development. This gives rise, in turn, to another contrast, with the characteristic though not exclusive interest of nineteenth-century historians informed by historicist ways of thinking, particularly in Germany, in the history and interplay of nations and states, considered as unique and contending historical individualities. The contrast here is with 'Social Evolution' in its subsumption of the categories of nation and state into wider sociological typologies of the forms of civil society. Herbert Spencer, England's leading nineteenth-century social evolutionist sociologist, for example, was scornful of the details supplied in most of the corpus of historical knowledge; 'struggle', certainly, was an important explanatory category, but the state was merely the organ of 'Society', one social institution among others. The narratives of political history, therefore, were for him irrelevant; what mattered was the discrimination, at the most abstract level, of the social typologies which could be converted into a kind of hypothetical universal history if seen as the outcome of general laws of social evolution.

We have, therefore, at the outset, a double contrast, predicated on the idea of Individuality or its absence; first between a mode of understanding consisting in grasping the unique historical configuration and its inner meaning, its animating principle or idea, and on the other hand would-be 'scientific' comparison, classification, and the postulation of general laws; second between historical narrative, predominantly political, with the state as its most characteristic protagonist, and on the other hand the construction of a hypothetical sequence of social forms considered as social evolution. We have, therefore, something like a potential spectrum of generality, from the individual to the universal and from the State to Civil Society.

In trying to map these contrasted categories on to the other contrast with which we are concerned here, between German and English ideas of history, we have, of course, to beware of oversimplification. It would clearly be as absurd to imply that political history was a German monopoly as that universal history was an Anglo-French one. Before the middle of the nineteenth century it might, indeed, have been more plausible to claim that the reverse was true. Nevertheless, from around the mid-century the situation is noticeably altered. Not only did universal history take root in England in the sociological guise of 'social evolution', but English political and institutional historians began with good reason to think of themselves as in some sense, and almost for the first time (the influence of Niebuhr in the second quarter of the century, and a perceived debt to Jacob Grimm, were the most notable exceptions), in tutelage to German historiography.

One major reason for this, of course, was the notion, insistently propagated by the Anglo-German Acton, and by others, that the 'school of Ranke', in particular, had set new standards of professionalism in historiography, above all in 'scientific' source criticism. As history became more 'professionalized' in the second half of the century it also became more 'Germanized'. It is therefore sensible to ask how much of the characteristic metaphysical foundations of much German historiography—already familiar to English audiences in directly didactic form from the 1830s in the work of Carlyle—considered as the sense of glimpsing the underlying ideas, the animating individualities, in their concrete embodiment in specific historical situations, made its way into English political historiography and the historical study of institutions, alongside the new standards of professional rigour.

One of the most obvious cases for examination, Acton, is too complex for consideration here; he was, in any case, hardly typically English, though there were certainly English strands in his intellectual make-up. It is certainly true that he tends to see historical moments and episodes as the embodiment of principles, as (partial) revelations, even, as it were, epiphanies. His presentation of them, however, which we may take as the inarticulated components of his great unwritten *History of Liberty*, seems more straightforwardly progressive than is characteristic of the Rankean tradition. For Acton history was above all the successive attainment by human beings to a progressively more adequate perception of the great truth of natural law: individual liberty and the absolute right of individual conscience. If this is not altogether distant from a more philosophically coherent and idealist version of the history of the successively more adequate embodiment and consciousness of freedom, in, for example, Hegel, it more obviously derives from a Catholic and Enlightenment universalism, expressed in the language of natural law, often taken as the antithesis of Historicism. It is also accompanied by a notable hostility to the concept of the sovereign state, which he sees as amoral. His general view of progress, moreover, is clearly in many ways consistent with the key idea of a successively more securely grounded and comprehensive heritage of political and individual liberty found in the English Whig tradition, though Acton was fond of mocking the latter for its lack of system and universality.

The Whig tradition in historiography, though mostly, as in Macaulay, fiercely anti-metaphysical, was perhaps not always so. I have argued elsewhere,[1] in particular, that in Stubbs's account of English constitutional development the central working notion, abstract but constantly hinted at in Stubbs's choice of metaphors, is something like the German metaphysical idea of a concrete universal. I need not repeat the argument here; it is, in any case, conjectural, based only on a reading of the text; any specific intellectual influence, which would draw Stubbs closer to Coleridge and the liberal Anglican school of historians than he is usually placed, remains undemonstrated. Here then I want to take neither

---

[1] J. W. Burrow, *A Liberal Descent: Victorian Historians and the English Past* (Cambridge, 1981), 147–8.

Acton nor Stubbs as my central case of German metaphysical influence, but the perhaps more initially implausible case—implausible given his not undeserved positivist reputation—of Sir John Seeley, and particularly his work *The Growth of British Policy* (1895).

Seeley is interesting not only for his key position in relation to history in Cambridge before Acton but also because of the balance of elements he represented. He seems in many ways the most positivistic of serious nineteenth-century English historians. He had fallen under the influence of Comtean positivism at University College London,[2] and the conception of 'science' in his advocacy of a science of politics in his Cambridge inaugural lecture seems a very positivistic one, with its stress on classification and induction, very remote from the German sense of 'scientific history' as source criticism; Seeley even used the analogy of specimen-collecting in biology and said that anyone could do it.[3] It is not surprising that J. R. Green, for one, saw Seeley's lecture as an attack on history as a subject.[4] Seeley's successor Acton perhaps thought so too. In his own inaugural, which was in part a celebration of the achievement of Rankean historical scholarship, he discharged his ritual obligation to his predecessor by giving him the shortest possible shrift, reducing Seeley's conception of a science of politics to the platitude that we can sometimes learn from experience, and denying that contemporary history, which Seeley had advocated, could be written, because its sources were inaccessible.[5] Seeley wanted to make the historian the ally and servant of the statesman. Acton saw these two as predestined enemies, the former being professionally committed to uncover the truth, the latter, ex officio, to concealing it and covering his tracks.

All this places Seeley at a large conceptual distance from

---

[2] Deborah Wormell, *Sir John Seeley and the Uses of History* (Cambridge, 1980), 18, 29–32.

[3] J. R. Seeley, 'The Teaching of Politics', in id., *Lectures and Essays* (London, 1870), 14.

[4] On Seeley's position generally see the fuller discussion in S. Collini, D. Winch, and J. Burrow, *That Noble Science of Politics* (Cambridge, 1983), 225–34.

[5] See John E. E. D. Acton, *Selected Writings of Lord Acton*, ed. J. Rufus Fears, 3 vols. (Indianapolis, 1985–8), ii. 504–5.

any kind of historicism, though German influences of another sort, that of the geographer Carl Ritter, for example, are clearly evident.[6] In the light of this it may seem paradoxical to place Seeley, along with Carlyle and Acton himself, as one of the most 'German' of practising nineteenth-century British political historians, and in a fashion common enough in Germany but almost peculiar to himself in Britain. Not for nothing was he the author of a life of Stein. He was unusual among nineteenth-century British historians and felt himself to be so. He was contemptuous of what might be thought to be the two central, and sometimes combined, British historiographical traditions, of Whig parliamentary history and of 'literary history', both of which he despised.[7] What was Germanic, even historicist, about him was not, however, an attention to the rigours of source criticism, nor to institutional history, but rather the direction of his attention away from the traditional focus of Whig historiography, parliament, to the state, above all in its external aspect, in foreign affairs. He was interested in power politics and in Britain as a great power. Though Seeley is known chiefly as the leading publicist of imperialism, and his best-known work is *The Expansion of England* (1883), his kind of imperialism is not really that of the racist Anglo-Saxonism found in other imperialists like J. A. Froude or Cecil Rhodes.

For him it seems the great-power aspect of imperialism was uppermost. Without any notable traces of its vocabulary he seemed to come closer than any other nineteenth-century British historian except perhaps Stubbs to the Hegelian conception of the nation-state so influential in nineteenth-century German historicism: the nation-state, that is, as a self-realizing idea, coming, as a state, to consciousness and realization of its national individuality, which was, in turn, to be seen as a movement of the World Mind or World Spirit, recognizing itself in its encounters with other states, in accordance with the Hegelian principle that the self needs the not-self to recognize its own identity,

---

[6] *Introduction to Political Science* (London, 1896), ch. 2.
[7] For example, ibid. 4. Also 'History and Politics', *Macmillan Magazine*, 40 (1879), 295, 371–3.

becoming an individuality, something other than a mere crowd or aggregation in its struggles to preserve its identity and autonomy in the arena of power politics and international warfare. It is the conception of the nation-state we find outlined in paragraphs 320 to 352 of Hegel's *Philosophy of Right* (and later, for example, in book one of Treitschke's *Politik*) in which the claims of universality and individuality are supposedly reconciled and in which eighteenth-century notions of public virtue, struggle, and bellicosity are incorporated into German universal history for transmission to the nineteenth century. My argument presupposes that nineteenth-century German historicism was decisively shaped by the drive to the achievement of the nation-state, and it is here that the analogy can be found. The most significant work is Seeley's *The Growth of British Policy*,[8] in which the Whig history (Seeley did not call it that, though he deprecated organizing British history around the concept of Party) of the constitution is turned inside out. It was still Whig history, in which Britain moved haltingly towards its destiny, but the protagonist was the English state (the union with Scotland marks the book's terminus) in its external relations, discerning itself as an autonomous, sovereign power. The sinister opponent was the same as in parliamentary Whig history: the Stuarts. But the *telos* was different: not the securing of internal political liberty but a consistent foreign policy devoted to the pursuit of national rather than dynastic interests. Until this occurred the nation had not achieved its full autonomy, its national will as a great power.

It is probably not fanciful to pursue the Hegelian analogy further and to say that, in Seeley's account, only where the national interest was consistently and consciously pursued in the nation's external policies did the nation, long existing, become fully conscious of itself as a nation among others, rather than a kingdom whose rulers' policies often did not express but ran counter to the national will. Having achieved this autonomy and self-consciousness, as England and as Britain, it was ready to move on, in the fashion of a Hegelian Idea, to its wider and fuller, more comprehensive embodiment

[8] J. R. Seeley, *The Growth of British Policy*, 2 vols. (Cambridge, 1895).

in *The Expansion of England*, and perhaps to its political consummation in Imperial Federation. It can be questioned whether a Hegelian nationalist Seeley will be found convincing; perhaps the argument of this essay merely demonstrates the flexibility with which idealist metaphysical formulae can be applied to anything, as, indeed, they were intended to be. Certainly the distinctive language, and therefore the full textual warrant, is absent. It may be enough to claim Seeley as the nearest counterpart nineteenth-century England was to produce to a representative of the 'Prussian school' of nationalist historiography. Yet that itself is significant: metaphysics can shape thought in ways of which its inheritors need not be fully conscious, and it is surely at least highly plausible that Seeley's reading of German historiography and the interplay of national and dynastic considerations in the era of Stein left a residue in his English nationalism of which he may not have been himself fully aware.

With this example, at all events, we leave historicism as political history and push on along our assumed spectrum, from the individual to the universal. Constitutional history *per se* may be just as individual, as nationally peculiar, as political history, though it requires a longer sweep. Traditionally English constitutional history had been seen in this way, but in the nineteenth century it became more comparative in becoming more emphatically Teutonic. Personal links between English and German historians were partly a consequence of the way the history of English institutions was seen not in isolation, though its distinctive features were fully recognized, but as a branch of *die Germanische* (not *Deutsche*) *Rechtsgeschichte* in the full Tacitean sense. This included, as Stubbs and Freeman agreed, both Dithmarschen and Wessex; Stubbs's second chapter of his *Constitutional History* is devoted to Tacitus. And this leads to a further push along the spectrum to a more general category, focused on the history of institutions, which Freeman called 'Comparative Politics', Henry Maine 'The Comparative Method' and 'The Early History of Institutions', and Henry Sidgwick 'The Development of European Polity'. Even Seeley's 'science of politics', despite his professed concern with the contemporary, was so thoroughly historicized that his chief work on it virtually falls into the same category.[9] In the classic form which Maine and Freeman gave it in the 1860s, early English history was no longer in principle necessarily central, and nor indeed was German, but both became particularly significant cases subsumed under a wider category, derived from Friedrich Schlegel and from German philology, that of 'Aryan' institutions, which allowed one to include also the Greek and Roman worlds and, in Maine's case, India also.

In terms of the spectrum of generality this takes us a significant step toward the widest generality of all, that of the category of social evolution, though it does so without abandoning its scholarly roots in philology and *Rechtsgeschichte* for the wider and wilder shores of anthropology and biology. Even so, the lines of demarcation were blurred enough to provoke Maine and Max Müller into drawing them with some irritability:[10] however conjectural, the comparative studies of the Indo-European heritage were intended to establish specific historical connections and were grounded in legal and philological scholarship. They were distinguished by their practitioners from merely speculative evolutionary sequences constructed from contemporary examples drawn from all over the world and promiscuously jumbled together. This inhibition held at a distance works like Johann Jakob Bachofen's *Das Mütterrecht* (1861) and McLennan's *Primitive Marriage*, which were more readily assimilated to the genre of social evolutionism. But the sources invoked chiefly by Maine, or in Freeman's *Comparative Politics*, were also those used, perhaps more circumspectly, by Stubbs: Konrad von Maurer on the *Mark* and Georg Waitz's *Deutsche Verfassungsgeschichte* (8 vols., 1844–78), to which Freeman was happy to add Grote for Greece, while Maine drew on Savigny and Ihering for Rome.

The final step to social evolution, as the name implies, is the acceptance or proclamation of a continuity between biological evolution and human social development, in a cosmic chain as universal and unbroken as, for example,

---

[9] See Collini, Winch, and Burrow, *That Noble Science of Politics*, 229 and ch. 7 *passim*.
[10] J. W. Burrow, *Evolution and Society* (Cambridge, 1966), 163.

Hegel's account of the relation between spirit and the world. The continuity could be thought of in two ways: as the evolution of distinctive, human psychological and behavioural traits from animal physiology and habits, as in Herbert Spencer's *Principles of Psychology* (1857) or Darwin's *Descent of Man* (1871) or, more relevantly here, as the claim to demonstrate that human societies developed under the same evolutionary 'law' as animal organisms and species. The outcome, exemplified above all in Spencer, was a universal, conjectural history of mankind, from animal or at least 'savage' origins, shaped by concepts borrowed from biology. Here at last German intellectual tutelage seems largely to have been left behind, though perhaps to some extent replaced, for the earlier part of the century, by that of the French, in particular Lamarck.

But the English were indisputably pioneers, beginning in the 1860s, that marvellous decade. Works in the genre that came to be spoken of as 'Social Evolution' include Spencer's *Principles of Sociology* (1876–82) and indeed virtually all his major works, Walter Bagehot's *Physics and Politics* (1866), W. H. Mallock's *Aristocracy and Evolution* (1884), Benjamin Kidd's *Social Evolution* (1894), and Leslie Stephen's *The Science of Ethics* (1882), not to mention those innumerable more casual references to evolutionary struggle that are often loosely grouped together as 'Social Darwinism'. They often appear, towards the end of the nineteenth century and after, in conjunction with race, frequently in the context of imperialism or of the contemporary European power struggle. These, of course, were not uncommon in Germany either, yet with social evolution, at least in its liberal-individualist, Spencerian form, the far end of the spectrum seems to have been reached, with German historicism as its other pole: positivist rather than idealist; focused on civil society, with the state and war often seen as early or primitive features of social evolution destined to be superseded; utilitarian rather than sacrificial. Everything that was taught at the time as history, and was regarded as constituting it by, for example, Ranke or Acton, was dismissed by Spencer as trivially particular and accidental. History at most provided, like ethnographic data, examples to be grouped together in classifications from which, in the inductive science of society, generalizations could be derived.[11]

There is truth in these characterizations, but they are arguably not the whole story. In terms of the national comparison it can certainly be pointed out that like is not being compared with like. For German counterparts to social evolution, despite their differences, one should be looking at the academic schools of *Völkerkunde* and *Völkerpsychologie*, the latter dominated by the ubiquitous Theodor Waitz. Though ideas of social development were of course, present, expressed in the distinction between *Naturvölker*, and *Kulturvölker*, a distinction between 'non-historical' and 'historical' peoples which goes back to Hegel and the eighteenth century, there is a stronger emphasis in the German traditions on individuality, on the particular characters of particular peoples, while in Britain distinctively ethnographic interests were subsumed, in the later nineteenth century, under the old Enlightenment conception of 'stages'. The emphasis came to be placed on hypothetically tracing the supposed structural evolution of particular institutions, of marriage, kingship, religion, illustrated by ethnographically miscellaneous examples detached from their local provenance. The intellectual tradition at work seems distinctively that of the French and Scottish Enlightenments, while in Germany that of Herder remains active in *Völkerpsychologie*.

But what of Spencer, widely regarded on the Continent as the archetypal English positivist individualist of the later nineteenth century, in succession to J. S. Mill and Buckle? Was his intellectual make-up so entirely devoid of Germanic influences as this characterization implies? The strictly factual answer is 'no'; what is difficult is the assessment of its significance. To attempt this, Spencer's central concept, his particular version of the idea of evolution, needs to be explored first. He characterized it in terms of the opposite but reciprocal concepts of individuation and differentiation: each implied the other. An organism or species became distinct from others, individualized, by the differentiation of

[11] Ibid. 198–9.

organs. But differentiated organs also imply individuation in the sense of integration and direction. Highly evolved organisms with an assemblage of specialized organs require a coordinating mechanism of brain and nervous system, through which the organism becomes self-directing; a simple, segmented organism does not. The external controlling influence was adaptation to an environment. This was Spencer's Lamarckianism.

Differentiation, specialization, was a form of the division of labour in relation to an environment, just as differentiation in the organism itself in evolutionary development was an internal form of the division of labour. Spencer applied this formula to the development of integrated societies, each successively elaborating more and more specialized institutional forms corresponding to the functions required by its relation to its environment and its own life-processes: productive systems, communicating systems, judicial systems, and so on. The notion of progress as differentiation of functions was not, in the 1860s and 1870s, confined to Spencer. In particular the separation of legal from executive decisions, and of religious and secular authority are a feature of a number of seminal works: Maine's *Ancient Law*, Fustel de Coulanges's *La Cité antique*, Ranke on the papacy, and Stubbs on the Anglo-Norman bureaucracy. The lines of intellectual connection, though some may be just parallels, generally lie far back, rather than laterally in contemporary influences: in *Rechtsgeschichte* and in the Smithian concept of the division of labour, though we also have to allow, in the mid-nineteenth century, for new fashionable liberal notions of secularization, of emancipation from religious control against which young scholars in all countries were tending to chafe. There were differing views of the state, but theocracy was virtually universally condemned.

But none of this answers the questions raised earlier, namely whether there are any German trace elements in Spencer's conception of evolution, given the unquestionable importance of the concept of the division of labour and the Lamarckian idea of adaptation. The answer is clearly, on Spencer's own testimony, an affirmative. However, the question of how important it is remains open. Spencer records as a significant moment his encounter, mediated through Coleridge, with Schelling's concept of life as 'the tendency to individuation'. Important for him too, as for Darwin, was the embryological work of von Baer.[12] Von Baer's own intellectual matrix was *Naturphilosophie*, which here touches Spencer's apparently fundamentally Lamarckian evolutionism. Further, embryology is inescapably teleological, that is, the working out to its end of a programme or idea. There seems no reason to doubt that Spencer derived his concept of differentiation at least partly from von Baer.

Spencer also attended the anatomical lectures of Richard Owen, though he said he found Owen's mode of reasoning too 'Platonic'.[13] What he was registering here, clearly, was the grounding of Owen's lectures, as Nicolaas Rupke has recently shown, in *Naturphilosophie*. Rupke points out that for the scientific community, as opposed to the general public, the central biological issue of the mid-nineteenth century was not creationism versus transmutation, but between different versions of transmutation, respectively those of *Naturphilosophie* and Anglo-French functionalism.[14] In the latter utility was the central explanatory concept. The utility of an organ to its possessor was also its explanation—a notion which married easily with the English utilitarian tradition in ethics to which Spencer at least partly belonged. Both were epitomized in the Natural Theology of William Paley, utilitarian moralist and demonstrator, as proof of providential design, of the correlations of form and function in the natural world. Darwin was to stand this causal explanation on its head while retaining the correlation. Function, because of its survival value, explained structure. The world was not adapted to the requirements of species but they to it.

In the tradition of *Naturphilosophie*, however, anatomical structure was explained not as a product of function but as the working-out of an archetypal Idea underlying a whole family of species. It was transmutationist but not evolutionist in the full sense because there was no single overall Idea.

[12] D. Duncan, *The Life and Letters of Herbert Spencer* (London, 1908); appendix B (by Spencer), 'The Filiation of Ideas', 541, 546.   [13] Ibid. 553.
[14] Nicolaas A. Rupke, *Richard Owen, Victorian Naturalist* (New Haven, 1994), esp. ch. 4.

The archetypes or ground-plans set limits not so much to the extent as to the directions in which species could develop. The signature of German idealist metaphysics seems as evident in *Naturphilosophie* as it is in historicism. It therefore becomes a matter of significance to try to measure the *naturphilosophische* element in Spencer's evolutionism compared with its utilitarian-functionalist and Lamarckian-adaptative components. No clear answer is perhaps ascertainable, but it is worth noting the view of the most perceptive modern interpreter of Spencer's evolutionism, J. D. Y. Peel. In Peel's highly persuasive interpretation,[15] what Spencer required, above all, for emotional and ideological reasons, was not just a theory of adaptation and differentiation, as Darwin's was, but a directional theory of Evolution, a guarantee of future 'progress' of a discernible kind. But this, Peel argues, a theory of adaptation cannot provide, for adaptation is always adaptive to something, to a mutable natural world in whose instability there is no guarantee that the Spencerian yearning for the inevitability of progress ensured by natural laws will be served.[16] The latter in fact requires a programmatic and directional evolutionism of the kind which could be found in von Baer's embryology, which accordingly underwrote Spencer's progressive evolutionism in a way that the theories of Lamarckian adaptation and Darwinian natural selection alone could not. If this is so, the spectrum unfolded in this chapter has, in Spencerian social evolutionism, bent back on itself into an almost complete circle, arriving, if not at historicism, then certainly somewhere in its intellectual vicinity.

[15] J. D. Y. Peel, *Herbert Spencer. The Evolution of a Sociologist* (London, 1971), ch. 6.
[16] Ibid. 153–5.

14
'Peoples without History' in British and German Historical Thought

JÜRGEN OSTERHAMMEL

I

In the summer of 1810, Barthold Georg Niebuhr considered resuming his earlier studies of Arabic, and envisaged a work on the history of the Orient. The 34-year-old son of the famous Arabian traveller Carsten Niebuhr had just been raised to the dignity of Historiographer to the Prussian Court.[1] The plan came to nothing, and only weeks later Niebuhr embarked upon his *Roman History*, but it is revealing that in the early nineteenth century, a major German intellectual, one of the coming founders of the new scientific study of the past, could still seriously contemplate dedicating his time and energy to the history of the East. Few of Niebuhr's contemporaries would have been surprised. Ever since the multi-volume English *Universal History from the Earliest Account of Time to the Present* (1736–65), a collective work whose non-European parts were much more innovative and original than those dealing with Europe, and Voltaire's famous championing of China in his *Essai sur les mœurs* of 1756, non-Western civilizations had figured prominently in surveys and philosophies of world history. These were based not only on travellers' reports, but also on early modern traditions of oriental and Far Eastern learning.[2] A glance at the references in Johann Gottfried Herder's *Ideen zur Philosophie der Geschichte der Menschheit* (1784–91), or at the

---
[1] Gerrit Walther, *Niebuhrs Forschung* (Stuttgart, 1993), 296.
[2] Cf. Jürgen Osterhammmel, 'Neue Welten in der europäischen Geschichtsschreibung (ca. 1500–1800)', in Wolfgang Küttler, Jörn Rüsen, and Ernst Schulin (eds.), *Geschichtsdiskurs*, ii (Frankfurt am Main, 1994), 202–25.

footnotes to the chapters on Middle Eastern and Central Asian history in Edward Gibbon's *Decline and Fall of the Roman Empire* (1776–88), indicates the wealth of material already available towards the end of the eighteenth century.

The years around 1800 were a period of renewed imperial expansion, and much important historiographical work was subsequently done by diplomatic and colonial practitioners on the spot, although it has so far rarely been acknowledged in general histories of historical writing. In India, many agents of the East India Company enhanced their personal prestige and added a cultural gloss to their conquest of Asian peoples by writing the history of the vanquished. Sir John Malcolm, a famous general and colonial governor, authored a *History of Persia* (1815) that was not superseded for almost a century.[3] The *History of the Mahrattas* (1818), that is, of Britain's strongest military antagonist in India, written from a broad range of Persian and Marathi documents by James Grant Duff, an administrator of the Bombay government, is a work of supreme scholarship, used for reference to the present day.[4] At least as broad and thorough in its research, but also an attractive and still highly readable specimen of the narrative craft, is the masterly *Geschichte des Osmanischen Reiches* (1825–35) by Joseph von Hammer-Purgstall, an Austrian interpreter and diplomat at the Sublime Porte, disciple of Johannes von Müller and orientalist adviser to Goethe.[5] However, when Hammer's tenth and final volume, taking the story as far as 1774, came out in 1835, it attracted less attention and more hostile comments than the previous volumes. By then, oriental history was no longer regarded as a subject worthy of a respectable historian. If one is looking for a symbolic caesura, the silencing of Arnold Hermann Ludwig Heeren, the last German proponent of a broad Enlightenment vision of world history, by a chorus of vicious

---

[3] Cf. M. E. Yapp, 'Two British Historians of Persia', in Bernard Lewis and P. M. Holt (eds.), *Historians of the Middle East* (London, 1962), 343–51.

[4] Stewart Gordon, *The Mahrattas 1600–1818* (Cambridge, 1992), 2–3.

[5] Cf. the discussion of Hammer's achievement by a modern Osmanist: Klaus Kreiser, 'Clios's Poor Relation: Betrachtungen zur osmanischen Historiographie von Hammer-Purgstall bis Stanford Shaw', in Gernot Heiss and Grete Klingenstein (eds.), *Das Osmanische Reich und Europa 1683 bis 1789: Konflikt, Entspannung und Austausch* (Munich, 1983), 25–30.

criticism in 1832[6] marks the end of an epoch, at least in Germany.[7] Like the other members of the famous Göttingen school, above all August Ludwig Schlözer, Heeren had always been interested in the social and cultural history of Asian civilizations. This was now considered improper for a professional historian. At about the same time, the systematic cultural sciences, too, narrowed their scope. In its early and embryonic stages in the eighteenth century, comparative linguistics, for example, represented by scholars such as Peter Simon Pallas and Johann Christoph Adelung, had encompassed the broadest possible range of languages; Wilhelm von Humboldt, the student of Chinese, of Indo-Malayan, and of American languages, was a late heir to this universalist tradition. *Vergleichende Sprachwissenschaft* (comparative linguistics) was now reduced to the 'Indo-germanic' languages including, of course, classical Sanskrit—a language, however, that seemed to bear no relation to the India of modern times, just as it was difficult to see how the downtrodden Indian subjects of British colonialism could possibly be the descendants of the noble Indo-Aryans of earlier ages.

In the second quarter of the nineteenth century the idea that the peoples of Asia possessed no history, or at least no history worth knowing, became widespread or even predominant. Leopold Ranke in Germany, and James Mill and Thomas Babington Macaulay in Britain did at least study Ottoman or Indian history, but came to the conclusion that it hardly mattered within a world-historical context.[8] Oriental history seemed to follow the laws of necessity rather

---

[6] Horst Walter Blanke, ' "Verfassungen, die nicht rechtlich, aber wirklich sind": A. H. L. Heeren und das Ende der Aufklärungshistorie', *Berichte zur Wissenschaftsgeschichte*, 6 (1983), 156–7.

[7] It 'marks the end of the phase in which historians of non-European peoples were still criticized as historians. From this point on, no criticism was necessary, for ethnological historians were simply no longer historians but rather second-rate scholars working on another research programme.' James N. Ryding, 'Alternatives in Nineteenth-Century German Ethnology', *Sociologus*, 25 (1975), 20.

[8] Cf. Ernst Schulin, *Die weltgeschichtliche Erfassung des Orients bei Hegel und Ranke* (Göttingen, 1958), 147 ff., esp. 155; Javed Majeed, *Ungoverned Imaginings: James Mill's 'The History of British India' and Orientalism* (Oxford, 1992); and, still unsurpassed: Duncan Forbes, 'James Mill and India', *Cambridge Journal*, 5 (1951), 19–33.

than the calls of freedom. To many observers, the Chinese provided the most spectacular example of a general pattern that was confirmed by the historical trajectory of almost all non-European peoples and nations. After an early flowering of cultural achievement and political inventiveness, gracefully acknowledged by the triumphant West, they had succumbed to luxury and a fatal relaxation of effort—some would say to the natural tendencies of an effeminate race. For centuries or even millennia they had passed through one dynastic cycle after the next without achieving noteworthy spiritual or material progress and rejuvenation. A stagnant, eventless, and therefore infinitely boring civilization, seemingly devoid of *welthistorische Individuen* (individuals of world-historical significance)—much the same was said of Islam in its post-medieval form—offered no challenge to historians committed to the idea of development through struggle. Even Kurt Breysig, a daring innovator of world-history-writing at the turn of the century, believed that China had never outgrown the stage of antiquity.[9] The old notion that civilization itself had originated in the East and only later spread to the barbarian West—*ex oriente lux*—was tacitly abandoned.[10] Being deficient of history in the sense applied to the peoples of Europe, the Orient could now become an object of study for the philological disciplines, for *Religionsgeschichte* (the study of the history of religions),[11] and archaeology.

The reintegration of Asia into the historiographical mainstream did not begin until the twentieth century, and this process is still far from complete, much less so in Germany than in Britain. An ingenious strategy was early on adopted by Otto Franke, whose massive and authoritative *Geschichte des Chinesischen Reiches* (1930–52), unrivaled as a narrative in

---

[9] Kurt Breysig, *Der Stufenbau der Weltgeschichte* (2nd edn., Stuttgart, 1927), 55–6. On Breysig as a universal cultural historian cf. Stefan Haas, *Historische Kulturforschung in Deutschland 1880–1930: Geschichtswissenschaft zwischen Synthese und Pluralität* (Cologne, 1994), 221–6.

[10] The notion was revived in an original way by Oscar Montelius in 1899. Cf. Bruce G. Trigger, *A History of Archaeological Thought* (Cambridge, 1989), 155–61.

[11] Cf. Martin Rade, 'Religionsgeschichte und Religionsgeschichtliche Schule', in *Religion in Geschichte und Gegenwart*, iv (Tübingen, 1913), cols. 2183–200, esp. cols. 2194 ff..

any Western language, is one of the masterpieces of German *Späthistorismus* (late historicism). Franke placed himself explicitly into the Rankean tradition. He wrote the history of China from early times to the thirteenth century as the magnificent story of the unfolding of the Confucian idea of the state.[12] Franke, one of the founders of German Sinology, thus outwitted the guardians of German historiographical orthodoxy by presenting China, of all countries, as the paragon of the virtue dearest to mainstream political historians: state-building.[13]

The alleged *Geschichtslosigkeit* (lack of history) of the stagnant oriental civilizations no longer posed a serious problem at a time when their history was made *for* them by the European colonial powers. Paradoxically, the orientals with their old chronicles and ancient refinement could be dispensed with much more easily than the so-called 'savages' of America, Africa, Australia, and the South Seas, broadly defined as all those peoples who lived close to nature and did not produce written records. The problem was one created by the famous 'comparative method' of the eighteenth century.[14] Was it conceivable that today's 'naked savages' were leftovers ('survivals' as the anthropologist Edward B. Tylor was to say) of early phases of human development? Did they permit regressive analogies with our own unknown ancestors?

'Savages' had occupied the European imagination for centuries. Two major Enlightenment figures, William Robertson in his *History of America* (1777),[15] and Alexander

---

[12] He explained his historiographical principles in Otto Franke, *Geschichte des Chinesischen Reiches*, i (Berlin, 1930), pp. xix–xxi.

[13] Franke also contradicted the Spenglerian notion of isolated and incommensurable cultural monads (ibid., pp. xii–xiii). On his aspect of Spengler's work cf. Detlef Felken, *Oswald Spengler: Konservativer Denker zwischen Kaiserreich und Diktatur* (Munich, 1988), 54, 64.

[14] Cf. George W. Stocking, *Victorian Anthropology* (New York, 1987), 15; John Burrow, *Evolution and Society* (Cambridge, 1966), 12; Stephen K. Sanderson, *Social Evolutionism: A Critical History* (Cambridge, Mass., 1990), 37–41; Kenneth E. Bock, 'The Comparative Method in Anthropology', *Comparative Studies in Society and History*, 8 (1966), 269–80.

[15] Cf. David Armitage, 'The New World and British Historical Thought: From Richard Hakluyt to William Robertson', in Karen Ordahl Kupperman (ed.), *America in European Consciousness, 1493–1750* (Chapel Hill, NC, 1995), 64–70.

von Humboldt in numerous historical remarks scattered throughout his enormous œuvre,[16] had carried on the tradition of sixteenth-century Spanish ethnohistory and had argued in favour of a place for at least the native South and Central Americans in the history of the world. By the end of the eighteenth century, a large amount of ethnographic material from all over the world was available. However, enormously different conclusions could be drawn from it. The 'savage' state of mankind had been an essential ingredient of three of the main eighteenth-century attempts to explain the emergence and constitution of European society: the model of the social contract, the model of a cyclical movement of fragile de-barbarization (as in the work of Giambattista Vico), and the model of material progress through stages of development. Each of these models assumed a certain anthropological continuity between savage man and civilized man, providentially connected through the Great Chain of Being. The savages bore the germs of subsequent improvement.

This idea came under attack in the early nineteenth century. Influenced by racial doctrines of polygenesis, or at least by the classification of mankind into immutable physical types,[17] historians and other cultural scientists emphasized the ontological gap between civilized and, as the new term went, 'primitive' human beings. The idea, quite alien to the Enlightenment, gained ground that primitives had a special cast of mind, a magic and irrational mentality that followed its own more or less incomprehensible laws. The second quarter of the nineteenth century was the high (or rather, the low) point of this image of the ignoble savage. Many contemporaries would have agreed with Friedrich Christoph Schlosser, who asserted in his widely read *Weltgeschichte für das deutsche Volk* (1843–57) that the 'Caucasian race'—a term coined by the eighteenth-century anthropologist Johann Friedrich Blumenbach—was the only one on earth to have developed 'a progressive culture'. It has

---

[16] Cf. Charles Minguet, *Alexandre de Humboldt: Historien et géographe de l'Amérique espagnole (1799–1804)* (Paris, 1969).
[17] Cf. Michael Banton, *Racial Theories* (Cambridge, 1988), 28–64.

since time immemorial been the 'summit of our kind' and, says Schlosser, forms 'the core of mankind and the hub around which the entire history of the world turns'.[18] Such self-confidence went hand in hand with the bleakest possible picture that could be extracted from travel reports of the savagery of the 'primitives'. They led lives devoid of reason, in an eternal present, without a notion of past or future, subsisting improvidently from hand to mouth, indulging in beastly sexual pleasures, and so on. As the theologian and historian of religion Adolf Wuttke says in his book *Die ersten Stufen der Geschichte der Menschheit* (1852): 'They are just flora in human shape.'[19] They do not lead lives, they vegetate. The general expectation was that primitive peoples and tribes would soon be swept away by the advance of European civilization. Was it imaginable that mankind had evolved from such revolting barbarism? The common answer was a flat No. The miserable condition of contemporary primitives was the result of a long process of degradation from a much higher level of cultural achievement that was, however, shrouded in the mist of time.

The actual condition and behaviour of non-Western peoples was mainly a problem for colonial administrators and frontier fighters and gave rise, for example in British India, to a remarkable colonial ethnography and sociology. It was not considered to be one of the major problems of contemporary European culture. Yet there was a related problem: the beginning of history. During the second quarter of the nineteenth century the old biblical time-scale was discredited and discarded for good, not just by intellectuals, but also in popular consciousness.[20] The development of

[18] Friedrich Christoph Schlosser, *Weltgeschichte für das deutsche Volk*, i (Frankfurt am Main, 1843), 4.

[19] 'Sie sind nur eine menschliche Pflanzenwelt.' Adolf Wuttke, *Die ersten Stufen der Geschichte der Menschheit: Entwickelungsgeschichte der wilden Völker, so wie der Hunnen, der Mongolen des Mittelalters, der Mexikaner und der Peruaner* (Breslau, 1852), 200, quoted in Hans-Jürgen Hildebrandt, *Der Evolutionismus in der Familienforschung des 19. Jahrhunderts* (Berlin, 1983), 73; Hildebrandt cites numerous other references of a similar kind (pp. 71–80).

[20] Cf. Edoardo Tortarolo, 'Die Angst des Aufklärers vor der Tiefenzeit: Oder: Die Euthanasie der biblischen Chronologie', in Gangolf Hübinger, Jürgen Osterhammel, and Erich Pelzer (eds.), *Universalgeschichte und Nationalgeschichten: Ernst Schulin zum 65. Geburtstag* (Freiburg im Breisgau, 1994), 31–50; and for the

geology, palaeontology, and early archaeology contributed to this crucial reshaping of the historical continuum.[21] The bottom dropped out of history, and a new space opened up for 'prehistory', *Urgeschichte, Frühgeschichte*, in short, for constructs of a deep past that reached back far beyond the earliest recorded events of Graeco-Roman and oriental Antiquity. Human remains and artefacts of an apparently *very* old age were sought and found in increasing numbers from the 1820s onwards. Finally, the discovery of *homo neanderthalensis* in 1856 marked the beginning of a new age for natural history and the history of man. The Deluge had gone forever.

Universal historians now had to decide not only on the spatial extent of their purview, but also on its temporal dimension. Schlözer, in 1772, could still confidently decree that the world was 6,000 years old and that universal history proper, as documented by the ancient historiographers, began with the building of Rome 3,700 years after the creation.[22] His and other Enlightenment histories of mankind benefited from a strictly observed biblical chronology. It gave them a firm shape. When an interest in world history as the history of human civilization re-emerged towards the end of the nineteenth century—Karl Lamprecht and especially Kurt Breysig were its main protagonists in Germany—such a firm grounding was no longer available. Introducing the first volume of the vast *Propyläen-Weltgeschichte* in 1931, its editor-in-chief, Walter Goetz, admitted that the boundary between history and nature was impossible to draw with any degree of plausibility.[23] Consequently a chapter on the emergence of man was placed before that on prehistory. In the same vein, William

---

background in the geological theories of Thomas Burnet, James Hutton, and Charles Lyell: Stephen Jay Gould, *Time's Arrow, Time's Cycle: Myth and Metaphor in the Discovery of Geological Time* (Cambridge, Mass., 1987).

[21] On the origins of prehistory see Hans Gummel, *Forschungsgeschichte in Deutschland* (=*Die Urgeschichtsforschung und ihre historische Entwicklung in den Kulturstaaten der Erde*, i) (Berlin, 1938); Glyn E. Daniel and Colin Renfrew, *The Idea of Prehistory* (Edinburgh, 1988).

[22] August Ludwig Schlözer, *Vorstellung seiner Universal-Historie*, i (Göttingen, 1772), 60.

[23] Walter Goetz, 'Einleitung', in id. (ed.) *Propyläen-Weltgeschichte*, i (Berlin, 1931), p. xxiv.

McNeill, in 1963, opens his famous book *The Rise of the West* with the statement: 'In the beginning human history is a great darkness.'[24] He then plunges into a discussion of skulls and bones. This would have been unacceptable to the major authors of high historicism in the second half of the nineteenth century. In 1889 Ernst Bernheim, who himself strongly opposed the reduction of historical science to the realm of the so-called civilized peoples (*Kulturvölker*),[25] listed the usual arguments in support of the exclusion of prehistory: prehistoric man created language and religion, but lacked individuality and personal agency, memory organized by means of script, objectified cultural achievements, and above all the capacity to build states.[26] The charges that primitive peoples had developed magic instead of scientific thinking, and that they had no stable territorial settlements, could be added. A few years earlier Ranke had wisely started his world history (*Weltgeschichte*) with the ancient Egyptians. 'But the nations whose characteristic is eternal repose form a hopeless starting-point for one who would understand the internal movement of Universal History.'[27] The 'peoples of eternal stagnation', either in the deep past or in the primitive present, were no business of the historian.

To demarcate the realm of the Historical from the sphere of the Non-historical was one of the major operations of the historicist discourse. All static (or slow-moving) and all collective (rather than individual) phenomena were 'non-historical'. Nature was divorced from history, the realm of necessity from the realm of freedom. There was little support for Karl Lamprecht's later attempt to reaffirm the romantic unity of nature and history, of matter and spirit.[28] Primitive peoples (*Naturvölker*) were not endowed with historical meaning and

---

[24] William H. McNeill, *The Rise of the West: A History of the Human Community* (Chicago, 1963), 3.
[25] Ernst Bernheim, *Lehrbuch der historischen Methode* (2nd edn., Leipzig, 1894), 37.   [26] Ibid. 34.
[27] Leopold von Ranke, *Weltgeschichte*, i: *Die älteste historische Völkergruppe und die Griechen* (Leipzig, 1881), p. viii, here quoted from the trans., *Universal History: The Oldest Historical Group of Nations and the Greeks*, ed. G. W. Prothero (London, 1884), p. xi (preface).
[28] Cf. Luise Schorn-Schütte, *Karl Lamprecht: Kulturgeschichtsschreibung zwischen Wissenschaft und Politik* (Göttingen, 1984), 144–6.

dignity. The question (one that had greatly interested Edward Gibbon) of how to deal with those *Naturvölker* who quite suddenly, and without any recognizable prior experience of being 'polished', had seized the world-historical initiative, as the Arabs had done in the seventh century and the Mongols in the thirteenth, was left unanswered or even unasked.

II

This closure of discourse and discipline in Germany, which seems not to have been challenged by any major British historian of the nineteenth century after Henry Thomas Buckle, had some obvious advantages which are easily overlooked. It is facile to lament the parochialism and Eurocentrism of the classic historicist vision of history. In a way, the caution and modesty of mainstream historiography allowed other spheres of knowledge to unfold, above all ethnology. The affinity between ethnology and history had been obvious from the very beginning. Both in Britain and in Germany and across the various schools of thought, ethnology (*Völkerkunde*) was unanimously conceived of as a study of change over time. The idea of ethnology as a synchronic, ahistorical science appeared in Britain only after the First World War with the emergence of Social Anthropology in the shape of Bronislaw Malinowski's functionalism and A. R. Radcliffe-Brown's French-inspired structuralism.[29] These programmes never caught on in Germany, where ethnology continues to have a strong historical orientation to the present day. With very few exceptions, German (and Austrian) ethnologists saw themselves as contributors to cultural *history*.[30]

---

[29] On the distance of functionalism towards history cf. Karl-Heinz Kohl, *Ethnologie: Die Wissenschaft vom kulturell Fremden. Eine Einführung* (Munich, 1993), 139–40. Malinowski rejected any kind of historical approach in favour of participant observation. But E. E. Evans-Pritchard is quoted by Meyer Fortes as saying, in 1951, 'that, as things are, Social Anthropology is, in fact, more akin to certain types of historical study than it is to a natural science like chemistry'. Quoted in Jack Goody, *The Expansive Moment: The Rise of Social Anthropology in Britain and Africa 1918–1970* (Cambridge, 1995), 62.

[30] The main exceptions were Richard Thurnwald, Wilhelm E. Mühlmann, and a few other ethnologists who subscribed to what they called *Ethnosoziologie*.

Yet, 'change over time' could mean quite different things, including the tension between evolution and history. From around 1860 to the rise of Social Anthropology as a method of investigation and a subfield of sociological theory in the early twentieth century, evolutionism was the dominant paradigm of British thought about early and primitive man, or, to be more precise, of Anglo-Saxon thought, since the most uncompromising and influential evolutionist was the American lawyer Lewis Henry Morgan.[31] Evolutionism continued where the 'philosophical history' of the eighteenth century had left off, adopting, for example, the old Scottish concept of development through stages.[32] It aimed for a universal history of technical inventions, social institutions (above all, kinship), and related belief-systems. Even though the *telos* of the developmental process was firmly located in the glorious, yet further improvable, present of High Victorianism, the scope of evolutionist thought was truly global and in no way restricted to the prehistoric foundations of national history. Like the protagonists of German historicism, the evolutionists regarded man as a creative being, but they were not interested in the great and heroic individual. For them, progress was, as a modern historian of the discipline has put it, 'the sum product of innovations that were made every day by ordinary people'.[33] The Hegelian idea of a privileged Western path to political superiority and cultural perfection did not follow automatically from evolutionist assumptions; these assumptions did not necessarily underwrite a Eurocentric conception of history. Nor was it mandatory for evolutionists, close as they were to current developments in physical anthropology, to condone racism. In contrast to the conviction of a deep cleavage between savagery and civilization that was characteristic of the second quarter of the nineteenth century, most evolutionists agreed

---

[31] There is a huge literature on evolutionism in the cultural sciences. For a survey of the main topics and writers cf. Hans-Joachim Koloss, 'Der ethnologische Evolutionismus im 19. Jahrhundert: Darstellung und Kritik seiner theoretischen Grundlagen', *Zeitschrift für Ethnologie*, 111 (1986), 15–46.

[32] Morgan was especially close to the model of stages. Cf. Adam Kuper, *The Invention of Primitive Society: Transformations of an Illusion* (London, 1988), 66.

[33] Henrika Kuklick, *The Savage Within: The Social History of British Anthropology, 1885–1945* (Cambridge, 1991), 75.

on the spiritual unity of mankind. If there was a particular *pensée sauvage*, it differed from the reasoning capacity of civilized man by degree rather than kind.[34] But it differed all the same—and thus, as John Burrow argued in his pioneering book *Evolution and Society*, evolutionism avoided the strict relativism that was to be a hallmark of other schools of ethnological thought and in different ways also of historicism.[35]

The response to evolutionism, as distinct from Darwinism, in Germany is a little-researched subject. Morgan's theories, translated by Karl Kautsky, canonized by Friedrich Engels, and popularized by August Bebel, passed into the *Weltanschauung* of the Social Democratic movement and its socio-cultural milieu. Among historians, the unconventional Gustav Schmoller, his iconoclastic pupil Kurt Breysig, the heterodox Karl Lamprecht, and at one stage even Heinrich von Treitschke, took a keen interest in authors such as Morgan, Edward B. Tylor, or John McLennan.[36] However, unlike Schmoller most historians did not consider the early history of the human family, for example, to be a subject located within their realm of interest and competence. If they took any notice at all of recent developments in evolutionism, it was with a view to sealing off the discipline from obnoxious influences. The ancient historian Eduard Meyer, a respected leader in the field, wrote his *Anthropology*, a rather traditional work with a promising title, explicitly in order to stem the evolutionist tide.[37]

---

[34] Kuklick, *The Savage Within*. 82.

[35] Burrow, *Evolution and Society*, 42, 99, 102.

[36] Cf. Erhard Lucas, 'Die Rezeption Lewis H. Morgans durch Marx und Engels', *Saeculum*, 15 (1964), 152–76; Bernhard vom Brocke, *Kurt Breysig: Geschichtswissenschaft zwischen Historismus und Soziologie* (Lübeck, 1971), 58–60; Schorn-Schütte, *Karl Lamprecht*, 129–37, 164–5. Gustav Schmoller's excellent knowledge and sympathetic reading of contemporary British and American anthropology and sociology (especially Herbert Spencer) is documented in his article 'Die Urgeschichte der Familie: Mutterrecht und Gentilverfassung', *Schmollers Jahrbuch*, 23 (1899), 1–21.

[37] Eduard Meyer, *Geschichte des Altertums*, i. 1st half: *Einleitung: Elemente der Anthropologie* (3rd edn., Stuttgart, 1910). Cf. Wilfried Nippel, 'Prolegomena zu Eduard Meyers "Anthropologie"', in William M. Calder III and Alexander Demandt (eds.), *Eduard Meyer: Leben und Leistung eines Universalhistorikers* (Leiden, 1990), 315, 326–7. For a different view see Friedrich Tenbruck, 'Max Weber and Eduard Meyer', in Wolfgang J. Mommsen and Jürgen Osterhammel (eds.), *Max Weber and his Contemporaries* (London, 1987), 234–67.

It is curious that the *second* generation of German ethnologists—the *first* generation (Theodor Waitz, Gustav Klemm, and others) were mostly collectors and compilers of material with a limited interest in theoretical questions[38]—behaved coolly towards the evolutionist challenge. The Anglo-Saxon theorists on the one hand, and scholars such as Adolf Bastian and Rudolf Virchow on the other, who had founded the German Society for Anthropology, Ethnology, and Prehistory (Deutsche Gesellschaft für Anthropologie, Ethnologie und Urgeschichte) in 1869,[39] shared basic liberal persuasions and a commitment to a developmental view of the world.[40] Yet the German ethnologists were much more interested in cultural diversity than in uniformity, and they distrusted the concept of a movement of stages.[41] At the same time, in the scientific culture of the Kaiserreich, there was little room for the respected amateur. New fields of study had to fight for a place in academia. Thus Bastian and Virchow pursued the strategy of establishing the young discipline of ethnology as an offshoot of the prestigious natural sciences. This involved a high degree of empiricism and an inductive methodology, an aversion to a priori reasoning, and a concept of scientific laws that did not look for secular patterns of change but to constant regularities. In the huge œuvre of Bastian, an inveterate traveller, collector, and organizer, the tension between romanticism and positivism remained conspicuously unresolved. He never rejected a historical approach in the way Malinowski would do some decades later. He wrote learned, if messy, historical books such as his rambling history of the Indo-Chinese people (*Geschichte der Indochinesen*) of 1866,[42] and he even elaborated a vision of the organic cultural development of

---

[38] Cf. Woodruff D. Smith, *Politics and the Sciences of Culture in Germany 1840–1920* (New York, 1991), 59–61.

[39] The Anthropological Society of London had been founded a few years before, in 1863. In its early years, its orientation was diffusionist rather than evolutionist (Burrow, *Evolution and Society*, 122–3).

[40] Smith, *Politics and the Sciences of Culture*, 110.

[41] Models of stages, by contrast, had played a certain role in German historical economics (Bruno Hildebrand, Gustav Schmoller, Karl Bücher *et al.*).

[42] Adolf Bastian, *Die Voelker des oestlichen Asien: Studien und Reisen*, i: *Die Geschichte der Indochinesen: Aus einheimischen Quellen* (Leipzig, 1866).

mankind.[43] But he also believed that the ethnographic record of mankind could be scientifically reduced to a handful of recurring *Elementargedanken* (elementary ideas), prefigurations, as it were, of C. G. Jung's 'archetypes', and that everywhere and in every epoch the human mind worked according to immutable psychological laws.[44] Bastian's somewhat rudimentary epistemology was unambiguously anti-historicist. He was interested neither in historical specificity, nor in interpretative approaches.

Ethnology's mimicry of the dominant natural sciences, repeating the success story of academic geography, paid off. It yielded results in the form of a few professorships and positions in museums.[45] Whereas mainstream historiography firmly rejected a preoccupation with 'peoples without history', the natural sciences at least tolerated a tiny enclave on the margins that applied some of their methods to phenomena of cultural history. Bastian was the institutional founding father of German ethnology, and moreover, a theorist in the same class as Edward B. Tylor and Lewis H. Morgan. His concepts dominated the field until about 1910. However, alongside Bastian a more openly historical tendency survived and increasingly asserted itself, a tradition of a universal cultural history that preserved the intentions of the late eighteenth century through the age of unchallenged historicism. This tradition was kept alive not by historians and ethnologists, but by geographers.

The last major German historian of the non-European world before the revival of interest in universal history around the turn of the century was Carl Ritter. From 1825

---

[43] Annemarie Fiedermutz-Laun, *Der kulturhistorische Gedanke bei Adolf Bastian* (Wiesbaden, 1970), 108–12; ead., 'Adolf Bastian (1826–1905)', in Wolfgang Marschall (ed.), *Klassiker der Kulturanthropologie: Von Montaigne bis Margaret Mead* (Munich, 1990), 109–36, esp. 122–7; ead., 'Adolf Bastian und die Begründung der deutschen Ethnologie', *Berichte zur Wissenschaftsgeschichte*, 9 (1986), 167–81; Klaus-Peter Koepping, *Adolf Bastian and the Psychic Unity of Mankind: The Foundations of Anthropology in Nineteenth-Century Germany* (St Lucia, 1983), provides a translation of a selection of Bastian's works.

[44] Fiedermutz-Laun, *Der kulturhistorische Gedanke*, 77–107, esp. 77; ead., 'Adolf Bastian', 119–21; Fritz Kramer, *Verkehrte Welten: Zur imaginären Ethnographie des 19. Jahrhunderts* (Frankfurt am Main, 1977), 74–81.

[45] Ryding, 'Alternatives', 25–6.

until his death in 1859 Ritter occupied a chair of 'Geography, Ethnology, and History' ('der Länder- und Völkerkunde und der Geschichte') at the University of Berlin. During this time he worked on the second edition of his *Erdkunde*. It finally ran to twenty-one massive volumes and still did not cover anything but Asia. Ritter and (in a different way) his contemporary Alexander von Humboldt were the first modern European scholars to take geography beyond the purely descriptive and statistical, and to redefine its subject as the cultural history of mankind in relation to the physical environment.[46] Ritter combined new romantic concepts of nature and landscape with an older environmentalism and with Herder's idea of peoples as collective and organic individualities to create a vision of the 'historical process' as the slow peopling and cultivation of the earth by mankind. Like Ranke, his colleague at Berlin (who used Ritter's rich works as sources of information on non-European history),[47] he was not a systematic thinker. One has to dip into the 20,000 pages of his *Erdkunde* to get an idea of the vividness and attention to detail with which he described the cultural and economic history of regions such as India, China, and Asia Minor. Ritter was one of the best-informed people of his time. He had an unprecedented mastery of European travel literature in all languages, knew whatever oriental materials were available in translation, and kept abreast of current reporting from the frontiers of European expansion. His temporal scope reached from Antiquity to current developments such as the opening up of China and the settlement of the American West, developments whose momentous significance he prophetically understood. Ritter provided an empirically based, decidedly non-speculative universal history of human civilization in the *longue durée*, ethnographically sensitive and always related to the natural environment. While he shared with his historicist contemporaries a language pervaded with key concepts such

---

[46] On Ritter as a historian cf. Klaus E. Müller, 'Carl Ritter und die historische Völkerkunde', *Paideuma*, 11 (1965), 24–57; Jürgen Osterhammel, 'Geschichte, Geographie, Geohistorie', in Wolfgang Küttler, Jörn Rüsen, and Ernst Schulin (eds.), *Geschichtsdiskurs*, iii (Frankfurt am Main, 1997), 257–71.

[47] Schulin, *Die weltgeschichtliche Erfassung des Orients*, 149, referring to the 1820s.

as 'individuality', 'development', 'perception', 'context', and 'living whole', he neglected the lines of demarcation that had been drawn by the legislators of Rankean New History. The distinction between historical and non-historical peoples made as little sense to him as the strict dichotomy between nature and history.

Ritter had a certain influence in Russia, the United States, and France (where Michelet was one of his admirers), but his posthumous impact on the German academic scene was practically nil. Both the historians and the geographers, drifting rapidly apart, rejected his grandly synthetic approach. It was another outsider of more than one discipline who took up some of Ritter's ideas. Friedrich Ratzel, zoologist and geographer, was a professor at Leipzig University from 1886 to 1904, where he became a close friend of Karl Lamprecht and a member of his circle.[48] Ratzel was no less of a polymath than Ritter, but he belonged to an entirely different intellectual world, one no longer dominated by the pious idealism of the romantic period, but by the matter-of-fact atmosphere of positivist science. The first volume of his famous *Anthropogeographie* (1882) bore the subtitle 'Elements of an Application of Geography to History'. Here and on numerous other occasions Ratzel ridiculed the preposterous idea that history should be confined to the peoples of the white race, and he opposed all attempts at an open or camouflaged racial denigration of non-Europeans, including the *Naturvölker* whom he consistently declined to call 'primitives'. Ratzel's own historical analyses were mainly devoted to issues of migration, colonization, and cultural borrowing in early ages, both among *Naturvölker* and in the present world. His first book was a careful analysis of Chinese coolie emigration in the nineteenth century. In his three-volume *Völkerkunde* (1885–8), characteristically translated into English as *The History of*

---

[48] Schorn-Schütte, *Karl Lamprecht*, 87–8; Roger Chickering, *Karl Lamprecht: A German Academic Life (1856–1915)* (Atlantic Highlands, NJ, 1993), 289–97. On innovative aspects of Ratzel's work see Jürgen Osterhammel, 'Raumerfassung und Universalgeschichte im 20. Jahrhundert', in Hübinger *et al.* (eds.), *Universalgeschichte und Nationalgeschichten*, 51–72, esp. 57–66.

Mankind (1896–8),[49] he initiated two related developments in ethnological theory—diffusionism and the concept of *Kulturkreise* (culture areas).[50]

Diffusionism, a belief with a long ancestry going back to the Old Testament,[51] was something like the German answer to evolutionism. It postulated that cultural elements and material innovations were created only once, and then spread through processes of transmission which could be documented even in the absence of written records.[52] Diffusionism expressed a less optimistic world-view than evolutionism: the amount of creative capacity in the world is limited,[53] and the spread of cultural achievements does not converge in an overall process of linear improvement. Thus, the diffusionists retreated from the grand designs of the Victorian evolutionists. Diffusionism was also closer to the concerns of contemporary historians, lending itself to empirical archaeological and historical research, at best even in connection with something like a precise chronology. Often the usual range of historical sources was available for documenting migrations and contacts between peoples and civilizations. Today's ethnohistory rests on the same principle, the use of observers' reports (mainly travel writing) about illiterate ethnic groups.

The *Kulturkreislehre* (theory of culture areas) was a direct consequence of diffusionism, if not a necessary one.[54] The

---

[49] The English edition included a preface by E. B. Tylor.

[50] A good introduction is Wilhelm Schmidt, *Handbuch der Methode der kulturhistorischen Ethnologie* (Münster, 1937); id., *The Culture Historical Method of Ethnology*, trans. S. A. Sieber (New York, 1939). See also Robert H. Winthrop, *Dictionary of Concepts in Cultural Anthropology* (New York, 1991), 61–3.

[51] See e.g. Manfred Petri, *Die Urvolkhypothese: Ein Beitrag zum Geschichtsdenken der Spätaufklärung und des deutschen Idealismus* (Berlin, 1990).

[52] Cf. Kohl, *Ethnologie*, 132–7. On diffusionist tendencies in British ethnology cf. Kuklick, *The Savage Within*, 121–33, and in Germany cf. Smith, *Politics and the Sciences of Culture*, 140–61. Diffusionist influences from Germany and Austria were felt in Britain after about 1910, in particular, on the psychologist and ethnologist W. H. R. Rivers, 'and began to undermine the orthodox evolutionism of the British school' (Kuper, *Invention*, 152). Cf. the detailed account in George W. Stocking, Jr., *After Tylor: British Social Anthropology 1888–1951* (Madison, 1995), 179–232.

[53] This is pointed out by Trigger, *History of Archaeological Thought*, 154.

[54] On Ratzel und the early history of the concept of 'Kulturkreis' cf. Paul Leser, 'Zur Geschichte des Wortes Kulturkreis', *Anthropos*, 58 (1963), 1–36, esp. 3–19 (with an interesting assessment of the English translation of Ratzel's *Völkerkunde*).

distribution of cultural artefacts—this was its basic idea—could be traced on maps, and their frequency, density, and clustering could be read as indicating spatially separate 'culture areas' or 'spheres of civilization'. Ratzel himself did not elaborate this theory beyond a few elementary sketches. It later became the cornerstone of the *kulturhistorische Schule* of ethnology, the paramount ethnological tendency in the German-speaking countries during the first half of the twentieth century.[55] The proponents of *Kulturkreislehre* regarded their science as a branch of history, more particularly, as the foundation for the history of literate civilizations.[56] Significantly, its best theoretician, Fritz Graebner, was a trained medievalist with a strong interest in questions of historical method.[57]

In their methodology, Graebner and his colleagues borrowed heavily from Dilthey and the neo-Kantian philosophers. They also insisted on the rigours of a technical critique of the sources.[58] In actual practice, however, ambitious speculations outgrew an as yet slender empirical basis. Ethnographic field research was neglected. Evolutionism crept back and ultimately, in the hands of Pater Wilhelm Schmidt, the head of the Vienna school, turned into a Christian history of salvation.[59] Mainstream *political* historians

[55] Leo Frobenius was a remarkably independent thinker. He soon parted company with the *Kulturkreislehre* whose mechanistic idea of culture he attempted to replace with his own idealistic and holistic concept of 'Paideuma', a revival of Herder's theory of 'Volksgeist' (genius of a people). Cf. Helmut Straube, 'Leo Frobenius (1873–1938)', in Marschall (ed.), *Klassiker der Kulturanthropologie*, 151–70. A sample of Frobenius's work is available in English: Eike Haberland (ed.), *Leo Frobenius 1873–1973: Eine Anthologie* (Wiesbaden, 1973). Frobenius, a busy traveller and collector, was the only German ethnologist of his generation who had a broader public appeal.

[56] Klaus E. Müller, 'Grundzüge des ethnologischen Historismus', in Wolfdietrich Schmied-Kowarzik and Justin Stagl (eds.), *Grundfagen der Ethnologie: Beiträge zur gegenwärtigen Theorie-Diskussion* (Berlin, 1981), 193–231, esp. 205, 207. To Willy Foy, writing in 1911, ethnology was 'a branch of historical studies' (quoted in Jürgen Contag, *Zur Methodik der deutschsprachigen Völkerkunde*, D.Phil. thesis, Marburg, 1971, 3). Schmidt, *Handbuch*, 14, saw his own brand of ethnology as a 'special branch of the science of history'.

[57] Cf. Fritz Graebner, *Methode der Ethnologie* (Heidelberg, 1911), 3; and for a critical assessment Christoph Marx, *'Völker ohne Schrift und Geschichte': Zur historischen Erfassung des vorkolonialen Schwarzafrika in der deutschen Forschung des 19. und frühen 20. Jahrhunderts* (Stuttgart, 1988), 324–9.

[58] Müller, 'Grundzüge', 195–7.

[59] Cf. Marx, *'Völker ohne Schrift und Geschichte'*, 341–2. In this, Schmidt was not unlike Arnold J. Toynbee in his later writings.

in Germany never showed any interest in a historically minded ethnology. A brief, but intense dialogue between *cultural* historians and ethnologists came to an end in the mid-1920s.[60] From the beginning, it was marred by a divergent understanding of the term 'Kulturgeschichte': whereas in ethnology 'Kulturgeschichte' stood for a non-evolutionist position, historians who rallied around this flag were much more open-minded than their colleagues in political history towards mildly evolutionist approaches borrowed from neighbouring disciplines.[61]

A new *rapprochement* between history and anthropology in Germany had to wait until the 1980s. Since then, Clifford Geertz in particular has enjoyed a formidable reputation as the master of a hermeneutics of the supposed 'Other'. Ironically, the warm welcome offered to a leading representative of symbolic or interpretative anthropology by a number of German historians today[62] means a kind of homecoming. The link between German historicism and the study of 'peoples without history' that failed to materialize in Germany itself was forged by one of the great pioneers and innovators of the generation of Karl Lamprecht, Otto Hintze, Friedrich Meinecke, and Max Weber: Franz Boas, who later became the towering father-figure of American Cultural Anthropology.[63]

Franz Boas was born in 1858 in Minden in Westphalia, the son of a well-to-do Jewish merchant family with liberal leanings. Carl Schurz was an old friend of the family. Boas's studies of chemistry, physics, and especially geography took him to Heidelberg, Bonn, Kiel, and finally to Berlin. He admired

---

[60] Haas, *Historische Kulturforschung*, 305–8. The historian Fritz Kern (at Bonn University from 1922 to 1937) was crucial in this exchange.

[61] This misunderstanding was pointed out in Erich Rothacker, 'Zur Methodenlehre der Ethnologie und der Kulturgeschichtsschreibung', *Vierteljahresschrift für wissenschaftliche Philosophie und Soziologie*, 36 (1912), 85.

[62] See, for example, Ute Daniel, ' "Kultur" und "Gesellschaft": Überlegungen zum Gegenstandsbereich der Sozialgeschichte', *Geschichte und Gesellschaft*, 19 (1993), 82–4.

[63] 'there is no real question that he was the most important single force in shaping American anthropology in the first half of the twentieth century.' George W. Stocking, Jr., 'Introduction: The Basic Assumptions of Boasian Anthropology', in id. (ed.), *A Franz Boas Reader: The Shaping of American Anthropology, 1883–1911* (Chicago, 1974), 1.

Alexander von Humboldt and his universalist vision of science. He studied Friedrich Ratzel's writings on anthropogeography and ethnology, and worked with Adolf Bastian and later with Rudolf Virchow, who impressed him deeply as a scientist and a liberal politician. His first field-research was conducted among the Canadian Inuit (or Eskimos) in 1883–4.[64] Having failed to obtain satisfactory employment in Germany, Boas emigrated to the United States in 1886. Ten years later, he joined the staff of Columbia University and in 1899 was appointed to its newly created chair of anthropology.[65]

Boas's mature ideas that shaped two generations of American anthropologists are rooted in the German period of his life when he received a humanistic education and a thorough scientific training, and absorbed the general intellectual atmosphere of the time.[66] Boas advocated strict empiricism and a research orientation[67]—a proclivity shared by German natural scientists and professional historians alike. He did not deny the limited validity of developmental or evolutionist ideas, but regarded most of them as unsupported (or even unsupportable) by evidence.[68] He likewise objected to a strict environmental determinism. He replaced the conjectures and loose analogies of the comparative method[69] with the certainties of what he called the 'histori-

[64] Cf. Cathleen Carol Knötsch, *Franz Boas bei den kanadischen Inuit im Jahre 1883–1884* (Bonn, 1992).

[65] Cf. Erich Kasten, 'Franz Boas: Ein engagierter Wissenschaftler in der Auseinandersetzung mit seiner Zeit', in *Franz Boas: Ethnologe, Anthropologe, Sprachwissenschaftler. Ein Wegbereiter der modernen Wissenschaft vom Menschen* (Berlin, 1992), 7–37, at 23. For biographical information see Volker Rodekamp (ed.), *Franz Boas 1852–1942: Ein amerikanischer Anthropologe aus Minden* (Bielefeld, 1994).

[66] Robert Lowie was the first commentator to draw attention to Boas's German background (*The History of Ethnological Theory*, New York, 1937). A good summary of German influences is Egon Renner, 'Franz Boas' Historismus und seine Rolle bei der Begründung der amerikanischen Ethnologie', in *Franz Boas: Ethnologe, Anthropologe, Sprachwissenschaftler*, 125–67.

[67] Cf. Wolfgang Rudolph, *Der Kulturelle Relativismus: Kritische Analyse einer Grundsatzfragen-Diskussion in der amerikanischen Ethnologie* (Berlin, 1968), 17–19.

[68] George W. Stocking, Jr., 'Franz Boas and the Culture Concept in Historical Perspective', in id., *Race, Culture and Evolution: Essays in the History of Anthropology* (2nd edn., Chicago, 1982), 211.

[69] Franz Boas, 'The Limitations of the Comparative Method of Anthropology' (1896), in id., *Race, Language and Culture* (New York, 1940), 270–80. On Boas's objections to evolutionism see Renner, 'Franz Boas' Historismus', 134–41.

cal method' based on observation and turning on the central question of what was—in the case of an individual ethnic group—original and what was borrowed.[70] Cultural phenomena were the results of specific and complex historical processes.[71] Boas took Ratzel's point that history ought to be conceived of in terms of migrations and cultural influences, while he objected to a notion of culture limited to the mechanical addition of individual elements and features. His main argument against Graebner's diffusionist *Kulturkreislehre* was that it excluded the cognitive dimension by neglecting psychology and the analysis of meaning. Instead, Boas advocated investigations of 'the different interpretations and attitudes of the people themselves toward the phenomenon present in the principal material'.[72] More rigorously than any of his predecessors in the German tradition of cultural (or anthropo-) geography, he applied the quintessentially historicist principle of individuality to the study of culture. He was one of the first authors to have consistently used the word 'culture' in the plural.[73]

The alleged difference between *Naturvölker* (primitive peoples) and *Kulturvölker* (civilized peoples) made little sense to him. In Boas's view, there existed only a plurality of cultures, each with its own pattern of internal development, and none of them normatively superior to others.[74] The rise of civilization in Europe seemed to him to have been the outcome of contingent factors, not the result of a providential plan.[75] Some of his students later turned this into a full theory of radical 'cultural relativism'. Boas was a determined academic critic and political opponent of all forms of racism and Eurocentrism.[76] By reviving the notion, going back to

[70] Stocking, 'Franz Boas', 206.   [71] Ibid. 211.
[72] Franz Boas, 'Review of Graebner, "Methode der Ethnologie" ' (1911), in id., *Race, Language and Culture*, 296. Pater Wilhelm Schmidt attempts to refute Boas's (and Alfred L. Kroeber's) criticism of the 'kulturhistorische Methode' in his 'Die kulturhistorische Methode und die nordamerikanische Ethnologie', *Anthropos*, 14–15 (1919–20), 546–63.
[73] Stocking, 'Franz Boas', 203.
[74] In contrast to Oswald Spengler, Boas did not deny the value of comparisons. He retained an 'elementaristic comparativism inherited from the natural sciences' (ibid. 207).   [75] Ibid. 213.
[76] He continued to publish on this subject in German. See his *Kultur und Rasse* (Berlin, 1914).

Herder, of a culture as an integrated way of life,[77] as a living microcosm held together by a few basic ideas or organizing principles,[78] he took part in the 'holistic revolution' of the early twentieth century. Neither evolutionist nor diffusionist ethnology were particularly interested in cultural wholes, and Boas went his own original way, as he also did on other issues. Lamprecht in his later years,[79] Breysig, and the German advocates of *Volksgeschichte* (ethnic history)[80] shared similar ideas, as did the pioneers of Gestalt psychology[81]— and perhaps, if one accepts a very broad meaning of the term 'holism', even some of those historians who were now talking about 'synthesis' or 'histoire totale'. Boas's holism was, however, of a particularistic kind. It ruled out the writing of universal history, at least at the present level of knowledge.[82]

During the second decade of the twentieth century, the national schools of ethnology parted ways. Evolutionism, the last and only paradigm of universal stature, was now in limbo everywhere (it was soon to re-emerge as neo-evolutionism without ever recovering its Victorian prominence). The British school was dominated by Malinowski's functionalism and had lost interest in any kind of history. German and Austrian ethnologists saw themselves as cultural historians of non-literate peoples, but got bogged down in the tracing of specific diffusions and influences, and were unable to arrive

[77] Stocking, 'Franz Boas', 229. Boas even used the expression 'genius of a people', an exact translation of Herder's 'Volksgeist'. See Stocking, 'The Basic Assumptions of Boasian Anthropology', 6–7.

[78] But Boas, the strict empiricist, distanced himself from Leo Frobenius's speculative holism. In a review of one of Frobenius's books he wrote: 'By following the methods presented in this book, anything and everything can be proved. It is fiction, not science.' Quoted in Marvin Harris, *The Rise of Anthropological Theory: A History of Theories of Culture* (New York, 1968), 260.

[79] Cf. Schorn-Schütte, *Karl Lamprecht*, 84–6. In this respect, the decisive influence on Lamprecht was that of the philosopher and psychologist Wilhelm Wundt.

[80] Cf. Willi Oberkrome, *Volksgeschichte: Methodische Innovation und völkische Ideologisierung in der deutschen Geschichtswissenschaft 1918–1945* (Göttingen, 1993).

[81] Cf. Michael G. Ash, *Gestalt Psychology in German Culture, 1890–1967: Holism and the Quest for Objectivity* (Cambridge, 1995).

[82] 'We must understand the process by which individual culture grew before we can undertake to lay down the laws by which the culture of all mankind grew.' Franz Boas, *The Growth of Indian Mythologies* (1896), quoted in Rudolph, *Der Kulturelle Relativismus*, 20.

at a non-mechanistic concept of culture. The German traditions of holism, relativism, hermeneutics, methodical empiricism, and linguistic research were finally amalgamated in the work of Franz Boas, a sober romantic in the New World. He took central tenets of German historicism and drew conclusions from them that would have surprised the nineteenth-century German masters of historiography. As Boas implicitly demonstrated, the exclusion or even denigration of 'peoples without history', so commonplace in German mainstream historical writing, was not a *necessary* consequence of historicist principles. Franz Boas's *translatio* of German historicism created a new interpretative and empirical science of man in nature and history which preserved impulses of the Herder–Ritter–Ratzel countertradition. For Boas, history knew no boundary between an active Western core and a sluggish non-Western periphery. 'Peoples without history' had ceased to exist.

15

'Westward the course of empire takes its way'

Imperialism and the Frontier in British and German Historical Writing around 1900

BENEDIKT STUCHTEY

When his viceroyalty in India ended with his resignation in 1905, Lord Curzon, the statesman noted for his influential policy in Asia, became Chancellor of Oxford University. Here, where he himself had been educated in an imperial spirit,[1] he delivered widely acclaimed lectures on colonial questions, one of which he entitled simply: 'Frontiers'.[2] Curzon is well remembered for the formation of the North-West Frontier Province during his Indian administration, and as Foreign Secretary under Lloyd George he became fascinated with what he regarded as the mobile frontier of Persia,[3] which was highly significant for British imperialism in Asia in the early twentieth century.

His practical politics certainly did not lack a theoretical basis. In his lecture on frontiers Curzon pointed out that this subject had so far been wholly ignored, although 'frontier policy is of the first practical importance, and has a more profound effect upon the peace or warfare of nations than any other factor, political or economic'; it was common to

---

[1] Richard Symonds, *Oxford and Empire: The Last Lost Cause?* (Oxford, 1986), 36–40.
[2] Lord Curzon of Kedleston, *Frontiers* (The Romanes Lecture 1907; Oxford, 1924, New York, 1969).
[3] Lord Curzon of Kedleston, *Persia and the Persian Question*, 2 vols. (London, 1892).

speak of Great Britain as the greatest sea power, but despite its colonial possessions in North America, Africa, and Asia, nobody really took into account 'that she is also the greatest land-power in the Universe'.[4] He went on to describe how the history of the extension of the frontier had shaped the character of the British Empire, and how the process of expanding the imperial frontier could be compared with the settlement of North America. Curzon's creation of the North West Frontier Province in India in 1901 was, in his view, analogous to the 'reservation' system of the Indian territories that had developed in North America a century earlier.[5] In both cases he discovered what he called the 'influence of Frontier expansion upon national character',[6] the emergence of the individual settler and his self-confident, earnest, and restless manhood, and the adventurous life of conflict between savagery and civilization. In Curzon's opinion, British character built the Empire, just as the Empire shaped the pioneering character of its officers, who experienced an ennobling and invigorating stimulus in the highlands of the Indian border or in the equatorial forests of Africa. In short, the frontier and its experience as described by Curzon was a crucial part of British imperialism. It contributed to the understanding of the Empire's past and it possessed a character-building element for future imperial tasks.[7]

What Curzon did not spell out in detail, but what played a crucial part in nineteenth-century British imperial history, was that while the London government rarely initiated frontier policy, expanding the Empire's frontier was deliberately pursued by the men on the spot. Trying to stabilize the frontiers in the colonies by means of new annexations, governors effectively produced new frontier problems. The result was an empire which, for reasons of security, 'grew in spite of itself', even at the time of Cobden and Bright, when expansionism was not uncontroversial.[8]

---

[4] Curzon, *Frontiers*, 4, 7. [5] Ibid. 30.
[6] Ibid. 54–8, quotation at 55.
[7] For this question in general compare Kathryn Tidrick, *Empire and the English Character* (London, 1992).
[8] John S. Galbraith, 'The "Turbulent Frontier" as a Factor in British Expansion', *Comparative Studies in Society and History*, 2 (1959–60), 150–68, at 168.

Assuming that the Empire was, and to a certain extent probably still is, at the heart of English national identity, some scholars have argued that the imperial frontier could be a constitutive (historiographical) category. In the older colonial historiography the British Empire had been compared to a living organism capable of expansion and contraction. In the early twentieth century, when it emerged that the Empire could not expand much further, global frontiers seemed to be closing in.[9] In the context of American historiography of this time, Frederick Jackson Turner's famous study of 1893, *The Significance of the Frontier in American History*, comes to mind. Turner has been characterized as an important exponent of US imperialist ideologies since the late nineteenth century.[10] In fact, Curzon himself drew attention to modern American historical writing which 'has devoted itself with patriotic ardour to tracing the evolution of the national character as determined by its western march across the continent. In no land and upon no people are the evidences more plainly stamped.'[11] Turner had developed the idea that the American nation had been formed by its westward movement: American national characteristics such as individuality and the pioneering spirit were shaped on the frontier between civilization and wilderness. This western frontier was an expanding frontier, the edge of settlement, and in the words of Bishop George Berkeley it had a constitutive element: 'Westward the course of empire takes its way.'[12]

The important influence of Turner's thesis on American historiography has been constantly examined and has remained a source of inspiration ever since.[13] Whether there

[9] Bill Schwarz, *The Expansion of England: Race, Ethnicity and Cultural History* (London, 1996), 2; an impressive recent survey is by Peter J. Cain and A. G. Hopkins, *British Imperialism*, 2 vols. (London, 1993).

[10] Hans-Ulrich Wehler, *Der Aufstieg des amerikanischen Imperialismus. Studien zur Entwicklung des Imperium Americanum 1865–1900* (Göttingen, 1974), 34 ff.

[11] Curzon, *Frontiers*, 55.

[12] George Berkeley, *Verses on the Prospects of Planting Arts and Learning in America* (1752), quoted from Matthias Waechter, *Die Erfindung des amerikanischen Westens: Die Geschichte der Frontier-Debatte* (Freiburg, 1996), 38.

[13] There is a great deal of literature on the frontier thesis. See the relatively recent studies by Wilbur R. Jacobs, *On Turner's Trail: 100 Years of Writing Western History* (Lawrence, Kan., 1994), and John Mack Faragher, 'The Frontier Trail:

are any possible parallels between the American example and British and German imperial thinking is the question this essay addresses, bearing in mind, of course, that Turner's thesis applied only to America and that it was heavily criticized even in his own time.[14] The American author Mark Twain, for example, who had certainly been formatively influenced by the world of the pioneers, later became a stronger critic of the idea of the frontier. In his great travel book *Following the Equator. A Journey around the World* (1897) Twain, although rather Anglophile, criticized the expansion of the British Empire. He described it to his readers, accompanying them from Sydney and Melbourne to Ceylon, Calcutta, Cape Town, and Johannesburg, where he witnessed the South African War. This book is certainly more than just good literature; it also gives some impression of amateur historiography as Twain always integrated historical accounts with travel descriptions.[15] Moreover, the author clearly criticized the white settler's contempt for native traditions, stating that the difference between slavery and colonial experience was not very great. The analogy with the frontier thesis was obvious: here the small American entrepreneur, the individual settler; there the 'man on the spot' in British India, or the adventurer in the gold mines of South Africa. Twain, a member of the Anti-Imperialist League, did not hide his detestation of the destructiveness of colonial exploitation; what he ironically described as the 'blessings' of Western civilization was indeed, in his eyes, the 'white man's burden', but the other way round. Twain, with a good number of other American and European intellectuals, drew attention to what he called 'The person sitting in darkness', the title of one of his anti-imperialist essays, showing

Rethinking Turner and Reimagining the American West', *American Historical Review*, 98 (1993), 106–17; cf. also Peter Novick, *That Noble Dream: The Objectivity Question and the American Historical Profession* (Cambridge, 1988). Linda Colley, *The Significance of the Frontier in British History* (Austin, Texas, 1995).

[14] For a survey of Turner's work and the debate on the frontier thesis to the present see Waechter, *Die Erfindung*, esp. 141 ff. on the reception of Turner's thesis in the early 20th century.

[15] Mark Twain, *Following the Equator and Anti-Imperialist Essays*, ed. Shelley Fisher Fishkin, with an introduction by Gore Vidal and afterword by Fred Kaplan (Oxford, 1996).

that American and European frontier imperialism had no fewer dark sides than bright ones.[16] Yet the historians examined in this essay took only the glamour into account.

It should be also noted, however, that Turner himself was not an active imperialist and that he did not advocate American overseas expansion. It was mainly the motive behind his thesis that attracted other scholars to adopt it for their own work—or to think in its terms, parallel to Turner. He concentrated only on a 'white' perspective, that is, the viewpoint of the dominant, colonial side. As Jürgen Osterhammel has shown in an article about the cultural frontier, Turner was not interested in intercultural societies located between civilized and noncivilized territory. Instead, he focused on the 'white' frontiersmen.[17] Turner thus took a traditional standpoint and did not consider exploring the mutual cultural perceptions of the colonizing and the colonized peoples. In this way imperial history illustrated and justified the 'winner's' perspective without paying attention to the historiographical opportunities that lay beyond the frontiers: the significance of cultural difference, the chance for cultural reconciliation, and the construction of identities formed by the frontier. It required a historian with experience of and interest in intercultural societies to point out the danger of colonial arrogance and the problem of 'an increasing tendency to override local knowledge, and to apply English standards and methods of government to wholly un-English conditions'.[18] As W. E. H. Lecky said: 'Government by telegraph is a very dangerous thing.'[19] This was a significant statement for a British intellectual with an

---

[16] On anti-colonialism at this time cf. Benedikt Stuchtey, 'The International of Critics: German and British Scholars during the South African War (1899–1902)', *South African Historical Journal*, 41 (1999), 1–23; Bernard Porter, *Critics of Empire: British Radical Attitudes to Colonialism in Africa, 1895–1914* (London, 1968); A. P. Thornton, *The Imperial Idea and its Enemies: A Study in British Power* (London, 1966); Miles Taylor, 'Imperium et Libertas? Rethinking the Radical Critique of Imperialism during the Nineteenth Century', *Journal of Imperial and Commonwealth History*, 19 (1991), 1–23.

[17] Jürgen Osterhammel, 'Kulturelle Grenzen in der Expansion Europas', *Saeculum: Jahrbuch für Universalgeschichte*, 46 (1995), 101–38.

[18] W. E. H. Lecky, 'The Empire: Its Value and its Growth', in *Historical and Political Essays*, ed. Elisabeth Lecky (London, 1908), 43–67, quotation at 57.

[19] Ibid.

Anglo-Irish background and a continuing concern for England's oldest colony, Ireland. In more than this matter, Lecky was a noteworthy exception among British historians.

The present essay examines British historians such as Froude, Seeley, Egerton, and Lucas, before it turns to some German historians. It may be no coincidence that most historians discussed in this essay held nationalistic political opinions: the idea, if not myth, of the pioneer carried with it a certain cultural and social brutality, hypocrisy, and sometimes even plain racism. But they did not discuss these aspects. Further, none of the historians discussed in this essay took any notice of the gender dimension of colonialism, namely, that in the nineteenth century women were often at the frontier of settlement. Whether in America or Australia, women carried arms and, in effect, became pioneer feminists. Interestingly, in the same year (1907) in which Curzon gave his lecture on the 'Frontiers', the German historian Karl Stählin published his Heidelberg inaugural lecture on exactly the same topic.[20] It seems that in both countries scholars developed an interest in the same subject, probably without knowing of each other's work. The German side necessarily looked to British history as its own colonial experience was relatively short and consequently colonial historiography was just beginning.

This observation can be confirmed by a closer study of the work of German historians such as Heinrich von Treitschke and Dietrich Schäfer, both of whom were certainly Anglophobe in political terms, but who also, on the other hand, admired the British Empire as a historical phenomenon. For Stählin history had an educational function, but this lay less in justifying political decisions than in making them intelligible to his readers. Therefore his essay, which is a plea for the idea of the frontier, looked far back into Scottish and English history in order to try to understand contemporary questions posed by the Indian border; for this purpose he made extensive use of works that gave him the historical background of Scotland (Froude), and insights

---

[20] Karl Stählin, 'Die Politik der englischen Landgrenze von einst und jetzt: Die schottische und die indische Frage', *Historische Zeitschrift*, 98 (1907), 55–115.

into the contemporary politics of India (Curzon). Stählin's thesis was that it was the union between England and Scotland, bringing stability and peace to the island, which prepared the ground for the country to build up a world-wide empire. From this he reasoned that only by stabilizing and extending the Indian frontier would the Empire's future existence be guaranteed: a process of the past and a condition of the present were closely connected. This was based on the historical as well as contemporary experience of the frontiersman, whose 'peaceful, civilizing "forward policy" ' was the military and political prerequisite for subsequent cultural prosperity in the newly conquered land.[21] Without mentioning Turner's frontier thesis, but clearly arguing along the same lines, Stählin explained what he understood by the civilizing achievements of the pioneers on the moving imperial frontier, whether in the Scottish or the Indian borderlands:

> Filled with the warrior's and the hunter's love of adventure, and supported by the missionary activity of the English church, they press forward into areas, some of which have not been entered by Europeans before, and settle, surrounded by a hundred dangers and exposed to the inclement climate, alone or with their families, in the remotest posts. They take the field against robber bands and, with endless diplomatic tact, overcome the mistrust of the peaceful population. They tirelessly ride through the country, exploring it; they study new languages and dialects, and make them available for science, scholarship, and practical use in the border service by writing dictionaries. They build houses, roads, and villages; set up hospitals in the hills; turn dirty Oriental living places into European residences, obsolete fortifications into modern forts, and within twenty years transform a large country, previously subjected to permanent chaos, into a peaceful and flourishing province.[22]

Expanding and defending the frontier were two sides of the same imperial coin. Yet Stählin, who admired this recipe for British imperial success, did not recommend it to German imperialism. In fact, unlike other historians such as Schäfer, who contrasted the German and the British cases,

[21] Ibid. 89.   [22] Ibid. 91–2.

Stählin did not compare them at all in his lecture. He regarded the frontier as a genuine Anglo-American phenomenon applicable only to British or American colonial expansion, and at the very core of the existence of these states.[23]

To the present day the idea of a colonizing frontier (*Erschließungsgrenze*) is an important metaphor in both American and European historical writing.[24] This may partly be because the frontier thesis 'provides us with an important tool of analysis to explain the cultural dynamics of self-identification through exclusion'.[25] The colonizing, expanding frontier was controlled by individuals and private initiatives. They saw their civilizing, missionary tasks as secondary to their main aim of cultivating the land. In contrast to Turner's society of 'white' frontiersmen, the colonizing frontier should not be understood as a clearly defined borderline, but as a territory where mutual perception between settler and 'wilderness' could take place. The frontier offered a chance to define one's own identity *and* to construct the other as a result of the experience of contrasting one's own culture with the other. It thus provided a mechanism for exclusion or inclusion. Therefore, it had an additional quality to the pedagogical one described by Curzon, because the (cultural) frontier was not limited to geographical or political borders.[26] According to Stählin's account, however, there was not much intercultural contact from which the colonial power would profit, and it was up to the frontiersman alone to decide what was best for the people he met on the borderline.

This cultural process, together with the myth of endless land for settlement, can also be reconstructed taking the example of southern Africa,[27] which definitely played a

---

[23] Ibid, 115.
[24] See Osterhammel, 'Kulturelle Grenzen', 111 ff.; also William H. McNeill, *The Global Condition: Conquerors, Catastrophes, and Community* (Princeton, 1992), 3–63.
[25] Gerard Delanty, 'The Frontier and Identities of Exclusion in European History', *History of European Ideas*, 22 (1996), 93–103, at 94.
[26] Osterhammel, 'Kulturelle Grenzen', 116.
[27] Jörg Fisch, 'Der Mythos vom leeren Land in Südafrika oder Die verspätete Entdeckung der Afrikaner durch die Afrikaaner', in Heinz Duchhardt, Jürg A. Schlumberger, and Peter Segl (eds.), *Afrika: Entdeckung und Erforschung eines Kontinents* (Cologne, 1989), 143–64.

crucial role in the imperial thinking of British and South African historians. For the latter the Great Trek and the 'trekking Boer' were *the* constitutive elements of South African history.[28] Consequently, what Turner thought he had developed for American history as a unique process and a singularly American experience was in fact a widespread phenomenon applicable to other colonial processes as well. While this demonstrates Turner's one-sidedness, it does not reduce the importance of his thesis and its possible applicability to classic British and German imperial historiography at the turn of the century.[29]

It has been observed also that in Britain imperial and colonial studies were often integrated into general historical studies;[30] further, British historians did not form the same sorts of 'schools' with explicit methodological and political implications as did their German colleagues. A number of common aspects are evident, for example, that most British historians regarded the colonies not as beyond the British Isles but as part of them. In this respect Canada or Australia were as close to London as Kent or the Scottish Highlands. Moreover, they regarded imperial affairs in terms of external dynamics, so that there was no real division between English history at home (internal) and colonial history abroad (external). The two formed a unity, which meant that the existing dualism between European and non-European history was to be overcome.

The American version of the frontier and the British varieties of imperial expansion developed certain similiarities: first, in forming a national sentiment as a reflection of 'this noble heritage of achievement and suffering' into which 'the entire nation, purified and united in its search for the

---

[28] Cf. Martin Legassick, 'The Frontier Tradition in South African Historiography', in Shula Marks *et al.* (eds.), *Economy and Society in Pre-industrial South Africa* (London, 1980), 44–79.

[29] Howard Lamar and Leonard Thompson (eds.), *The Frontier in History: North America and Southern Africa Compared* (New Haven, 1981). See esp. the theoretical, highly instructive introduction by the editors, 3–40.

[30] Jürgen Osterhammel, 'Epochen der britischen Geschichtsschreibung', in Wolfgang Küttler, Jörn Rüsen, and Ernst Schulin (eds.), *Geschichtsdiskurs*, i: *Grundlagen und Methoden der Historiographiegeschichte* (Frankfurt am Main, 1993), 157–88, at 167.

Frontier, both of its occupation and its manhood, has proudly entered'; and secondly, in believing that the construction of the frontier had an 'ennobling and invigorating stimulus' for youth, 'saving them alike from the corroding ease and the morbid excitements of Western civilization'.[31] The defence of the ideals of the frontier carried with it an implicit criticism of current imperial policy. Because the adherents of frontier ideology regarded the state of the Empire as unsatisfactory, they advocated a policy that was basically rooted in conservative opinions.

It was based on the conviction that the history which was taught to young people who went to administer the colonies needed to serve categories of 'masculine' authority. As Stefan Collini has pointed out in his account of the 'idea of character' in the late Victorian age, society envisaged the individual, even the isolated individual, as a 'governing value', typified, for example, by the soldier or explorer, whose struggles against adversity were a test of his 'manliness' and of the Empire's capacity to survive.[32] Those who explored new frontiers, and those who defended them provided the Empire with a positive and encouraging model.

General surveys based on the chronological approach were typical of British imperial historiography. Case studies were rare. But this was only to be expected given that the attention of the public was to be drawn to the development of the Empire as a whole. If imperial history was to be employed as a vehicle for educational propaganda only a historical synthesis could really serve this aim. It was believed that broad lines, such as the growth or decline of imperial government, economic influence, or administrative control, were the principles by which imperial historians should orientate themselves. Constitutional themes, not least the evolution of a centralized empire into a partnership and commonwealth, played an important role in understanding imperial history. In this respect the Whig concept had not yet been abandoned.

---

[31] Curzon, *Frontiers*, 56, 57.
[32] Stefan Collini, *Public Moralists: Political Thought and Intellectual Life in Britain, 1850–1930* (Oxford, 1991), 116 f.; cf. Mrinalini Sinha, *Colonial Masculinity: The 'Manly Englishman' and the 'Effeminate Bengali' in the Late Nineteenth Century* (Manchester, 1995).

However, imperial history was not fully accepted for some time. The British colonies did not become a subject for study in schools and a part of the curriculum of Cambridge and Oxford, for example, until the 1890s.[33] At the same time the older approach to teaching colonial history, based on large compendia proceeding fact by fact and year by year,[34] was replaced by more interpretative insights into the imperial context. This was a significant shift because with the method and tone, the authorship of the texts also changed. While in the middle of the nineteenth century amateurs had formulated the Whig interpretation of the nation's rise and triumph that secured the spirit of English liberty and reform, at the end of the century it was increasingly professional academics who developed an interest in topics such as patriotism and particularly imperial expansion.

Among the historians of this generation who lived through this historiographical change was James Anthony Froude. He is an obvious starting point, both as regards the southern Africa problem already mentioned, and in connection with the idea of the frontier. Supposedly Thomas Carlyle's most important disciple, although he did not display the same interest in Germany, Froude is best known for his works on sixteenth-century English history.[35] Though he studied original sources and numerous manuscripts in the Public Record Office, the British Museum, and other archives, Froude approved neither of Henry Buckle's positivism nor of William Stubbs's scientific and Germanophile methods. Probably, after Thomas Babington Macaulay and Lecky, Froude was one of the most widely read British historians in the nineteenth century, but his works, written in an elegant and narrative style, sometimes lack balanced judgement, and are often based on superficial research.

[33] John MacKenzie, *Propaganda and Empire: The Manipulation of British Public Opinion, 1880–1960* (Manchester, 1984), 174 ff.

[34] Ibid. 177; for example: James Hewitt, *Geography of the British Colonies and Dependencies* (London, 1869); William Francis Collier, *History of the British Empire* (London, 1880).

[35] J. A. Froude, *History of England from the Fall of Wolsey to the Defeat of the Spanish Armada*, 12 vols. (London, 1856–70); see G. P. Gooch, *History and Historians in the Nineteenth Century* (1913; London, 1935), 332–9.

Consequently he was vigorously attacked by Stubbs and Edward A. Freeman. Ironically, Froude was to be appointed Freeman's successor as Regius Professor of Modern History at Oxford for the last two years of his life.

Froude's historical thinking was conditioned by his belief in the English Reformation as the basis of England's constitutional and religious triumph over the Catholic world of its rivals, Spain and Rome. The defeat of the Armada was the beginning of English naval greatness (described in his *English Seamen in the Sixteenth Century*, 1895) and of the colonial Empire. Thus England's liberty was rooted in its defeat of its rivals' power in the church and on the oceans. While traditional Whig historiography paid little attention to the Tudors, Froude made their history an accepted field of research. But he also had firm opinions on contemporary imperial problems. Froude's essays on South Africa, Australia, New Zealand, and the British West Indies as well as his books on Ireland were all highly popular, not least because he had visited all these places and could describe them vividly.[36]

Behind his belief in England's imperial power lay Froude's conviction that colonial expansion would not have been possible without Protestantism. As he thought that Catholicism was politically dangerous, Froude detested everything connected with Catholic resurgence while glorifying the Protestant mission both at home and abroad, thereby justifying British imperialism.[37] However, Froude regarded England's domestic political stability, as compared with Bismarck's Germany, as under threat because of the influence which the Irish clericals and the Home Rule movement had on governments in London. In contrast to England, Germany, in Froude's view, had successfully resisted Catholic demands which would have undermined liberal values, and German Protestantism had guaranteed

---

[36] Waldo Hilary Dunn, *James Anthony Froude: A Biography*, 2 vols. (Oxford, 1961, 1963), ii. 388–417, 517–57; Jeffrey Paul von Arx, *Progress and Pessimism: Religion, Politics and History in Late Nineteenth-Century Britain* (Cambridge, Mass., 1985), 173–200.

[37] For this in general see Barbara Schwegmann, *Die Protestantische Mission und die Ausdehnung des Britischen Empires* (Würzburg, 1990).

Imperialism and the Frontier 301

the creation of the German Empire after the defeat of Catholic France.[38]

In Froude's view England's task was certainly to resist the forces that threatened the unity of the Empire, whose rise and condition he described in a number of remarkable texts.[39] His imperialism started somewhat traditionally with Ireland. He advocated the rule of the Protestant Ascendancy in Ireland by explaining that the Catholic Irish majority was incapable of self-government in political, economic, and even moral terms. Lecky, himself a liberal Protestant unionist and in his late days a defender of Empire, ruthlessly criticized Froude's picture of Ireland. The pattern which Lecky discerned in Froude's texts about Ireland was also visible in most of Froude's imperial writings: it was his open racism, the belief that the English were superior to all colonial races, who needed Britain's paternalistic administration and institutions.[40]

Moreover, England needed the colonies for its own benefit as well, particularly to defuse tension at home. Froude's article 'England and her Colonies' was inspired by the contemporary emigration to the colonies, which Froude regarded as a necessary outlet for the overpopulated English industrial cities. He also saw it as a means of strengthening the morale of a generation which, he believed, had already

---

[38] James Anthony Froude, 'Condition and Prospects of Protestantism', in id., *Short Studies on Great Subjects*, 4 vols. (London, 1898–1900), ii (1900), 146–79; in general see Karl Rohe, 'The British Imperialist Intelligentsia and the Kaiserreich', in Paul Kennedy and Anthony Nicholls (eds.), *Nationalist and Racialist Movements in Britain and Germany before 1914* (London, 1981), 130–42; Percy Ernst Schramm, 'Englands Verhältnis zur deutschen Kultur zwischen der Reichsgründung und der Jahrhundertwende', in Werner Conze (ed.), *Deutschland und Europa. Historische Studien zur Völker- und Staatenordnung des Abendlandes. Festschrift für Hans Rothfels* (Düsseldorf, 1951), 135–75; Günter Hollenberg, *Englisches Interesse am Kaiserreich: Die Attraktivität Preußen-Deutschlands für konservative und liberale Kreise in Großbritannien 1860–1914* (Wiesbaden, 1974); Manfred Messerschmidt, *Deutschland in englischer Sicht: Die Wandlungen des Deutschlandbildes in der englischen Geschichtsschreibung* (Düsseldorf, 1955).

[39] In particular: 'South Africa once more', *Fortnightly Review*, 26 (1879), 449–73; *Oceana or England and her Colonies* (London, 1886); 'England and her Colonies' and 'The Colonies once more', in *Short Studies*, ii. 180–216 and 397–438; *The English in the West Indies* (London, 1888).

[40] Benedikt Stuchtey, *W. E. H. Lecky (1838–1903): Historisches Denken und politisches Urteilen eines anglo-irischen Gelehrten* (Göttingen, 1997), 139–60.

been too much shaped by materialist tendencies.[41] All in all, he thought that England's colonial policy was dictated too much by political parties and too little by a national spirit. But, he believed,

> it is no party question; all ranks, all classes are equally interested, manufacturers in the creation of new markets, landowners in the expansion of soil ... Most of all is it the concern of the working men. Let broad bridges be established into other Englands, and they may exchange brighter homes and brighter prospects for their children for a life which is no life in foul alleys of London and Glasgow.[42]

Among the English 'public moralists', Froude was one of the earliest to advocate the strengthening of ties between the colonies and England.[43] When Australia and Canada developed more responsible governmental structures, he endorsed an imperial federation, long before this argument became fashionable among intellectuals and before it was taken up again by John Robert Seeley. But in contrast to Seeley, Froude advocated a federation less on political than on spiritual grounds.[44] In his widely read and impressionistic, even meditative, travel book *Oceana*, published in 1886, Froude expressed his conception of an English commonwealth of nations.[45] As Collini, Winch, and Burrow have shown,[46] in this book Froude drew quite pessimistic imperial analogies with ancient Rome. He tried to prove that the reasons for the decline of Rome could become the cause of a decline of the British Empire: luxury, corruption, and finally the loss of virtue—the very virtue which had originally been gained at the frontier—would lead to the collapse of the Empire once built in pride.[47] According to Froude, the

---

[41] Ilse Grossklaus, *James Anthony Froude und seine politische Ideenwelt im Spiegel der Entwicklung des Britischen Empire 1870–1880: Unter besonderer Berücksichtigung Südafrikas* (Frankfurt, 1981), 45 ff.   [42] Froude, 'England and her Colonies', 215.

[43] Cf. Collini, *Public Moralists*, 216.

[44] Dunn, *James Anthony Froude*, ii. 351 ff.

[45] J. A. Froude, *Oceana, or England and her Colonies* (London, 1886).

[46] Stefan Collini, Donald Winch, and John Burrow, *That Noble Science of Politics: A Study in Nineteenth-Century Intellectual History* (Cambridge, 1983), 190.

[47] For the parallels between ancient and modern history see R. F. Betts, 'The Allusion to Rome in British Imperialist Thought', *Victorian Studies*, 15 (1971), 149–59; another famous example is by Charles Prestwood Lucas, *Greater Rome and Greater Britain* (Oxford, 1912). Cf. the recent study by Norman Vance, *The Victorians and Ancient Rome* (London, 1997).

reason for the decline and fall was the dominance of commercial interests, which therefore needed to be kept under control by a strengthened class of farmers and small independent freeholders. The argument of lost virtue together with a critique of imperial policy which could no longer be identified with the frontier philosophy often emerged when the British Empire experienced a major crisis. A good example of this was the South African War (1899–1902), when the military and liberal intellectuals alike criticized an imperial policy that was dangerously reminiscent of the causes of the decline of the Roman Empire.[48]

Those who had cultivated the land and thus guaranteed security and stability were, in fact, the frontiersmen of Turner's philosophy. But the soldier, probably even more than the civilian, furnished the type of the frontiersman whose combination of courage and conciliation, of patience and pioneering initiative, of physical and intellectual training, was supposed to be an ennobling and invigorating example to the young generation, in short, the stimulus that was to save them from the bad influences of modern civilization. This argument can be found in much of the colonial literature at this time. In order to find evidence in support of his convictions Froude had travelled widely in North America, Australia, South Africa, and the West Indies. In his travel books he noted the desire of the peoples in the colonies to stay united with England in loyalty and interest, and to preserve unbroken the integrity of the Empire. At the centre of his colonial thinking lay the need for the creation of a worldwide commonwealth of English-speaking peoples that was to be united by the spirit of English culture. Therefore his ultimate aim was reunification with the United States in a commonwealth, in the hope that 'there will no longer be Englishmen and Americans, but [that] we shall be of one heart and mind, and perhaps of one name'.[49]

In the late nineteenth century this idea of a 'special relationship' with the United States emerged strongly among

---

[48] Keith Surridge, ' "All you soldiers are what we call pro-Boer": The Military Critique of the South African War, 1899–1902', *History*, 82 (1997), 582–600.
[49] Froude, *Oceana*, 353.

British intellectuals, and became a factor in British foreign policy.[50] It was rooted in Britain's response to the growth of the USA as a world power, and can be interpreted as an emotional search for support against growing competition from Europe, and Germany in particular. For the Boers in South Africa it was a similar case. The Boer War provided an opportunity to assert a sense of identity by means of comparison: parallels were sought with the American Civil War, and in both cases, here the Boers, there the American North, the struggle was for political freedom and free institutions. The freedom, however, was restricted to whites only, and in both countries those who were ruled were not to enjoy what the others demanded for themselves.[51]

Froude admired the American colonial settlements, but he feared that if England did not take its responsibility for its colonies seriously enough, they might apply for membership of the American Union. Thus he justified the need for English colonial settlement by the twofold argument that first, the English had to be earlier than the Americans, and second, they had to employ the same means as the Americans. Vast spaces were to be utilized and cultivated, and Froude wondered whether 'we may not exchange England for an English Empire in which every element shall be combined which can promise security to the whole'.[52] If the colonies were occupied by subjects of the British crown, this would, in Froude's opinion, consolidate patriotism in the British Isles as well as establish a sense of belonging to a common history in the colonies: 'The yet unexhausted vigour of our people, with boundless room to expand, will reproduce the old English character and the old English strength over an area of a hundred Britains. The United States of America themselves do not possess a more brilliant prospect.'[53] This idea of numerous reproductions of England in the colonies was repeated in later imperial historiography, becoming something of a topos.

---

[50] Ronald Hyam, *Britain's Imperial Century 1815–1914. A Study of Empire and Expansion* (London, 1976), 202 ff.

[51] Iain R. Smith, *The Origins of the South African War 1899–1902* (London, 1996), 10–11; G. M. Frederickson, *White Supremacy: A Comparative Study in American and South African History* (Oxford, 1981).

[52] Dunn, *James Anthony Froude*, ii. 354.   [53] Ibid. 355.

In another article, 'The Colonies once more', which Froude published on the outbreak of the Franco-Prussian War (1870), he warned that European politics might at some time drag England into the problems of the Continent. Emigration as a means of consolidating the Empire would reinforce England's insularity and special character within Europe, argued the Eurosceptic Froude. In fact, in his view, Britain did not belong to Europe at all. The Channel was much wider than the Atlantic. Britain's future should be westward orientated. Withdrawing from continental affairs meant turning to America and thus formulating interests common to the English-speaking world. In this amalgamation of English and Americans, Australians, South Africans, Canadians, etc. Froude saw the solution for every possible imperial problem: 'The British Empire will be held together by a magnetism which no local or selfish ambition can decompose. All difficulties will vanish then.'[54]

Froude's discussion of the significance of emigration for the Empire clarified his definition of 'colonies'. Colonies, in his view, were the territories which had been gained by more or less peaceful settlement and which were predominantly populated by English or 'white' settlers (Australia, New Zealand, South Africa, Canada), in contrast to imperial dependencies such as India, which had been gained by the sword and could only be defended in the same manner. Here the analogy between India and Ireland is all too obvious. Unlike the colonies, which according to Froude belonged to England because they wished to do so, both India and Ireland were to be treated as English possessions and, for racial and religious reasons, would never be fit for Home Rule.[55]

The role of the imperial historian was very much a public and a political one. This is also well demonstrated by what is generally considered to be the most famous and influential

[54] Ibid. 359.
[55] S. B. Cook, *Imperial Affinities: Nineteenth Century Analogies and Exchanges between India and Ireland* (New Delhi, 1993); cf. T. G. Fraser, 'Ireland and India', in Keith Jeffery (ed.), *'An Irish Empire'? Aspects of Ireland and the British Empire* (Manchester, 1996), 77–93.

British historical work of the second half of the nineteenth century, Seeley's *The Expansion of England*. Originally a lecture course on the British Empire delivered in 1881–2, this book was subsequently published in 1883, that is, shortly after the British occupation of Egypt, and sold 80,000 copies within two years. By 1901 it had gone through seventeen editions. It remained in print until 1956.

As one of Seeley's disciples, Hugh Edward Egerton, put it in 1897, this book 'threw a powerful searchlight on the development of British empire, and brought home to thousands of readers, who have never before thought of it, the sense that, after all, our Colonies are only England beyond the seas—a greater England but all the same'.[56] To popularize imperialism was one of Seeley's aims, and to identify imperialism with modern British history the other. Imperialism in this respect replaced the Whig concept of liberty as the main object of British history. Seeley's book, which used the term 'imperialism' only twice, and then in order to illustrate despotic rule, was henceforth regarded as the Bible of British imperial historiography.

Seeley was among those British historians who, *par excellence*, played an important part in public and political life.[57] In the late Victorian period an extensive literature on the Empire reflected popular sentiment and a public awareness of colonial concerns. The nature of imperial expansion, the value of colonies, and the future of the Empire were vividly discussed, essentially, however, in descriptive narratives such as travel accounts. To study the Empire in a distinctly historical context was something new. In 1884 Seeley, who taught history at Cambridge University from 1869 to 1895, was among the founding members of the Imperial Federation League, which was a movement trying

---

[56] Hugh E. Egerton, *A Short History of British Colonial Policy* (London, 1897), 6; see Richard Aldrich, 'Imperialism in the Study and Teaching of History', in J. A. Mangan (ed.), *'Benefits bestowed'? Education and British Imperialism* (Manchester, 1988), 23–38, at 25; in general see Eric Williams, *British Historians and the West Indies* (Trinidad, 1964); V. Harlow, *The Historian and British Colonial History* (inaugural lecture as Beit Professor of Colonial History; Oxford, 1951).

[57] For a detailed examination see Deborah Wormell, *Sir John Seeley and the Uses of History* (Cambridge, 1980); Peter Burroughs, 'John Robert Seeley and British Imperial History', *Journal of Imperial and Commonwealth History*, 1 (1972–3), 191–211.

to find a compromise between imperial unity and colonial nationalism.

If history was to be a popular and useful subject, then it could not be written in too complicated a manner. Only those historical facts and figures should be highlighted that could be portrayed as having contributed to England's progress towards the imperial world of the late nineteenth century. For obvious reasons Disraeli's romantic imperialism and his association of the monarchy with the Empire were more acceptable than Gladstone's more complex political ideas. Thus in school-books, for example, Disraeli was described as a lover of the pomp of Empire while Gladstone was shown as representing an overcautious Little-Englandism. Consequently Disraeli was more appropriate to join the list of imperial heroes which started in the Tudor period and included Cromwell and Livingstone.[58] Ironically, Gladstone appointed Seeley to his Cambridge Regius Professorship of Modern History in succession to Charles Kingsley.

School-books of this time drew their information from the classic nineteenth-century historians such as Macaulay, Froude, and Lecky, but most of all from Seeley. The reason for this probably lay in his special talent for simplification, and also for selecting from the past those bits which in his opinion had led to the rise of the nation-state and, in particular, the British Empire as the apogee of a state which had achieved a universal political order. For Seeley, history could be employed as a stimulating moral force, as a means to raise the morale of the nation.

In Seeley's opinion history could banish the pessimism of the late nineteenth century, it could form a national party and class consensus, and it could bridge political divisions, always assuming that the history of expansion taught a state patriotism. History, intertwined with politics, was the vision of a patriotic expansion of the state. In this reinterpretation of British history, the traditional emphasis of Whig historians on the progress of constitutional liberties gave way to an examination of the growth of the English state. The gradual

[58] MacKenzie, *Propaganda*, 176.

transformation of England into Greater Britain constituted the country's most striking achievement and fulfilled a providential destiny that finally guaranteed England's security. This idea was not necessarily based on original research. Rather, it required the ability to create syntheses with a political message. Seeley was interested in history as a teacher of morals. He needed generalizations, broad coherences, general principles, and comprehensive ideas. What he actually had to say on imperialism, or indeed on the idea of 'Greater Britain', was not novel.

What was new, however, was the lesson he drew from the history of the United States, particularly the notion that in spite of vast territories and a civil war, this federal state was a nation. Predicting the emergence of the United States and Russia as the new superpowers, Seeley urged Britain to become a federal empire if there was to be any future for its Empire. He justified this objective by references to history. According to Seeley, the British Empire was very different from most previous empires. Especially in the 'white' dominions of Australia, New Zealand, and Canada, it represented an extension of British culture into countries which were hardly populated so far. In fact, little conquest had taken place. Imperial rule had been achieved in a somewhat unplanned manner, or as Seeley put it in the much quoted phrase, 'in a fit of absence of mind'.[59] One could even say that expansion was England's destiny or the law of its history, based on the principle of mutual benefit, and on England's historical development as 'a maritime, colonising and industrial country'.[60] This point would later be taken up by Curzon who believed that expansion had become more than a law of history. It was now a pressing necessity for the future if great powers were to satisfy the economic needs of a growing

---

[59] John Seeley, *The Expansion of England* (London, 1883), 10; other lesser-known works by Seeley in which he expressed his views on imperial history are: *Her Majesty's Colonies* (1886) and *Our Colonial Expansion* (1887). Seeley's study *The Growth of British Policy* (1895) is not addressed in this essay in detail as it plays a central role in John Burrow's contribution to this volume; for an evaluation of Seeley's position in British historiography cf. Benedikt Stuchtey, 'Literature, Liberty, and Life of the Nation: British Historiography from Macaulay to Trevelyan', in Stefan Berger *et al.* (eds.), *Writing National Histories: Western Europe since 1800* (London, 1999), 30–46, esp. 36–7. [60] Seeley, *Expansion*, 80.

population.[61] Although the weak points in Seeley's analysis are relatively obvious—for example, he hardly examined the perspective of the colonized population—his contribution to imperial historiography was none the less highly influential because he drew attention to the problem of the imperial frontier. And this, the work of colonial settlement, was what counted, or in the words of Stählin referring to Seeley: 'And in the first instance this work benefits the imperialist idea and the defence of the Anglo-Indian Empire.'[62]

Seeley regarded history as a science which was able to correlate, analyse, and explain, and he rejected a merely entertaining, picturesque evocation of past times such as that practised by amateur historians. As can be seen also from his other important work, *The Growth of British Policy* (1895), Seeley wanted the historian to work like the scientist and draw lessons from historical laws in order to make forecasts about the future. These were the laws by which states rise and expand, or decline and fall. In a somewhat Carlylian fashion Seeley agreed that the nation's history was its Bible, and the historian a preacher, a public propagandist who taught history as the school of statemanship.

As far as seeing the historian as a political educator is concerned, Seeley could well be compared with the Prussian school of German historians which also discussed the usefulness of historical study for political socialization and for understanding both the present and the future.[63] A sentence such as: 'We shall all no doubt be wise after the event; we study history that we may be wise before the event,'[64] may as well have been written by Johann Gustav Droysen, for example. The future could be more confidently faced with knowledge of the past. The opening passage of *The Expansion of England* leaves us in no doubt as to where Seeley's historical education was intended to lead:

---

[61] Curzon, *Frontiers*, 7. [62] Stählin, 'Landgrenze', 92.
[63] Gangolf Hübinger, 'Geschichte als leitende Orientierungswissenschaft im 19. Jahrhundert', *Berichte zur Wissenschaftsgeschichte*, 11 (1988), 149–58; see also Rüdiger vom Bruch, 'Gelehrtenpolitik und politische Kultur im späten Kaiserreich', in Gustav Schmidt and Jörn Rüsen (eds.), *Gelehrtenpolitik und politische Kultur in Deutschland, 1830–1930* (Bochum, 1986), 77–106.
[64] Seeley, *Expansion*, 169.

It is a favourite maxim of mine that history, while it should be scientific in its method, should pursue a practical object. That is, it should not merely gratify the reader's curiosity about the past, but modify his view of the present and his forecast of the future. Now if this maxim be sound, the history of England ought to end with something that can be called a moral.[65]

For Seeley this moral involved some form of imperial federation. In order to avoid the mistakes that had led to the American Revolution, Britain should maintain a liberal relationship with its colonies. Seeley contrasted this high idealism with the commercial materialism of the first Empire. The idea of Empire was thus welcomed as a moral support when Britain's power was increasingly under threat towards the end of the century. In contrast to others Seeley regarded the Empire not as a means to stave off a decline in Britain's commercial position, but as an idealistic concept that could focus the collective consciousness of the nation at home and abroad. Moreover Seeley was largely responsible for establishing imperial studies as a recognized field of historical research within British historiography. He influenced many later historians, especially as regards his distinctive moralizing approach to the history of the Empire which had hitherto been virtually neglected. After Seeley the Whig notions of destiny and progress were translated into the teleological view of an essentially evolutionary growth of the British Empire. That in fact he argued backwards in order to project the Empire's future may sound absurd, but it became fashionable in his succession.

Seeley's preoccupations lay with the colonies of white settlement—South Africa, Canada, Australia, New Zealand, and, although not logically, the West Indies. He certainly expressed opinions on India. India would actually be part of an empire, while the dominions represented merely an extension overseas of English nationality, which was itself territorially unbounded. Settling abroad basically meant carrying the English state, its rights, institutions, and traditions, with oneself, thereby producing a common identity of interest. According to Seeley, colonies should no longer be regarded as possessions but as an

[65] Seeley, *Expansion*, 1.

integral part of the English nation. Consequently Seeley rejected those critics who, in his view, were too insular and represented a cautious Little-Englandism in thinking that emigration would be ruinous for Britain because it would deprive the country of its most industrious population.

That emigrants did not remain Englishmen overseas, and that they were thus no longer serviceable to their country, was an argument mainly developed by anti-colonialists, but some supporters of the imperial idea such as Treitschke also used it. According to Seeley, the first Empire collapsed because the other side of the Atlantic was seen only in the categories of tobacco, fisheries, and sugar, but not as an English community. Seeley sharply contrasted this with the later success story of the United States where in his view 'the constant movement of the population westward, the constant settlement of new Territories, which in due time rise to be States, is not regarded as either a symptom or a cause of weakness, not at all as a draining-out of vitality, but on the contrary as the greatest evidence of vigour and the best means of increasing it'.[66]

Consequently to question the material value of the colonies was senseless, because they were part of the mother country, and the colonists were fellow countrymen, not foreign enemies. A 'Greater Britain' as he understood it was the enlargement of the English state and the English governmental heritage. Therefore, there was no question of the pros and cons of imperial expansion, and thus no argument against emigration because emigrants would remain Englishmen and would still be serviceable to the English commonwealth. Here lay the difference from Germany, for example, as despite a constant stream of German emigration to America 'no Greater Germany comes into existence, because these emigrants, though they carry with them and may perhaps not altogether lose their language and their ideas, do not carry with them their state'.[67] When Treitschke published his important essay on the 'Early Attempts of German Colonial Policy' just a year after the first edition of Seeley's *Expansion*, he picked up exactly this argument

[66] Ibid. 71.   [67] Ibid. 50.

defending the need for German colonies, given that thousands of emigrants left Germany every year for America without being of any further benefit to their mother-country. If Germany had its own colonies where the emigrants could go, this would fulfil, in Treitschke's terms, the European task of civilizing the rest of the still uncivilized world ('die neuen Kulturaufgaben'), thereby giving European history a new dimension. It would also allow Germany to pursue its 'natural rights', like all other great nations.

Inherent in his argument for the need of German colonies was a line of thought that is clearly reminiscent of the frontier philosophy, or, in Treitschke's words, 'die unbestimmte Sehnsucht nach dem Westen' (an indeterminate longing for the west). Colonialism was a 'question of being' for the state ('Kolonisation zur Daseinsfrage'); it was a perfect means for overcoming the deleterious effects of too much luxury, comfort, and laziness at home; it was a school for youth in learning virtue.[68] Treitschke also referred to Dilke's book *Problems of Greater Britain*, claiming that it was hardly known in Germany. The limits of mutual perceptions and transfers were quite obvious.[69] Central to his plea for colonies was his belief that the 'natural difference between colony and mother-country' would soon totally vanish and that both would become part of a greater entity.[70] The imperial idea could not be stopped; the movement of the frontier simply followed the Hegelian World Spirit, in both Seeley's and Treitschke's thinking, and was heading towards fulfilling the goal set by history.

Both historians were equally influential in forming public opinion in their countries. But Treitschke, for his part, was certainly the more nationalistic, if not chauvinistic intellectual whose impact on German imperialist thinking in the late nineteenth century cannot be underestimated.[71]

[68] Heinrich von Treitschke, 'Die ersten Versuche deutscher Kolonialpolitik' (1884), in *Heinrich von Treitschke: Aufsätze, Reden und Briefe*, ed. Karl Martin Schiller, 4 vols. (Meersburg, 1929), iv (*Schriften und Reden zur Zeitgeschichte*), 665–76, quotations at 671, 670.   [69] Ibid. 675.   [70] Ibid. 668.
[71] Peter Winzen, 'Treitschke's Influence on the Rise of Imperialist and Anti-British Nationalism in Germany', in Kennedy and Nicholls (eds.), *Nationalist and Racialist Movements in Britain and Germany before 1914*, 154–70; see now Ulrich Langer, *Heinrich von Treitschke: Politische Biographie eines deutschen Nationalisten* (Düsseldorf, 1998), 331–5.

Although he tried to remain vague as regards an explanation of the phenomenon of German imperialism ('The desire to roam, like a dark, elemental power over the minds of the people'),[72] he did not hesitate to predict a great conflict between British and German colonial interests. It is certainly true that fascination for German *Weltpolitik* was widespread among German scholars in the late nineteenth century. Max Weber, for example, was no exception. He temporarily took the lead in this movement before he cancelled his membership of the Pan-German League in 1899. In his famous Freiburg inaugural lecture on 'Der Nationalstaat und die Volkswirtschaftspolitik' (1895), he enthusiastically addressed the question of German colonial expansion: 'We must understand that unifying Germany was a youthful prank which the nation played in its old age. However, it would have done better not to have played this expensive trick if it was intended as the end, not the beginning, of a policy aiming to make Germany a world power.'[73]

Using a more widespread definition, German historians in the later nineteenth century such as Treitschke, Heinrich von Sybel, and Droysen are often described as 'Borussian' historians. Most of them taught at the University of Berlin and constantly expressed their loyalty to the Protestant-dominated Hohenzollern state. In their view Prussia equalled Germany. The first requirement, Germany's unification under Prussia's lead, having been fulfilled, it was simply logical that *Weltpolitik* would be dominated by Prussian values. Thus the imperialist movement was the next degree of nationalism after the nation-state. A cultural-imperial ideology such as Treitschke's, based on bourgeois nationalism, claimed a continuity between the past and future power and greatness of the state.[74] In short, according

---

[72] Treitschke, 'Versuche', 671.
[73] Quoted from Wolfgang J. Mommsen, 'Max Weber: Ein politischer Intellektueller im Deutschen Kaiserreich', in Gangolf Hübinger and Wolfgang J. Mommsen (eds.), *Intellektuelle im Deutschen Kaiserreich* (Frankfurt am Main, 1993), 33–61, at 38; Wolfgang J. Mommsen, *Max Weber und die deutsche Politik*, 2nd edn (Tübingen, 1974).
[74] Wolfgang Hardtwig, 'Von Preußens Aufgabe in Deutschland zu Deutschlands Aufgabe in der Welt: Liberalismus und borussianisches

to the Borussian historians, Germany's national mission of defining its frontiers corresponded to its international mission of expanding frontiers. The dynamics of history demanded that the aim of national unity should develop into the claim for an international role for the state. In this concept, and in the view of most Prussian historians, Anglo-German rivalry was the natural outcome.[75]

The ties of sentiment and common heritage at home and abroad also counted most for Seeley, who therefore did not understand those intellectuals who, after the fall of the old colonial system in America, had voiced an unseemly scepticism towards an Empire no longer capable of exacting commercial tribute from the colonies. As Goldwin Smith put it in a review of Seeley's *Expansion,* this unsatisfactory notion of Greater Britain carried with it the belief that the earth was still the centre of the universe. That is, it completely disregarded the fact that a feeling of separate nationality, a colonial nationalism, was already growing up in the colonies.[76]

Geschichtsbild zwischen Revolution und Imperialismus', in id., *Geschichtskultur und Wissenschaft* (Munich, 1990), 103–60, at 137; Wolfgang J. Mommsen, 'Wandlungen der liberalen Idee im Zeitalter des Imperialismus', in Karl Holl and Günther List (eds.), *Liberalismus und imperialistischer Staat: Der Imperialismus als Problem liberaler Parteien in Deutschland 1890–1914* (Göttingen, 1975), 109–47; Lothar Gall, ' "Sündenfall" des liberalen Denkens oder Krise der bürgerlich-liberalen Bewegung? Zum Verhältnis von Liberalismus und Imperialismus in Deutschland', ibid. 148–58. However, in a fascinating comparison between the English historian James Bryce and the German historian Georg Waitz as regards the different ideas of the Middle Ages at times of contemporary political controversy such as the Sybel--Ficker controversy, Thomas Kleinknecht states that the Prussian contribution to the German Reich is generally overestimated, cf. Thomas Kleinknecht, 'Mittelalterauffassung in Forschung und politischer Kontroverse: Zu den Beiträgen von James Bryce und Georg Waitz', in Heinz Dollinger, Horst Gründer, and Alwin Hanschmidt (eds.), *Weltpolitik, Europagedanke, Regionalismus: Festschrift für Heinz Gollwitzer zum 65. Geburtstag* (Münster, 1982), 269–86.

[75] Willy Schenk, *Die deutsch-englische Rivalität vor dem Ersten Weltkrieg in der Sicht deutscher Historiker: Mißverstehen oder Machtstreben?* (Aarau, 1967); Charles E. McClelland, *The German Historians and England: A Study in Nineteenth-Century Views* (Cambridge, 1971), 161–236, esp. 191 ff.

[76] Goldwin Smith, 'The Expansion of England', *Contemporary Review*, 45 (Apr. 1884), 531; see Burroughs, 'John Robert Seeley', 200; see also John Eddy and Deryck Schreuder (eds.), *The Rise of Colonial Nationalism: Australia, New Zealand, Canada, and South Africa First Assert their Nationalities, 1880–1914* (Sydney, 1988).

Many contemporary reviewers agreed that Seeley's preference for the federal solution of 'Greater Britain' over the Disraelian notion of imperialism was quite fashionable at a time when the liberal Victorian intelligentsia was converting to the imperial cause.[77] Yet it was essentially the effectiveness and persuasion of his arguments, the book's broad historical perspective, and Seeley's ability to produce a philosophical frame around imperial issues that made his book stand out. *The Expansion of England* probably contributed to the late nineteenth-century crisis of Victorian liberalism. Attitudes towards the Empire, Ireland, and liberalism at home changed, and a shift took place from the 'old' to the 'new' liberals who had a much more positive attitude to the Empire. In this context Seeley was a typical late Victorian imperialist and advocate of the unifying bonds of Anglo-Saxondom. His main historiographical value was in having stimulated works on imperial history and established techniques of modern historical research.

This, in fact, became a trend among subsequent generations of imperial historians,[78] among them, for example, the above-mentioned Egerton as well as Arthur Percival Newton and Charles Prestwood Lucas, whose scholarly surveys were limited to the 'white' dependencies and left out the tropical areas and the 'informal' empire. Thanks to Dietrich Schäfer, Egerton and Lucas were not unknown in Germany. Having published his acclaimed *Short History of British Colonial Policy* in 1897, Egerton was appointed the first Beit Professor of Colonial History at Oxford in 1905.[79] This professorship, especially created for colonial history, was named after the German financier Alfred Beit, who with Cecil Rhodes had been an ardent imperialist engaged in southern Africa.

---

[77] John Roach, 'Liberalism and the Victorian Intelligentsia', *Historical Journal*, 13 (1957), 58–81.

[78] J. G. Greenlee, 'A Succession of Seeleys: The *Old School* Re-examined', *Journal of Imperial and Commonwealth History*, 4 (1975), 266–82; J. G. Greenlee, 'Imperial Studies and the Unity of Empire', *Journal of Imperial and Commonwealth History*, 7 (1979), 321–35.

[79] Other important works by Egerton are *The Claims of the Study of Colonial History upon the Attention of the University of Oxford* (Oxford, 1906), and *Federations and Unions within the British Empire* (London, 1911); for the following see Richard Aldrich, 'Imperialism', 27 ff.

Newton became the first Rhodes Professor of Imperial History at the University of London in 1919, and Lucas was chairman of the Royal Colonial Institute from 1915. Lucas had enjoyed a distinguished career at the Colonial Office from 1877, and until his retirement he remained closely devoted to Joseph Chamberlain. Newton was the youngest of the three, and supposedly also the most enthusiastic.

These three historians were not only responsible for promoting the study of imperial history at the universities. They also made imperial studies more popular by giving numerous public lectures and advocating Empire Day as an important symbol for raising the imperial consciousness of the nation as a whole. All three historians were much influenced by Seeley in that they believed that the general public did not yet sufficiently appreciate the benefits of Empire. In particular, they believed that the working class needed to be taught history as a means of strengthening national morale in wartime. This was felt especially after the South African War, which not only highlighted the Empire's military weakness, but also called into question its moral foundations. To show the superiority of the British concept of Empire over the German was one of the aims Lucas pursued in his book *The British Empire*,[80] originally given as six lectures addressed to the Working Men's College and published in 1915. Here he tried to demonstrate that the British Empire was characterized by toleration, loyalty, and unity, qualities that gave crucial support to the war effort during the First World War.

In addition Lucas pointed especially to the old individualist ideal, frequently expressed in imperial writings, which saw the history of Empire as representing individualism at its purest and best.[81] Imperial history, for Lucas, was not the history of the institutions of the mechanical network administering the colonies, but human history, the personal involvement of individuals, the record of biographies. Lucas wrote about what he called 'the obvious outcome of men and women, who were really men and women, not contin-

---

[80] C. P. Lucas, *The British Empire* (London, 1915).
[81] See Christopher Parker, *The English Historical Tradition since 1850* (Edinburgh, 1990), 136 f.

Imperialism and the Frontier 317

gent remainders in a complicated legal-constitutional-social-industrial system'. Thus imperial history was the history of enterprise and individual initiative, in a word, the history of the frontiersman who conquered unknown land and brought fame to his country. It was the history of the experiences of a heroic individual whose character could be viewed as setting an example for future generations. Of course, this was also the basis for myth-building, for example, in the case of David Livingstone, *the* national model for missionary exploration, discoveries, and extending the frontiers of civilization into the wilderness. A living history was fabricated about him to an extent hardly matched by any other Victorian imperialist.[82] Finally, imperial history was an alternative to institutional, and also to constitutional, history. In a way it was even a new method of writing history, as Lucas put it in order to contrast it with traditional historiography:

> On the overseas side of English history private individuals, and combinations of private individuals, have done more, and Governments, Parliaments, laws, constitutions have done less than on the home side. It is to the story of our Overseas Empire that we point to illustrate the private initiative on which Englishmen pride themselves. And, obviously, the more elementary the conditions of land and living are, the more depends upon the human factor as opposed to laws and systems.[83]

While Newton in his book *The Old Empire and the New*, published in 1917, stressed that especially in wartime nothing should be given greater prominence than overseas history,[84] Egerton contributed to a series of Oxford pamphlets which, on the outbreak of war, set out to explain why British imperialism had succeeded and German imperialism had failed. Pamphlets such as *The Germans, their Empire, and What They Covet* warned of the dangers posed by the territorial ambi-

---

[82] Catalogue of the exhibition *David Livingstone and the Victorian Encounter with Africa* (National Portrait Gallery, London, 22 Mar.–7 July 1996), see esp. the articles by Tim Barringer, 'Fabricating Africa: Livingstone and the Visual Image 1850–1874', 169–97; John M. MacKenzie, 'David Livingstone and the Wordly After-Life: Imperialism and Nationalism in Africa', 201–17.
[83] Quoted from Parker, *English Historical Tradition*, 136.
[84] A. P. Newton, *The Old Empire and the New* (London, 1917), introd.

tions of the pan-German school, and the pamphlet *The Germans, their Empire, and How They Made it* gave a historical account of Prussian policy since the seventeenth century.

What these historians shared was the belief that imperial history could no longer be treated as a mere subfield of general English history, as this greatly underestimated the significance of Empire. Basically it was the other way round: English history could not be thought of without imperial history, and as England's past and future lay beyond its shores, English history was, in the words of Lucas, 'the record of the human growth of an island into an Empire'.[85] A new definition of English history was on the way, with important implications for English historiography. In his inaugural lecture of 1906 Egerton underlined his debt to Seeley by pointing out how important he believed was the practical use of history for politics and for predicting the future. He also said that the time had come 'when the history of England should be identified with the history of the English Empire'.[86] Moreover, going beyond Seeley, Egerton believed it necessary for English imperial historians to take other historical perspectives into account. In this context he especially looked to North America.[87] And in this context, too, the idea of the frontier in its character-forming quality again became the link as formulated by Curzon in his lecture:

> the British Empire may be seen shaping the British character, while the British character is still building the British Empire. There, too, on the manifold Frontiers of dominion, now amid the gaunt highlands of the Indian border, or the eternal snows of the Himalayas, now on the parched sands of Persia or Arabia, now in the equatorial swamps and forests of Africa, in an incessant struggle with nature and man, has been found a corresponding discipline for the men of our stock. Outside of the English Universities no school of character exists to compare with the Frontier.[88]

Egerton, the former Colonial Office official, had lectured comprehensively on British colonial history, but he resolved that his university position should not be used for political

---

[85] Greenlee, 'Succession', 273.
[86] Egerton, *Claims*, 21; see Aldrich, 'Imperialism', 29.
[87] Egerton, *Claims*, 23.   [88] Curzon, *Frontiers*, 56.

propaganda.[89] What he in fact produced was cultural propaganda *par excellence*. He argued that the justification for imperialism lay in the moral good it brought to England itself. Not only the welfare of the colonies, but also the moral benefit that the colonists derived was the final result of British expansion. Thus Egerton was ready 'to bow down with reverence before the majestic fabric of British imperial development',[90] which he admired because of what he considered the special genius of the British race for bringing good to the world at large. In this respect Egerton, Newton, Lucas, and several other disciples of Seeley adopted a passionate, emotional, almost religious tone in praising the political value of the British Empire, and also in formulating their role in it. Their writings could be described as what Seeley had once called 'bombastic', that is, elevating emotional appeals above historical accuracy. Arguably Seeley would have deplored the dangerously romantic attitudes of his disciples who did not fully adopt the rational perspective which Seeley had found necessary for a substantive appraisal of the historical development of the Empire. Yet, at a time of international anxiety before the First World War, a 'lost in wonder' attitude was more easily carried through.

In some respects these historians also owed much to Froude, in particular, their concept that expansion was the expression of a natural enlargement of the state, the genuine character of English history, an imaginable organic growth. The Empire was thus explained in terms of a living organism, that is, it was an entity with a significance of its own, and therefore more than the sum of its parts. These ideas had originally been put forward by Froude in his *The English in the West Indies* (1888), a book in which he had tried to link these islands with the organic body of the whole Empire.

To come back to the German perspective, Treitschke's student Dietrich Schäfer[91] was probably the most active

---

[89] Symonds, *Oxford and Empire*, 51 ff.
[90] Quoted from Greenlee, 'Succession', 272.
[91] Cf. Rüdiger vom Bruch, *Wissenschaft, Politik und öffentliche Meinung: Gelehrtenpolitik im wilhelminischen Deutschland (1890–1914)* (Husum, 1980), 206 ff.; Charles E. McClelland, 'Berlin Historians and German Politics', in Walter Laqueur and George L. Mosse (eds.), *Historians in Politics* (London, 1974), 191–221.

reviewer of British colonial literature in German scholarly journals, in particular in the *Historische Zeitschrift*. Against the background of his conviction that in Germany academic study of the history of colonialism was still in its very first beginnings, Schäfer published a survey of this subject in 1903.[92] A trained medievalist, his major field of study until the turn of the century had been the Hanseatic League, but now he increasingly concentrated on the history of German colonialism in the eastern provinces since the fourteenth century. Schäfer was one of the leading German scholars who advocated German colonial expansion into eastern Europe (*Drang nach Osten*) and the world, and he was a member of the Pan-German League. For him, this intellectual interest had clear political implications: historiography was to be serviceable to contemporary politics; in addition to its scholarly aspect it had an ideological one. To name but a few, he was loosely or directly associated with men such as Gustav Schmoller, Otto Hintze, Hans Delbrück, Hermann Oncken, Max Lenz, and Erich Marcks, some experts, others non-experts on Britain. The latter turned to British history at a later stage only because of their interest in Britain as a global and maritime power.

Schäfer did not, at least not before 1914, advocate German settlements in France or the Netherlands, which was one of the dreams of the Pan-Germans. But as an admirer of a strong nation-state at home and a powerful German fleet abroad, he supported German expansionism into the so-called *Ostmarken* in order to stop Polish advances in this region.[93] Expansion towards the east at a time of colonial dreams was driven by motivations similar to those behind the westward movement—the east was regarded as 'darkest Africa', far from civilization, foreign, and in need of missionary cultivation. But the pioneers who were prepared—or forced—to go to the eastern frontier saw their work also as a civilizing, moral task for themselves, as

---

[92] Dietrich Schäfer in his review of Alfred Zimmermann's book 'Die Kolonialpolitik Großbritanniens', *Historische Zeitschrift*, 84, NS 48 (1900), 141–3, at 141; id., *Kolonialgeschichte* (Leipzig, 1903).

[93] Dietrich Schäfer, 'Unser Recht auf die Ostmarken', in id., *Aufsätze, Reden und Vorträge*, 2 vols. (Jena, 1913), ii. 305–20.

well as a counterbalance to the corrupting temptations of modern life.[94] Whether westward or eastward expansion, the way in which Schäfer argued and his justifications of colonial policy were quite similiar to Seeley's or Froude's. Of course, the eastern frontier had gained in significance only after the turn of the century. The historians named here were members of the conservative, educated bourgeoisie, and their ideology of *Lebensraum* in the east' was an intellectual preparation for the revisionist historiography which, after Versailles, aspired to compensate for defeat through new territorial acquisitions, and whose terminology led over into the racism and radicalism of the 1930s.[95] Already as the outbreak of the Great War drew closer, the opinions of Schäfer and of many German public figures of his time became more radical in the service of a politics that saw Britain as the rival in international conflicts. The fact that Schäfer thought in these terms, and that he regarded history as *magistra vitae*, revealed his debt to Treitschke.[96]

More than most of his German contemporaries, however, Schäfer acknowledged that the British were 'our teachers in matters concerning imperialism'.[97] These 'matters' were, after all, the business of the building of a strong fleet to which, together with the Navy League, many scholars lent their support. Unlike earlier generations of German liberal historians who, possibly influenced by Macaulay, had admired England because of its constitution and exemplary parliamentary tradition, Schäfer merely took into account the British Empire's success story as an expanding imperial frontier in industrial and naval matters. For Schäfer England

---

[94] See Rolf Lindner (ed.), *'Wer in den Osten geht, geht in ein anderes Land': Die Settlement-Bewegung in Berlin zwischen Kaiserreich und Weimarer Republik* (Berlin, 1997).

[95] Klaus Zernack, ' "Ostkolonisation" in universalgeschichtlicher Perspektive', in Gangolf Hübinger, Jürgen Osterhammel, and Erich Pelzer (eds.), *Universalgeschichte und Nationalgeschichten* (Freiburg, 1994), 105-16; Osterhammel, 'Kulturelle Grenzen', 112.

[96] See Roger Chickering, *We Men Who Feel Most German: A Cultural Study of the Pan-German League, 1886–1914* (London, 1984), esp. 74 ff.; id., 'Dietrich Schäfer and Max Weber', in Wolfgang J. Mommsen and Jürgen Osterhammel (eds.), *Max Weber and his Contemporaries* (London, 1987), 334–44.

[97] According to his reviewer, Theodor Kükelhaus, *Historische Zeitschrift*, 94, NS 58 (1905), 322.

was Germany's 'teacher' only as far as colonial exploitation and naval power were concerned. British economic policies and power politics worked hand in hand. The country's unhesitating application of military force was the backbone of its imperial power, which, for example, was also Schmoller's argument in his plea for a stronger German fleet to defend German overseas trade. Looking for historical examples of English supremacy in world affairs, German scholars sometimes went back as far as the Tudors and Stuarts.[98] But naturally, British imperial history was often presented in negative terms, as, for example, in Schäfer's account of ruthless English commerce in rivalry with the German Hansa.[99] Moreover, some German historians attempted to demonstrate that past and present hardly differed from each other in the derogatory accounts they gave of British imperialism in the early twentieth century. Only Schmoller, Lujo Brentano, and a few other scholars tried to remain as objective as possible.[100]

According to McClelland colonialism predominantly served as an excuse for the fleet. In fact, national-conservative historians of the late nineteenth century were not really original in finding explanations other than those already used by Treitschke.[101] Germany must expand in order to supply land to a vast emigrating population which would otherwise be lost through German emigration to British colonies or to America; the 'civilizing mission' of German

[98] Erich Marcks, 'Die Einheitlichkeit der englischen Auslandspolitik von 1500 bis zur Gegenwart', in id., *Männer und Zeiten: Aufsätze und Reden zur neueren Geschichte*, 2 vols. (Leipzig, 1911), ii. 235–63; id., 'Im England der Elisabeth', ibid. 25–45; Felix Salomon, *Die Grundzüge der auswärtigen Politik Englands vom 16. Jahrhundert bis zur Gegenwart* (Berlin, 1910); Gustav Schmoller, 'Die englische Handelspolitik des 17. und 18. Jahrhunderts', *Schmollers Jahrbuch*, 23 (1899), 1211–41; cf. McClelland, *German Historians*, 201–13.

[99] Dietrich Schäfer, 'Deutschland und England im Welthandel des 16. Jahrhunderts', *Preußische Jahrbücher*, 83 (1896), 268–81.

[100] See e.g. Gerhard von Schulze-Gaevernitz, *Britischer Imperialismus und englischer Freihandel zu Beginn des 20. Jahrhunderts* (Leipzig, 1906); Otto Hintze, 'Der britische Imperialismus und seine Probleme', *Zeitschrift für Politik*, 1 (1908), 297–345; id., 'Imperialismus und Weltpolitik' (1907), in id., *Historische und politische Aufsätze*, 4 vols. (Berlin, 1908–9), iv. 144–59; Gustav Schmoller, 'Die künftige englische Handelspolitik, Chamberlain und der Imperialismus', *Schmollers Jahrbuch*, 28 (1904), 829–52; cf. also the bibliographical essay in McClelland, *German Historians*, 258 ff.

[101] McClelland, 'Berlin Historians', 203.

Kultur and the long-term economic rewards would provide ideological and economic compensation for what seemed initially to be a costly adventure; and finally, a great power such as Germany had to keep pace with the other world powers. In view of the rising Anglo-German antagonism, these arguments among others were put forward, for example, by Schäfer, Delbrück, and Oncken.[102] Naval policy and imperialism complemented each other, especially after the Berlin government and Admiral Tirpitz had given the political signals in 1897, and the Prussian historians sacrificed scholarly objectivity and independence of mind to political aims.[103]

Theodor Kükelhaus's review of Schäfer's book on colonialism (*Kolonialgeschichte*, 1903) was highly favourable because he had set out not only to integrate colonial studies into the field of political historiography, but also to popularize them; while there was a long tradition of Dutch, French, and British colonial historiography, the Germans had a lot to catch up. This must also be seen in the context of the popularity of British imperial historiography. The same reviewer remarked in his critique of Harry H. Johnston's book *A History of the Colonization of Africa by Alien Races* (1899) that British history books were noteworthy for their exemplary liberal approach, but that despite their merits they would not be paid any attention in Germany as long as they remained untranslated.[104] Fortunately a German translation of this study was soon provided by Max von Halfern.

---

[102] Dietrich Schäfer, *Deutschland zur See* (Jena, 1897), reprinted in id., *Deutschland und England* (Leipzig, 1915); Hans Delbrück, 'Deutschland und England' (1904), in id., *Vor und nach dem Weltkrieg* (Berlin, 1926), 50–60; Hermann Oncken, 'Deutschland und England: Heeres- oder Flottenverstärkung?', in id., *Historisch-politische Aufsätze und Reden*, 2 vols. (Munich, 1914), i. 121–44.

[103] For the historical background cf. Paul M. Kennedy, *The Rise of the Anglo-German Antagonism 1860–1914* (London, 1980); R. K. Massie, *Die Schalen des Zorns: Großbritannien, Deutschland und das Heraufziehen des Ersten Weltkrieges* (Frankfurt am Main, 1993); on the impact of military history see Arden Bucholz, *Hans Delbrück and the German Military Establishment* (Iowa City, 1985), esp. 19–51; Cain and Hopkins, *British Imperialism*, i. 456 ff.; still useful is Pauline Anderson, *The Background of Anti-English Feeling in Germany, 1890–1902* (Washington, 1939).

[104] *Historische Zeitschrift*, 94, NS 58 (1905), 324; see Peter Wende's contribution to this volume for a detailed examination of the mutual reviewing of British and German history books.

Reviewing Egerton's *The Origin and Growth of the English Colonies and of their System of Government* (1903) and Lucas's *A Historical Geography of the British Colonies* (1888–1901), Schäfer himself praised the quality of the work of his British colleagues and stated that, together with Egerton's *Short History of British Colonial Policy* (1897), these books were especially convincing in showing the historical process of British overseas expansion in combination with its geographical conditions. He concluded his reviews with the observation that these authors often underlined the significance of German colonialism as a driving force for the strengthening of British colonial rule.[105] Thus Schäfer did not have to look for a justification of imperialism: it was a widespread, 'natural' European phenomenon which was displayed by all 'healthy' states.

He praised Hereford B. George's treatment of the expansion of the frontier in his *A Historical Geography of the British Empire* (1904) as the formative part of the emergence of the empire. According to Schäfer, George showed that the British Empire was not an artificial construct but a living organism, 'that it grew out of itself, that inherent in things was the necessity to expand'.[106] This is clearly reminiscent of Froude's and Seeley's concept of 'Greater Britain', namely that the British people and their empire had become one entity, the result of which, for Schäfer, could be seen in the majestic power of a state that rested on the security of its imperial strength. As far as the United States of America were concerned, he argued, again in Hegelian terms, that the expansion of the frontier was a historical necessity for the formation of the nation. It resulted in the belief, first, that the aim of American expansion was the freedom of humanity, and secondly, that it would benefit the American people.[107]

Schäfer also followed this paradigm in his own studies. His *Kolonialgeschichte* attached greater importance to the historical process of expansion and the work of the pioneering

---

[105] *Historische Zeitschrift*, 94, NS 58 (1905), 325–31, at 331.
[106] *Historische Zeitschrift*, 96, NS 60 (1906), 511–13, at 512.
[107] Schäfer in his review of Albert Bushnell Hart, *The Foundations of American Foreign Policy* (1901), *Historische Zeitschrift*, 94, NS 58 (1905), 331–4, at 334.

frontiersman than to the actual administrative, economic, or cultural state of the colonies themselves. Adopting Rudyard Kipling's notion of 'the white man's burden', Schäfer justified the necessity of German colonies in terms of the moral duty which the Western, Christian cultures had simply as the result of their allegedly higher standards of civilization. As the African and Asian 'tribes', according to this argument, could not govern themselves, European colonial rule and missionary work would be an 'endless blessing' to these continents.[108] The motifs of burden and duty are central to his work.

Schäfer emphasized that for better or for worse, Germany had to follow the general trend to acquire colonies before it was too late. Because imperialism was a 'powerful movement which had gripped all nations', it was the 'duty of humanity' to participate in what was not only a burden, but also a matter of pride.[109] Although he believed in the British Empire as a model for all other colonial movements and referred particularly to C. P. Lucas's work, Schäfer insisted that it was Germany's colonial endeavours in the late nineteenth century that had motivated the British and French to keep up. Even the Americans, who were without competition on their vast continent, could not resist colonial expansion. Schäfer believed the critics of colonialism were running counter to modernity and the general tendencies of the times. The move towards new frontiers thus fell into a third category. As well as being a burden and a matter of pride, states striving for colonial expansion were following a straightforward 'natural' law. The fact that Germany now acquired colonies in Africa and in the Pacific for itself was nothing but a historical, inevitable necessity after Germans had worked abroad for so long for the benefit of other colonial powers.[110] Two years before the outbreak of the war, this was certainly intended as anti-British rhetoric.

Schäfer repeated his convictions in another article of the same year, leaving no doubt that he regarded German

---

[108] Dietrich Schäfer, 'Weltlage und Kolonialpolitik', in id., *Aufsätze*, 242–9, at 248. [109] Ibid. 242, 247.
[110] Dietrich Schäfer, 'Was bedeutet dem Deutschen sein Reich?' (1912), in id., *Aufsätze*, 321–40, at 329.

Weltpolitik as an absolute necessity ('Naturnotwendigkeit'). 'We desperately need an area in which to settle.'[111] Settlement, finally, would be merely an extension of the mother-country abroad. And in this aspect, German imperialist historiography drew on patterns similiar to those used by British historical writing. Froude, Seeley, and Dilke, for example, had justified the ideology of British imperialism in terms of the historical development of the Empire, which was nothing less than a law inherent in English history.[112] Moreover, just as German historians emphasized the dominant role of Prussia, so did British historians underline England's dominant role for the Empire. Both were entrusted with the task of guaranteeing peace in the universal system of states: here the imperial 'Pax Britannica', there the conviction that only Germany's imperialism could ensure a balance between western and eastern powers.

If traces of T. B. Macaulay can be found in late nineteenth-century British imperial historiography, especially as regards the heritage of the Whig belief in constitutional progress, the near perfection of British institutions, and liberty as the outcome of a prosperous empire and a politically stable nation, echoes of Leopold von Ranke's work are also traceable in the writings of German imperial historians.[113] In this context it may be not unimportant to note that Seeley himself was strongly influenced by Ranke.[114] The Rankean paradigm, of which Treitschke and Schäfer—although not in matters of method—were outstanding disciples, had reached a crisis at the end of the nineteenth and beginning of the twentieth centuries. None the less a Ranke renais-

---

[111] Dietrich Schäfer, 'Englands Weltstellung und Deutschlands Lage' (1912), in id., *Aufsätze*, 341–62, at 359.

[112] Wolfgang J. Mommsen, 'Nationale und ökonomische Faktoren im britischen Imperialismus vor 1914', *Historische Zeitschrift*, 206 (1968), 618–64; Hardtwig, 'Preußens Aufgabe', 137–8; Lord Rosebery could possibly be included in this line, cf. Helmut Reifeld, *Zwischen Empire und Parlament: Zur Gedankenbildung und Politik Lord Roseberys, 1880–1905* (Göttingen, 1987), 32 ff.

[113] James Joll, *National Histories and National Historians: Some German and English Views of the Past* (German Historical Institute London: 1984 Annual Lecture; London, 1985), 17 ff.; for a comprehensive study of the problem of national identity in German historical writing see Stefan Berger, *The Search for Normality: National Identity and Historical Consciousness in Germany since 1800* (Providence, RI, 1997).

[114] John L. Herkless, 'Seeley and Ranke', *Historian*, 43 (1980), 1–22.

sance seems to have been relatively widespread.[115] Not surprisingly, it was also open to Seeley's ideas.

Ranke's concept of the Great Powers, expressed in his early essay 'Die grossen Mächte', was eagerly adopted, but seriously misinterpreted, by national historians before the First World War, who took the model of a universal peace system for granted in order to tie to it the claim that Germany played a leading role in the world.[116] As Dehio has convincingly shown, neo-Rankeans described Britain's 'new' imperialism as a threat to the hegemonial system in which a stronger German imperial position would provide the necessary balance. The Berlin historian Max Lenz, for example, is well remembered for his timely book *Die großen Mächte: Ein Rückblick auf unser Jahrhundert* (1900), which was a discreet departure from Ranke although it used his premises. By trying to translate Ranke's system of European balance into a universal system, Lenz and especially Delbrück produced scholarly arguments in favour of Tirpitz's political aims. The danger was not only that their neo-idealism was far removed from reality, but also that they offered an uncritical version of history in the service of Prussian policy.[117]

Macaulay, whom James Joll called 'an imperialist historian since he was concerned about British public indifference to the history of India',[118] had been able to justify his belief that Britain had played a leading role in the drama of history by pointing to the Glorious Revolution. Britain's mission,

---

[115] Georg G. Iggers, 'The Crisis of the Rankean Paradigm in the Nineteenth Century', in id. and J. M. Powell (eds.), *Leopold von Ranke and the Shaping of the Historical Discipline* (Syracuse, NY, 1990), 170–9; Elisabeth Fehrenbach, 'Rankerenaissance und Imperialismus in der wilhelminischen Zeit', in Bernd Faulenbach (ed.), *Geschichtswissenschaft in Deutschland* (Munich, 1974), 54–65.

[116] Leopold von Ranke, 'Die grossen Mächte', *Historisch-politische Zeitschrift*, 2 (1833), 1–51; Ludwig Dehio, 'Ranke und der deutsche Imperialismus', *Historische Zeitschrift*, 170 (1950), 307–28; for a comprehensive interpretation of Ranke's essay see Ulrich Muhlack's afterword in his new edn. of Leopold von Ranke, *Die grossen Mächte. Politisches Gespräch* (Frankfurt am Main, 1995), 115–39; for the misinterpretation of Ranke by the neo-Rankeans see Ernst Schulin, 'Universalgeschichte und Nationalgeschichte bei Leopold von Ranke', in Wolfgang J. Mommsen (ed.), *Leopold von Ranke und die moderne Geschichtswissenschaft* (Stuttgart, 1988), 37–71.

[117] Hans-Heinz Krill, *Die Rankerenaissance: Max Lenz und Erich Marcks. Ein Beitrag zum historisch-politischen Denken in Deutschland 1880–1935* (Berlin, 1962), 139 ff.

[118] Joll, *National Histories*, 16.

according to Macaulay, was to bring British civilization and political culture to the so-called backward peoples. By extending the cultural frontier, Britain would integrate, even assimilate, these new lands into British history. That the allegedly uncivilized peoples possessed their own identity and culture was acknowledged, but it was not seen as really important. In contrast to British history, German history could not offer an event such as a peaceful revolution to demonstrate that the progress of the history of civilization guaranteed the success of the history of the nation.[119]

Therefore the contemporary history of German unification and the emergence of the Bismarckian empire were not only the culmination of the struggles of the past, but also a new starting point for German history that formed the background to colonial expansion. Participants in the Ranke renaissance adopted Ranke's doctrine that the true actors in history were the great nation-states. By developing his notion of universal history and his idea of an interplay between the European nations, they translated it into a concept of colonial struggle between nations in which Germany had to maintain its place and to fight for a *Weltstellung*, a position in the world. In this regard they were influenced by Seeley, yet his argument had a different political and imperial background, namely that of an expanding British Empire whose existence could be justified but did not need to be declared.

The disciples of Ranke and Seeley emphasized one particular point which Seeley had admired in the Prussian statesman Baron Stein, whose biographer he was: the central role of the state. Or, as Seeley put it: 'history is not concerned with individuals except in their capacity as members of a State.'[120] As well as disciples, they were also epigones in so far as they, in contrast to British imperialist historians, could merely complain that Germany had come late into the international concert of nations. Naturally, this would not happen without a good deal of envy and frustration, especially in view of British imperial power.[121] One of the many

---

[119] Jürgen Osterhammel, 'Nation und Zivilisation in der britischen Historiographie von Hume bis Macaulay', *Historische Zeitschrift*, 254 (1992), 281–340.
[120] Seeley, *Expansion*, 7–8. [121] Cf. Joll, *National Histories*, 19.

aspects of the rising Anglo-German antagonism was rooted in these circumstances. And as a result, historians of the Ranke renaissance were, in political terms, certainly not Anglophile—at least not in the liberal sense of the word associated with German scholars such as Theodor Mommsen, Lujo Brentano, or Theodor Barth, who admired the British constitution.[122]

Among the historians of the Ranke renaissance was Erich Marcks, who wrote a number of studies on individuals in British history, and on questions relating to the British Empire. Politically formed by the events of 1871 Marcks was convinced of the importance of individuals in history; his greatest hero was Otto von Bismarck, and his biography of him was a best-seller in the early twentieth century. Karl Stählin, the author of the study on the English frontier mentioned at the beginning of this essay, wrote a comprehensive obituary of Marcks in which he drew special attention to the historian's closeness to the politics of his time. Against the background of Weber's idea of charismatic leadership, Marcks's Carlylian hero-worship was nurtured by his personal experience of Treitschke and Bismarck.[123] Although he considered himself unpolitical, Marcks strongly approved of Germany's *Weltpolitik* and became associated with the Pan-German movement during the First World War.[124]

The article which shows Marcks at his best as a defender of the Rankean paradigm and a historicist interpreter of foreign policy, but also, to a certain extent, as a defender of the Anglo-German cultural common ground, is his 'Deutschland und England in den grossen europäischen Krisen seit der Reformation'. He gave it as a lecture to London's German community in 1900.[125] In this lecture Marcks tried to counterbalance rising Anglophobia in

---

[122] Percy Ernst Schramm, 'Deutschlands Verhältnis zur englischen Kultur nach der Begründung des neuen Reiches', in Walter Hubatsch (ed.), *Schicksalswege deutscher Vergangenheit: Festschrift für S. Kaehler* (Düsseldorf, 1950), 289–319.
[123] Karl Stählin, 'Erich Marcks zum Gedächtnis', *Historische Zeitschrift*, 160 (1939), 496–533, at 502.
[124] Krill, *Rankerenaissance*, esp. 188–96; McClelland, *German Historians*, 215 ff.
[125] Reprinted in Marcks, *Männer und Zeiten*, ii. 201–31.

Germany by providing a scholarly account of English and German political and cultural communities since the Reformation. He strove to achieve an objective, 'non-party' historiography without a commitment to ethical considerations: only political history counted, and this was the history of foreign affairs between powerful states. However, the scholarly detachment which Marcks, Lenz, and other neo-Rankeans claimed in the spirit of Ranke was definitely more self-delusion and lip service than reality. But it is remarkable how this generation of Prussian historians remained untouched by the widespread pessimism so strongly felt in philosophy or in the arts. In contrast, they regarded their work as supplying a theoretical preparation for German imperialism. Therefore, state power was more than a fact; it was the ultimate objective.[126]

As regards the publications which Marcks devoted to British history, his essays on the 'idea of imperialism' and on Pitt the Younger are certainly the most interesting for the present study.[127] Marcks was fascinated by Pitt the statesman whose peculiar 'Prussian rulership' he admired. In his view this also applied to the best representatives of the English state since Elizabethan times, or, to be more precise, since 1588. The destruction of the Armada had laid the basis for Britain's imperial self-confidence, argued Marcks, thus confirming what Froude had made the credo of his voluminous *History of England*, published about half a century earlier, namely, that Protestantism and the power of the state were the two pillars of imperial success. And Marcks's story concentrated on the individuals who guaranteed this success, whether in the sixteenth century, or Pitt in the eighteenth century, or characters such as Joseph Chamberlain and Cecil Rhodes in the present.[128] In addition to being historical figures, these characters symbolized a 'cultural type' which is reminiscent of the frontiersman.

---

[126] Cf. Georg G. Iggers, *Deutsche Geschichtswissenschaft: Eine Kritik der traditionellen Geschichtsauffassung von Herder bis zur Gegenwart* (Munich, 1971), 169 ff.

[127] Erich Marcks, 'Die imperialistische Idee in der Gegenwart' (1903), in id., *Männer und Zeiten*, ii. 267–91; id., 'Der jüngere Pitt und seine Zeit' (1906), ibid. i. 123–53.

[128] Marcks, 'Der jüngere Pitt', 147; cf. McClelland, *German Historians*, 216 f.

According to Marcks, Pitt was like a rock around which world affairs surged when England was fighting for domination over the seas. The Anglo-French struggle in the eighteenth century was a worldwide conflict which Marcks described in terms of political and economic power politics. Powerful statesmen such as Pitt and his father, the Earl of Chatham, pursued a higher object by being superior to a corrupt and Little-England-orientated aristocracy: the triumph of the idea of the state. He proclaimed this as the central message of his essay on the 'idea of imperialism'.[129] Elisabeth Fehrenbach has shown how the idea of a strong state and the image of a powerful statesman served as a stronghold against the unleashing of social movements. Behind imperial aims stood a conservative social programme whose philosophy was that only the mighty could secure the peace, whether at home or abroad.[130]

To a certain extent the Rankean notion can also be found in Lecky's eight-volume *History of England in the Eighteenth Century* (1878–90). In it, he wrote about what he considered the basis of Britain's rise to become *the* world power, namely, the consolidation of state power as the prerequisite for colonial expansion. For Lecky, Pitt had played an indisputably central political role.[131] This explanation for a well-controlled and consciously directed colonial policy in India, Canada, and elsewhere—in Ranke's words the 'Primat der Außenpolitik' (the primacy of foreign policy)—was the opposite of Seeley's famous claim, quoted above, that the Empire had been acquired in a 'fit of absence of mind'.[132] The German scholar Marcks, still relatively Anglophile but becoming slightly critical of Britain mainly for political reasons, and the Irishman Lecky, who against the background of his country's history longed for some sort of historiographical balance, concurred in the conviction that the

---

[129] Marcks, 'Die imperialistische Idee', esp. 270 f.

[130] Fehrenbach, 'Rankerenaissance', 59; see also Wolfgang J. Mommsen, 'Ranke and the Neo-Rankean School in Imperial Germany: State-Orientated Historiography as a Stabilizing Force', in Iggers and Powell (eds.), *Leopold von Ranke and the Shaping of the Historical Discipline*, 124–40, at 128.

[131] Cf. W. E. H. Lecky, 'William Pitt', in *Chambers's Encyclopedia: A Dictionary of Universal Knowledge*, viii (London, 1891), 203–6; for this and the *History of England* see Stuchtey, *W. E. H. Lecky*, 168–213. [132] Seeley, *Expansion*, 10.

British Empire was the result not of historical accident, but of *Machtpolitik*, the quest for power of the state, the mission of the concept of 'Greater Britain'. In Marcks's opinion this was possible because of the following qualities which were, finally, the characteristics of the frontiersman:

economic daring and prudence at the same time, being active and diligent, a healthy sense for what is real and tangible, robust political-national pride, political flexibility and allowing the personal development of the individual, his powers, his rights, and his inner life, knuckling down to things, ruthless violence and serious, profound cultural work—everything under the direction, advice, and ordering force of a state which remained in lively contact with its citizens. Settler and cleric, but also merchant, sailor, soldier, and statesman have always worked together happily, more happily than anywhere else.[133]

Marcks did not leave it at that. The description of Pitt, of his political achievements, and of the duel between France and Britain was, unlike McClelland's interpretation, probably not meant as a direct criticism of 'England's aggressive quest for power'.[134] Rather Marcks, the admirer of the British imperial system as a system as such, tried to extract the educational aspects from his historical examples in the service of political ends from which contemporary Germany would naturally profit. In the past Germany had had to watch its European neighbours founding colonies, but now the time had come to imitate them. How could this be better done than by taking the successful history of British imperialism as an example and looking at the efforts and performance of the frontiersman?[135] In parallel, Marcks discussed the case of America, which he described as a model for the history of an expanding frontier, and thus as another example of a country which defined its national character by means of settlement, something he still missed in

---

[133] Marcks, 'Der jüngere Pitt', 147.
[134] McClelland, *German Historians*, 217.
[135] Marcks, 'Der jüngere Pitt', 151; this observation is confirmed by Marcks's essay 'Die imperialistische Idee in der Gegenwart', see esp. 271–82. Here Marcks even expressed his admiration for Chamberlain (cf. 280), compared Chamberlain with Bismarck (290), and confessed that no other country had impressed him as deeply as Britain as far as the 'idea of imperialism' was concerned (cf. 281).

Germany.[136] But above all, and quite distinctively, Britain had a Dilke, a Froude, and a Seeley as preachers of colonial expansion. According to Marcks, these historians expressed in words what the imperial practitioners demonstrated in deeds, whereby both found the meaning of British history in the country's expansion.[137] Did Marcks perhaps want to be a German Seeley?

Casting a look at the opening twentieth century Max Lenz expressed his belief that a historical law valid for all states and all centuries would also stand in the future: the instinct of self-preservation. This he regarded as equally important as the state's will to grow and expand. The survival of the state depended upon its ability to expand its frontiers.[138] Lenz went on to explain that the new, widespread European imperialism was a positive, encouraging sign of modernity, and that those nations were most democratic which fostered the expansion of their trade and which increased their colonial acquisitions. The critics of empire, pacifists, and socialists, he dismissed as mere soap bubbles without a future.[139] On this point he agreed with Dietrich Schäfer. The fact that the future which Lenz predicted optimistically, while also being ideologically dazzled, ended in the trenches of the First World War was to a certain extent prepared for by historians like himself who uncritically allowed themselves to be used for nationalist and imperialist political ends.

While Britain already had the largest empire in world history, which needed some justification but mainly required to be maintained, Germany, the late-comer, longed to possess some remaining bits on the world map. Therefore historians in those countries had different tasks. In Britain the imperial past was used to renew pride in the nation, an Empire Day was inaugurated, and the existence of at least three different types of colonies (the ones settled predominantly by British people; India; the tropical empire and recently acquired land in Africa) needed to be explained. Froude and Seeley, for example, concentrated on the

---

[136] Ibid. 283–4.   [137] Ibid. 277.
[138] Max Lenz, 'Ein Blick in das zwanzigste Jahrhundert' (1900), in id., *Kleine historische Schriften* (Munich, 1910), 589–95, at 590.   [139] Ibid. 594.

British-populated colonies. In Germany, on the other hand, the justification of the acquisition of an empire was based on the unification of the country, the nation-state, and the concept that powerful states needed colonies for their survival.[140] In the historical writings of both scholarly communities the idea of the frontier, although it was more popular in American historiography, attracted some considerable attention, whether directly as in the case of Curzon and Stählin, or indirectly as, for example, in the studies by Egerton and Schäfer. It was no great step from Treitschke's Anglophobia and the later historical rationalization of Germany's *Weltpolitik* to the propaganda written by scholars during the First World War. And when war broke out many of the national-conservative German historians discussed in this essay as well as their British colleagues were ideologically well prepared.[141] Now Anglo-German relations had definitely arrived at the 'turning point'.[142]

---

[140] Cf. Joll, *National Histories*, 15.

[141] For this see the fascinating studies by Stuart Wallace, *War and the Image of Germany: British Academics 1914–1918* (Edinburgh, 1988), and Rolf-Peter Sieferle, 'Der deutsch-englische Gegensatz und die "Ideen von 1914" ', in Gottfried Niedhart (ed.), *Das kontinentale Europa und die britischen Inseln. Wahrnehmungsmuster und Wechselwirkungen seit der Antike* (Mannheim, 1993), 139–60; cf. also Krill, *Rankerenaissance*, 211–25.

[142] Otto Becker, 'Die Wende der deutsch-englischen Beziehungen', in Richard Nürnberger (ed.), *Festschrift für Gerhard Ritter zu seinem 60. Geburtstag* (Tübingen, 1950), 353–400.

16

The Role of British and German Historians in Mobilizing Public Opinion in 1914

HARTMUT POGGE VON STRANDMANN

State and nation were the prime subjects of most modern historians in both Germany and Britain before the First World War. Whatever their political outlook historians tended to look upon themselves as high priests of a school of thought through which they were able to demonstrate to the political establishment and its leaders how much their political actions were embedded in some sort of positive historical continuity. There was a tendency amongst British and German historians to emphasize in their history-writing the special character and uniqueness of their own particular state and its political culture. Their outlook was nationalist. As a consequence they tended to sacrifice the critical and comparative dimensions of their academic discipline to an emphasis on national identity.

In Britain a number of historians at that time strongly identified with the evolution of political values in their country, and showed how this evolution culminated in a 'growing national commitment to the state'.[1] At the outbreak of the war in 1914 these historians had little difficulty in committing themselves to their government's actions and extolling the virtues of their own country's history in the face of enemy propaganda. As all governments participating in the war firmly stated that they

---

I am grateful to Peter Foden of Oxford University Press for helping me with my research in the archives of the OUP. I should also like to thank Dr Niall Ferguson for his advice on the manuscript.

[1] Reba N. Soffer, *Discipline and Power: The University, History and the Making of an English Elite, 1870–1930* (Stanford, Calif., 1994), 129.

were involved in fighting a defensive war, the great majority of historians justified their own country's involvement in the war and disputed the enemy's claim to be doing the same.

Historians in each country were attempting to occupy the higher moral ground and so the question of who caused and started the war became of paramount concern. Yet a systematic analysis of events leading up to the war was rarely undertaken. Most historians seemed to have a different concern. As the existence of their state was challenged by war the nation also appeared endangered and thus the interpretation of national history was perceived as having been put at risk. Historians therefore felt obliged to rally to the defence of nation, state, and their view of their own history.

Historians in each country rose to the occasion and tried to pursue two aims. First they tried to justify and thus legitimize the involvement of their respective governments and their own nations in the war. Secondly they were in the forefront of those analysing and challenging the enemy's justification for the claim that it was the one fighting a defensive war. Following from this they tried to pin the responsibility for the war firmly on to the other side. Thus in this sense the post-1918 'war guilt question' began to occupy historians right from the beginning of the war.

It has been argued that the fact that academic historians in Germany were civil servants inclined them to act as pillars of the German nation-state and defenders of the existing constitution. However, the context of German academic historians' pay and service was probably less important to the interpretation of their role in society than their adherence to the historicist school. Nevertheless the authors of the well-known German manifestos had indeed collaborated with government departments when drafting their texts.[2]

As the history of these manifestos shows, the authors' collaboration with the government distinguished the early propaganda of German historians from that of their British colleagues. And there was another area in which there was a

---

[2] J. H. Morgan's article in the *Times Educational Supplement*, 1 Sept. 1914. Klaus Schwabe, *Wissenschaft und Kriegsmoral: Die deutschen Hochschullehrer und die politischen Grundfragen des Ersten Weltkrieges* (Göttingen, 1969), 21–45. See also C. R. L. Fletcher, *The Germans: Their Empire and How they have Made it* (Oxford, 1914), 17–18.

marked difference in the position of German and British historians. During the war and during the peace conference afterwards a number of British historians were directly involved with, or even employed by, various government departments, sometimes in leading positions. Their pre-war proximity to government circles in Britain had made it easier for many academic historians to enter a service in which their expertise and general views appeared to be appreciated. This particular wartime service had no equivalent in Germany.

But when it came to propaganda activities in the broadest sense, the similarity between British and German historians was closer. Both sides created and repeated national stereotypes. On the British side the *Whig Interpretation* of English history made a 'national' interpretation of the English past easier, and it also provided a basis on which historians could take a moral stance against Germany and its assumed responsibility for the outbreak of the war. The gradual development of what was called English liberty, the story of the emerging nation which had successfully overcome racial, linguistic, and religious barriers, the widespread belief in the uniqueness of the English political system at central and local levels, and pride in its representative institutions provided the background from which it appeared easy to criticize German politics and the views put forward by German historians during the war.

I

Whatever the political opinions of British historians were in the last few weeks before the outbreak of hostilities, for many *The Times* played a pivotal role in focusing their thoughts on the possibility of a forthcoming European conflict. As early as 22 July the paper talked of danger to Europe. It was feared that Austria–Hungary would submit a 'note' to Serbia which might result in a European war because 'it is not clear that Austria–Hungary, did she draw the sword, would localise the conflict if she could, and it is clear that the decision would not rest with her alone'.[3]

---

[3] *The Times*, 22 July 1914.

Thus the paper was ready for intervention even before the British cabinet had made up its mind. England should be involved in a war right from the beginning as the anticipated German occupation of Dunkirk, Calais, and Belgium would put Britain's vital security interests at stake. 'Interest, duty, and honour' should justify British intervention. *The Times* also put forward a new reason for an early entry into the war. It would be cheaper to invervene early because Britain would join the other powers fighting Germany and thus prevent a French defeat. Otherwise Britain might face Germany alone later, an effort which would financially be 'ruinous'.[4]

On 1 August three letters addressed the imminent threat of war. The Oxford historian J. A. R. Marriott, later a Conservative MP, thanked *The Times* 'for the lead it has given' over the last few days.[5] As the international crisis worsened, the interventionist line which *The Times* had pursued over the previous days had provoked a number of liberals to plead for British neutrality by publishing peace manifestos in various newspapers. Their efforts were crowned when *The Times* published the now famous 'Scholars' Protest Against War with Germany' on the same day as it printed Marriott's letter. This proclamation was sent from Cambridge and signed by nine scholars of whom at least one was a historian, namely F. J. Foakes-Jackson from Jesus College, Cambridge, who apparently was also the leading spirit behind it.[6] The

[4] *The Times*, 25, 27, and 31 July 1914.

[5] See also J. A. R. Marriott, *Memories of Fourscore Years: The Autobiography of the Late Sir John Marriott* (London, 1946); Soffer, *Discipline and Power*, 108.

[6] See H. Pogge von Strandmann, 'Britische Historiker und der Ausbruch des Ersten Weltkrieges', in W. Michalka (ed.), *Der Erste Weltkrieg: Wirkung, Wahrnehmung, Analyse* (Munich, 1994), 930. See also Stuart Wallace, *War and the Image of Germany: British Academics 1914–1918* (Edinburgh, 1988), 24 and 250. Wallace lists only eight signatories. The protest is also mentioned in D. Pick, *War Machine: The Rationalisation of Slaughter in the Modern Age* (New Haven, 1993), 152. A. J. P. Taylor mentions a figure of eighty-one who were supposed to have signed the letter. See his *The Troublemakers* (London, 1969), 117. One of the nine signatories, W. M. Ramsay, Professor Emeritus from Aberdeen, wrote to *The Times* on 15 August declaring that he no longer wished to be associated with the letter. He did not regret that he had originally agreed to sign the letter without having actually seen it, but believed now that Germany's attempt to enslave Europe must be resisted by war. Professor Alfred Marshall from Cambridge wrote to *The Times* on 26 August to say that he had also been asked to sign the Scholars' Protest. He had declined and had

signatories protested against a war with Germany 'in the interest of Serbia and Russia'. It would be 'a sin against civilisation'. They demanded at the end of their letter: 'At this juncture we consider ourselves justified in protesting against being drawn into the struggle with a nation so near akin to our own, and with whom we have so much in common.'

A similar letter was published two days later by Graham Wallas, a historian at the London School of Economics, who had organized a Neutrality Committee.[7] All these efforts were however unlikely to be successful because, as *The Times* put it, the war challenged British security and therefore appealed to the 'instinct for self-preservation'. Even the Scholars' Protest made clear that 'if by reason of honourable obligation we are to be unhappily involved in war, patriotism might still our mouths'. But at the very end of July they still objected to the new resoluteness for war which was finding growing support.

II

Opposition to war was continuously voiced in the *Manchester Guardian* until Britain's declaration of war on 4 August, but it did not provoke the same reaction as the 'Scholars' Protest' in *The Times*. Generally speaking *The Times* appeared to have made up its mind by giving substantial space to the arguments of the interventionists. Thus Valentine Chirol felt that Britain was morally obliged to help France regardless of the costs involved. He also detected German machinations behind the crisis and he was not far from the truth when he wrote: 'By provoking, or rather by instigating, Austria–Hungary to provoke a fresh European crisis over Serbia, Germany has brought Russia first of all into the forefront of the controversy, knowing full well that Russia for many reasons enjoys much less popular sympathy in this country than France.'[8]

suggested instead that 'we ought to mobilise instantly and announce that we shall declare war if the Germans invade Belgium'. See also the forthcoming article by John Clarke, 'All Souls and the War of the Professors'. I am very grateful to J. Clarke (University of Buckingham) for providing me with a draft of his article.

[7] Wallace, *War and the Image of Germany*, 25.   [8] *The Times*, 3 Aug. 1914.

Whereas Chirol did not specifically refer to the 'Scholars' Protest', the Oxford historian Stuart Jones did when his letter appeared in *The Times* just before Britain declared war on Germany.[9] In it he criticized his academic colleagues from Oxford and Cambridge for glorifying the achievements of German culture and science without pointing to the militarist and expansionist traditions represented by authors such as Treitschke, Bernhardi, and even former Chancellor Bülow. He also reminded them that Germany was not 'governed by scholars but by statesmen who solemnly believe that might confers not only the right but the duty of attacking the weaker states'. Moreover, Jones objected to the notion that Germany had rendered intellectual services to the world.

Whilst Jones rehearsed some of the arguments which were to become staple fare in the later campaign of words against Germany, some liberal historians continued to voice opposition to British involvement in a war. During the Boer War most liberals opposed British intervention. By contrast at the beginning of the First World War liberals preferred to demonstrate national solidarity by joining the war effort. When the war finally broke out the public was not completely unprepared. Nor were most historians in any way surprised. Some had feared a European conflict for some time. G. Lowes Dickinson had warned against an Anglo-German war in late 1907. He wrote: 'There may, indeed, be war between Germany and England, but, if so, it will be because the Government and peoples of those countries have willed it; not because of any necessity to be.'[10]

In his book *The Great Society*, published in 1914, Graham Wallas had bidden farewell to liberal hopes of peace in Europe and hoped that his appeal to the strengthening of international law would help to prevent wars.

A third historian who should be mentioned here is John Adam Cramb, whose reflective lectures on Germany and England were published in book form in 1914, a year after his death. Cramb, labelled the 'English Treitschke', had actually

---

[9] *The Times*, 4 Aug. 1914; Wallace, *War and the Image of Germany*, 26.
[10] Ibid. 113, see also Pogge von Strandmann, 'Britische Historiker', 930.

attended Treitschke's lectures in Berlin in the 1880s. By 1913 he still believed that Treitschke was the most influential German historian; this assumption was widely accepted by other historians in Britain, although W. J. Allen noted that Treitschke had been superseded by names such as Erich Marcks, Max Lenz, Hermann Oncken, and Friedrich Meinecke. Cramb 'paints for us a Germany', as the *Times Literary Supplement* noted, 'expanding rapidly in opulence, in power, in the mastery of practical life, and deeply imbued with the teaching of Nietzsche'.[11]

Cramb regarded the triad of Bernhardi, Nietzsche, and Treitschke as having enormous influence in Germany, and thus fed into an existing stereotype among many British academic observers of Germany. He also noted that in Germany contempt for England was widespread, and that a feeling that Britain was blocking Germany at every corner would inevitably lead to war between the two nations. Cramb's influence was considerable, partly because his book had appeared a few weeks before the outbreak of hostilities, partly because he was associated with Lord Roberts and his campaign for compulsory military service and had lectured at various military institutions, and finally because his message was outspoken and undifferentiated.

The warnings against harbouring any illusions about German politics put forward by a few historians were not accepted by all sectors of public opinion until after the war had begun. In any case it looks as if a majority of historians backed England's entry into the war, at least at the time of the British declaration of war on 4 August. A typical example of a change of mind was the Cambridge historian J. Holland Rose, author of a book on the *Development of the European Nations 1870–1900*, who had signed a letter on 2 August in favour of preserving neutrality. But a day later, when it became clear that Germany had begun to invade Belgium, he withdrew his signature and advocated that Britain should repel German aggression by force.[12]

---

[11] *Times Literary Supplement*, 13 Aug. 1914. [12] *The Times*, 10 Aug. 1914.

III

The rallying of historians behind the war effort meant that they almost automatically took their part in 'educating the nation'. This was an important task which was also claimed by German historians. But there were differences in how these two national groups fulfilled it. Brochures, newspaper articles, and pamphlets were used by both sides, but addressing lay audiences had been a particular preoccupation of British historians since Victorian times. In the twentieth century Gilbert Murray, G. M. Trevelyan, G. P. Gooch, A. D. Lindsay, H. A. L. Fisher, H. W. C. Davis, and E. Barker, to name but a few, embodied this tradition. They were keen to put their talents at the service of the wider public.[13] These historians also maintained close connections with the political élite in Westminster and Whitehall. A certain degree of interaction was a consequence of the special position of Oxford and Cambridge, but the deliberate attempt by academics to gain greater public influence may have formed part of a trend towards greater cultural integration in Britain.[14]

It is difficult to ascertain in this context to what extent historians acted as opinion leaders, or to what extent they were reacting to a public discussion outside the confines of academia. In so far as historians were part of a British 'intellectual aristocracy' (to use Noel Annan's term) which lent a special flavour to the world of letters, they tended to shape public opinion, but the conversion of anti-war historians to the cause of national solidarity showed that they also followed public opinion. Inspired by the growing campaign for British intervention, a group of Oxford historians, namely E. Barker from New College, H. W. C. Davis from Balliol College, C. R. Fletcher from Magdalen College, A. Hassall from Christ Church, L. G. Wickham Legg from New College, and F. Morgan from Keble College, organized itself to write spontaneously a book entitled *Why we are at War*.

---

[13] Julia Stapleton, *Englishness and the Study of Politics: The Social and Political Thought of Ernest Barker* (Cambridge, 1994), 15.
[14] Ibid. 17.

Great Britain's Case, which Oxford University Press published between 26 August and 14 September 1914.[15] Because of the significance of this group the present essay concentrates in the following on historians from Oxford.

The *spiritus rector* of the group effort was either H. W. C. Davis of Balliol College, later Regius Professor of Modern History at Oxford, or Ernest Barker of New College, who in the 1930s was to hold the first chair of Political Science at Cambridge. One of their main sources was the German White Book which they translated. Further ammunition was probably provided by a letter Rudolf Eucken and Ernst Haeckel wrote to the *Vossische Zeitung*, in which they protested against Britain's intervention in the war which they explained by arguing that Britain was envious of Germany.[16] This letter has been regarded as the opening shot in what was to become the 'war of the professors'; obviously it was rejected by Gilbert Murray, John Cowper Powys, and Ford Madox Hueffer (later Ford).

The final spark for the erupting war of propaganda may have been a German pamphlet campaign which had been started in neutral Italy to win over public opinion to the German cause. Another contributing factor may have been the early publication in the middle of August 1914 of a German pamphlet *Die Wahrheit über den Krieg* (*The Truth about the War*), which also appeared in an English translation.[17] This pamphlet had been written at the behest of the propaganda department of the Naval Office. It appears that the Germans were quicker off the mark than the British in the very first phase of the war of words.

Responding to the German efforts, the Oxford dons

---

[15] The book has recently been referred to by Wallace, *War and the Image of Germany*, 60–1; J. M. Winter, 'Oxford and the First World War', in B. Harrison (ed.), *The History of the University of Oxford*, viii: *The Twentieth Century* (Oxford, 1994), 15–16; Soffer, *Discipline and Power*, 46.

[16] S. Hynes, *A War Imagined. The First World War and English Culture* (London, 1990), 70. The protest was published on 20 August 1914. For the response see ibid. 71.

[17] J. and W. von Ungern-Sternberg, *Der Aufruf 'An die Kulturwelt': Das Manifest der 93 und die Anfänge der Kriegspropaganda im Ersten Weltkrieg* (Stuttgart, 1996), 119 is the most recent publication quoting the latest studies of the German propaganda effort.

stated in their preface that they were not politicians, but that they did 'belong to different schools of political thought'.[18] Whether this meant different party affiliations or different approaches to history is not clear. But they wanted to stress that they 'had some experience in the handling of historic evidence, and that they had endeavoured to treat this subject historically'. They examined the evidence available and confirmed something which turned out to be a foregone conclusion. However, the book was surprisingly sober and dispassionate, as Peter Sutcliffe wrote in his history of the Oxford University Press, 'when all about them was a mindless fervour'.[19] The authors blamed Germany's obsession with power and militarism, and held that England's intervention was based on the need to uphold international law. They were, of course, convinced of England's moral superiority and that 'if we have harped on England's interest, it must not for a moment be supposed that we have forgotten England's duty'. According to the five authors, both combined gave Britain's intervention a special thrust.

Contrary to Sutcliffe's benevolent interpretation the book could, however, be seen as a strong attack on Germany's political system. In a self-righteous tone the Oxford dons referred in the final chapter to a firm link between Englishness and law. The five authors in Oxford assumed that other nations could not be guided by similar principles, and they seemed unaware of the concurrent belief of German liberals that Germany was a *Rechtsstaat*, that is, that it was governed by the rule of law. Guided by their own preconceptions, the authors equated Germany's theory of the state with 'absolute sovereignty' and the glorification of war. England, by contrast, 'stands for the idea of public law of Europe, and for the small nations which it protects'. As Ernest Barker was to dwell on this aspect of Gladstonianism in his writings during the war, Julia Stapleton concludes that Barker 'would seem to have played an instrumental role in the book's conclusion'.[20] This may well have been the case

[18] Members of the Oxford Faculty of Modern History, *Why we are at War: Great Britain's Case* (Oxford, 1914), 5.
[19] P. Sutcliffe, *The Oxford University Press: An Informal History* (Oxford, 1978), 173.
[20] Stapleton, *Englishness*, 95.

and could be the explanation for the later difference of opinion between Barker and Davis.

The *Times Literary Supplement* reviewed the book favourably and found it 'refreshing to turn from the morass of gross mendacity and diatribe to the solid ground of ascertained facts and authoritative documents'.[21] The review ends with the judgement that it placed 'upon the conduct of Germany the least unfavourable interpretation compatible with the evidence'. In Germany this claim was rejected and a number of its historians criticized the Oxford volume. In response, Ernest Barker rejected the German historians' accusation 'of misusing science for political objectives'.[22] He at first simply returned the charge, but then realized that this method would not have much effect. Instead he believed that he had tried 'to conquer a very natural national prejudice' which had not been an easy task. He therefore concentrated on six points which, to his mind, revealed that the German authors were unfamiliar with either the available evidence or simple facts. He refuted the arguments in defence of the construction of the German battle fleet, rejected the criticism of British imperialism and British diplomacy in St Petersburg, saw through the plan as to why the Kaiser had been absent from Berlin until 26 July, upheld the Belgian right to neutrality, and did not accept the declaration of the German love of peace.

The Oxford don William Sanday appreciated Barker's letter and recommended publishing the German professors' attack. But H. W. C. Davis objected to Barker entering into an argument with the German professors by publishing a pamphlet.[23] He thought that Barker's 'stuff is not worth printing. The "war of the professors" has already become a byeword and if Barker wants to defend the Red Book "Why we are at War" any further, he had better do it somewhere else.'[24] As it turned out this was to be the end of Barker's particular effort.[25]

[21] *Times Literary Supplement*, 17 Sept. 1914.
[22] *The Times*, 9 Dec. 1914.
[23] Oxford University Press Archive, 1217, Davis to Chapman, 17 Dec. 1914.
[24] Ibid. 1743, Davis to Cannan, 20 Dec. 1914.
[25] Although Davis had eventually agreed with Barker's proposal Cannan probably persuaded Barker not to proceed with this particular project.

The emerging rivalry between Barker and Davis had deteriorated further because of another incident which unfortunately occurred at the same time. As Britain and Germany were especially concerned to win over hitherto neutral Italy to their causes the British Admiralty planned to join the fray by asking Davis and the Clarendon Press to produce a pamphlet for Italy.[26] The Admiralty simply informed Davis that it wanted half a million copies in Italian as quickly as possible which the Foreign Office, if its agreement could be secured, was then to circulate in Italy. 'Why the Admiralty should take up the publicity business is more than I can guess,' Davis told Chapman, but he was willing to accept an order from outside Oxford which was aimed more directly at clear propaganda purposes. Barker was asked to write the pamphlet 'quam promptissime', as Davis put it, so that it could be translated in London. Barker set to work immediately and produced a draft in the shortest time, reminiscent of the speed with which he had produced crucial sections of *Why we are at War*. When he took it to London he could not find anyone at the Admiralty who would accept his pamphlet, and he then blamed Davis for this mishap. Cannan received an explanation from Davis as to why Barker's manuscript had never reached him: 'I was expecting it until I heard from him that he had handed it over to the National Health Insurance Committee.'[27] The porter at the Admiralty was not allowed to divulge Davis's department. As a result Barker was angry and Davis had 'to try and find another pamphleteer for Italy'. As far as can be made out he did not succeed, and Barker published his tract *Great Britain's Reasons for going to War* in London in 1915.

In his article John Clarke has given two explanations for the clash between Barker and Davis.[28] On the one hand he has argued that the quarrel between the two may have had something to do with their different interpretations of democracy. However, there is not really enough evidence to support this view. Davis's somewhat élitist opinion that new

---

[26] Oxford University Press Archive, 1226, Davis to Chapman, 15 Dec. 1914.
[27] Ibid. 1743, Cannan to Barker, 29 Dec. 1914.
[28] Clarke, 'All Souls and the War of the Professors'.

ideas do not appear at the bottom level of society but trickle downwards from the top of the social pyramid may have differed from Barker's views in this respect, but they both shared an Oxford-based élitist outlook which included a certain educational and social concern for less well-educated groups of society. In addition, Barker appeared to be no friend of the new social history which Davis later also rejected in public. On the other hand, Clarke has referred to their different views on Treitschke. In his Oxford pamphlet Barker followed the wartime trend in England, and by the autumn of 1914 he was highly critical of Nietzsche and denounced Treitschke. In 1914, however, Davis managed to publish a booklet on Treitschke's political thought which was not characterized by the usual wartime denunciations. Instead he tried to be fair to a historian for whom he must have felt considerable respect. The book was not, as Davis's biographer, J. R. H. Weaver, has argued, 'written with a controversial purpose'.[29] Their differences in interpreting Treitschke are possibly indicative of another problem which concerns the pamphlets. Whereas Davis seemed to follow the rules of fairness towards Germany and wanted this to be reflected in the pamphlets, Barker displayed a more belligerent attitude and was perhaps even hostile towards Germany. Therefore his pamphlets were different in character from those Davis had written and it is possible that the latter was determined to adhere more to historical standards at this time than Barker.

IV

Just before *Why we are at War* came on to the market in September 1914, Oxford University Press wrote to the Foreign Secretary and sent him three advance copies. Grey, who had not known about the forthcoming book, was very impressed with it and offered to buy a number of copies including trans-

---

[29] J. R. H Weaver, *Henry William Carless Davis 1874–1928: A Memoir* (London, 1933), 35. Weaver's article on Davis in the *Dictionary of National Biography* hardly mentions his involvement with the Oxford Pamphlets. *DNB 1922–1930* (Oxford, 1937), 249.

lations which were to be distributed through the various embassies.[30] Even without the Foreign Office's purchase of 3,300 copies the book proved to be a success. It ran through several editions, and, including translations, sold about 50,000 copies by 1928. The proceeds were given to the Belgian Relief Fund. The first payment worth £728 1s. was sent to the Belgian Minister in London in November 1915.[31] How much the volume was appreciated can be gauged from two letters, one by the British ambassador in Washington, Cecil Spring Rice, and the other by the former British ambassador to Berlin, Sir Edward Goschen. Spring Rice wrote to Oxford University Press that he liked the Oxford manifesto: 'I have no doubt it will carry conviction abroad! The people here have pretty well made up their minds as to who began the war. They don't question any more what Germany did. What they are now chiefly interested in is that those who are fighting for liberty and public law should fight well. They get indignant at any disaster as they would at a baseball match if their side didn't play well.'[32] Spring Rice also pleaded for more openness and less British censorship as the Americans wanted to know the German side of the arguments as well. Obviously he had no fear that this might weaken Britain's case. The other reaction came from Goschen, who had received the German translation of *Why we are at War* (*Warum wir Krieg führen*). He praised the completeness and historical accuracy of the book and regretted that there was no hope that it would be widely read in Germany. Otherwise it would counteract the 'legend so widely spread throughout that country by the ruling class that the war was engineered by Great Britain for her own nefarious purposes'.[33]

Outside Oxford historians like D. J. Medley (Glasgow) and Ramsay Muir (Manchester) published their criticism of Germany in *Why Britain is at War* and *Britain's Case against Germany*. A different line of publications appeared in

---

[30] Oxford University Press Archive, 58, Grey to Cannan, 8 Sept. 1914, and Grey to Davis, 11 Sept. 1914.
[31] Sutcliffe, *Oxford University Press*, 172–3.
[32] Oxford University Press Archive 1743, Cecil Spring Rice to Cannan, 17 Oct. 1914.
[33] Ibid. 131, Goschen to Delegates, 31 Jan. 1915.

September 1914. It looked as if it had been prompted by G. W. Prothero, formerly at Edinburgh and editor of the *Quarterly Review*. In a letter to *The Times* of 20 August, headed 'A Fight to a Finish', he had suggested setting up an organization whose task would be to convert working men in the north and the centre of England to the cause of Britain's involvement in the war.[34] He was reacting to various reports that the war effort had not fully united the nation behind the government. The historians' claim to be the nation's educator in this hour of need would sound hollow if they did not turn their attention to this particular problem and help to unify the nation. Prothero thought that such addresses should explain that 'we have to cope with an unscrupulous aristocracy, with a military caste and principles that Might makes Right'. He also wanted it to be made clear that this war would be a 'struggle to the end'. The idea that indifferent country folk and workers in the north should be made aware of Britain's good reasons for being involved in the war appealed to a number of education-minded letter-writers who offered their advice for such a publicity campaign. Among the first were C. Grant Robertson, Fellow and Bursar of All Souls, and the economist Alfred Marshall from Cambridge.[35] They were followed by many others, for example by Stuart Jones, historian from Trinity College, who wanted to appeal to the Americans to convene a conference of neutrals and Hague Convention signatories to condemn Germany.[36] A number of complaints were directed against the editorial in *John Bull*, written by Horatio Bottomley: 'To Hell with Serbia!', which appeared before 8 August and which argued that Serbia was not worth British involvement in the war and that the Balkan state should be wiped out. And E. Littelton from Eton College wanted a special notion to be addressed which to his mind existed 'among many of our working men . . . that if Germany wins they will be no worse off than they are now'.[37] A. L. Smith echoed this information and added that 'there

---

[34] *The Times*, 20 Aug. 1914. See also Wallace, *War and the Image of Germany*, 167–8. Soffer, *Discipline and Power*, 47.   [35] *The Times*, 21 Aug. and 22 Aug. 1914.
[36] Ibid. 26 Aug. 1914.
[37] Ibid. 24 Aug. 1914. Dalton supported this statement by referring to the general 'ignorance in rural districts'. Ibid. 31 Aug. 1914.

are still large sections of the community who fail to realise the vastness of the issues at stake, the formidable nature of the forces ranged against us, and the true inner significance of the struggle'.[38] Prothero's proposals were also endorsed by the Cambridge historian J. Holland Rose who firmly believed that it was a duty of those who had studied 'continental affairs' to enlighten the public about the causes of the war: 'The more they are studied, the more complete and overwhelming is the case in favour of Great Britain.'[39]

When Prothero's suggestions received Curzon's support it was not long before the Prime Minister reacted by sending a letter to *The Times*, stipulating that a publicity campaign should be initiated in the major cities in which the 'justice of our cause' was to be explained. He also counted on co-operation between cities, education authorities, and voluntary organizations, and announced that a Parliamentary Committee was to be set up with the backing of Bonar Law to oversee the forthcoming campaign.[40] A well-organized series of public lectures was started by the Oxford University Extension Delegacy, the Workers' Educational Association (WEA), the Victoria League, the Cavendish League, the Business Men's League, the Rural League, and the Social Service Bureau, all of which used historians to educate audiences about the legitimacy of Britain's involvement in the war, and its moral obligation to fight. Prothero then set up a Central Committee to co-ordinate the propaganda efforts 'as to the reason, justice and necessity of the war'.[41]

The centralizing efforts did not succeed right from the beginning. Thus the WEA, which defined itself as a strictly educational body, protested against being drawn into a propaganda campaign.[42] Because of its emphasis on infor-

[38] Wallace, *War and the Image of Germany*, 168.
[39] *The Times*, 27 Aug. 1914.
[40] Ibid. 28 Aug. 1914, and Curzon's second letter, ibid. 1 Sept. 1914. See also ibid. 3 Sept. 1914.
[41] Ibid. 5 Sept. 1914. In Germany similar efforts were made to create a central organization which was to direct its propaganda activities abroad. See J. and W. von Ungern-Sternberg, *Der Aufruf*, 126–35.
[42] *The Times*, 7 Sept. 1914. See now L. Goldman, *Dons and Workers: Oxford and Adult Education since 1850* (Oxford, 1995), 195; Wallace, *War and the Image of Germany*, 168–9.

mation the WEA attracted the criticisms of 'pacifism and pro-Germanism', as Goldman has put it. But as the border between propaganda and educational information was not clearly defined, the WEA accepted lectures given by historians as long as the state was supported in its hour of need. The historian J. A. R. Marriott was to write later about his activities in the WEA: 'Propaganda in the narrower sense was not within our proper province. But we substituted for our usual lecture subjects, courses which had a direct bearing on the war, its antecedents and issues.'[43]

As more and more books appeared supporting Britain's case for being involved in the war, an authors' declaration appeared in *The Times* giving full support to the government's course of action.[44] In their letter the authors, many of whom were historians who before the war had been ardent champions of Germany, pacifists, and critics of Grey's foreign policy, denounced Germany's claim that its culture was so superior to the civilization of other nations that all political decisions were justified. They also attacked Germany's will to conquer, and denied it the right to defend small nations. Among the signatories were the following: the two Trevelyans, the Wards, H. A. L. Fisher, who was going to publish his own version of *The War: its Causes and Issues* later that year, the Hammonds, Ensor, Tawney, and the former pacifist Gilbert Murray.

While the book *Why we are at War* was being printed, Prothero was launching his campaign of educating the less motivated, and while the Declaration by Authors was appearing, the Oxford War Pamphlets were born spontaneously without government interference.[45]

[43] Wallace, *War and the Image of Germany*, 169. Goldman maintains that, contrary to Marriott's impression, many lectures presented 'a fiercely patriotic and anti-German case', ibid.
[44] *The Times*, 18 Sept. 1914.
[45] Rüdiger vom Bruch's assertion that the 'war of professors' was directed by the British Foreign Office is made without evidence and actually mistaken. R. vom Bruch, 'Krieg und Frieden: Zur Frage der Militarisierung deutscher Hochschullehrer und Universitäten im späten Kaiserreich', in J. Dülffer und K. Holl (eds.), *Bereit zum Krieg. Kriegsmentalität im wilhelminischen Deutschland 1890–1914* (Göttingen, 1986), 74. In his otherwise comprehensive study Stuart Wallace has underestimated the significance of the Oxford Pamphlets and neglected the self-mobilizing role Oxford historians played in 1914.

V

The first time the forthcoming Oxford Pamphlets were mentioned was in a letter by Henry Jackson from Trinity College, Cambridge, to Cannan who had asked the Cambridge academic to write one of the pamphlets. Jackson, who indulged in wartime hatred of anything German, thanked Cannan for sending him copies of the first pamphlets, which he liked: 'I had thought that pamphleteering had been killed by the magazines; you have now the opportunity of reviving it.'[46]

It is likely that the initiative for the pamphlets originated with Davis who found willing collaborators in Cannan and Chapman from Oxford University Press. He called together a number of Oxford historians and other eminent academics during the second half of August 1914 to produce a series of pamphlets for the general education of the public. Although Davis recruited heavily in Oxford he later also contacted the authors of articles in various journals and asked them to convert their pieces into pamphlets. A case in point was W. G. S. Adams's pamphlet No. 3, *The Responsibility for the War*, which was first published in the *Political Quarterly*.[47] The Secretary and Assistant Secretary to the Delegates of the Press were also busy winning over contributors to the series of pamphlets. They made good use of their contacts in Oxford and thus were able to come up with a number of suggestions. One example may suffice. Through Chapman, Davis heard that F. S. Marvin, from St John's College and HM Inspector of Schools, would like to write a pamphlet. The Balliol historian regarded this 'as good news' and went on in his letter to Gilbert Murray: 'I am told his title will be *The Bloody Present*. But whatever he wishes to write about ... will be very welcome.'[48] In fact Marvin's later pamphlet (No. 42) dealt with German aspirations and was published under the title: *The Leadership of the World*.

---

[46] Oxford University Press Archive, 1208, Jackson to Cannan, 10 Sept. 1914. On 18 September Jackson informed Cannan that he did not know enough to write a pamphlet.   [47] Ibid. 1207, Davis's note of 17 Oct. 1914.

[48] Ibid., Davis to Murray, 16 Oct. 1914.

The purpose of the Oxford Pamphlets, as Davis explained in a condescending manner to Chirol whom he recruited as one of the pamphleteers, was as follows: 'The series is intended for the intelligent working man, and therefore the method of treatment to be adopted is simple, even elementary.'[49] And Davis went on: 'The contributors belong to very different schools of opinion; but they are all anxious to confirm the ordinary elector in his present admirable attitude towards the war, and to warn him against the dangers of making peace on terms which settle nothing.' Two months later Davis had slightly modified the objective of the series. Now it was 'to provide useful information on the War and all questions connected with it'.[50] He still wanted to reach classes 'who do not buy books of reference because they cannot afford the luxury, but do wish for exact information'.

Among the contributing authors there were also those who volunteered to join the emerging 'band of sharpshooters' because they wanted to put across a particular view. Sir Erle Richards, Professor of International Law and a Fellow of All Souls, who had coined the term 'sharpshooters', quickly retracted it because it gave the impression of partiality which he wanted to avoid at all costs. This was especially welcomed by the Assistant Secretary to the Delegates of the Press because he believed that an impartial assessment of the international legal situation would favour Britain and would therefore be much more effective.[51] Thus Richards agreed later to write a pamphlet on international law because he thought it necessary to expose Germany, which had struck 'at the whole root of the Law of Nations'.[52] But on the whole Richards tried to be objective, especially when the issue of German atrocities in the war in Belgium came up. Davis himself was not particularly concerned about Richards's scruples as long as the facts were correct. 'The great difficulty', he foresaw, 'is of persuading the artisan to buy and read any point of view which is not his own. I am trying to

[49] Ibid., Davis to Chirol, 14 Sept. 1914.
[50] Ibid. 1743, Davis's note about a pamphlet for Japan, 17 Nov. 1914.
[51] Ibid., Chapman to Richards, 11 Sept. 1914.
[52] Ibid., Richards to Chapman, 11 Sept. 1914.

get in touch with various labour organisations which may help us.'[53] In this way he found out that the question which interested working men and women was not so much why this war was necessary, but rather 'why any war should ever be necessary'. He used this question to convince Gilbert Murray to write a pamphlet entitled: *How can War ever be Right?*[54]

Having started the series with very few authors (Sanday, Hassall, and Fletcher), Davis threw himself into action in Balliol's Tower to win over more academics from Oxford. He successfully approached Sir Walter Raleigh, Professor of English Literature, W. G. S. Adams, Gladstone Professor of Political Theory and Institutions, Spencer Wilkinson, Chichele Professor of Military History, Keith Feiling from Christ Church, and Murray Beaven from Aberdeen. Nine of the first batch of pamphlets were written by historians, eight from Oxford and one from Aberdeen. The historically orientated brochures deal with topics such as the 'Responsibility for the War', 'Great Britain and Germany', the 'German Violation of Belgian neutrality', the 'Creation of the German Empire' and 'The Political Ambitions of the Germans', the slogan 'Might is Right', 'Austrian Policy since 1867', and 'Italian Policy since 1870'. The first ten pamphlets were free of any hate campaigns. Whereas Adams, the author of *Responsibility for the War*, emphasized that this war meant a struggle of 'freedom against militarism', Murray Beaven from Aberdeen simply analysed Austrian foreign policy. He blamed Aehrenthal's 'forward policy' as crucial for the outbreak of the war, as well as Germany's efforts, namely 'that the hour has struck to translate her vision of Weltmacht into substance'. Beaven's analysis was relatively unbiased, a judgement which applies neither to Ernest Barker's Francophile pamphlets, nor to the oversimplifications of Robert S. Rait's (Professor at Glasgow) brochure: *Why we are Fighting Germany: A Village Lecture.*

For the next ten pamphlets Davis engaged the historians F. Morgan from Keble College, F. F. Urquhart and A. D. Lindsay

---

[53] Oxford University Press Archive, Davis to Kilbracken, 18 Sept. 1914.
[54] Ibid., Davis to Murray, 18 Sept. 1914.

from Balliol College, H. A. L. Fisher and Barker from New College, and Ramsay Muir from Manchester. Non-historians were Paul Vinogradoff, Professor of Jurisprudence, Gilbert Murray, Regius Professor of Greek, and Sir Valentine Chirol, a well-known publicist. As Peter Sutcliffe has pointed out, these first pamphlets were written 'with intense conviction, and a spontaneity that distinguished them from works written later to manipulate public opinion or promote the war effort'.[55] Most of the first pamphleteers were moderate in their criticism of Germany and more forceful in their rejection of defensive arguments provided by German scholars. They were also keen to free themselves from a previously strong German academic influence. The German pronouncements which identified militarism with culture were interpreted as a perversion of true culture and civilization. The Oxford authors regarded themselves as far better guardians of these values than their German colleagues. They often differentiated between Prussia and the other German states, the ruling caste and the ordinary peace-loving German, the military and civilian circles, in short, the 'good' and the 'bad' German. German academics refuted this British approach which in their eyes tried to 'contrast the spirit of German intellectual and natural sciences with Prussian militarism'.

Hynes has argued that by denouncing German scholars and German culture the British historians 'were warring against their own past'.[56] They had taken over German rationalism, scientific methods and thoroughness, the emphasis on research into primary sources as well as source criticism, and as far as music and literature were concerned, the romantic tradition. However, Hynes goes too far in his generalization. Certainly, there were members of the British educated classes who, during the war, rejected anything linked to Germany. But the majority of historians held that the German academic community had perverted the values it had once promoted and that it was no longer justified in believing that it was the holder of the grail of objectivity.

One of the pamphleteers, Spencer Wilkinson, who had

[55] Sutcliffe, *Oxford University Press*, 173. [56] Hynes, *A War Imagined*, 78.

helped to organize the British Navy League in the 1890s, took J. W. Burgess, the American political scientist from Columbia University, to task over his defence of the German cause.[57] He subjected Burgess's published letters to a textual analysis and accused him of blatant partiality through which he had neglected his duty as a historian. Both had paid tribute to the German influence on their professional development, but whereas Wilkinson emancipated himself from his intellectual indebtedness to Germany at the beginning of the war, Burgess became a little more doubtful of his ties to Germany only after the American entry into the war.

Although Davis might have appreciated Wilkinson's dialectical method, he was probably much happier with E. A. Sonnenschein's approach. In his pamphlet *Through German Eyes*, which he had offered to Davis in December 1914, he was fairer even to Treitschke than, for instance, Barker. Davis told Cannan that Sonnenschein 'really knows Germany and the Germans and he seems to have studied all the apologetic literature that they have produced'.[58] Thus Davis had been able to attract a great variety of authors who deployed different methods and approaches in their tracts. What they had in common was that they had liberated themselves from an overbearing German intellectual influence. As the Principal of Manchester College in Oxford put it: 'The age of German footnotes is on the wane.'[59]

As might be expected there were also some failures in Davis's and Cannan's campaign to recruit authors for 'the band of sharpshooters'. Among them were Henry Jackson from Cambridge, Gordon, Professor of Literature at Leeds, Robert Bridges, the Poet Laureate, Kilbracken, Benecke, who had attended Treitschke's lectures in the past, Herbertson, Professor of Geography at Oxford, D. G. Hogarth, Keeper of the Ashmolean Museum, Lord Rosebery, and A. L. Smith, who later wrote a pamphlet on *The Christian Attitude to War*. Some plans, such as Grant

---

[57] Spencer Wilkinson, *Great Britain and Germany*, pamphlet No. 4 (Oxford, 1914).
[58] Oxford University Press Archive, 1217, Davis to Cannan, 25 Dec. 1914. Sonnenschein's pamphlet was published as No. 61 in 1915.
[59] Wallace, *War and the Image of Germany*, 37.

Robertson's *Great Britain's Continental Policy*, never materialized, and other projects, such as those by Namier or Headlam, were rejected.

Davis proved to be a strong-minded unofficial editor of the Oxford Pamphlets. When writing to Benecke about Treitschke, Davis criticized Cramb's influential book as of 'no use', and he told Fletcher that 'we have been enjoying [your] *The Germans, their Empire and what they covet* in the office. My wife says it made her ill with laughing.'[60] Initially Davis was not keen to let anything be written about the German colonies because 'it would look as though we had gone to war to grab colonies'.[61] But he later included a pamphlet on the subject by the librarian of the Royal Colonial Institute, Evans Lewin, who had been recommended by Egerton, the Beit Professor of Colonial History, possibly because German excesses in the war had been discussed by Dawson in his book on *The Evolution of Modern Germany*.[62] Kipling's poems were also scanned to see whether any could be included after the poet had offered them because 'he couldn't wave a louder flag'.[63] But the plan foundered because it was difficult to find anything suitable, and because of objections made by Cannan's daughters who, since the beginning of the war, had been working at Oxford University Press.[64]

A number of projects did not materialize for a variety of reasons. Rosebery regarded himself as too old to write a pamphlet; Namier was too difficult to deal with when alterations to his manuscript were suggested; and Headlam was regarded by Davis as sound 'but not exciting' enough.[65] Hogarth actually completed his pamphlet, but did not like it.

[60] Oxford University Press Archive, 1208, Davis to Benecke, 15 Sept. 1914, and Davis to Fletcher, 18 Sept. 1914.
[61] Ibid., Davis to Herbertson, 16 Sept. 1914.
[62] Ibid. 1206, Davis's note on a typed copy of schoolmaster Coombes's letter to the Press, 25 Oct. 1914.
[63] Ibid., Milford to Cannan, 19 Sept. 1914.
[64] Ibid., Davis to Fletcher, 18 Sept. 1914.
[65] Ibid., Davis to Namier, 18 Sept. 1914, ibid., Rosebery to Cannan, 29 Sept. 1914, ibid. 1207, Davis's note of 17 Oct. 1914. Ibid. 1221, Davis to Milford, 6 May 1915. Davis wrote: 'Namier has definitely refused to cut down his remarks on Poland and Prussia to the limits of a pamphlet.' He wanted to submit a manuscript of 20,000 words, 'but I said no'.

He finally withdrew his script mainly because he did not trust Grey's and Asquith's public assertions about the diplomatic origins of the war.[66] A pamphlet on German atrocities in Belgium was vetoed by the Press because it was doubted that it could be written in good style.[67]

In November 1914 Professor Hadow from the University of Durham wanted to change his original proposal for a pamphlet. Instead of publishing merely a translation of Wilhelm Wundt's war brochure he wanted to add Oncken's defence of the German case, 'the manifestoes of the German Scholars, the manifestoes of the German Theologians etc., or a sufficient selection from these'.[68] He did not want to select passages because 'the enemy always accuses one of fraudulently leaving out passages which were on his side'. In order to fulfil a later demand to hear the other side as well he suggested a booklet 'which shall reprint the best that has been said on the other side by its most distinguished apologists, and show how easily the points can be answered'. Davis went along with Hadow's suggestion but thought that to 'reprint all the German apologists would be . . . a great waste of time'.[69] Thus Davis believed that the academic from Durham and his translator sister should produce an anthology of German apologetic arguments, but this part of the project did not see the light of day.[70] At the end of 1914 Davis had various ideas as to how the pamphlets should be continued. A historian from University College, Oxford, Cecil Jane, had written a pamphlet about the naval action near Helgoland on 28 August 1914. In December 1914 Davis asked him to write another one, namely a comparative survey of the British and German fleets. Jane agreed but nothing further was heard of his second script ever being submitted.[71]

On the whole the series of pamphlets was a success. Eighty-seven had appeared by September 1915 and the print-run

---

[66] Oxford University Press Archive, 1208, Hogarth to Cannan, 4 Oct. 1914.
[67] Ibid. 1186, Cannan to Davis, 13 Nov. 1914.
[68] Ibid., Hadow to Cannan, 13 Nov. 1914.
[69] Ibid. 1223, Davis to Hadow, 14 Nov. 1914.
[70] Ibid. 1217, Davis to Cannan, 23 Dec. 1914.
[71] Ibid. 1224, Jane to Davis, 9 Dec. 1914.

approached the half-million mark.[72] With very few exceptions prices were kept low at one penny, twopence, or threepence. They were intended to be informative, educational, and occasionally even practical, such as *The War and the Cotton Trade* (No. 73), or *Prices and Earnings in Time of War* (No. 75). The tone of the pamphlets is generally judgemental and critical of Germany, but they do not contain hateful and aggressive remarks. Between 5,000 and 8,000 words long, the pamphlets were mainly sold to schools, universities, military institutions, educational clubs and associations, and to private citizens in Britain. Outside Britain they were sold in the neutral countries and in the Empire.

The Clarendon Press was anxious 'not to give the impression that our pamphlets are propaganda'.[73] This claim is understandable as the term had many negative associations especially with regard to lies and disinformation. But the purpose of the pamphlets was not an objective discussion of the issues involved, even if Davis insisted on a fair one. The information they provide was to help the public rally behind the government and the nation's war effort. In that sense the series was part of a national propaganda effort. There were also plans to translate some of the pamphlets into French and Italian, but it is not clear whether these plans were carried out or not. Sales of the series started sluggishly, but this was to change rapidly after October. By January 1915 Milford reported that the recent boom in sales had begun to fade, and that the latest pamphlets had not sold as well as the first ones, 'but it takes time to get each new one known'.[74] In any case by January 1915 total sales had reached 'just under 300,000'.[75]

There is no trace of direct government interference with

---

[72] On 31 Oct. 1914 Humphrey Milford, the London manager of the Press, informed Cannan that according to very rough estimates 100,000 pamphlets had been sold. Ibid. 1743. A higher figure was, however, much more likely. The final figure mentioned here had been calculated by looking through the account books.

[73] Ibid. 1215, Chapman to Crum, 11 Jan. 1915.

[74] Ibid. 1743, Milford's memo of 18 Jan. 1915.

[75] Ibid. 19 Jan. 1915. Vinogradoff's pamphlet was the most successful at this stage with 24,000 copies sold. Among the others Barker's pamphlet on Nietzsche and Treitschke sold 12,000, Fletcher I and II sold 12,000 and 11,500 copies respectively, and Morgan and Davis 7,000.

the Oxford Pamphlets. However Davis, Cannan, and Chapman co-operated with Wellington House, a secret government propaganda organization. In September 1914, C. R. L. Fletcher, author of two of the Oxford Pamphlets, informed Cannan that his brother-in-law, Sir Claud Schuster, 'seems to be in charge of a bureau (at the F.O.?) which intends much the same set of tracts as ours'.[76] Schuster was apparently interested in co-operating with the Press and wanted to see copies of the first pamphlets produced in Oxford.

Fletcher recommended that 'we might work with his gang', a suggestion which was taken up by Davis and Cannan. Subsequently Wellington House was sent copies of the pamphlets as they emerged from the Press and then Schuster decided whether he wanted to buy them or not. During the following weeks Wellington House bought several thousand copies from the Press which were either sold or given away. As for the price, Chapman had suggested to Milford that if Schuster 'pays something over the cost of machining and paper and carriage I suppose that may content us'.[77] A few days later Schuster ordered 10,000 copies of Vinogradoff's pamphlet.[78] He was reluctant to buy Fletcher's and thought Trevelyan's pamphlet on India dull, a judgement with which Milford agreed.[79] In October Schuster wanted 'ten copies "in proof" of each pamphlet that we publish, so that various members of his staff ... should have plenty of time to consider what steps they will not take'.[80]

It is difficult to ascertain how many copies Wellington House bought from the Press, but it looks as if Wellington House contributed in no small manner to the wide distribution of the pamphlets. This allowed Schuster and 'his gang' to make suggestions to the Press about new pamphlets. Thus in January 1915 Gowers, Schuster's second-in-command, proposed that three articles which Wellington House had

[76] Ibid. 1208, Fletcher to Cannan, 14 Sept. 1914.
[77] Ibid., Chapman to Milford, 18 Sept. 1914.
[78] Ibid., Milford to Cannan, 23 Sept. 1914.
[79] Ibid., Milford to Cannan, 24 Sept. 1914.
[80] Ibid., Milford to Cannan, 14 Oct. 1914.

commissioned for publication in the Russian paper *Novoe Vremya* should be put together into one Oxford Pamphlet.[81] In Russia it had been felt 'that we were not pulling our weight in the war'. Sir Edward Cook, Buchan, and Thursfield had therefore been asked to correct this impression by writing about military, naval, and political matters. Gowers was very pleased when Davis accepted his proposal and agreed in turn to Davis's suggestion that they should be extended and published as separate pamphlets.[82] Buchan's and Thursfield's articles appeared as pamphlets Nos. 66 and 67, *Britain's War by Land* and *Sea Power and the War*. Davis did not feel particularly sorry that he had been unable to persuade Sir E. T. Cook to expand his article, and told Gowers 'between ourselves, I thought his article the least effective of the three'.

The Oxford effort began to wane in the spring of 1915, when the government's own propaganda machine, however improvised at the beginning, had become much more dominant. By June 1915 official propaganda was handled by the Press Bureau, the Neutral Press Committee, and the Foreign Office's News Department.[83] Wellington House itself had commissioned and published 2.5 million books and pamphlets in seventeen different languages.[84] This was roughly five times as many as the figure reached by Oxford University Press, but this does not provide a sufficient reason for the neglect of the Oxford Pamphlets in recent academic accounts of the British propaganda effort during the war.

The difference in style between the Oxford Pamphlets and the productions of Wellington House was growing and may have been a factor in stopping publication of the Oxford pamphlets. Most of the latter were more academic in character and provided political and historical information, refuted German arguments, and justified British intervention. The main purpose of the publications prepared by

---

[81] Ibid. 1215, Gowers to Milford, 8 Jan. 1915.
[82] Ibid. 1216, Gowers to Davis, 14 Jan. 1915, and Davis to Gowers, 15 Jan. 1915.
[83] M. L. Sanders and P. M. Taylor, *British Propaganda during the First World War, 1914–18* (London, 1982), 38–42.
[84] G. S. Messinger, *British Propaganda and the State in the First World War* (Manchester, 1992), 41–3.

Wellington House, however, was to whip up feelings against the Central Powers in Britain and in the USA. By 1916 Wellington House was reorganized and its propaganda output became increasingly the province of journalists, until the press barons Northcliffe and Beaverbrook took over the propaganda organization in 1918. Historians who had worked for Wellington House, such as Toynbee, Headlam, Namier, and Zimmern, were transferred to the Foreign Office. Unlike the Oxford-selected authors and their pamphlets, the historians working for Wellington House were 'unhampered by needless scrupulosity'.[85]

But there may have been other reasons for the end of the Oxford Pamphlets. The market appeared to be saturated with pamphlets and as the last ones did not sell very well the Delegates to the Press, probably on Cannan's recommendation, decided on 29 March 1915 to wind up the series.[86] In addition, the Delegates may have felt that Davis's work in the Trade Clearing House, which was closely linked to the Admiralty and the Board of Trade, would take more and more of his time and that it would be too difficult to continue without the original *spiritus rector*, especially as Barker had been drafted to work for the Ministry of Labour. Nevertheless the timing of the Delegates' decision had not been anticipated by Davis. As late as 7 March 1915 Barker wrote to Cannan telling him that Davis approved strongly of his latest proposal for a pamphlet on the nationalities within the German Empire.[87] But Cannan must have told him about the pending decision to discontinue the series and probably advised him to publish it elsewhere. Thus it appeared separately in 1915 under the title *The Submerged Nationalities of the German Empire*.

Although his day-to-day co-operation with the Clarendon Press had come to an end, Davis had other projects in the pipeline which he discussed with the Press. One was a volume on Shakespeare's England and the other was an official history of the war. But neither of them was to material-

---

[85] Wallace, *War and the Image of Germany*, 173.
[86] Clarke, 'All Souls and the War of the Professors'.
[87] Oxford University Press Archive, 1209, Barker to Cannan, 7 Mar. 1915.

ize. Nevertheless the war accelerated Davis's transformation from a medieval historian into a modern one.

VI

The demise of the Oxford Pamphlets had the effect of safeguarding the reputation of some of the historians who did not join the campaign of hatred against Germany. This was left to historians like Arnold Toynbee who, writing for Wellington House, tried to expose 'German frightfulness'. However, crass displays of jingoism were counterproductive if they were intended either to sway German public opinion or to win over the minds of educated people in the neutral states. Although most of the English pamphlets represented a war of words directed against Germany during the war they were not readily available in Germany or Austria–Hungary. The main effort of the 'pamphleteering' shadow-boxing, therefore, was either aimed at public opinion in the neutral countries like the USA, Italy, Holland, Switzerland, and the Scandinavian kingdoms, or intended for consumption at home and in the dominions. The British public was reminded of these goals by a letter to *The Times* signed, among others, by Asquith, Rosebery, Balfour, and Prothero.[88] The letter stated that 'British public opinion may well prove to be the deciding factor in this great struggle' and that 'victory must not expose Great Britain to a revival of the German menace'. In the campaign for the minds of the British people the Oxford Pamphlets and the millions of others played a significant role. It is therefore not surprising that the first catalogue of pamphlets was published a few months after August 1914. The *Times Literary Supplement* noted that 'all historical experiences of pamphlets pale with the pamphlets in the second half of 1914'.[89] And the paper noted that 'people walked surprising distances, systematising the causes, motives, extent, and range of the disaster in a manner satisfactory to their own preconceived views or knowledge'. *The Times* echoed its

---

[88] *The Times*, 21 Nov. 1914.   [89] *Times Literary Supplement*, 4 Feb. 1915.

supplement a few days later by pointing out that the vogue for pamphlets provided 'more argument than abuse'.[90] Although at the beginning of the war, German replies and counter-attacks were taken up by some British papers, by contrast in the Oxford Pamphlets the war of words developed into a war without a direct enemy who could reply immediately. Hynes therefore concluded that the war of the professors was not really a war. Nobody lost his life and nothing was destroyed 'except the scholar's vision of a community of scholars'.[91]

After the war, *The Times* thought no one would be likely to read the huge number of pamphlets 'unless some German professor makes them the subject of his research and there is no pleasure in the thought that we may fill a German professor with impotent patriotic rage some twenty years hence'. *The Times* concluded that most of the pamphlets were for consumption on the home front, and in that field the paper accepted that the German pamphlets were as useful for a German readership as the British ones for a British audience. Milford from Oxford University Press in London disputed this statement in a letter to *The Times* and pointed to the fact that the Oxford Pamphlets had included an English translation of a German pamphlet in order to expose 'the weakness of the German case'.[92]

Looking back at the position of British historians during the war, we could say that their position was characterized by an attempt to take the high ground of moral superiority. The analysis of German politics was often superficial and revealed surprising gaps in knowledge. Only a few historians, such as Dawson or A. W. Ward, seemed to be informed about German political institutions and certain aspects of political life. It is not surprising, therefore, that many historians singled out German militarism and referred to the widespread German belief in Social Darwinism as well as to the adoration of naked power. Seen from this point of view it was understandable that the triad of Nietzsche, Treitschke, and Bernhardi figured so prominently. Only the conservative

---

[90] *The Times*, 9 Feb. 1915.
[92] *The Times*, 10 Feb. 1915.
[91] Hynes, *The War Imagined*, 74.

historian George W. Prothero discussed social imperialist reasons for Germany's determination to start the war:

> It can hardly be doubted that the spectre of Socialism and the menace of a revolutionary proletariat have contributed to make the great capitalists, the dominant military party and the Emperor himself, already inclined on other grounds to war, more ready to adopt this solution as an alternative.[93]

As regards the outbreak of the war most British historians in 1914 held that Austria–Hungary and Germany had been willing for some time to strike at the international status quo. Therefore the two powers were seen as chiefly responsible for the outbreak of the war in late July and early August 1914. As the initiative for the war came from Berlin and Vienna, British historians were convinced that the Entente powers had reacted more in response to the willingness for war of the Central Powers than the other way round. Stuart Wallace was one of the first historians to point out that modern research tends to confirm the British historians' tendency to locate the origins of the war in Berlin and Vienna for hegemonial, expansionist, and militarist reasons. Despite this outlook the tone of most of their writings during the first few months of the war differs from some of the more blatant propaganda brochures, which painted Germany in the blackest colours, and in which the alliterative trio of *Kaiser*, Krupp, and *Kultur* stood for all possible negative images.[94]

The German historians' salvoes in the 'war of the professors' dismayed those British colleagues who had previously held a positive image of Germany. Yet the self-mobilization of British historians was only to some extent a reaction to German proclamations. They may have provided the catalyst for some of the British reactions, but British historians were also keen to demonstrate national solidarity especially when a number of them had, with their liberal leanings, been wary of British intervention until August. This seems to have been the main intention of those who signed the Declaration by Authors which was published in *The Times* on 18 September 1914. This letter was followed by more signatures on 22 and

[93] Wallace, *War and the Image of Germany*, 66.
[94] This was also the title of a wartime pamphlet. Ibid. 36.

23 September which included a growing number of historians. In their recent publication about the Manifesto of the 93, the von Ungern-Sternbergs appear to have confused the Declaration with the two conferences which Masterman had convened in Wellington House earlier that month to start an official propaganda campaign.[95] The German side had gone into action before that when Haeckel and Eucken published their strongly worded anti-British invective in the middle of August 1914 and when some German scholars decided to return the honours they had received from British institutions.[96]

In addition, the German side had published some pamphlets in Italy in August. It thus looks as if the war of words was triggered by German actions and had a snowball effect on the British side. However, the British outcry against German brutalities during the advance through Belgium appeared in the British and French press, and it was this reaction which pushed the German side into a defensive overdrive and which led to the drafting of the Manifesto of the 93 between the middle of September and early October. Key figures on the German side were the popular dramatist Ludwig Fulda, the Berlin Mayor Georg Reicke, and the author Hermann Sudermann.[97] They were patriots rather than nationalists, and had gained a reputation as liberals who objected to government interference in the world of arts and sciences. In that way their efforts were comparable to those of English historians who contributed to the escalation of the war of words, but there was one noticeable difference.

As the von Ungern-Sternbergs discovered, the German Manifesto of the 93, published on 4 October, had been initiated by the propaganda department of the German Naval Office (Captain Löhlein), and then drafted by a very select

---

[95] J. and W. von Ungern-Sternberg, *Der Aufruf*, 19, 113–14. The two conferences actually took place on 2 and 7 Sept. 1914. Sanders and Taylor, *British Propaganda*, 39.

[96] Schwabe, *Wissenschaft und Kriegsmoral*, 23 and 196.

[97] B. vom Brocke, 'Wissenschaft und Militarismus: Der Aufruf der 93 "An die Kulturwelt!" und der Zusammenbruch der internationalen Gelehrtenrepublik im Ersten Weltkrieg', in W. M. Calder, H. Flashar, and T. Lindken (eds.), *Wilamowitz nach 50 Jahren* (Darmstadt, 1985), 648–719.

group in co-operation with the Foreign Office (Theodor Wiegand, Director of the Berlin Museums), whereas the Oxford Pamphlets, the Red Book, and the Declaration of Authors were spontaneous undertakings without governmental co-operation or interference.[98] It is not quite clear whether any government institution was in any way involved with the drafting, printing, and distribution of the German Manifesto of Academic Teachers which was published on 16 October. The main author of this appeal was the classicist Ulrich von Wilamowitz-Moellendorff, whose invective attracted nearly 4,000 signatures, mostly collected by the Pan-German historian Dietrich Schäfer. The two German manifestos were signed by a number of historians, but in comparison with their British colleagues the role of German historians seems to have been less instrumental. One explanation for this might be that in 1914 the academic discipline of history was much more closely connected with the political establishment in England than in Germany.[99] And contrary to the impression put forward by some historians that German professors, unlike their English counterparts, regarded themselves as a public authority, British historians had a fairly high reputation in the eyes of the British public.[100]

Another difference concerned the styles in which the Anglo-German war of words was conducted. The German proclamations were written in the form of statements as well as theses, and expressed convictions. There was little space in them for reasoned arguments. Perhaps British historians found it easier to argue more effectively in their pamphlets. Those who have analysed the German proclamations suggest that their net effect was counterproductive. Some were criticized in Germany, even by signatories, although this mostly came to light after the war.

---

[98] J. and W. von Ungern-Sternberg, *Der Aufruf*, 27–49.
[99] Bruch, 'Krieg und Frieden', 88–9. Bruch has argued that German historians were, however, heavily involved with the press and that their opinions were at least registered by the Kaiser, the Chancellor, and the Foreign Office.
[100] R. vom Bruch, ' "Militarismus", "Realpolitik" und "Pazifismus": Außenpolitik und Aufrüstung in der Sicht deutscher Hochschullehrer (Historiker) im späten Kaiserreich', *Militärgeschichtliche Mitteilungen*, 39 (1986), 37–58.

British historians may have been helped in their propaganda activities by a tradition of public-speaking engagements in which they addressed lay audiences. The Oxford adult education programme in particular, in which a number of historians were involved, strongly emphasized teaching and social contacts. German universities with their emphasis on research had not developed anything similar. Lawrence Goldman goes a step further and sees the Oxford tutorial system, with its 'open dialogue between tutor and student' and its informality, as a way of disseminating knowledge more effectively than the formal teaching methods employed by most German academics.[101] Thus workers' education programmes may have helped to improve the solidarity on the British home front. A third, but less dramatic statement was published by the Kulturbund deutscher Gelehrter und Künstler (Cultural League of German Scholars and Artists) in the autumn of 1914 in response to a proclamation by British academics. This reply was signed by 150 people, more than a third of whom were academic postholders. A number of historians also signed this latest manifesto which was linked to the Manifesto of the 93 and its signatories.[102]

German historians launched two attacks on their British colleagues in the autumn of 1914. The first salvo was fired by the historians of Bonn University in the middle of October and was inspired by the Prussian Ministry of Education. The second appeared on 3 December and was signed by twenty-six scholars among whom the names of Marcks, Meinecke, Oncken, Schäfer, and Schiemann were most noticeable.[103] This last declaration was directed against the authors of *Why we are at War* and rejected the Oxford attempt to put the responsibility for the war onto Germany's shoulders as 'slanderous'.[104] Klaus Schwabe listed thirty-five out of a total of forty-three history professors who had joined 'the war of the professors', and who firmly believed that Germany was fighting a defensive war

[101] Goldman, *Dons and Workers*, 317–18.
[102] J. and W. von Ungern-Sternberg, *Der Aufruf*, 136–43.
[103] Schwabe, *Wissenschaft und Kriegsmoral*, 23–4.
[104] For Ernest Barker's reply, see *The Times*, 9 Dec. 1914.

for its existence against, as E. Meyer had put it, a 'band of robbers'.[105]

Despite these differences the two groups were comparable, at least at the beginning of the war, in their uncritical identification with state and nation to such an extent that it is possible to speak of a 'pathos of identification'.[106] But whereas the Germans lifted the term *Kultur* onto the platform of war propaganda, the British side emphasized law and honour in their campaign. The German academics protested against the supposed lies and calumnies which the Allies had used against Germany at a time when they thought their fatherland was involved in a struggle for its existence. The so-called lies referred mainly to the German responsibility for the war, the violation of Belgian neutrality and international law, and the atrocities in Belgium. What British historians did not understand was why their German colleagues demonstrated so few traces of what they had propagated as the merits of 'German science', and why so many accepted uncritically the militarist arguments in favour of war. Therefore the reference in the Manifesto of the 93 to the German army and the German people being one may have suggested to many British observers that the German academics had abdicated their role as responsible citizens by linking *Kultur* and militarism, which of itself implied a massive degradation of culture.

Why did German historians combine *Kultur* with militarism? Were they not aware of the effect that this would have on international public opinion, especially at the beginning of the war? Most historians were not warmongers, and only a few, such as Schäfer, aimed for a hegemonic clash with Britain.[107] Most historians pleaded for German expansion under the slogan 'World Politics and no War', but this did not make them into pacifists or advocates of world peace. Perhaps, in their defence of nationalism, they overreacted to cover up the offensive conduct of German politics in 1914. A case in point was the ancient historian Eduard Meyer, who changed from a patriot into an ardent

[105] Schwabe, *Wissenschaft und Kriegsmoral*, 290.
[106] H. Lübbe, *Politische Philosophie in Deutschland* (Basle, 1963), 237. See Schwabe, *Wissenschaft und Kriegsmoral*, 44 and 210.
[107] Bruch, 'Krieg und Frieden', 87.

nationalist, and who, together with many others, defended the German invasion of Belgium.[108] Despite these different premisses, British and German historians differed only by degree in their response to the call of nationalism and in their neglect of historical virtues such as objectivity, detachment, and impartiality.

The question is whether the similarities in the reactions of British and German historians outweighed what was perceived at the time as fundamental differences between the two sides. Whilst the two groups hurled offensive clichés and stereotypes at each other in order to win the upper hand in the war of propaganda, some historians tried to find 'deep' reasons for the unnecessary and rather senseless slaughter of the war.[109] In one way the 'war of words' fulfilled the historians' desire to become active in a people's war, even if only with the pen, and in another it used ideas and national history to defend Germany's and Austria-Hungary's straight war of aggression, which on the opposite side found ready and willing defenders. Cast in the role of the attackers, most German historians tried to avoid confronting the issues involved in Germany having started the war by lifting this debate on to a higher level where 'German culture' seemed to be threatened and needed to be defended, even at the cost of linking militarism with culture. Friedrich Meinecke joined the defensive chorus of nationalist historians, but rejected the notion that cultural differences explained international political conflicts.[110]

Not even in Germany did all historians pursue the same nationalist line. What is astonishing but perhaps not surprising is that historians in both countries let themselves be blinded by the need for national solidarity, and ultimately seriously damaged the ethics of their subject in the name of nationalism. In the USA historians were dismayed to see the

---

[108] J. von Ungern-Sternberg, 'Wie gibt man dem Sinnlosen einen Sinn? Zum Gebrauch der Begriffe "deutsche Kultur" und "Militarismus" im Herbst 1914', in Wolfgang J. Mommsen (ed.), *Kultur und Krieg: Die Rolle der Intellektuellen, Künstler und Schriftsteller im Ersten Weltkrieg* (Munich, 1996), 79.

[109] Wolfgang J. Mommsen, 'Die deutschen kulturellen Eliten im Ersten Weltkrieg', ibid. 2–4.

[110] Stefan Meineke, 'Friedrich Meinecke und der "Krieg der Geister" ', ibid. 112.

loss of historical virtues in Germany and Britain in 1914.[111] In 1915 and in 1916 American historians were therefore warned by the American Historical Association not to lose sight of objectivity, impartiality, and scepticism, but when America entered the war in 1917 most historians joined the nationalist enthusiasm in the same way as their European counterparts had done before. Their previous appeal for the maintenance of historical virtues was swept aside.

[111] Peter Novick, *That Noble Dream: The 'Objectivity Question' and the American Historical Profession* (Cambridge, 1988), 111–32.

17
British Conservative Historiography and the Second World War

REBA N. SOFFER

Assumptions about human nature, society, and the state tend to be either relatively optimistic and indeterminate or relatively pessimistic and fixed. Throughout most of the nineteenth century and into the 1930s, liberals began with an optimistic belief in the regeneration of human nature and the salutary transformation of institutions. For the succeeding three decades their labour and socialist successors attempted to convert the liberals' meliorist theories into practice. Conservatives, beginning at the opposite pole with a pessimistic suspicion of individuals and their works as irremediably flawed, remained generally consistent throughout the twentieth century in their dismissal of liberal, labour, and socialist expectations as naïve and dangerous. After the Second World War, Lord Coleraine, the only surviving son of Bonar Law, worried that conservatives were forgetting their traditionally sceptical approach to political, social, and economic problems. By the 1960s, he was deeply disappointed with the tendency of post-war conservatism to embrace 'progress' or 'consensus'. Conservatism and liberalism were irreconcilable *Weltanschauungen*. Unless that fundamental dichotomy was maintained, Coleraine warned, conservatism would become an irrelevant set of beliefs. He urged conservatives to reject the progressive assumptions that 'every man is a creature capable of unlimited improvement, moral as well as material, granted only that he has the right environment'; and that 'it is within the power of the state, as it is its duty, to create that environment'.[1]

[1] Coleraine had been a moderately successful Conservative politician who served in the pre-war Foreign Office and then held a position in Churchill's post-

Although English liberals and conservatives were divided in the ways Coleraine describes, they tended similarly, until the Second World War, to approve the course of their national history. History continued to testify to the permanent, resilient values of British institutions, private and public virtues, and a constitution based upon law. The First World War, no matter how ravaging its effect on the participants and those who cared for them, hardly changed either the study or the writing of history. In the myth- and ritual-making about the Great War that continued well into the 1930s, historians echoed and reinforced the larger, patriotic national mood. Public sanctification of the war was evident in the phenomenal sales of Ernest Raymond's novel *Tell England* (1922) which, together with the play *Journey's End* by Bob Sherriff, became 'English-language talkies in 1930 while the works of Graves and Sassoon still await film treatment'.[2] For most historians, the Great War was neither an unmitigated disaster nor a definitive break with the past, but rather a regrettable aberration in the essentially progressive course of events. The militaristic aggression of Germany, a country without English restraints of law and character, ensured its defeat.[3]

By the end of the 1920s, the great depression created a crisis of faith for economists and for those without prospect of work. Established historians were less apprehensive. J. H. Clapham, who still dominated the teaching of economic history at Cambridge, was notorious among his students for dismissing the economic crisis as a historical mishap, sobering, but transient.[4] Within a decade, historians who were assured of Britain's historically successful trajectory could point to Britain's economic flexibility and endurance in comparison to the USA or the Continent. Britain continued

---

war government, Lord Coleraine, *For Conservatives Only: A Study of Conservative Leadership from Churchill to Heath* (London, 1970), 45, 49, 55.

[2] John Ramsden, 'The Legacy of the Great War', *Contemporary European History*, 5/1 (1996), 136. See, too, Rosa Maria Bracco, *Merchants of Hope: British Middlebrow Writers and the First War, 1919–1939* (Oxford, 1993).

[3] See Reba Soffer, *Discipline and Power: The University, History and the Making of an English Elite, 1870–1930* (Stanford, Calif., 1994), esp. 46–52 for a discussion of historians' reactions to the Great War.

[4] For J. H. Clapham see ibid. 156.

to dominate the world's economy because its Empire spanned the earth, expanding and guaranteeing trade, international community, and power to demonstrate the vitality of British character.

When the depression's economic and political denouement was intensified by the appearance of totalitarian regimes in the 1930s, historians were harder put to find reassuring historical continuity. In the decade before the Second World War, politics within Britain were marked by the rise of a radical left, articulate but small in numbers, and a still smaller, less reputable, radical right. University students found the left especially appealing while the proto-fascist right satisfied a xenophobia never content with the settlement of the First World War. These minority views, magnified in importance by the Spanish Civil War and the rise of Mussolini in Italy, Hitler in Germany, and Stalin in the Soviet Union, led to a new debate about the meaning of citizenship, the state, and justice. But the study of history at Oxford and Cambridge, which set the curricula for teaching history throughout British universities, grammar, and primary schools, remained largely untouched by events that occurred after the Great War. For most historians, revolutionary fascism and communism were unsatisfactory responses among peoples without equitable political systems or a devoted, altruistic governing class. Those few British historians who admired the radical left, such as the young A. J. P. Taylor, felt that British political, social, and economic institutions required remedy. To them, the radical left offered the possibility of a more just society.[5] The radical right attracted very few historians. Some, like Arnold Toynbee, saw *rapprochement* with Hitler as preferable to war.[6] Appeasers were almost always conservatives, but their motives varied. Opposition to the communists was the major

---

[5] A. J. P. Taylor had 'no illusions about Stalinism' in the 1930s, but he was 'unshakably pro-Russian' and saw the 'Five Year Plan as a demonstration of socialism in action'. *A Personal History* (New York, 1983), 124.

[6] See A. L. Rowse, *Appeasement: A Study in Political Decline, 1933–39* (New York, 1961), 38. Rowse argues that many of the appeasers such as Geoffrey Dawson and John Simon were decent men who did not know the kind of men Hitler and his associates were because they 'were ignorant of Europe and European history', 116. Toynbee could not be included in that ignorance.

issue for many. Others were pacifists. Very few admired the fascists.[7]

Unlike the Great War, the Second World War jolted British historians into questioning a confident understanding of national and imperial history that had prevailed since the establishment of their profession as a university discipline in the 1870s. Traditional accounts of history became increasingly untenable as the war was finally concluded and the civilian cost became more widely known. The Holocaust and Hiroshima were without historical precedent, and the question of guilt assumed new moral and international dimensions. At the war's end, James B. Conant, presiding over a memorial service for Harvard men and women, mourned the Americans who 'gave their lives' in 'a close and bitter struggle between two worlds: one groping towards a goal of light, the other committed to a reign of evil'. That was what Allied leaders said consistently during and after the war. But Conant emphasized further that the 'victory was decisive, but the margin was slight'. History had very nearly gone wrong. Good had barely conquered evil, and only at terrible human cost.[8] Britain, a 'good' victor, emerged from

---

[7] The popular historian Arthur Bryant was the rare exception in his admiration of Hitler and the new Germany. See Reba N. Soffer, 'The Long Nineteenth Century of British Conservatism', in George Behlmer and Fred Leventhal (eds.), *Singular Continuities: Tradition, Nostalgia, and Society in Modern Britain* (Stanford, Calif., 2000). See, too, Richard Griffiths, *Fellow-Travellers of the Right: British Enthusiasts for Nazi Germany 1933–39* (London, 1980), and Andrew Thorpe (ed.), *The Failure of Political Extremism in Inter-war Britain* (Exeter, 1989). When the Conservative Party defeated Labour in the election of 1959, a spate of books appeared by historians politically sympathetic to Labour who linked Conservatism to appeasement. They included A. L. Rowse's *Appeasement*, Colin Cross's *The Fascists in Britain* (1961), and Martin Gilbert and Richard Gott's *The Appeasers: The Decline of Democracy from Hitler's Rise to Chamberlain's Downfall* (1963). Gilbert and Gott's *The Appeasers* was dedicated to A. J. P. Taylor. R. A. C. Parker, in *Chamberlain and Appeasement: British Policy and the Coming of the Second World War* (New York, 1993) argues that the 'evidence shows that Chamberlain, first, became the most active exponent of an agreed policy towards Germany and, then, as others came to doubt and hesitate, argued and manœuvred to continue it'. Chamberlain dominated the making of British policy and pursued appeasement because 'he thought it was correct'. Parker finds that 'Chamberlain was wrong when he argued that no effective methods of securing British safety and prosperity were possible other than those he advocated', 364–5.

[8] Quoted in John T. Bethell, 'Harvard and the Arts of War', *Harvard Magazine* (Sept.–Oct., 1995), 48.

the war as a small power which would never again regain its world standing. Moreover, although the war destroyed fascism, it fortified communism.

Explanations of the consequences of the war were more manageable for post-war historians on the left than on the right. The left sided with progress and the future. For them, pre-war social, economic, and political institutions, and the arbitrary class order on which they were based, were not worth preserving. They understood fascism as a logical consequence of growing corporate dominance over helpless individuals. The year 1945 signalled a decisive turning point by ending a regrettable past and introducing new opportunities. The empirical demonstration of progressive direction was the general election of June 1945 which brought Clement Attlee's government to power. For these critical, left-leaning historians, the past was hardly a sound and evolutionary demonstration—even within England—of special achievements in individual and public arenas. The study of history revealed rather a chronicle of egregious errors, wrong turns, and the economic exploitation of the weak.[9] In the early 1960s, post-war historians were succeeded by a 'new left' generation inspired by E. P. Thompson's *The Making of the English Working Class* (1963), a panegyric to self-conscious working-class groups determining their own future.

During the first two post-war decades the right, in contrast to the left, was limited in its attempt to produce a radical historiography by lingering public suspicion about conservatism's contamination by pre-war fascism. When the left basked in political power in 1945, the right found themselves without a programme and without a reliable constituency. What had characterized conservatives throughout the nineteenth century and well into the twentieth was that they possessed power derived from land, local authority, money, social status, and religion. Conservative privilege, vested in property, the monarchy, the constitution, and the religious and cultural authority of the Church of England, was

---

[9] See G. D. H. Cole and Raymond Postgate, 'Epilogue', in *The British Common People, 1746–1946* (London, 1947).

extended to embrace Greater Britain with the adoption of imperial ambitions during the last quarter of the nineteenth century.[10] As late as the Abdication Crisis of 1936 Stanley Baldwin was cheered by a receptive audience of the faithful when he described the strength of conservatism as an alliance of Church, throne, and Empire. Those who believed in the rectitude of conservative ascendancy continued to exercise prerogatives throughout the first six decades of the twentieth century. Even though the Conservative Party had made great efforts to broaden its membership, the selection of Harold Macmillan as Prime Minister in the mid-1950s was still presided over by an impeccable aristocrat, the fifth Marquess of Salisbury.

A distinction has to be made between the appeal and success of the Conservative political party and 'conservatism' as a fundamental mediator of beliefs and practices. Throughout the twentieth century, the party presented itself as the historic protector of law, order, and property rights within a nation unified by ancient institutions. Between 1880 and 1991 that message won the Conservatives sixteen of the twenty-eight general elections. The party's electoral success rested, in great part, on its compliance with changing circumstances. A slow shift from landed to commercial

[10] In 1836, the young Benjamin Disraeli wrote that 'England has become great by her institutions. Her hereditary Crown has in a great degree insured us from the distracting evils of a contested succession; her Peerage, interested, from the vast property and the national honours of its members, in the good government of the country, has offered a compact bulwark against the temporary violence of popular passion; her House of Commons, representing the conflicting sentiments of an estate of the realm not less privileged than that of the Peers, though far more numerous, has enlisted the great mass of the lesser proprietors of the country in favor of a political system which offers them a constitutional means of defence and a legitimate method of redress; her ecclesiastical establishment preserved by its munificent endowment from the fatal necessity of pandering to the erratic fancies of its communicant, has maintained the sacred cause of learning and religion, and preserved orthodoxy while it has secured toleration; her law of primogeniture has supplied the country with a band of natural and independent leaders, trustees of those legal institutions, which pervade our land, and which are the origin of our political constitution.' 'The Spirit of Whiggism' (1836), in William Hutcheson (ed.), *Whigs and Whiggism: Political Writings* (New York, 1914), 327–8. See, too, 'Vindication of the English Constitution' (1835), in *Whigs and Whiggism*, 111–232, and the Crystal Palace Speech, 24 June 1872, in which Disraeli brought his party up to date by adding Empire to the Conservative standard, in R. J. White (ed.) *The Conservative Tradition*, (New York, 1957), 238–40.

wealth, begun in the nineteenth century, continued during the inter-war years to allow Conservative MPs to remain a plutocracy. Although many post-war changes were not really effective until the 1980s, the post-war party moved from 'both local and Parliamentary elites of squires and business magnates to leaders and representatives drawn from professional and managerial backgrounds'. By the 1970s, these groups were joined 'increasingly by the ranks of professional politicians'.[11] Protestants who were not Anglican, as well as Catholics and Jews, found the Conservative Party congenial. But 'Christianity' continued to inform conservative political thought and to be 'seen as essential for the bonding and well-being of society'.[12]

While the Conservative Party demonstrated considerable pragmatism in its appeal to a changing electorate, 'conservatism' as a basic set of beliefs endured remarkably unchanged. Recently, John Barnes found that twentieth-century conservative ideas consistently stressed distrust of human nature, pessimism about progress, emphasis upon authority, the relationship between law and property, limitation of the power of the state, constitutionalism, and imperialism.[13] Until the Second World War conservatives selected certain ideas from the canon and rejected others. But most continued to understand history as a coherent narrative about the maintenance and transmission of those institutions, laws, prescriptions, and proscriptions that guaranteed a distinctly British society. After 1945, conservatives were hard put to reconcile that reading of history with the mass extermination of peoples, the wartime bombing of Britain, the liquidation of Empire, a socialist government, and the perceived threat to everything they valued as histor-

---

[11] Byron Criddle, 'Members of Parliament', in Anthony Seldon and Stuart Ball (eds.), *Conservative Century: The Conservative Party since 1900* (Oxford, 1994), 166, 165. See tables indicating occupations of MPs on 147, 152, and 160. For the late 19th and early 20th centuries, see Peter Marsh, *The Discipline of Popular Government: Lord Salisbury's Domestic Statecraft 1881–1902* (Hassocks, 1978).

[12] Peter Catterall, 'The Party and Religion', in Seldon and Ball (eds.), *Conservative Century*, 670.

[13] John Barnes, 'Ideology and Factions', in Seldon and Ball (eds.), *Conservative Century*, 315–45. The title of his essay places it squarely within contemporary political analysis in its treatment of interests and ideas as inseparable.

ically 'English'. Historians of the right could not accept, let alone explain, international events over which Britain had lost all control. It was equally perplexing to interpret domestic issues which culminated in the loss of 185 seats for the Conservative Party, the most serious defeat in forty years.

Post-war conservative historians were a diverse group. Very few were born to privilege or involved consistently in Conservative politics.[14] By the late 1970s, the first generation had been succeeded by 'new' conservatives who embraced and sped on the Thatcher revolution. They contemptuously rejected welfare state 'consensus' and its secular foundations as well as those Conservative politicians of the 1950s and 1960s who had appeared to accept Labour and its ideals. The first generation of post-war conservative historians, pilloried by their Thatcherite successors, lived intellectual lives shaped by an expressed, compelling need. While radical conservative historians today dismiss the immediate post-war historians as naïve, the radicals are the linear descendants of their predecessors' determination to find in history antidotes to the horrors of the Second World War. Through their study of history they tried to explain the meaning of the post-war world. The Australian historian Robert Bosworth, in an important study of the historiography of Auschwitz and Hiroshima, has argued that the publication of A. J. P. Taylor's *The Origins of the Second World War* (1961) and E. P. Thompson's *The Making of the English Working Class*

---

[14] The Post War Problems Central Committee was created in 1941 and at its first meeting on 24 July R. A. Butler was elected chairman with David Maxwell-Fyfe as his deputy and Sir Robert Topping as secretary. Butler sent out a circular letter from his office at the Board of Education, asking for help in the new venture and outlining his understanding of its purpose: 'we are setting up a series of sub-committees on various aspects of national life . . . [and] I am anxious to associate with them figures who, though of general sympathy with the party faith are not of the party machine. Thus I want to bring in new blood.' Among those who offered help were the historians George Kitson Clark, G. M. Young, Keith Feiling, Arthur Bryant, George Clark, Kenneth Pickthorn, Arnold Toynbee, and Sir Charles Petrie. John Ramsden, *The Making of Conservative Party Policy: The Conservative Research Department since 1929* (London, 1980), 97–8. By the last quarter of the 20th century, Julian Critchley points out, the new Conservative activist was far more likely to be the car dealer on the Kingston bypass than a historian. Julian Critchley, *Some of Us: People Who Did Well under Thatcher* (London, 1992), 58.

(1963) led to a major shift in the British understanding of the 'long Second World War'. He finds it significant that these new directions have not produced any subsequent radical revolution within the historiography of the left. Instead, the new, self-conscious, revolutionary radicals such as Jonathan Clark and Norman Stone stand provocatively and productively on the far right.[15]

That attempt to make sense of a war which profoundly altered their lives was evident especially among three Cambridge historians, Herbert Butterfield, George Kitson Clark, and Geoffrey Elton. They were not the only conservative historians at Cambridge, and Cambridge was certainly not the only university to nourish a conservative historiography. But each thought that the defence of conservative principles was their personal obligation, and they shared a fundamental understanding of conservatism that they transmitted to at least one generation of historians. Butterfield and Kitson Clark were deeply religious, and Elton passionately secular. During their professional lives at the same university they avoided each other, concentrated on different periods, and emphasized contrasting methods. But the collapse of Britain's traditional political and imperial authority led them each to look at history through a conservative prism. Elton was a Jew who immigrated from Prague in 1939, Butterfield was a lower middle-class Yorkshire scholarship boy who preached as a lay Methodist minister until 1937, and Kitson Clark was an Anglican from a privileged upper middle-class family in Leeds. Despite their differences of background and temperament, they assumed three common axioms of faith. First, that historic institutions and habits must be maintained because their soundness was tested by their survival; second, that practice always had greater virtue than ideas; and third, that human nature was a formidable barrier to a better future. Butterfield and Kitson Clark agreed further that the role of circumstances was more compelling than the role of individuals, while Elton saw the strong individual as a shaper of institutions.

---

[15] Robert Bosworth, *Explaining Auschwitz and Hiroshima: History Writing and the Second World War, 1945–1990* (London, 1993), 51–2.

Of the three Butterfield, more than any other historian of his time, set out deliberately to transform the post-war study of history according to his fundamentally religious and conservative views of both past and present. While neither Kitson Clark nor Elton made their colleges magnets for conservative historiography, Butterfield's Peterhouse created an enduring school of high politics with an increasingly conservative bent. Conservative historians at Peterhouse included Maurice Cowling, Edward Norman, John Vincent, and Jonathan Clark, as well as the political philosopher Roger Scruton. Butterfield's influence was strengthened by his appointments as Professor of Modern History at Cambridge, 1944–63, as Regius Professor, 1963–8, as Master of Peterhouse, 1955–68, and as Vice-Chancellor of the University, 1959–61. University College, Dublin, staffed by history teachers taught by Butterfield, became very nearly an Irish extension of Peterhouse, and Butterfield became the External Examiner of the National University of Ireland.[16] Noel Annan described Butterfield as a 'fascinator whose chief pastime was academic intrigue'.[17] Cowling saw him rather as an 'Asquithean' and despaired because Butterfield never belonged to the 'bloody-minded' right that Cowling admired.[18] While Cowling begot Michael Portillo, the 'bloody-minded' Tory right's great hope in July 1995, Butterfield always preferred conciliation to confrontation, but for reasons very different from Asquith's. The Liberal leader brought opponents together as a matter of political

[16] See the Butterfield Papers, Cambridge University Library.

[17] Noel Annan, *Our Age: Portrait of a Generation* (London, 1990) 270. Hugh Trevor Roper was on the Committee of Electors for the Regius Professorship in Modern History in 1963. Butterfield's close friend Desmond Williams sent Butterfield an extract of a letter he received from Trevor Roper, who wrote: 'I shall listen demurely and cast my vote with the Cambridge majority.' He thought the candidates would be Jack Plumb, Elton, and George Kitson Clark. He found Elton unpopular and a stiff opponent of reform, 'but no denying his energy and ability'. For Plumb, he could not 'vote *very* enthusiastically ... There is something small about his character, something vulgar about his *arrivisme*, something trivial about his attitude to history ... Rowse ... would probably vote for Plumb as a fellow-devotee of the great god Mammon ... Kitson ... is not very inspiring and a bit of an ass ...' He wanted to know if there was a dark horse such as A. J. P. Taylor. 29 May 1963, Butterfield Papers, W335. The chair went to Butterfield.

[18] Maurice Cowling, *Religion and Public Doctrine in Modern England* (Cambridge, 1980), 198, 229, 199.

expediency. Butterfield saw reconciliation as a means of forestalling latent violence and as a requirement of the Christian conscience.

Elton held a personal chair in Constitutional History from 1967 and was Regius Professor from 1983 until his retirement in 1988. He was without peers in his influence among historians of Tudor England, not only in Britain but throughout the English-speaking world. Elton created a following by his single-minded pursuit of a subject, particularly the Tudor revolution in government, through original investigation of high politics, narrated with verve and elegance.[19] Elton adopted his new country without reservation. To explain the origins of the nation that he admired he went back to the sixteenth century to reveal a constitution based on law and parliamentary consent. In his epochal *The Tudor Revolution in Government* (1953), Elton wrote that, belonging to a generation that knew 'despotism and a reign of terror' at 'first hand', he could exonerate the Tudors of similar charges. It was more accurate to describe the sixteenth century as 'a time when men were ready to be governed, and when order and peace seemed more important than principles and rights'.

Some of his peers, such as Joel Hurstfield, challenged Elton's attempts to rehabilitate Tudor government. Hurstfield also came from a family of *émigrés* and he turned to twentieth-century *émigré* experience to question Elton's arguments that the Tudors' reliance on law and consent proved that they were not tyrants. 'Everything Hitler did before 1943', Hurstfield argued, 'was within the framework of the law and the constitution although some of his deeds were the most barbarous in the history of mankind.' Elton replied that there were no personal differences between Hurstfield and himself because they equally hated oppression, deplored

---

[19] For Elton's influence see E. I. Kouri and Tom Scott (eds.), *Politics and Society in Reformation Europe: Essays for Sir Geoffrey Elton on his Sixty-fifth Birthday* (London, 1987); Claire Cross, David Loades, and J. J. Scarisbrick (eds.), *Law and Government under the Tudors: Essays Presented to Sir Geoffrey Elton, Regius Professor of Modern History in the University of Cambridge, on the Occasion of his Retirement* (Cambridge, 1988); and *Rules, Religion and Rhetoric in Early Modern England: A Festschrift for Geoffrey Elton from his Australasian Friends* (Sydney, 1988).

corruption, and disliked hypocrisy, but there were differences of method. Elton wanted understanding to come from 'inside the period studied' while Hurstfield brought to the sixteenth century a 'model' of a 'free society by means of which he tests' sixteenth-century events.[20] What Elton did not see was that he, too, brought a 'model' to his studies: Hurstfield's socialist sympathies and Elton's conservative sensibilities led each of them to very different understandings of liberty and justice.

Kitson Clark, unlike either Butterfield or Elton, remained a Fellow at Trinity College, Cambridge, and never achieved a university post higher than a Readership in Constitutional History, 1945–67. But he did have considerable power within the Cambridge History Faculty and was influential as a dedicated teacher whose students assumed important posts in Britain, North America, and Australia.[21] After producing *Peel and the Conservative Party 1830–41* (1929) and *Peel* (1936), Kitson Clark did not publish again until the late 1950s. In his teaching as well as writing, his message remained fairly consistent after the war. It was the 'development of social policy that led to the creation of the State as we know it nowadays in Britain'. That policy, between 1820 and 1880, was the result of actions taken by a great variety of people not as a result of principles or personality but because of 'the need to find a practical solution' to immediate problems.[22] The purpose of his 1929 study of Peel had been 'to describe first how Peel and his party were moulded and scarred by the years before 1832', and then how they 'set about protecting . . . the ancient institutions of their country'. The second edition, published in 1964 without alteration to the content, had a new introduc-

---

[20] Geoffrey Elton, *The Tudor Revolution in Government* (Cambridge, 1953), 1–2; Joel Hurstfield, 'Was there a Tudor Despotism after all?', *Transactions of the Royal Historical Society*, 5th ser., (1967), 17–96, reprinted in id., *Freedom, Corruption and Government in Elizabethan England* (London, 1973); and Geoffrey Elton, 'Hurstfield's "Freedom, Corruption and Government"', *Reviews in European History*, 1–2 (Sept. 1974), reprinted in id., *Studies in Tudor and Stuart Politics and Government*, iii: *Papers and Reviews 1973–1981* (Cambridge, 1983), 434.

[21] Those students include John Burrow in England, David Cressap Moore in the USA, and F. B. Smith in Australia.

[22] George Kitson Clark, *An Expanding Society: Britain, 1830–1900* (Cambridge, 1967), 147, 163. Based on lectures at the University of Melbourne as first George Scott Visiting Fellow in June and July 1964.

tion which emphasized instead that Peel was a man who was 'not to evade his destiny'.[23] After the war, Kitson Clark viewed conditions as more powerful than individuals.

In contrast to Elton and Kitson Clark, Butterfield continuously returned to the dilemma of the historian's part in 'the drama of human life in time'.[24] Neither Kitson Clark nor Elton was troubled by the historian's participation in the history that he wrote. In 1967, when he was 67, Kitson Clark published *The Critical Historian*. This is not an exploration of the historian's reading or writing of history, but rather a simple discussion of the craft of teaching. Elton believed that the role of the historian was to tell a story about high politics based upon a precise and objective study of evidence. 'Narrative history' was 'usually political history because narrative records movement, and the dynamic life of society (as I have stressed several times) equals political life'.[25] Only Butterfield genuinely suffered from the consequences of historical introspection and he alone became a deliberately polemical conservative. For many intellectuals after the war, the marginal victory of good over evil became a cautionary lesson about the futility of optimistic future goals. For Butterfield, who had never expected the future to be a marked improvement over the past or the present, the war confirmed dramatically his conviction that every person's nature was so defective, good would never triumph. Even though the tide had clearly turned in the Allies' favour by 1943, that conviction led him to urge the British government to make a separate peace with Hitler.[26]

---

[23] George Kitson Clark, *Peel and the Conservative Party: A Study in Party Politics, 1832–1841* (2nd edn., New York, 1964), 'Introduction to First Edition', p. xiv; 'Introduction to Second Edition', p. xxiv.

[24] Herbert Butterfield, *Christianity and History* (New York, 1949), 23. This book began as a series of lectures given to the Divinity faculty at Cambridge in 1948. They were then transposed into six lectures broadcast for the BBC from 2 Apr. to 7 May 1949 and amplified for publication.

[25] Geoffrey Elton, *Political History, Principles and Practices* (New York, 1970), 156–7; id., *The Practice of History* (1967), and his famous exchange with the economic historian Robert Fogel, in Robert Fogel and Geoffrey Elton, *Which Road to the Past?* (New Haven, 1983).

[26] Annan, *Our Age*, 392. During the war, Butterfield 'saw nothing odd when visiting Dublin as external examiner at the university in going to parties at the German Consulate'.

Twenty years earlier, when Butterfield had been Paul Velacott's student at Peterhouse, he had adopted a conservatism rooted in his wholehearted assent to Christianity and his equally wholehearted scepticism about everything human. But it was the trauma of Dunkirk that led him to reconsider his accountability as a historian who was also a Christian. The Second World War made sense to Butterfield only if he approached it with Christian resignation. Looking back in 1948 on the multitude of human tragedies in history, Butterfield took refuge in those fundamental Christian doctrines that made the burden of the modern historian bearable. The historian could write and explain history only if he accepted 'the doctrine of original sin, which affects any notion of history as judgment; the idea of a future life, with a redistribution of fortunes in another world; and the Christian scheme of salvation'.[27] Butterfield was able to write history because he could explain even the most incredible inhumanity as due to the evil that underlay human nature. That evil, uniform throughout time and place, meant that it was impossible for the historian either to praise or to blame, functions reserved exclusively to God. Absolving comfort was not to be sought in the study of history, but rather through emotional and spiritual investment in an internal spiritual life. All of Butterfield's ideas sprang from and returned to the conviction that history is incomprehensible unless approached through religion. It was, he wrote, 'the combination of history with a religion, . . . which generates power and fills the story with significances'.[28] After 1940, Butterfield's lectures in universities throughout Britain, Europe, and America, and on the BBC, his writing, and his remarkable personal influence within international academic life were all guided by conservative spiritual commitments that transformed his technical subjects.

Butterfield began and ended his study of history with the tragic consequences of original sin upon moral freedom. Every person, without exception, was to Butterfield what his friend George Kennan called a 'cracked vessel'.[29] Human

---

[27] Butterfield, *Christianity and History*, 77.   [28] Ibid. 23.
[29] 'The Cracked Vessel' is George Kennan's title for the first chapter of his *Around the Cragged Hill: A Personal and Political Philosophy* (New York, 1993).

frailty led Butterfield to insist upon moral neutrality and to be drawn repeatedly into a dialogue with the long dead Lord Acton. The second lecture in Butterfield's lectures on *Christianity in European History* (1952) is part of a continuing commentary on Acton and a rejection of his argument that historians must take the side of right. John Raymond, writing in the *New Statesman* in 1952 pointed out that for Acton historical events were to be judged by whether they promoted or failed to promote 'the delicacy, integrity and authority of Conscience'. Butterfield dismissed this as a crude, because moralistic, approach. But Raymond worried that the effect of Butterfield's dictum that 'Tout comprendre c'est tout pardonner' was that in 'a fallen world, the saint and the research scholar are somehow complementary'.[30] To Butterfield, the human condition meant that research scholars, saints, and everyone else necessarily lived in ignorance of the direction of their lives.

Butterfield could never entirely free himself from an ambiguous and troubled relationship with Acton. Elton, far more convinced of the rectitude of his methodology than Butterfield was of his, dismissed Acton as a fraud and once introduced a motion into the Academic Senate that would forbid future graduate students from writing doctoral dissertations about him.[31] Butterfield, however, admired Acton's ideal of presenting all sides of every issue, his 'historical sympathy', but disliked his predecessor's certitude about moral judgement in history. Beneath Acton's appeal to high ideals, Butterfield suspected his 'militant purpose' of making a historical case for liberal Catholicism.[32] Butterfield also found that Acton misused historical evidence because driven by his moralistic zeal. There was a rigidity and intellectual arrogance in Acton that sometimes 'forgot the shifting sands upon which much of our history is constructed, and regarded the student of history as the person who ought

---

[30] See John Raymond, review of *Christianity in European History* in *New Statesman*, 12 Apr. 1952.

[31] Personal conversation with Elton in June 1983.

[32] Herbert Butterfield, *Lord Acton* (London, 1948), 7–8, 13. For a perceptive discussion of Butterfield's ambiguity about Acton, see Owen Chadwick, 'Acton and Butterfield', *Journal of Ecclesiastical History*, 38/3 (July 1987).

to be the real Pope'.[33] To Butterfield, every other human being and institution, including religious leaders, churches, and historians, suffered from the same frustrating impotence. Ranke, rather than Acton, offered Butterfield a more kindred mind. The German scholar had argued that each generation was equally close to God, and he had tried to reconcile freedom with necessity and the unique with the general. Ranke especially appealed to Butterfield because his explanations of how fundamental decisions affected life always returned to religion.[34]

Religion taught Butterfield that free will was an illusion. Even intelligent and powerful men were likely to fail. Whatever succeeded was produced by the worst elements in human nature rather than by the best. Whenever anyone acted the most likely consequence was calamity.[35] There was 'a whole universe of countless alternative futures', but men were thrown into that universe with a will that was bound to be defeated even when well intentioned. A 'small handful of men' after the Great War had great confidence in their reformist plans. But the result of their planning was not peace and progress but rather the Second World War, 'one of the great landslides in history'.[36]

These convictions led Butterfield to argue that the way the world was, probably was the best that it could be.[37] He dismissed secular and utopian systems and system-makers such as the Marxists because they believed that significant changes could occur in society to improve the human condition. These system-makers were doomed to fail because they believed, mistakenly, that they could understand and consequently control events. The historically recurring 'new men' such as Napoleon or Hitler or Mussolini, who also believed

[33] Butterfield, *Lord Acton*, 8.
[34] Herbert Butterfield, *Man on his Past: The Study of the History of Historical Scholarship* (Wiles Trust Lecture, Nov. 1954; Boston, 1960), 186, 107.
[35] Herbert Butterfield, *The Englishman and his History* (Cambridge, 1944), 89.
[36] Herbert Butterfield, *The Present State of Historical Scholarship* (inaugural lecture; Cambridge, 1965), 24. See, too, the discussion of free will and necessity in *George III and the Historians* (revised edn., New York, 1959), 205 and *History and Human Relations* (London, 1951), 70.
[37] Butterfield, *Christianity and History*, 36, 34.

they could master history, were bound to miscarry.[38] What was to be valued in history and in the historian who studied it was moderation, conciliation, and compromise. Butterfield's reading of history supported his religious belief that moralistic ardour always led to excess and violence. The historian's role was to accept what was given as unsatisfactory circumstance and provide a 'reconciling mind that seeks to comprehend'. When Butterfield wrote in 1949 that the historian's reconciling understanding allows us at last perhaps to be a 'little sorry for everybody', were we to understand that we should be a little sorry for Hitler as well as very sorry for his victims?[39]

Kitson Clark, who shared Butterfield's strictures about the limits of free will and hence the historian's inability to judge moral conduct, was concerned about the rush to judgement as Britain entered the Second World War. In 1940, he warned against the habit, adopted in the Great War, of 'a continuous indulgence in moral condemnation'. Accepting that the men who controlled Germany were morally evil and that an 'ugly strain in German history and German thought' has 'prepared the way for them', he argued that Nazi Germany must be crushed. At the same time he urged that Britain must 'exercise what self-restraint we can, to give morality a rest, and to leave the attribution of moral guilt to God, or his very humble servants, the Historians'.[40] Twenty-seven years later he returned to the problems of moral guilt and judgement to write that unless 'the tribunal of history is a phantasy and a myth, it must pass judgement; though a study of the trials of some of the war criminals, particularly of some of the minor ones, may suggest how difficult are some of the moral problems which judgment involves'. That led him to conclude that 'it is desirable to stigmatize evil deeds but not to condemn people, and that in general the historian serves the general

---

[38] Butterfield, *The Englishman and his History*, 135. See too, *Christianity in European History* (The Riddell Memorial Lectures 195; London, 1952), 63.
[39] Butterfield, *Christianity and History*, 92.
[40] George Kitson Clark, 'Thoughts on War Thought', *Cambridge Review*, 11 Oct. 1940, reprinted in Eric Homberger, William Janeway, and Simon Schama (eds.), *The Cambridge Mind. Ninety Years of the Cambridge Review, 1879–1969* (London, 1970), 55–6.

interests of mankind better if he tries to understand and explain than if he assumes the position of a judge'.[41]

Providence governed history for both Kitson Clark and for Butterfield. But Butterfield went further to argue that the best exercise of free will that any person could attempt lay in co-operation with Providence. In the English, Butterfield found a historically tested national genius for such co-operation.[42] If God decided for his reasons to destroy humanity, co-operation with history implied that people would become God's means in carrying out that destruction. It would be typical of human history, Butterfield wrote in *Christianity and History* (1949), 'if—assuming that the world was bound some day to cease to be a possible habitation for living creatures—men should by their own contrivance hasten that end and anticipate the operation of nature or of time' because Divine judgement in history made men its agents.[43] To deny the role of divine Providence and to believe instead that human beings were in control was moral hubris, another subversive consequence of original sin.

When Butterfield wrote his first book on historiography, *The Whig Interpretation of History* (1931), he attacked that tradition because it was inconsistent with his conservative, fundamentally religious pessimism. The Whig interpretation was entirely secular and written 'on the side of the Protestants and the Whigs, to praise revolutions provided they have been successful, to emphasize certain principles of progress in the past and to produce a story which is the ratification if not the glorification of the present'.[44] Justification of the present was an approach that always distorted the past. Instead, Butterfield insisted, with Ranke, that every time was unique to God, the only possible interpreter of history. Since we cannot really understand the meaning, let alone direction of the historical process, we cannot let our current

---

[41] George Kitson Clark, *The Critical Historian* (New York, 1967), based on a paper for the educational section of the British Association at Manchester in 1962 on the teaching of history, 208, 209.
[42] Butterfield, *The Englishman and his History*, 2.
[43] Butterfield, *Christianity and History*, 66.
[44] Herbert Butterfield, *The Whig Interpretation of History* (London, 1931), p. v.

concerns affect our approach to the past.[45] Elton also rejected the Whig view and its emphasis on history as preparation for a superior present, but for secular and methodological reasons. In early 1956 he described Whiggish history as a wrong-headed attempt to seek 'the outlines of the future' or explanations of 'modern politics' in the past.[46]

In 1944, Butterfield turned again to historiographical problems in *The Englishman and his History* (1944). The book was based upon a series of lectures given in Germany before the war. After Dunkirk, the lectures were rewritten to provide a patriotic plea for a conservative reading of Whiggism. The valuable continuities within English history that Butterfield emphasized in the middle of the war were practical and non-doctrinaire. In 1944, Butterfield returned to the eighteenth century to identify a Whig tradition described admiringly as 'a moderate pace of reform, a cautious progress to whatever end may be desired: the Whiggism which, abhorring revolutionary methods, seems now mildly left-wing, now almost indistinguishable from conservatism'.[47] In 1931 he had disavowed a liberal Whig tradition; in 1944 when the continued existence of Britain was threatened, he discovered a conservative Whig tradition. One of his charges against the liberal Acton was that Acton had insufficiently recognized that the British constitution was made by Tories as well as Whigs. Acton was unaware that 'between the fanaticisms of right and left' there was a conservative kind of whiggism, that steered 'the country through perilous seas, measured the limits of what was practicable and prevented catastrophe by a maturer kind of political wisdom'.[48]

Although Acton was a liberal Catholic, Butterfield treated him as if he were in the secular camp because he saw Acton's thought as contributing to the displacement of religion by arrogant scholarship and moral vanity. Instead of the liberal ideal of individuality that Acton championed, Butterfield

---

[45] Herbert Butterfield, *The Statecraft of Machiavelli* (London, 1940), 15–16.
[46] Geoffrey Elton, 'Fifty Years of Tudor Studies at London University', *Times Literary Supplement*, 6 Jan. 1956, p. viii. Elton was talking specifically about the Tudor age and the work of A. F. Pollard and R. H. Tawney.
[47] Butterfield, *The Englishman and his History*, 92.
[48] Butterfield, *Lord Acton*, 20.

proposed a religious image of distinctive 'personality', or soul, given to everyone by God. Without the essential qualities of their personalities, no historian could write historical narrative informed by an understanding of mind and motive, hope and fear, passion and faith. Personality was the beating heart of history and in its depths lay self-consciousness, intellect, and the only kind of freedom that men possessed. Unpredictable and singular, personality was the sole arena for struggle between good and evil. Moral conflict did not occur between nations or creeds but within a 'deeper realm' out 'of reach' for the historian because it is 'within the intimate interior of personalities'.[49] But human personality flowered only when 'accompanied by a powerful affirmation on the spiritual side'. Personality was limited, too, by the force of events and it succeeded, for Butterfield, only in combination with Christianity: 'Since human beings are so wilful, it may be true that the modern western world, by giving so much rein to individuals, is a civilization perpetually in jeopardy through an excess of liberty. There is grave danger for humanity if, in the new situation, individuals do not by an autonomous act of judgement go over to the Christian religion.'[50]

Butterfield's mistrust of secularism led to an even deeper distrust of science. In *The Origins of Modern Science, 1300–1800* (1951), his most original and influential book, Butterfield denied the Whig-Liberal reading of science and offered instead a history mitigated by regress and blunder rather than a story of steady progress. The history of science, he argued, was like the history of everything else. The same innately conservative tendencies set new discoveries into a 'realm of "established facts" '. We 'must wonder', he speculated, 'both in the past and the present that the human mind, which goes on collecting facts, is so inelastic, so slow to change its framework of reference'.[51] Secular, liberal meliorism distorted the study of history, including the history of science, because it assumed that amelioration of

---

[49] Butterfield, *Christianity and History*, 28, 26, 91.
[50] Butterfield, *Christianity in European History*, 63.
[51] Herbert Butterfield, *The Origins of Modern Science, 1300–1800* (London, 1951), 32, 41.

the human condition was a realistic goal. That sanguine, evolutionary view depended upon blind faith in the rehabilitation of human nature. It was as pernicious as ignorance to Butterfield because it provided a specious justification for dismantling those safeguards set up and administered by government to constrain the essential evil in human nature.[52] Control and containment were reasonable strategies for Butterfield; progress was a disappointing illusion.

Once misleading expectations about the world were put aside, then practical, limited policies could be adopted to direct human affairs more rationally. To demonstrate the efficacy of common sense as opposed to idealism, Butterfield called upon political history to testify for him. As early as 1929, in *The Peace Tactics of Napoleon, 1806–1808*, Butterfield studied diplomacy as the practised art of international reconciliation.[53] In *Christianity and History* (1949) he continued to explore eighteenth-century diplomacy as an object lesson in the common-sense truth that war was not fought for 'righteousness'. Unlike the twentieth-century wars fought over abstract and unattainable moral issues, eighteenth-century leaders fought about provinces. It was much easier, Butterfield thought, to compromise about relative boundaries than absolute right.[54] Throughout his technical historical writing, studies of statecraft as accommodation in both domestic and foreign affairs allowed him to illustrate the compulsion of circumstances and the restricted role of men in responding to those circumstances.

Those restrictions did not mean that men planned or acted without purpose. On the contrary, we could not understand historical figures like Machiavelli or Cromwell unless we listened to their asserted intentions. *The Statecraft of Machiavelli* (1940), published as Britain was on the threshold of war, argues that although great men were strictly confined in their choices, some, like Machiavelli, were effective because they held non-doctrinaire views of politics and

---

[52] Butterfield, *Christianity and History*, 33–4.
[53] Herbert Butterfield, *The Peace Tactics of Napoleon, 1806–1808* (Cambridge, 1929), p. vii.　　　　[54] Butterfield, *Christianity and History*, 137.

searched for the highest 'practical good' rather than an illusory 'highest good'.[55] But Machiavelli was wrong in believing that men could defeat capricious time and chance. Machiavelli's contemporary Guicciardini was far more perceptive because he understood policy as 'a perpetual course of improvization', and he appreciated government as an art rather than as a science.[56] Among great men, the best track record went to those, independent of context or country, who pursued virtues Butterfield identified as English: practicality over doctrine, practice over ideology, and pragmatism over system.[57] *George III, Lord North and the People* (1949) demonstrates that conflict could be avoided by sensible policies, while *Christianity, Diplomacy and War* (1953) argues further that war and diplomacy were always much more about power than about ideals.[58] Even when the outcome appeared to be a triumph for moral or idealistic principles, the motives and methods were generally utilitarian. Butterfield explained Cromwell's intervention for the legal resettlement of the Jews as due largely to economic and political motives. Cromwell restored Jewish life in England not out of altruism but because he wanted the Jews to be helpful should war occur with Spain.[59]

Butterfield found his greatest inspiration in English history and he argued regularly that the narrative of high politics was central to history. But he never produced a school of disciples in his broader historical fields of eighteenth-century British studies, the history of science, or historiography although he personally influenced many students who became prominent historians.[60] Butterfield reached his most responsive constituency in the theory and

---

[55] Butterfield, *Machiavelli*, 19, reprinted in 1955 and 1960, and *Christianity and History*, 47.   [56] Butterfield, *Machiavelli*, 24–5.

[57] Butterfield, *The Englishman and his History*, 138.

[58] Ibid. 102; Herbert Butterfield, *George III, Lord North and the People 1779–80* (London, 1949), p. vi; id., *Christianity, Diplomacy and War* (The Beckly Social Service Lecture; New York, 1953), 115.

[59] Herbert Butterfield, *Historical Development of the Principle of Toleration in British Life* (the Robert Waley Cohen Memorial Lecture of 1956, published in association with the Council of Christians and Jews; London, 1957), 14–15.

[60] John Pocock, Peter Laslett, and Jonathan Steinberg were influenced by Butterfield, but their work and considerable reputations are unique to them.

practice of international affairs, understood as an attempt to explain the uses of power for public good. In his inaugural address as Regius Professor of Modern History in 1964, he urged his colleagues to be less insular and adopt a more international point of view.[61] When Geoffrey Elton gave his inaugural twenty years later, he urged instead that 'English history be given a dominant role in English historical studies'.[62] Butterfield's wider interest in the twentieth century was expressed through such books as his *International Conflicts in the Twentieth Century* (1960), an appeal to mutual accommodation in place of cold wars. He was also active in the Rockefeller Committee on International Politics in the late 1960s. Initially a study circle run by Kenneth Thompson and centred in the Department of International Affairs at Columbia, the Rockefeller Committee included George Kennan and some of Kennan's friends from the former Policy Planning Section of the State Department such as Louis Halle and Paul Nitze. They were joined by Reinhold Niebuhr and Arnold Wolfers of the International Relations Department at Yale. The group examined, among other issues, the foundation of diplomacy in ethics; why countries have a foreign policy; and how far foreign affairs were amenable to scientific treatment. Butterfield met with them occasionally and in 1968 set up a similar group in England.[63]

Butterfield's conservative historical imagination gave him a sympathetic audience among international politicians who agreed with him about the inability of people to control events and that the best of intentions were more likely to go

---

[61] Butterfield, *The Present State of Historical Scholarship*, 22.
[62] Geoffrey Elton, *The History of England* (inaugural lecture delivered 26 Jan. 1984; Cambridge, 1984), 11.
[63] Butterfield Papers W270, Letter from Butterfield to Desmond Williams, 28 Apr. 1968, 1–2. Letter from Williams to Butterfield, 2 May 1958, W272, 1–3 and 27 May 1958, W273. Butterfield to Williams, ? Sept. 1968, W279. Williams to Butterfield, 30 Sept. 1958. The first meeting was scheduled from 19–21 Sept. and the small group adopted the name 'Committee on International Politics'. For a comparison of British and American conservatism in the 20th century see Reba N. Soffer, 'Catastrophe and Commitment: Conservation and the Writing of History in Twentieth-Century Britain and America', in Fred Leventhal and Roland Quinton (eds.), *Anglo-American Attitudes* (Brookfield, Vt., 2000).

wrong than right.[64] Butterfield's authority as a historian sanctioned the arguments for negotiation on the basis of power when he wrote that it was difficult to deal with the 'problem of morality in a realm where force possesses a certain unanswerability'. The 'realm of international relations is the one most calculated to suffer at one and the same time from the cupidity of the wicked, the anxieties of the strong and the unwisdom of the virtuous. It is a field in which the problem of the self-righteousness of nations can be more deadly than the problem of national greed.'[65]

In common, Butterfield, Elton, and Kitson Clark never confronted the problem of evil that the Second World War represented so dramatically because they held men and not God responsible. In his novel *The Living End* (1979), Stanley Elkin's God does not justify his ways, but he does explain them. He tells Heaven that interest in the sanctity of the human will or in goodness was irrelevant to his actions. Rather he did what he did because 'it makes a better story'.[66] For the Cambridge conservative historians it was the only story and their only choice was to tell it. Instead of focusing on the war Butterfield treated it as the continuation of the First World War, that 'dismal birthday of modern battle and hatred'. The war of 1914–18 was the first modern war to abandon the concrete and attainable objects of limited warfare and the Second World War was its logical conclusion.[67] Butterfield's Christian conservatism led him to read history as a series of warnings against any activity undertaken for moral purposes and carried out by tragically flawed human beings in a world that always overwhelmed them. He was

[64] See Kenneth Thompson (ed.), *Herbert Butterfield: The Ethics of History and Politics* (Lanham, Md., 1980); the very perceptive and sympathetic *The Wisdom of Statecraft: Sir Herbert Butterfield and the Philosophy of International Politics* (Durham, NC, 1985) by Alberto R. Coll who shares Butterfield's religious and political commitments; and Butterfield Papers W270, Letter to Desmond Williams, 28 Apr. 1958, 1; W272, William's reply, on 2 May 1958, 1; W273, 27 May 1958, Williams to Butterfield; W279, n.d., Butterfield to Willliams; Williams to Butterfield, 30 Sept. 1958.

[65] Morality and Force. MS on the morality of international relations, University of Cambridge Library, Butterfield Papers, Butt/110, n.d., 1.

[66] Stanley Elkin, *The Living End: A Triptych* (New York, 1979), 136–44.

[67] Butterfield, *Christianity, Diplomacy and War*, 15 and *History and Human Relations*, 39.

equally unsympathetic to those who mistakenly believed in the beneficent presence of God in the world and those whose narrow secular experience prevented them from understanding the Augustinian God that governed Butterfield and his world.

Unlike Butterfield who studied not only eighteenth-century politics but the imperatives of twentieth-century foreign policy as well, his two colleagues entrenched themselves in the amenable, pre-world war past where they could document the efficacy of their conservative values.[68] Both Kitson Clark and Elton deserted the twentieth century for times when order was imposed upon disorder and the excesses of human nature were contained by institutions and their efficient administration. Kitson Clark was more comfortable in the first half of the nineteenth century where sensible men such as Robert Peel were not 'likely to defend what was indefensible, nor to press a principle beyond the point that practical politics allowed'.[69] Although Kitson Clark returned to Peel repeatedly, he increasingly minimized the influence of individuals and of ideas. The lesson of the mid-Victorian period was the 'influence in human affairs of the force of necessity, of the pressure of circumstances'. It seems 'impossible to doubt that given the circumstances of Britain in the nineteenth century something resembling what did happen would have happened, whoever the agents available might have been'. Men's 'intentions had to conform, not to what was recommended by theory, but to what was determined by fact, and they were not masters of the future'.[70]

Elton chose to live in the sixteenth century among powerful political leaders like Thomas Cromwell, who were able to restrain conflict by efficient administration and equitable law. He was a generation younger than Butterfield and

---

[68] Herbert Butterfield, *International Conflict in the Twentieth Century: A Christian View* (London, 1960).

[69] George Kitson Clark, MS of *Peel and the Corn Laws*, 52, written about 1950 and never finished. Trinity College Library, Cambridge, Add. MS a. 239.

[70] Kitson Clark, *An Expanding Society*, 181–3 and 'A Commentary' (1974–5), 7–8 (an unfinished essay on public health and medical practice until 1854). Trinity College Library, Cambridge, Add.MS a. 240.

Kitson Clark and he outlived them both by a generation. At the beginning of his career he urged Tudor historians to 'understand the true structure and ideas of so "governed" an age' and to see 'Matters not only from the point of view of the governed but also from that of the government'.[71] At the end of his career, his beliefs about the Tudors and the straightforward role of the historian as a narrator of political life had altered very little. When, in 1974, he was asked to revise his best-selling text *England under the Tudors*, issued in eleven editions since its publication in 1955, he admitted that he continued 'in general to stand by the view of the sixteenth century which I expressed here from the first'.[72] In 1992, two years before his death, he published *The English*, a personal tribute to the 'country in which I ought to have been born', where 'the centuries of a strong monarchy and a powerful system of legal rights' left the twentieth century a legacy of the toleration of variety and respect for the rights 'not of Man but of English men and women'.[73]

The Second World War and its consequences deepened and accelerated the conservative impetus that drove Elton, Kitson Clark, and Butterfield. Each of them called upon history to support their convictions that moral idealism was futile, that policy could be guided only by pragmatic ends, and that institutions must restrain the implicit violence and destruction present in everyone's nature. Suspicion of human motives and their effect upon conduct, and admiration for stability and continuity, led them to doubt historical evidence demonstrating successful morally inspired activism and selfless individual commitment. They were never able, moreover, to reconcile their university's high ideals and aspirations for human attainment with their own assessment of life as a dismal art. Still, as eminent Cambridge historians, they exercised authority and control over people and their lives. For one generation, they succeeded remarkably in at

---

[71] Geoffrey Elton, 'Fifty Years of Tudor Studies at London University', *Times Literary Supplement* (6 Jan. 1956), p. viii.

[72] Geoffrey Elton, 'Preface to the Second Edition', *England under the Tudors* (London, 1974), p. v.

[73] Geoffrey Elton, *The English* (Oxford, 1992), pp. xii, 234–5. See too *Return to Essentials* (Cambridge, 1991).

least one of three areas: the shaping of historians, the definition of fields of history, and foreign policy. They all left deep personal impressions on students who became distinguished historians and teachers on three continents. In addition, Butterfield's and Elton's methodological positions on the writing and contents of history provoked enduring and fruitful discussion among historians. Only Butterfield, among the three, transcended his academic setting to influence American and British Cold War thinking. It is ironic that their conservative view of history did not lead Butterfield, Elton, or Kitson Clark to doubt their own effectiveness as historians, academics, and men of the world.

18

The Web and the Seams

Historiography in an Age of Specialization and Globalization

PETER BURKE

This essay provides a brief overview of some recent tendencies in historical writing. The aim is not only to compare and contrast Britain and Germany, but also to place British and German trends in a wider perspective, indeed, to raise the question of whether it is any longer useful to speak of national tendencies or schools at all in an age which might be described as one of transition from *Nationalstaat* to *Weltbürgertum*. The metaphor in the title of this essay comes, of course, from Frederic William Maitland and the book he wrote with Sir Frederick Pollock on the history of English law in which they described history as a 'seamless web'. The point which this essay makes is that while history may still be a seamless web, current historiography is certainly not.

On the contrary, the most obvious characteristic of the historiography of our age, compared with earlier periods, is its specialization and fragmentation. There is obviously a danger of overestimating the homogeneity of nineteenth-century historical practice. In the German-speaking world, for instance, Jacob Burckhardt, Gustav Schmoller, and Leopold von Ranke all pursued very different historiographical models and aims. Even Ranke, as Rudolf Vierhaus, Felix Gilbert, and others have argued, was not as narrowly political in his approach as either his image or his disciples might suggest.[1] All the same, in Ranke's day, political history was central, and other kinds of history were more or less peripheral. Today by contrast we live in an age of historiographical polycentrism.

---

[1] Rudolf Vierhaus, *Ranke und die soziale Welt* (Münster, 1957); Felix Gilbert, *History: Politics or Culture? Reflections on Ranke and Burckhardt* (Princeton, 1990).

On the other hand, the present age is also one of globalization and standardization which must affect the production of historical writing. Yet we cannot be suffering simultaneously from fragmentation and standardization. To replace Maitland's metaphor from weaving with a metaphor from physics, this essay addresses the problem of the balance of centrifugal and centripetal forces within contemporary historical writing.

Some forms of fragmentation are traditional, but they persist. National styles of history are still perceptible, the British style and the German style among them. One way in which this may be perceived is to look at the time-lags in translation. It took over thirty years for Edward Thompson's *The Making of the English Working Class*, first published in 1963, to be translated into German. On the other side, it is doubtful whether the late Thomas Nipperdey ever enjoyed in Britain the reputation he surely deserved.

More generally, the contrast between the British cultural tradition of empiricism and methodological individualism, and the German tradition of holism and interest in theory, is still perceptible, even if it is less strong than it used to be. A generation ago, the late Arnaldo Momigliano used to complain that whenever he mentioned the word 'idea' in University College London, someone would give him the address of the Warburg Institute, brought to England from Hamburg in 1933.

The experience Momigliano had (or claimed to have had) would probably not be repeated today. All the same, the *Begriffsgeschichte* associated with Reinhart Koselleck and his school differs in important respects from the intellectual history practised in Britain, by John Burrow, for example, or Stefan Collini. The differences are associated with different attitudes to philosophy in our two countries, as well as with different philosophies. An example from the German side is Koselleck's interest (like that of Hans-Robert Jauss), in Gadamer, Husserl, and Heidegger, an interest particularly noticeable when he speaks of 'horizons of expectation'.[2]

---

[2] Reinhart Koselleck, *Vergangene Zukunft* (1979; English translation *Futures Past*, Cambridge, Mass., 1985), 46, 56, 64, 106, 186, 201, 267 ff.

Attitudes to historiography itself also differ in our two countries. For example, the resistance to theory remains strong in Britain, whereas in Germany the history of historiography is an acknowledged subdiscipline of history. The well-known stereotype of the British as a nation of empiricists contains as well as exaggerates an insight. To be a British historian is, of course, to have swallowed a double dose of empiricism. That some local as well as national traditions of historical writing have survived to the end of the twentieth century is suggested by the continuing use of expressions such as the 'Leicester school', 'Cambridge school', 'Bielefeld school', or 'Göttingen school' of historical writing. The milieu of universities with their masters and disciples, to say nothing of patrons and clients, encourages such persistence. W. G. Hoskins at Leicester makes an obvious example, a somewhat eccentric figure who transmitted his concern for local history, for communities, and for the history of the English landscape to disciples as diverse as Alan Everitt, Margaret Spufford, and Charles Phythian-Adams.

Traditional forms of fragmentation like these now coexist with newer ones. The explosion of historical writing, the multiplication of dissertations, books, articles, and journals has turned the historian's village, once a cosy if parochial community, into a constellation of suburbs. To the expansion of the profession and the printed words it produces, the expansion of the territory of the historian must also be added, in other words the increasing acceptance of the idea that everyone and everything has a history: the working class, women, children, dreams, the climate, gestures, laughter, and even smells and noises. It is tempting to invert Maitland's metaphor and to think of history as something like a fat man in an old suit, in which expansion has led to splitting along the seams.

These tendencies to fragment have been encouraged, ironically enough, by some of the very attempts to avoid fragmentation; in other words, by the practice of interdisciplinarity, especially when it is institutionalized. That is, in the pursuit of certain new topics or 'objects' some historians turned for assistance to economics, others to demography, ecology, sociology, anthropology, philosophy, or literature. The price, and the unintended consequence of these interdisciplinary efforts, and the rise of centres and journals such as those for historical demography or historical sociology, has been that the more thoroughly one group of historians learns the language of ecologists or anthropologists, the more difficult that group finds it to communicate with the remainder of their colleagues. Even without attempts at empire-building, which occur from time to time, the rise of subdisciplines is almost inevitable.

Such subdisciplines might have been arranged around a centre. Today, however, the decline of the hegemony of any single paradigm is becoming evident. A few years ago there were three major competitors for hegemony: the Rankean, the Marxian, and the Braudelian paradigms. The last of these three paradigms was less important in Britain and Germany, which resisted *Annales* for a long time, than for historians in many other parts of the world. Today, on the other hand, there is a superfluity of choices, a cornucopia of styles of history from which historians can select what appeals most—women's history, the old or the new cultural history, and many more.

This fragmentation is both justified and encouraged by the current critique of Grand Narrative, which asserts or assumes that attempts to write universal or national history are as impossible as they are undesirable.[3] British or German historians may not be very interested in this critique. All the same, the rise of interest in micro-history in both countries suggests that some do share certain of the attitudes Lyotard formulated so dramatically. After all, the challenge to Grand Narrative is not only a philosophical one, but social and political as well. It is linked to current debates about multiculturalism and to practical problems such as that of teaching the history of Britain to classes of young Bangladeshis, or the history of Germany to classes of young Turks.

All this fragmentation is taking place in what is supposed to be an age of globalization and cultural standardization. A

---

[3] Jean-François Lyotard, *The Post-Modern Condition* (Manchester, 1984; French original, 1979).

useful definition of globalization is given in a recent study by Malcolm Waters: 'a social process in which the constraints of geography on social and cultural arrangments are receding', together with a consciousness of this process.[4] The recession is the result of what has been called 'time-space compression' and so, ultimately, of technology.[5] The term 'globalization' is a recent one, rarely used before the mid-1980s. The idea of a shrinking world is of course much older. Some Enlightenment historians, French, British, and German, had a global vision of the past. More recently, when they relaunched their journal *Annales* after the Second World War, both Lucien Febvre and Fernand Braudel expressed the sense of living in a 'global village'—a phrase, incidentally, which Febvre quoted from Gaston Roupnel at a time when Marshall McLuhan was still unknown outside Canada.[6]

In the fifty years since Febvre and Braudel made this point, the impact of globalization on the everyday life of historians has become more and more palpable. The rise of English as a world language has come to affect historical practice. On the other side, English-speaking historians have become more conscious of non-English theories and disciplines. Within the relatively narrow field of the history of historiography, there is also increasing interest in a global vision of the past.[7] But what are the consequences of these intensifying intercontinental contacts? In the first place, certain new historiographical trends, or perhaps fashions, spread rapidly. A well-known case is that of the international acclaim for a pair of books which appeared at almost the same time in Paris and Turin, were based on the same kind of source, and offered a similar vision of the past: Emmanuel Le Roy Ladurie's *Montaillou* (1975), and Carlo Ginzburg's *Il formaggio e i vermi* (1976).

In the second place, the internationalization of models and trends is associated with an international, interdisciplinary interest in a small group of theorists, German speakers such as Norbert Elias, Jürgen Habermas, and Hans-Robert Jauss, and

---

[4] Malcolm Waters, *Globalization* (London, 1995), 3.
[5] David Harvey, *The Condition of Postmodernity* (Oxford, 1989), ch. 15.
[6] Pierre Daix, *Fernand Braudel* (Paris, 1995), 216.
[7] Jörn Rüsen (ed.), *Westliches Geschichtsdenken: Eine interkulturelle Debatte* (Göttingen, 1999).

English speakers such as Clifford Geertz and Hayden White (to say nothing of the French). The discussion and, to a lesser extent, the practice of a self-consciously post-modern history (defined in terms, for example, of the 'linguistic turn', 'constructivism', or the collapse of the wall between history and fiction) has become an intercontinental movement. This internationalization mitigates the fragmentation discussed earlier.

Assessing the current importance and future significance of these trends is, of course, a more difficult task. How far have they gone, geographically speaking? Are they discussed in Sofia or Lima with the same interest as they are in Budapest or São Paulo? How deeply have the new trends affected professional practice? As reception theorists emphasize, the problem is to discover how different ideas or authors have been interpreted by individuals and groups in different places. A well-known piece of sociological research on the reception of *Dallas* in different parts of the world suggests caution. For example, Russian Jews recently arrived in Israel perceived the serial as a critique of capitalism.

A historiographical parallel to this example might be 'history from below', a term notoriously difficult to translate into other languages. Its Indian equivalent, Subaltern Studies, centred in Delhi, both is and is not part of the same trend as History Workshop. When he founded his group, Ranajit Guha was certainly aware of the work of History Workshop, but he was also interested in French theory. In any case, writing the history of a colonial regime from below is necessarily different from writing the history of the working class. And the Latin American movement to write the history of the vanquished (*La Vision de los vencidos*, as the Mexican Miguel Léon-Portillo calls it) began in the 1950s, before the slogan 'history from below' was launched. The movement is as different from the Subaltern Studies movement as the colonial situation in India differed from that in Latin America. It is only in the 1990s that contacts between the two movements have begun.[8]

---

[8] Florencia E. Mallon, 'The Promise and Dilemma of Subaltern Studies: Perspectives from Latin American History', *American Historical Review*, 99 (1994), 1491–515.

This essay now returns to the comparison between Britain and Germany, focusing on four sectors of historical writing, two in which the parallels seem to be relatively close and two in which the differences are more obvious: history from below, micro-history, historical anthropology, and the history of the everyday.

1. History from below. The British History Workshop, founded by Raphael Samuel and his friends in the 1960s, and the German *Werkstätte* inspired by it offer similar combinations of socialism and feminism. Edward Thompson has been an inspiration to this German movement, despite the time-lags in translation already mentioned. The two groups of historians appear to have been marching in the same direction.

2. Again, in the case of micro-history, the British and German trends seem to be roughly parallel. It would, of course, be possible to write a micro-history of micro-history, in other words, of each local movement for micro-history, in Bologna, Leicester, and elsewhere. In the case of Germany, it would be interesting to know whether micro-historians were aware of the essays of Aby Warburg, which in my view are micro-historical *avant la lettre*, and whether they saw him as a predecessor or not.[9] Despite the different traditions, however, the differences between the village studies produced by Hans Medick or Wolfgang Behringer in one country and those by Margaret Spufford and Keith Wrightson in the other do not seem to be very great.[10]

3. In the case of historical anthropology the situation is a little different. What makes it different is above all the contrast between the tradition of social anthropology in Britain and that of *Völkerkunde* in Germany. Folklore has

---

[9] Peter Burke, 'Aby Warburg as Historical Anthropologist', in Horst Bredekamp, Michael Diers, and Charlottte Schoell-Glass (eds.), *Aby Warburg* (Hamburg, 1991), 39–44.

[10] Hans Medick, *Leben und Überleben in Laichingen, 1650–1900. Lokalgeschichte als allgemeine Geschichte* (Göttingen, 1996); Wolfgang Behringer, *Chronrad Stoeckhlin und die Nachtschar* (Munich, 1994); Margaret Spufford, *Contrasting Communities* (Cambridge, 1974); Keith Wrightson and R. Levine, *Poverty and Piety in an Essex Village* (New York, 1979); id., *The Making of an Industrial Society: Whickham 1560–1765* (Oxford, 1991).

always had an academically marginal position in Britain, especially in England, despite a long tradition of amateur interest in the subject. On the other hand, British anthropology, although small in scale, was a respected and innovative discipline. Although there was a time when the majority of British anthropologists virtually ignored history, one leading figure, Edward Evans-Pritchard, kept open the lines of communication, and at the end of the 1950s inspired a young historian in his college (his fellow-Welshman Keith Thomas) to take anthropology seriously. One result of this encounter was that British historians of British witchcraft approached it via Africa (that is, via British anthropologists working on Africa, notably Evans-Pritchard himself on the Azande).

In Germany, the roles were reversed. In other words, it was *Völkerkunde* which was central while the anthropology of 'the other' was marginal, despite certain traditions of interest in the cultures of Africa, the Amerindians and so on. If the slogan in Germany today is historical 'anthropology', and not 'ethnology' (as it is in Scandinavia or Hungary), this looks very much like a deliberate break with tradition, a reaction against the associations which *Volkskunde* acquired during the Third Reich.

4. Finally we come to *Alltagsgeschichte* (history of the everyday), a term which should be left in German because it has not been as successful in Britain as in Germany, or indeed in other countries such as France and Brazil. In attempting to explain why not, it is not sufficient to say that we already have the phrase 'social history', because the history of the everyday is a particular kind of social history, one which is indeed practised in Britain but rather less self-consciously than elsewhere. As in the case of *Begriffsgeschichte*, the difference between British and German practice may be linked to contrasting attitudes to philosophy, and contrasting philosophies. *Alltagsgeschichte* is associated with a philosophy and sociology of the everyday, linked to Husserl, Schutz, and Max Weber's idea of *Veralltäglichung*, or in the case of Jürgen Kuczynski, one of the pioneers in this field, to the ideas of the Marxist philosopher-sociologist Henri Lefebvre.

In conclusion, it must be said that we are paying a high price for the variety of history as described in this essay.

Moreover, globalization has not led to *histoire globale* in the Braudelian sense of that term. A self-consciously postmodern position would be to embrace fragmentation, but I regard this as defeatism. The problem for the future seems to be how to combine the interest in alternative histories, in pluralism, and in multiple viewpoints with a concern for *histoire totale*, the seamless web, *Gesamtgeschichte*. There is obviously no simple solution, but that does not mean that there is nothing that we can do. In teaching and writing history, we can all work for 'decompartmentalization', whether the compartments we are trying to demolish are disciplinary or national.

Select Bibliography

This bibliography contains a selection of the modern titles cited in this volume, as well as some additional works in both English and German.

ANTONI, CARLO, *From History to Sociology: The Transformation in German Historical Thinking* (London, 1962).
ARNSTEIN, WALTER L., *Recent Historians of Great Britain: Essays on the Post-1945 Generation* (Ames, Ia., 1990).
ARX, JEFFREY PAUL VON, *Progress and Pessimism: Religion, Politics and History in Late Nineteenth-Century Britain* (Cambridge, Mass., 1985).
ASHTON, ROSEMARY, *The German Idea: Four English Writers and the Reception of German Thought, 1800–1860* (Cambridge, 1980).
AUSUBEL, HERMAN, et al. (eds.), *Some Modern Historians of Britain: Essays in Honor of R. L. Schuyler* (New York, 1951).
BANN, STEPHEN, *The Clothing of Clio: A Study of the Representation of History in Nineteenth-Century Britain and France* (Cambridge, 1984).
BARNES, HARRY ELMER, *A History of Historical Writing* (New York, 1963).
BEN-ISRAEL, HEDVA, *English Historians on the French Revolution* (Cambridge, 1968).
BERGER, STEFAN, *The Search for Normality: National Identity and Historical Consciousness in Germany since 1800* (Providence, RI, 1997).
——, DONOVAN, MARK, and PASSMORE, KEVIN (eds.), *Writing National Histories: Western Europe since 1800* (London, 1999).
BLAAS, P. B. M., *Continuity and Anachronism: Parliamentary and Constitutional Development in Whig Historiography and in the Anti-Whig Reaction between 1890 and 1930* (The Hague, 1978).
BLANKE, HORST WALTER, and FLEISCHER, DIRK (eds.), *Theoretiker der deutschen Aufklärungshistorie*, 2 vols. (Stuttgart, 1990).
—— *Historiographiegeschichte als Historik* (Stuttgart, 1991).
—— and RÜSEN, JÖRN (eds.), *Von der Aufklärung zum Historismus: Zum Strukturwandel des historischen Denkens* (Paderborn, 1984).
BOSWORTH, RICHARD, *Explaining Auschwitz and Hiroshima: History Writing and the Second World War, 1945–1990* (London, 1993).
BOWLER, PETER J., *The Invention of Progress: The Victorians and the Past* (Oxford, 1989).

Select Bibliography

BOYD, KELLY (ed.), *Encyclopedia of Historians and Historical Writing*, 2 vols. (London, 1999).
BRADY, CIARAN (ed.), *Ideology and the Historians* (Dublin, 1991).
BRANDI, KARL, *Geschichte der Geschichtswissenschaft* (2nd edn., Bonn, 1952).
BRANTLINGER, PATRICK, *Rule of Darkness: British Literature and Imperialism, 1830–1914* (Ithaca, NY, 1988).
BRECHENMACHER, THOMAS, *Großdeutsche Geschichtsschreibung im 19. Jahrhundert: Die erste Generation (1830–48)* (Berlin, 1996).
BREISACH, ERNST, *Historiography. Ancient, Medieval, and Modern* (Chicago, 1983).
BROWN, STUART C., *British Philosophy and the Age of Enlightenment* (London, 1995).
BROWNLEY, MARTINE WATSON, *Clarendon and the Rhetoric of Historical Form* (Philadelphia, 1985).
BRUCH, RÜDIGER VOM, *Wissenschaft, Politik und öffentliche Meinung: Gelehrtenpolitik im wilhelminischen Deutschland (1890–1914)* (Husum, 1980).
BRUNDAGE, ANTHONY, *The People's Historian: John Richard Green and the Writing of History in Victorian England* (Westport, Conn., 1994).
BRYANT, ARTHUR, *Macaulay* (New York, 1979)
BURKE, PETER, *Varieties of Cultural History* (Ithaca, NY, 1997).
BURLEIGH, MICHAEL, *Confronting the Nazi Past: New Debates on Modern German History* (London, 1996).
BURROW, JOHN W., *A Liberal Descent: Victorian Historians and the English Past* (Cambridge, 1981).
—— *Whigs and Liberals: Continuity and Change in English Political Thought* (Oxford, 1988).
—— *Evolution and Society: A Study in Victorian Social Theory* (Cambridge, 1966).
—— *Gibbon* (Oxford, 1985).
BUSSMANN, WALTER, *Treitschke: Sein Welt- und Geschichtsbild* (2nd edn., Göttingen, 1981).
BUTTERFIELD, HERBERT, *George III and the Historians* (1957; London, 1988).
—— *Man on his Past: The Study of the History of Historical Scholarship* (Cambridge, 1955).
—— *The Whig Interpretation of History* (1931; London, 1965).
CAMERON, JAMES R., *Frederic William Maitland and the History of English Law* (Norman, Okla., 1961).
CAMPBELL, JAMES, *Stubbs and the English State* (Reading, 1989).
CANNADINE, DAVID, *G. M. Trevelyan: A Life in History* (London, 1993).

CANNON, JOHN (ed.), *The Blackwell Dictionary of Historians* (Oxford, 1988).
CELOTTI, JOSEPH D., 'The Political Thought and Action of Friedrich Christoph Dahlmann' (Ph.D. thesis, Stanford University, 1970).
CHADWICK, OWEN, *Acton, Döllinger and History* (1986 Annual Lecture of the German Historical Institute London; London, 1987).
—— *Acton and History* (Cambridge, 1998).
CHANCELLOR, VALERIE, *History for their Masters: Opinion in the English History Textbook, 1800–1914* (New York, 1970).
CHICKERING, ROGER, *Karl Lamprecht: A German Academic Life (1856–1915)* (Atlantic Highlands, NJ, 1993).
—— *Imperial Germany. A Historiographical Companion* (Westport, Conn. and London, 1996).
CHINNICI, J. M., *The English Catholic Enlightenment: John Lingard and the Cisalpine Movement, 1780–1850* (Shepherdstown, 1980).
CHRIST, KARL, *Von Gibbon zu Rostovtzeff: Leben und Werk führender Althistoriker der Neuzeit* (Darmstadt, 1972).
CLIVE, JOHN, *Macaulay: The Shaping of the Historian* (Cambridge, Mass., 1987).
COLEMAN, D. C., *History and the Economic Past: An Account of the Rise and Decline of Economic History in Britain* (London, 1987).
COLLEY, LINDA, *Lewis Namier* (London, 1989).
COLLINI, STEFAN, *Public Moralists: Political Thought and Intellectual Life in Britain, 1850–1930* (Oxford, 1991).
—— et al., *That Noble Science of Politics: A Study in Nineteenth-Century Intellectual History* (Cambridge, 1983).
CRADDOCK, PATRICIA B., *Young Edward Gibbon, Gentleman of Letters* (Baltimore, 1982).
—— *Edward Gibbon, Luminous Historian, 1772–1794* (Baltimore, 1989).
CULLER, A. DWIGHT, *The Victorian Mirror of History* (New Haven, 1985).
DALE, P. A., *The Victorian Critic and the Idea of History: Carlyle, Arnold and Pater* (Cambridge, Mass., 1977).
DAMICO, HELEN and ZAVADIL, JOSEPH B. (eds.), *Medieval Scholarship: Biographical Studies on the Formation of a Discipline* (New York, 1995).
DANN, OTTO, OELLERS, NORBERT, and OSTERKAMP, ERNST (eds.), *Schiller als Historiker* (Stuttgart, 1995).
DAVIS, H. W., *The Political Thought of Heinrich von Treitschke* (Westport, Conn., 1973).
DOCKHORN, KLAUS, *Der deutsche Historismus in England: Ein Beitrag zur englischen Geistesgeschichte des 19. Jahrhunderts* (Göttingen, 1950).
—— *Deutscher Geist und angelsächsische Geistesgeschichte: Ein Versuch der Deutung ihres Verhältnisses* (Göttingen, 1954).

DORPALEN, ANDREAS, *Heinrich von Treitschke* (New Haven, 1957).
DOTTERWEICH, VOLKER, *Heinrich von Sybel: Geschichtswissenschaft in politischer Absicht (1817–1861)* (Göttingen, 1978).
DUA, J. C., *British Historiography, Eighteenth Century Punjab: Their Understanding of the Sikh Struggle for Power and Role of Jassa Singh Ahluwlia* (New Delhi, 1992).
DUNN, WALDO HILARY, *James Anthony Froude: A Biography*, 2 vols. (Oxford, 1961–3).
ELTON, GEOFFREY R., *F. W. Maitland* (London, 1986).
ERDMANN, KARL DIETRICH, *Die Ökumene der Historiker: Geschichte der Internationalen Historikerkongresse und des Comité International des Sciences Historiques* (Göttingen, 1987).
EVANS, ARTHUR HENRY, *English Historians and Welsh History: An Examination* (London, 1975).
EVANS, RICHARD, *Re-reading German History: From Unification to Reunification 1800–1996* (London, 1997).
EYCK, FRANK G., *G. P. Gooch: A Study in History and Politics* (London, 1982).
FASBENDER, THOMAS, *Thomas Carlyle: Idealistische Geschichtssicht und visionäres Heldenideal* (Würzburg, 1989).
FASNACHT, GEORGE E., *Acton's Political Philosophy: An Analysis* (London, 1952).
FAULENBACH, BERND, *Ideologie des deutschen Weges. Die deutsche Geschichte in der Historiographie zwischen Kaiserreich und Nationalsozialismus* (Munich, 1980).
FITZSIMONS, MATTHEW A., *The Past Recaptured. Great Historians and the History of History* (Notre Dame, Ind., 1983).
FORBES, DUNCAN, *The Liberal Anglican Idea of History* (Cambridge, 1952).
FRIEDMAN, BARTON R., *Fabricating History: English Writers on the French Revolution* (Princeton, 1988).
FUCHS, ECKHARDT, *Henry Thomas Buckle. Geschichtsschreibung und Positivismus in England und Deutschland* (Leipzig, 1994).
FUETER, EDUARD, *Geschichte der Historiographie* (3rd edn., Munich, 1936; new edn., New York, 1968).
FUHRMANN, HORST, *'Sind eben alles Menschen gewesen'. Gelehrtenleben im 19. und 20. Jahrhundert. Dargestellt am Beispiel der Monumenta Germania Historica und ihrer Mitarbeiter* (Munich, 1996).
FULDA, DANIEL, *Wissenschaft aus Kunst: Die Entstehung der modernen deutschen Geschichtsschreibung, 1760–1860* (Berlin, 1996).
FUSSNER, F. SMITH, *The Historical Revolution: English Historical Writing and Thought, 1580–1640* (Westport, Conn., 1976).
GALL, LOTHAR, 'Geschichte im Selbstverständnis der Deutschen', in

Dieter Hein, Andreas Schulz, and Eckhardt Treichel (eds.), *Lothar Gall: Bürgertum, liberale Bewegung und Nation. Ausgewählte Aufsätze* (Munich, 1996), 349–61. English original: *Confronting Clio: Myth-Makers and Other Historians* (1991 Annual Lecture of the German Historical Institute London; London, 1992).

GAWLICK, GÜNTHER, and KREIMENDAHL, LOTHAR, *Hume in der deutschen Aufklärung: Umrisse einer Rezeptionsgeschichte* (Stuttgart, 1987).

GEYL, PETER, *Debates with Historians* (Groningen, 1955; Fontana, 1962).

GILBERT, FELIX, *History: Politics or Culture? Reflections on Ranke and Burckhardt* (Princeton, 1990).

GOOCH, GEORGE P., *History and Historians in the Nineteenth Century* (London, 1913).

GRIFFITHS, RICHARD, *Fellow-Travellers of the Right: British Enthusiasts for Nazi Germany 1933–39* (London, 1980).

GUGGISBERG, HANS R. (ed.), *Umgang mit Jacob Burckhardt: Zwölf Studien* (Basle, 1994).

HAAS, STEFAN, *Historische Kulturforschung in Deutschland 1880–1930: Geschichtswissenschaft zwischen Synthese und Pluralität* (Cologne, 1994).

HAINES, GEORGE, *Essays on German Influence upon English Education and Science, 1850–1919* (Hamden, Conn., 1969).

HALE, JOHN R., *The Evolution of British Historiography: From Bacon to Namier* (London, 1967).

HAMBURGER, JOSEPH, *Macaulay and the Whig Tradition* (Chicago, 1976).

HAMER, DAVID A., *John Morley: Liberal Intellectual in Politics* (Oxford, 1968).

HAMILTON, PAUL, *Historicism* (London, 1996).

HAMMERSTEIN, NOTKER (ed.), *Deutsche Geschichtswissenschaft um 1900* (Stuttgart, 1988).

—— *Jus und Historie. Ein Beitrag zur Geschichte des historischen Denkens an deutschen Universitäten im späten 17. und im 18. Jahrhundert* (Göttingen, 1972).

HANSEN, REIMER and RIBBE, WOLFGANG (eds.), *Geschichtswissenschaft in Berlin im 19. und 20. Jahrhundert. Persönlichkeiten und Institutionen* (Berlin, 1992).

HARDTWIG, WOLFGANG, *Geschichtskultur und Wissenschaft* (Munich, 1990).

HARRIS, RONALD W., *Clarendon and the English Revolution* (Stanford, Calif., 1983).

HARVIE, CHRISTOPHER, *The Lights of Liberalism: University Liberals and the Challenge of Democracy, 1860–1886* (London, 1976).

HEYCK, T. W., *The Transformation of Intellectual Life in Victorian England* (London, 1982).
HICKS, PHILIP STEPHEN, *Neoclassical History and English Culture: From Clarendon to Hume* (London, 1996).
HILL, BRIDGET, *The Republican Virago: The Life and Times of Catharine Macaulay, Historian* (Oxford, 1992).
HIMMELFARB, GERTRUDE, *Lord Acton. A Study in Conscience and Politics* (London, 1952).
—— *The New History and the Old: Critical Essays and Reappraisals* (Cambridge, Mass., 1987).
HOFFMAN, CHRISTHARD, *Juden und Judentum im Werk deutscher Althistoriker des 19. und 20. Jahrhunderts* (Leiden, 1988).
HÜBINGER, GANGOLF, *Georg Gottfried Gervinus: Historisches Urteil und politische Kritik* (Göttingen, 1984).
—— *Kulturprotestantismus und Politik. Zum Verhältnis von Liberalismus und Protestantismus im wilhelminischen Deutschland* (Tübingen, 1994)
HUDSON, JOHN (ed.), *The History of English Law: Centenary Essays on Pollock and Maitland* (Oxford, 1996).
IGGERS, GEORG G., *The German Conception of History. The National Tradition of Historical Thought from Herder to the Present* (Middletown, Conn., 1968).
—— *New Directions in European Historiography* (Middletown, Conn., 1975).
—— and POWELL, JAMES (eds.), *Leopold von Ranke and the Shaping of the Historical Discipline* (Syracuse, NY, 1990).
JAEGER, FRIEDRICH, *Bürgerliche Modernisierungskrise und historische Sinnbildung: Kulturgeschichte bei Droysen, Burckhardt und Max Weber* (Göttingen, 1994).
—— and RÜSEN, JÖRN, *Geschichte des Historismus: Eine Einführung* (Munich, 1992).
JÄGER, WOLFGANG, *Historische Forschung und politische Kultur in Deutschland: Die Debatte 1914–1980 über den Ausbruch des Ersten Weltkrieges* (Göttingen, 1984).
JANN, ROSEMARY, *The Art and Science of Victorian History* (Columbus, Oh., 1985).
JOLL, JAMES, *National Histories and National Historians: Some German and English Views of the Past* (1984 Annual Lecture of the German Historical Institute London; London, 1985).
KADISH, ALON, *Historians, Economists, and Economic History* (London, 1989).
KAPLAN, FRED, *Thomas Carlyle: A Biography* (Cambridge, 1983).
KENNEDY, PAUL, and NICHOLLS, ANTHONY, (eds.), *Nationalist and*

Select Bibliography

Racialist Movements in Britain and Germany before 1914 (London, 1981).

KENYON, JOHN, *The History Men: The Historical Profession in England since the Renaissance* (London, 1983).

KIDD, COLIN, *Subverting Scotland's Past: Scottish Whig Historians and the Creation of an Anglo-British Identity, 1689–c.1830* (Cambridge, 1993).

KLEINKNECHT, THOMAS, *Imperiale und internationale Ordnung. Eine Untersuchung zum anglo-amerikanischen Gelehrtenliberalismus am Beispiel von James Bryce (1838–1922)* (Göttingen, 1985).

KNORR, BIRGIT, *Autorität und Freiheit. Das Liberalismus-Verständnis des Bildungsbürgertums im Kaiserreich und in der Weimarer Republik im Spiegel der Historiographie über den Frühliberalismus* (Frankfurt, 1976).

KNUDSEN, JONATHAN B., *Justus Möser and the German Enlightenment* (Cambridge, 1986).

KOOT, G. M., *English Historical Economics, 1870–1926: The Rise of Economic History and Neo-mercantilism* (Cambridge, 1987).

KOSELLECK, REINHART, *Vergangene Zukunft: Zur Semantik geschichtlicher Zeiten* (Frankfurt, 1984).

KOZICKI, HENRY (ed.), *Developments in Modern Historiography* (Basingstoke and London, 1993)

KRIEGER, LEONARD, *Ranke: The Meaning of History* (Chicago, 1977).

KRUFT, HANNO-WALTER, *Der Historiker als Dichter: Zum 100. Todestag von Ferdinand Gregorovius* (Munich, 1992).

KUEHN, MANFRED, *Scottish Common Sense in Germany, 1768–1800: A Contribution to the History of Critical Philosophy* (Kingston, 1987).

KUKLICK, HENRIKA, *The Savage Within: The Social History of British Anthropology, 1885–1945* (Cambridge, 1991).

KÜTTLER, WOLFGANG, et al. (eds.), *Geschichtsdiskurs*, 5 vols. (Frankfurt, 1993–9).

LANG, TIMOTHY, *The Victorians and the Stuart Heritage: Interpretations of a Discordant Past* (Cambridge, 1995).

LAQUEUR, WALTER, and MOSSE, GEORGE L. (eds.), *Historians in Politics* (London, 1974).

LEVINE, JOSEPH M., *Humanism and History: Origins of Modern English Historiography* (Ithaca, NY, 1987).

LEVINE, PHILIPPA, *The Amateur and the Professional: Antiquarians, Historians and Archaeologists in Victorian England, 1838–1886* (Cambridge, 1986).

LEWIS, BERNARD and HOLT, P. M. (eds.), *Historians of the Middle East* (London, 1962).

MCCLELLAND, C. E., *The German Historians and England* (Cambridge, 1971).

McDowell, Robert Brendan, *Alice Stopford Green: A Passionate Historian* (Dublin, 1967).
McElrath, Damian, *Lord Acton: The Decisive Decade 1864–1874. Essays and Documents* (Louvain, 1970).
McKitterick, Rosamond, and Quinault, Roland (eds.), *Edward Gibbon and Empire* (Cambridge, 1996).
McNeill, William H., *Arnold Toynbee: A Life* (New York, 1989).
—— *Toynbee Revisited* (Austin, Tex., 1993).
Majeed, Javed, *Ungoverned Imaginings: James Mill's 'The History of British India' and Orientalism* (Oxford, 1992).
Malik, Dagmar, *Die Französische Revolution im Diskurs des 19. Jahrhunderts: Untersuchungen zur englischen Revolutionsgeschichtsschreibung* (Bochum, 1983).
Maltzahn, Christoph von, *Heinrich Leo 1799–1878: Ein politisches Gelehrtenleben zwischen romantischem Konservatismus und Realpolitik* (Göttingen, 1979).
Marx, Christoph, *'Völker ohne Schrift und Geschichte'. Zur historischen Erfassung des vorkolonialen Schwarzafrika in der deutschen Forschung des 19. und frühen 20. Jahrhunderts* (Stuttgart, 1988).
Mathew, David, *Lord Acton and his Times* (London, 1968).
Maurer, Michael, *Aufklärung und Anglophilie in Deutschland* (Göttingen, 1987).
Meineke, Stefan, *Friedrich Meinecke: Persönlichkeit und politisches Denken bis zum Ende des Ersten Weltkrieges* (Berlin, 1995).
Messerschmidt, Manfred, *Deutschland in englischer Sicht: Die Wandlungen des Deutschlandbildes in der englischen Geschichtsschreibung* (Düsseldorf, 1955).
Messinger, Gary S., *British Propaganda and the State in the First World War* (Manchester, 1992).
Metz, Karl Heinz, *Grundformen historiographischen Denkens: Wissenschaftsgeschichte als Methodologie, dargestellt an Ranke, Treitschke und Lamprecht* (Munich, 1979).
Mittal, Satish Chandra, *India Distorted: A Study of British Historians on India* (New Delhi, 1995).
Mommsen, Wolfgang J. (ed.), *Leopold von Ranke und die moderne Geschichtswissenschaft* (Stuttgart, 1988).
—— *Die Geschichtswissenschaft jenseits des Historismus* (Düsseldorf, 1971).
—— (ed.), *Kultur und Krieg: Die Rolle der Intellektuellen, Künstler und Schriftsteller im Ersten Weltkrieg* (Munich, 1996).
—— and Osterhammel, Jürgen (eds.), *Max Weber and his Contemporaries* (London, 1987).

MUHLACK, ULRICH, *Geschichtswissenschaft im Humanismus und in der Aufklärung: Die Vorgeschichte des Historismus* (Munich, 1991).
—— (ed.), *Leopold von Ranke: Die großen Mächte. Politisches Gespräch* (Frankfurt, 1995).
MUHS, RUDOLF, PAULMANN, JOHANNES, and STEINMETZ, WILLIBALD (eds.), *Aneignung und Abwehr: Interkultureller Transfer zwischen Deutschland und Großbritannien im 19. Jahrhundert* (Bodenheim, 1998).
NIPPEL, WILFRIED, *Public Order in Ancient Rome* (Cambridge, 1995).
NOLTE, ERNST, *Geschichtsdenken im 20. Jahrhundert: Von Max Weber bis Hans Jonas* (Frankfurt, 1991).
NORTEN, B., *Freeman's Life: Highlights, Chronology, Letters and Works* (Farnborough, 1993).
OBERKROME, WILLI, *Volksgeschichte: Methodische Innovation und völkische Ideologisierung in der deutschen Geschichtswissenschaft 1918–1945* (Göttingen, 1993).
OEXLE, OTTO GERHARD, and RÜSEN, JÖRN (eds.), *Historismus in den Kulturwissenschaften* (Cologne, 1996).
OKIE, LARID, *Augustan Historical Writing: Histories of England in the English Enlightenment* (Lanham, Md., 1991).
OLLARD, RICHARD, *Clarendon and his Friends* (Oxford, 1988).
OSTERHAMMEL, JÜRGEN, *China und die Weltgesellschaft* (Munich, 1989).
—— *Die Entzauberung Asiens: Europa und die asiatischen Reiche im 18. Jahrhundert* (Munich, 1998).
OZ-SALZBERGER, FANIA, *Translating the Enlightenment: Scottish Civic Discourse in Eighteenth-Century Germany* (Oxford, 1995).
PANDEL, HANS-JÜRGEN, *Historik und Didaktik: Das Problem der Distribution historiographisch erzeugten Wissens in der deutschen Geschichtswissenschaft von der Spätaufklärung zum Frühhistorismus* (Stuttgart, 1990).
PARADIS, JAMES, and POSTLEWAIT, THOMAS (eds.), *Victorian Science and Victorian Values: Literary Perspectives* (New Brunswick, NJ, 1985).
PARKER, CHRISTOPHER, *The English Historical Tradition since 1850* (Edinburgh, 1990).
—— *History as Present Politics* (Winchester, 1980).
PEARDON, THOMAS PRESTON, *The Transition in English Historical Writing, 1760–1830* (New York, 1933).
PHILLIPSON, NICHOLAS, *Hume* (New York, 1989).
PÖGGELER, WOLFGANG, *Die deutsche Wissenschaft vom englischen Staatsrecht: Ein Beitrag zur Rezeptions- und Wissenschaftsgeschichte (1748–1914)* (Berlin, 1995).
POIS, ROBERT A., *Friedrich Meinecke and German Politics in the Twentieth Century* (Berkeley and Los Angeles, 1972).
POPPER, KARL, *The Poverty of Historicism* (London, 1957).

PORTER, ROY, *Gibbon: Making History* (London, 1988).
QUESNE, A. L., *Carlyle* (Oxford, 1982).
RAMHARDTER, GÜNTHER, *Geschichtswissenschaft und Patriotismus: Österreichische Historiker im Weltkrieg 1914–1918* (Vienna, 1973).
REILL, PETER HANNS, *The German Enlightenment and the Rise of Historicism* (Berkeley and Los Angeles, 1975).
REINHARDT, VOLKER (ed.), *Hauptwerke der Geschichtsschreibung* (Stuttgart, 1997).
RINGER, FRITZ, *The Decline of the German Mandarins: The German Academic Community, 1890–1933* (Cambridge, Mass., 1969).
ROSENBERG, JOHN D., *Carlyle and the Burden of History* (Oxford, 1985).
ROTHBLATT, SHELDON, *The Revolution of the Dons: Cambridge and Society in Victorian England* (Cambridge, 1981).
ROWSE, A. L., *Froude the Historian: Victorian Man of Letters* (Gloucester, 1987).
RÜSEN, JÖRN, *Begriffene Geschichte: Genesis und Begründung der Geschichtstheorie J. G. Droysens* (Paderborn, 1969).
—— *Konfigurationen des Historismus: Studien zur deutschen Wissenschaftskultur* (Frankfurt am Main, 1993).
SCHENK, WILLY, *Die deutsch-englische Rivalität vor dem Ersten Weltkrieg in der Sicht deutscher Historiker: Mißverstehen oder Machtstreben?* (Aarau, 1967).
SCHMIDT, GUSTAV, *Deutscher Historismus und der Übergang zur parlamentarischen Demokratie: Untersuchungen zu den politischen Gedanken von Meinecke, Troeltsch, Max Weber* (Lübeck, 1964).
SCHÖNWÄLDER, KAREN, *Historiker und Politik: Geschichtswissenschaft im Nationalsozialismus* (Frankfurt, 1992).
SCHORN-SCHÜTTE, LUISE, *Karl Lamprecht: Kulturgeschichtsschreibung zwischen Wissenschaft und Politik* (Göttingen, 1984).
SCHÖTTLER, PETER (ed.), *Geschichtsschreibung als Legitimationswissenschaft 1918–1945* (Frankfurt, 1997).
SCHULIN, ERNST, *Die weltgeschichtliche Erfassung des Orients bei Hegel und Ranke* (Göttingen, 1958).
—— *Traditionskritik und Rekonstruktionsversuch: Studien zur Entwicklung von Geschichtswissenschaft und historischem Denken* (Göttingen, 1979).
—— *'The Most Historical of All Peoples': Nationalism and the New Construction of Jewish History in Nineteenth-Century Germany* (1995 Annual Lecture of the German Historical Institute London; London, 1996).
SCHULZE, WINFRIED, *Deutsche Geschichtswissenschaft nach 1945* (Munich, 1989).

SCHURMAN, DONALD M., *Julian S. Corbett, 1854–1922: Historian of British Maritime Policy from Drake to Jellicoe* (London, 1981).
SCHWABE, KLAUS, *Wissenschaft und Kriegsmoral. Die deutschen Hochschullehrer und die politischen Grundfragen des Ersten Weltkrieges* (Göttingen, 1969).
SCHWARZ, BILL, *The Expansion of England. Race, Ethnicity and Cultural History* (London, 1996).
SHEA, DONALD F., *The English Ranke: John Lingard* (New York, 1969).
SIEWEKE, GARIELE, *Der Romancier als Historiker: Untersuchungen zum Verhältnis von Literatur und Geschichte in der englischen Historiographie des 19. Jahrhunderts* (Frankfurt, 1994).
SIMMONS, JACK (ed.), *English County Historians* (East Ardsley, 1978).
SLEE, PETER R. H., *Learning and a Liberal Education: The Study of Modern History in the Universities of Oxford, Cambridge and Manchester 1800–1914* (Manchester, 1986).
SMITH, K. J. M., *James Fitzjames Stephen: Portrait of a Victorian Rationalist* (Cambridge, 1988).
SMITH, WOODRUFF D., *Politics and the Sciences of Culture in Germany 1840–1920* (New York, 1991).
SOFFER, REBA, *Ethics and Society in England: The Revolution in the Social Sciences, 1870–1914* (Berkeley, Calif., 1978).
—— *Discipline and Power: The University, History and the Making of an English Elite, 1870–1930* (Stanford, Calif., 1994).
SOUTHARD, ROBERT, *Droysen and the Prussian School of History* (Lexington, Ku., 1995).
STAPLETON, JULIA, *Englishness and the Study of Politics. The Social and Political Thought of Ernest Barker* (Cambridge, 1994).
STERN, FRITZ (ed.), *The Varieties of History: From Voltaire to the Present* (London, 1957).
STIEG, MARGARET, *The Origin and Development of Scholarly Historical Periodicals* (Tuscaloosa, Ala., 1986).
STOCKING, GEORGE W., *Victorian Anthropology* (New York, 1987).
—— *After Tylor: British Social Anthropology 1888–1951* (Madison, 1995).
STROMBERG, ROLAND N., *Redemption by War: The Intellectuals and 1914* (Lawrence, Kan., 1982).
STUCHTEY, BENEDIKT, *W. E. H. Lecky (1838–1903). Historisches Denken und politisches Urteilen eines anglo-irischen Gelehrten* (Göttingen, 1997).
TRIBE, KEITH, *Governing Economy: The Reformation of German Economic Discourse 1750–1830* (Cambridge, 1988).
—— *Strategies of Economic Order. German Economic Discourse, 1750–1950* (Cambridge, 1995).

TULLOCH, HUGH, *Acton* (London, 1988).
VANCE, NORMAN, *The Victorians and Ancient Rome* (London, 1997).
WALLACE, STUART, *War and the Image of Germany: British Academics 1914–1918* (Edinburgh, 1988).
WALTHER, GERRIT, *Niebuhrs Forschung* (Stuttgart, 1993).
WASZEK, NORBERT, *The Scottish Enlightenment and Hegel's Account of Civil Society* (Dordrecht, 1988).
WATKINS, DANIEL P. (ed.), *Spirits of Fire: English Romantic Writers and Contemporary Historical Methods* (London, 1990).
WECHSLER, V. G., *David Hume and the 'History of England'* (Philadelphia, 1979).
WEHLER, HANS-ULRICH (ed.), *Deutsche Historiker*, 9 vols. (Göttingen, 1971–82).
WEIGAND, WOLF VOLKER, *Walter Wilhelm Goetz 1867–1958: Eine biographische Studie über den Historiker, Politiker und Publizisten* (Boppard, 1992).
WENDE, PETER, *Geschichte Englands* (Stuttgart, 1995).
WHITE, HAYDEN, *Metahistory: The Historical Imagination in Nineteenth-Century Europe* (Baltimore, 1973).
WILLIAMS, ERIC, *British Historians and the West Indies* (Trinidad, 1964).
WILLIAMS, GARETH, *George Ewart Evans* (Cardiff, 1991).
WITTE, BARTHOLD C., *Der preußische Tacitus. Aufstieg, Ruhm und Ende des Historikers Barthold Georg Niebuhr 1776–1831* (Düsseldorf, 1979).
WITTKAU, ANNETTE, *Historismus: Zur Geschichte des Begriffs und des Problems* (Göttingen, 1992).
WOODWARD, ERNEST L., *British Historians* (London, 1943).
WORMELL, DEBORAH, *Sir John Seeley and the Uses of History* (Cambridge, 1980).

Notes on Contributors

PATRICK BAHNERS is an editor with the *Frankfurter Allgemeine Zeitung*. He has published articles on Tacitus, Gibbon, Heinrich von Sybel, Franz Schnabel, and Hayden White and is currently working on a Ph.D. thesis on Macaulay and Ranke.

PETER BURKE is Professor of Cultural History at the University of Cambridge and a Fellow of Emmanuel College. He concentrates on the history of early modern Europe and has written extensively on historiographical topics. His most recent books are *The Fortunes of the Courtier* (1995), *Varieties of Cultural History* (1997), and *The European Renaissance* (1998).

JOHN BURROW is Professor of European Thought at the University of Oxford and a Fellow of Balliol College. His past publications include *A Liberal Descent: Victorian Historians and the English Past* (1981) and *Whigs and Liberals: Continuity and Change in English Political Thought* (1988). Together with S. Collini and D. Winch he has written *That Noble Science of Politics: A Study in Nineteenth-Century Intellectual History* (1983). He is currently working on a history of ideas in Europe in the later nineteenth century.

JAMES CAMPBELL is Professor of Medieval History at the University of Oxford and a Fellow of Worcester College. Among his publications are *Essays in Anglo-Saxon History* (1986) and *Stubbs and the English State* (1989). He edited *The Anglo-Saxons* (1991), and gave the Ford Lectures on 'Origins of the English State' (Oxford, 1996).

ECKHARDT FUCHS is a Research Fellow at the German Historical Institute Washington. He has written a number of articles on German, English, and American intellectual history and is the author of *Henry Thomas Buckle: Geschichtsschreibung und Positivismus in England und Deutschland* (1994). He is co-author of *'J'accuse!': Zur Affäre Dreyfus in Frankreich* (1994), and has edited, with Benedikt Stuchtey, *Across Cultural Borders: Historiography in a Global Perspective* (forthcoming).

GANGOLF HÜBINGER is Professor of Cultural History at the Europa University Viadrina in Frankfurt an der Oder. He concentrates on intellectual history and the history of publishing, religious cultures, and the history of the social sciences and of liberalism. His publications include *Georg Gottfried Gervinus: Historisches Urteil und politische Kritik* (1984) and *Kulturprotestantismus und Politik: Zum Verhältnis von Liberalismus und Protestantismus im wilhelminischen Deutschland* (1994). He is co-editor of *Kultur und Kulturwissenschaften um 1900* (I, 1989; II, 1997).

ULRICH MUHLACK is Professor of the History and Theory of Historiography at the Johann Wolfgang Goethe University in Frankfurt am Main. Among his publications is *Geschichtswissenschaft im Humanismus und in der Aufklärung: Die Vorgeschichte des Historismus* (1991). He has edited *Leopold von Ranke: Die großen Mächte. Politisches Gespräch* (1995).

WILFRIED NIPPEL is Professor of Ancient History at the Humboldt University in Berlin. He has published numerous articles on the constitutional, social, and intellectual history of ancient Greece and Rome, the reception of ancient political theory in early modern times, and the history of classical scholarship. His books include *Mischverfassungstheorie und Verfassungsrealität in Antike und früher Neuzeit* (1980) and *Public Order in Ancient Rome* (1995).

JÜRGEN OSTERHAMMEL is Professor of Modern History at the University of Constance. He has published several articles on the history of European historiography. Among his books are *Britischer Imperialismus im Fernen Osten* (1983), *China und die Weltgesellschaft* (1989), *Colonialism: A Theoretical Overview* (1997), *Shanghai, 30. Mai 1925: Die Chinesische Revolution* (1997), and *Die Entzauberung Asiens: Europa und die asiatischen Reiche im 18. Jahrhundert* (1998). Together with Wolfgang J. Mommsen he has edited *Imperialism and After: Continuities and Discontinuities* (1986) and *Max Weber and his Contemporaries* (1987).

FANIA OZ-SALZBERGER is Senior Lecturer in History at the University of Haifa. Her research into the Scottish and German Enlightenments has produced several articles and a book, *Translating the Enlightenment: Scottish Civic Discourse in Eighteenth-Century Germany* (1995). She is the editor of the recent Cambridge edition of Adam Ferguson's *Essay on the History of Civil Society* (1995). Her current research focuses on the transmission of ideas across cultural and linguistic borderlines in eighteenth-century Europe.

HARTMUT POGGE VON STRANDMANN is Professor of Modern History at the University of Oxford and a Fellow and Praelector of University College. He has published several articles and books on Wilhelmine Germany, German–Soviet relations 1917–1941, industrial history,

Anglo-German relations, the revolutions of 1848–9, and European imperialism. Among his books in English are: *Ideas into Politics: Aspects of European History 1880–1950* (ed. with R. J. Bullen and A. B. Polonsky, 1984), *Walther Rathenau: Industrialist, Banker, Intellectual, and Politician. Notes and Diaries 1907–1922* (ed., 1985), and *Britain after 1945: The Beginning of a Modern Age?* (1988). With R. J. W. Evans he has published *The Coming of the First World War* (1991), and *The Revolutions in Europe, 1848–1849: From Reform to Reaction* (1999).

REBA N. SOFFER is Professor of History at California State University, Northridge, Immediate Past President of the North American Conference on British Studies, and was a Guggenheim Fellow for 1995–6. She has written extensively on late nineteenth- and twentieth-century intellectual, social, and institutional history. Her work includes *Ethics and Society in England: The Revolution in the Social Sciences, 1870–1914* (1978), and *Discipline and Power: The University, History and the Making of an English Elite, 1870–1930* (1994). She is now working on a comparative study of British and American historiography in the twentieth century.

BENEDIKT STUCHTEY is a Research Fellow at the German Historical Institute London. He has published articles on the history of historiography and on the history of imperialism, and is the author of *W. E. H. Lecky (1838–1903): Historisches Denken und politisches Urteilen eines anglo-irischen Gelehrten* (1997). He has edited, with Eckhardt Fuchs, *Across Cultural Borders: Historiography in a Global Perspective* (forthcoming). Currently he is working on anti-colonialism in the twentieth century in a comparative perspective.

KEITH TRIBE is Reader in Economics at Keele University. Among his publications are *Governing Economy: The Reformation of German Economic Discourse, 1750–1830* (1988) and *Strategies of Economic Order: German Economic Discourse, 1750–1950* (1995). He is at present working on the formation of the economics discipline in British universities, in connection with which he has recently edited a volume of interviews under the title *Economic Careers* (1997).

HUGH TULLOCH is Senior Lecturer in History at the University of Bristol. He has published *James Bryce's 'American Commonwealth': The Anglo-American Background* (1988) and *Acton* (1988). He has just completed a survey of the historiography of the American Civil War era.

NORMAN VANCE is Professor of English at the University of Sussex. He has published extensively on the social, intellectual, and religious contexts of English and Irish literature. His recent books include

Irish Literature: A Social History (2nd edn., 1999) and *The Victorians and Ancient Rome* (1997).

PETER WENDE is Director of the German Historical Institute London and Professor of History at the University of Frankfurt am Main. He has published on German and British history. Among his latest publications are *Rivalität und Partnerschaft: Studien zu den deutsch-britischen Beziehungen im 19. und 20. Jahrhundert. Festschrift für Anthony J. Nicholls* (ed. with Gerhard A. Ritter, 1999), *Englische Könige und Königinnen: Von Heinrich VII. bis Elisabeth II.* (ed., 1998), *Geschichte Englands* (2nd edn., 1995), and *Politische Reden* (ed., 3 vols., 1990–4).

Index of Names

Unless otherwise indicated, most people listed in the index were historians

Acton, Sir John Emerich Edward Dalberg, 1st baron Acton (1834–1902) 1n., 13, 15–16, 23, 27, 27n., 106, 111, 144, 146n., 152, 159–72, 174, 182, 233–4, 247n., 253–6, 260, 387–8, 391
Adams, William George Stewart (1874–1966), public servant 352, 354
Adelung, Johann Christoph (1732–1806), linguist 267
Aehrenthal, Alois von (1854–1912), statesman 354
Archenholz, Johann Wilhelm von (1743–1812) 50
Argyll, George Douglas Campbell, 8th duke of (1823–1900) 140n.
Aristotle (384–322 BC) 60, 197, 199–202, 208
Arnold, Matthew (1822–88), poet and critic 97, 186
Arnold, Thomas (1823–1900), professor of English literature 9, 83, 93–6, 134, 246
Ashley, Sir William James (1860–1927) 18, 213–20, 215n., 227–8
Asquith, Herbert Henry, 1st earl of Oxford and Asquith (1852–1928), statesman 358, 363, 382
Attlee, Clement Richard, 1st earl Attlee (1883–1967), statesman 377
Austin, John (1790–1859), jurist 123
Austin, Sarah (1793–1867), translator 123–6, 128n., 130, 136, 138–9, 141–3, 144n., 148

Bachofen, Johann Jakob (1815–87), anthropologist 259
Baer, Karl-Ernst von (1792–1876), natural scientist 263–4
Bagehot, Walter (1826–77), economist and journalist 260
Baldwin, Stanley, 1st earl Baldwin of Bewdley (1867–1947), statesman 378

Balfour, Arthur James, 1st earl of Balfour (1848–1930), philosopher and statesman 109, 363
Balfour, Gerald William, 2nd earl of Balfour (1853–1945) 109
Barker, Sir Ernest (1874–1960) 342–7, 354–6, 362
Barrow, Sir John (1764–1848), secretary to the Admiralty 87–8
Barth, Theodor (1849–1909), liberal politician 329
Bastian, Adolf (1826–1905), ethnologist 277–8, 284
Bayle, Pierre (1647–1706), philosopher and critic 89
Beattie, James (1735–1803), poet 50
Beaven, Murray 354
Beaverbrook, William Maxwell Aitken, 1st baron (1879–1964), newspaper proprietor 362
Bebel, August (1840–1913), socialist leader 276
Beck, Christian Daniel (1757–1832), philologist 58, 61
Beesly, Edward Spencer 235
Beit, Alfred (1853–1906), financier 315
Benecke, Georg Friedrich 356–7
Benson, Edward White (1829–96), archbishop of Canterbury 109
Berkeley, George (1685–1753), bishop of Cloyne 291
Bernays, Jacob (1824–81), classicist 72–3
Bernays, Michael (1834–97) 75n.
Bernhardi, Friedrich von (1849–1930), general 340–1, 364
Bernheim, Ernst (1850–1942) 273
Bethmann-Hollweg, Moritz August von (1795–1877), jurist 115
Bischof, Hermann 33, 40
Bismarck, Otto von (1815–98), statesman 118–19, 166, 300, 328–9, 332n.

Blackie, John Stuart (1809–95), man of letters 12
Blair, Hugh (1718–1800), divine 52
Blanc, Jean Joseph Louis (1811–82), socialist 124n.
Blumenbach, Johann Friedrich (1752–1840), natural scientist 87, 270
Boas, Franz (1858–1942), ethnologist and anthropologist 283–7
Boeckh, August (1785–1867), philologist and classicist 126n.
Böhm-Bawerk, Eugen Ritter von (1851–1914), economist 212
Bonar, James (1852–1941), political economist 219n.
Boretius, Alfred (1836–1900), jurist 245n.
Bottomley, Horatio William (1860–1933), journalist and financier 349
Braudel, Fernand (1902–85) 405
Brentano, Ludwig Joseph (1844–1931), economist 226, 322, 329
Brewster, Sir David (1781–1868), natural philosopher 232
Breysig, Kurt (1866–1940) 268, 272, 276, 286
Bridges, Robert Seymour (1844–1930), poet laureate 356
Bright, John (1811–89), orator and statesman 290
Brooke, Stopford Augustus (1832–1916), divine and man of letters 124
Brunner, Heinrich (1840–1915) 116, 120, 121n., 178, 180
Brunner, Otto (1898–1982) 14
Brutus, Lucius Junius (late 6th century BC), Roman statesman 84
Bryant, Sir Arthur Wynne Morgan (1899–1985) 376n., 380n.
Bryce, James, Viscount Bryce (1838–1922), jurist and statesman 169, 314n.
Buchan, John, 1st baron Tweedsmuir (1875–1940) 361
Bücher, Karl (1847–1930), economist and sociologist 277n.
Buchholz, Friedrich (1768–1843), publicist 236
Buckle, Henry Thomas (1821–62) 12, 19–20, 153–4, 157, 157n., 162, 192, 201, 230, 232–41, 244–9, 261, 274, 299

Bugg, George 87
Bülow, Bernhard Heinrich Martin von (1849–1929), politician 340
Bunsen, Christian Carl von (1791–1860) 136n., 139
Burckhardt, Jacob (1818–97) 401
Burgess, J. W. 356
Burke, Edmund (1729–97), political theorist 10, 104
Butler, Richard Austen (1902–82), politician 380n.
Butterfield, Sir Herbert (1900–79) 1n., 4, 16, 23, 381–99

Caesar, Gaius Julius (100–44 BC) 71, 136, 167
Cairnes, John Elliot (1823–75), economist 215n.
Caligula (AD 12–41), Roman emperor 55
Cannan, Charles (1858–1919), university publisher 346, 352, 356–7, 360, 362
Carlyle, Thomas (1795–1881) 12, 116, 169–70, 184, 234, 246, 253–6, 299
Casaubon, Isaac (1559–1614), philologist 91–2
Cassius Dio Coccieanus (AD 163–235) 75
Cecil, Robert Arthur James Gascoyne, 5th marquess of Salisbury (1893–1972), politician 378
Cervantes, Miguel de (1547–1616), dramatist and poet 124n.
Chamberlain, Joseph (1836–1914), statesman 316, 330, 332n.
Chamberlain, Sir Neville Bowles (1820–1902), field marshal 376n.
Chapman, Robert William (1881–1960), university publisher 346, 352, 360
Chirol, Sir (Ignatius) Valentine (1852–1929), travellor and author 339–40, 353, 355
Church, Richard William (1815–90), dean of St Paul's 143–4
Clapham, Sir John Harold (1873–1946) 374
Clarendon, see Villiers
Clarke, George Sydenham (1848–1933), administrator 380n.
Clement IX (1600–69), pope (1667–9) 128
Clement XIV (1705–74), pope (1769–74) 128

Index of Names

Cluvier, Philip (1580–1622), classical scholar and geographer 89
Cobden, Richard (1804–65), statesman 290
Coleraine, *see* Law, Richard Kidston
Coleridge, Samuel Taylor (1772–1834), poet and philosopher 104, 254, 263
Columbus, Christopher (1451–1506), explorer 169
Comte, Auguste (1798–1857), philosopher and mathematician 19, 167, 230–9, 244–6, 255
Conant, James B. 376
Condillac, Etienne Bonnot de (1715–80), philosopher 168
Conrad, Johannes Ernst (1839–1915), economist 226
Cook, Sir Edward Tyas (1857–1919), journalist 361
Copernicus, Nicolaus (1473–1543), astronomer 169
Cramb, John Adam 340–1, 357
Creighton, Mandell (1843–1901), bishop of London 152, 160
Cromwell, Oliver (1599–1658) 307
Cromwell, Thomas, earl of Essex (?1485–1540), statesman 393–4, 397
Cunningham, William (1849–1919) 18, 108, 213–14, 219–20, 222–8
Curzon, George Nathaniel, Marquess Curzon of Kedleston (1859–1925), statesman 289–91, 294–6, 308, 318, 334, 350
Cuvier, Georges (1769–1832), natural scientist 87

Dahlmann, Friedrich Christoph (1785–1860) 22, 174, 179, 193, 198–203, 206
Darwin, Charles Robert (1809–82) 97, 103, 230, 243, 246, 260, 263–4
David, Jacques-Louis (1748–1825), painter 84
Davis, Henry William Carless (1874–1928) 120–1, 342–3, 345–7, 352–4, 356–63
Delbrück, Hans Gottlieb (1848–1929) 320, 323, 327
Descartes, René (1596–1650) 167
De Vere, Aubrey Thomas (1814–1902), poet and author 127
Dickinson, Goldsworthy Lowes (1862–1932), humanist 340

Dilke, Sir Charles Wentworth (1843–1911), politician and author 312, 326, 333
Dilthey, Wilhelm (1833–1911), philosopher 243, 245n., 251, 282
Diocletian (284–305), Roman emperor 71
Dionysius of Halicarnassus (80/75 BC–after AD 7), Greek historian 75
Disraeli, Benjamin (1804–81), 1st earl of Beaconsfield, statesman and man of letters 185n., 307, 378n.
Döllinger, Johann Joseph Ignaz von (1799–1890) 153n., 160, 163–4, 171
Donne, William Bodham (1807–82) 94, 144n.
Droysen, Johann Gustav (1808–86) 19, 31, 34, 36, 39, 42, 45, 166, 181–3, 192–3, 201, 203, 205–6, 237–44, 237n., 248, 309, 313
Duff, James Grant (1789–1858) 266

Eberty, Eduard Gustav (1840–94) 184
Edgeworth, Maria (1767–1849), novelist 84
Edgeworth, Richard Lovell (1744–1817), author 84, 219n.
Edward I (1239–1307), king of England 119
Egerton, Hugh Edward (1855–1927) 294, 306, 315, 317–19, 324, 334, 357
Eliot, George (1819–80), writer 12, 91–2
Elton, Geoffrey (1921–94) 107, 381–5, 387, 391, 395–9
Engels, Friedrich (1820–95) 276
Ennis, John 127–9, 131, 133, 144
Ensor, Sir Robert Charles Kirkwood (1877–1958), journalist 351
Erasmus, Desiderius (?1466–1536), humanist 169
Erdmannsdörfer, Bernhard (1833–1901) 245n.
Eucken, Rudolf Christoph (1846–1926), philosopher 343, 366
Evans-Pritchard, Sir Edward Evan (1902–73), social anthropologist 274n., 408
Ewald, Heinrich (1803–75), orientalist 141
Ewald, Paul (1857–1911), theologian 182

Index of Names

Faraday, Michael (1791–1867), natural philosopher 246n.
Farrar, Frederick William (1831–1903), dean of Canterbury 141
Fawcett, Henry (1833–84), statesman 216
Febvre, Lucien (1878–1956) 405
Feder, Johann Georg Heinrich (1740–1821), philosopher 60
Feiling, Sir Keith Grahame (1884–1977) 354, 380n.
Ferguson, Adam (1723–1816) 4, 7, 9, 49–66
Feuerbach, Ludwig Andreas (1804–72), philosopher 94
Fichte, Johann Gottlieb (1762–1814), philosopher 30, 155, 163, 167
Ficker, Julius von (1826–1902) 314n.
Firth, Sir Charles Harding (1857–1936) 170
Fisher, Herbert Albert Laurens (1865–1940), historian and statesman 109, 121, 342, 351, 355
Fitzgerald, Edward (1809–83), poet and translator 94
Fletcher, Charles Robert Leslie (1857–1934) 342, 354, 357, 360
Foakes-Jackson, Frederick John (1855–1941), divine 338
Fontane, Theodor (1819–98), novelist and journalist 148
Forster, Johann Georg Adam (1754–94), naturalist 68
Foster, Elizabeth 125, 143
Foy, Willy (1873–1929), ethnologist 282n.
Franke, Otto (1863–1946), sinologist 268–9
Frederick II, the Great (1712–86), king of Prussia 55, 60, 170, 178, 187, 189, 202
Freeman, Edward Augustus (1823–92) 12, 14, 111, 169, 177, 181, 185–6, 219, 246, 258–9, 300
Frobenius, Leo (1873–1938), ethnologist and cultural philosopher 282n., 286n.
Froude, James Anthony (1818–94) 12, 16, 18, 151, 169, 174, 177, 182–3, 233–4, 246–8, 256, 294, 299–305, 307, 319, 321, 324, 326, 330, 333
Fueter, Eduard (1876–1928) 80, 180
Fulda, Ludwig (1862–1939), writer 366

Fustel de Coulanges, Numa Denis (1830–89) 262

Gadamer, Hans-Georg, philosopher 402
Galbraith, Vivian Hunter (1889–1976) 108
Gardiner, Samuel Rawson (1829–1902) 151, 170, 178
Garve, Christian (1742–98), philosopher 54, 63
Gatterer, Johann Christoph (1727–99) 8, 28n., 57, 59–60
Geertz, Clifford 283, 406
George, Hereford Brooke (1838–1910), historical writer 324
Gervinus, Georg Gottfried (1805–71) 193, 199–204, 207
Gibbon, Edward (1737–94) 4, 6, 8–9, 55, 67–81, 136, 183, 266, 274
Gierke, Otto Friedrich von (1841–1921) 14, 116–17, 200
Giesebrecht, Wilhelm von (1814–89) 28n., 35–6, 160, 177
Gladstone, William Ewart (1809–98) 141, 141n., 307
Gneist, Heinrich Rudolf von (1816–95), jurist and politician 117, 179, 182, 200
Godwin, William (1756–1836), philosopher and novelist 84
Goethe, Johann Wolfgang von (1749–1832) 51, 184, 266
Goethe, Ottilie von (1796–1872) 123
Goetz, Walter (1867–1958) 272
Gomperz, Theodor (1832–1912), classical philologist 237–8
Gooch, George Peabody (1873–1968) 16, 342
Gordon, Sir Alexander and Lady Duff 141n., 144n.
Goschen, Sir Edward 348
Graebner, Fritz (1877–1934), ethnologist 282, 285
Granville, Augustus Bozzi (1783–1872), physician 88
Granville, see Leverson-Gower
Graves, Charles (1812–99), bishop of Limerick and mathematician 137
Green, John Richard (1837–83) 12, 181, 246, 255

Index of Names

Greville, Charles Cavendish Fulke (1794–1865), clerk to the council v, 126n.
Grey, Sir Edward, Viscount Grey of Falloden (1862–1933), statesman 347, 351, 358
Grimm, Jacob (1785–1863), Germanist 14, 37–8, 115–16, 253
Gross, Charles 116
Grote, George (1794–1871) 259
Guicciardini, Francesco (1483–1540), political theorist 394
Güterbock, Karl Eduard (1830–1914) 116

Haeckel, Ernst (1834–1919), zoologist and natural philosopher 343, 366
Halfern, Max von 323
Hallam, Henry (1777–1859) 100–1, 120, 139
Halle, Louis 395
Hamann, Johann Georg (1730–88), philosophical writer 53
Hamilton, Sir William Rowan (1805–65), mathematician 137
Hammer-Purgstall, Joseph von (1774–1856), orientalist 266
Hammond, John Lawrence Le Breton (1872–1949), journalist 351
Hannibal (247/246–183 BC) 61
Hansemann, David (1790–1864), statesman and economic politician 203
Hare, Julius Charles (1795–1855), archdeacon of Lewes 9, 83, 86, 88, 139
Harnack, Adolf von (1851–1930), protestant theologian 34, 40
Harrison, Frederic (1831–1923), author and positivist 230, 235
Harwood, Philip (1809–87), journalist 136–7, 155
Hashagen, Justus 176
Hassall, Arthur 342, 354
Häusser, Ludwig (1818–67) 39n., 174, 178, 187
Haym, Rudolf (1821–1901), philosopher and political publicist 187, 238, 242n.
Headlam-Morley, Sir James Wycliffe (1863–1929) 357, 362
Heeren, Arnold Hermann Ludwig (1760–1842) 266–7

Hegel, Georg Wilhelm Friedrich (1770–1831), philosopher 11, 19, 51, 53, 65, 68, 161–2, 166–7, 170, 201, 207, 251, 254, 256–7, 260–1
Hegewisch, Dietrich Hermann (1746–1812) 68
Heidegger, Martin (1889–1976), philosopher 402
Heimpel, Hermann (1901–88) 35n.
Henry IV (1367–1413), king of England 153
Henzen, Wilhelm (1816–87) 70
Herder, Johann Gottfried von (1744–1803), writer and philosopher 28–9, 33, 35, 41, 59, 65–6, 68, 93, 163, 251–2, 261, 265, 279, 286–7, 286n.
Heyne, Christian Gottlob (1729–1812), classical philologist 60–1
Hildebrand, Bruno (1812–78), economist 17, 228, 277n.
Hinneberg, Paul (1862–1934) 243–4, 243n.
Hintze, Otto (1861–1940) 34, 193, 195, 207, 209, 283, 320
Hitler, Adolf (1889–1945) 375, 375n., 376n., 383, 385, 388–9
Hogarth, David George (1862–1927), scholar and traveller 356–7
Home, John (1722–1808), author 52
Homer (b. 800 BC) 89–90, 159
Horace, Quintus Horatius Flaccus (65–8 BC) 84
Hugo, Gustav (1764–1844), jurist 68
Humboldt, Alexander von (1769–1859), natural scientist and geographer 270, 279, 284
Humboldt, Wilhelm von (1767–1835), scholar and politician 30–1, 35, 187–8, 207, 238, 242, 267
Hume, David (1711–76), philosopher 4–6, 8, 50–1, 54–5, 57, 59, 64, 168
Hurstfield, Joel 383–4
Husserl, Edmund (1859–1938), philosopher 402, 408

Ihering, Rudolf von (1818–92), jurist 259
Iselin, Isaak (1728–82), philosophical writer 59, 61–2, 65–6

Jackson, Henry (1839–1921), scholar 352, 356

Index of Names

Jacobi, Friedrich Heinrich (1743–1819), writer and philosopher 49, 63, 66
Jameson, Anna Brownell (1794–1860), author 123
Jane, Cecil 358
Jefferson, Thomas (1743–1826), 3rd president of the USA 162
Jelf, Richard William (1798–1871), principal of King's College London 137
Jellinek, Georg (1851–1911), specialist in constitutional law 207, 209
Jevons, William Stanley (1835–82), economist and logician 212, 215n., 216
Joachimsen, Paul 177, 182
Johnston, Sir Harry Hamilton (1858–1927), explorer 323
Jones, H. Stuart 340, 349
Jowett, Benjamin (1817–93), classical scholar 91
Jung, Carl Gustav (1875–1961), psychoanalyst 278

Kames, Henry Home, Lord (1696–1782) 58
Kant, Immanuel (1724–1804) 50, 65, 168, 194
Kautsky, Karl (1854–1938), political theorist and publicist 276
Kelly, Walter Keating 124n.
Kennan, George 386, 395
Kern, Fritz (1884–1950) 283n.
Keynes, John Neville 213–14
Kidd, Benjamin (1858–1916), sociologist 260
Kilbracken, John Arthur Godley, 1st baron (1847–1932), civil servant 356
Kingsley, Charles (1819–75), author 124, 170, 233–4, 307
Kipling, Rudyard (1865–1936), author 325, 357
Kitson Clark, George Sidney Roberts (1900–75) 381–2, 384–5, 389–90, 396–9
Klemm, Gustav Friedrich (1802–67), ethnologist 277
Klopp, Onno (1822–1903) 181
Kluckhohn, August (1832–93) 177
Knies, Karl Gustav Adolf (1821–98), economist 208, 228
Köpke, Rudolf (1813–70) 18, 28

Laband, Paul (1838–1918), jurist 116
Lamarck, Jean-Baptiste Antoine Pierre de Monet, Chevalier de (1744–1829), natural scientist 260, 262–4
Lamprecht, Karl Nathanael (1856–1915) 20, 44, 177, 207, 272–3, 276, 280, 283, 286
Lansdowne, see Petty-Fitzmaurice
Lappenberg, Johann Martin (1794–1865) 177, 179
Lasaulx, Ernst von (1805–61) 146
Law, Andrew Bonar (1858–1923), statesman 350, 373
Law, Richard Kidston, 1st baron Coleraine (1901–80), politician 373–4, 373n.
Lecky, William Edward Hartpole (1838–1903) 12, 157, 157n., 235, 293–4, 299, 301, 307, 331
Lefebvre, Henri 408
Legg, L. G. Wickham 342
Lenz, Max (1850–1932) 34, 320, 327, 330, 333, 341
Leslie, Cliffe 18, 213n., 215–19
Lessing, Gotthold Ephraim (1729–81), writer and critic 49, 53, 132, 132n.
Leverson-Gower, Granville George, 2nd earl Granville (1815–91), statesman 160
Lewes, George Henry (1817–78), miscellaneous writer 148, 184, 232
Lewis, Sir George Cornewall (1806–63), statesman and author 97, 126, 140n.
Liebermann, Felix (1851–1925) 14, 120–1
Lindsay, Alexander Dunlop, 1st baron Lindsay of Birker (1879–1952), educationist 342, 354
Lingard, John (1771–1851) 12n.
Littré, Maximilian Paul Émile (1801–82), philosopher and linguist 237
Livingstone, David (1813–73), missionary and explorer 307, 317
Livy (59 BC–AD 17), Roman historian 75, 84, 88–9, 93–8
Lloyd George, David (1863–1945), statesman 289
Lockhart, John Gibson (1794–1854), author 89
Louis XIV (1638–1715), king of France 159

Index of Names

Lucas, Sir Charles Prestwood (1853–1931), civil servant 294, 302n., 315–19, 324–5
Luden, Heinrich (1778–1847) 193, 196–8
Luther, Martin (1483–1546) 139, 144n., 169
Lyell, Sir Charles (1797–1857), geologist 85

Macaulay, Thomas Babington (1800–59) v, 6n., 9, 12, 17, 18, 45–7, 96–8, 126n., 140n., 145–51, 153, 156, 174, 178, 187–9, 191, 254, 267, 299, 307, 321, 326–8
Macdonald, James 50–1
Machiavelli, Niccolò (1469–1527) 169, 201–2, 393–4
McLennan, John Ferguson (1827–81), sociologist 259, 276
Macmillan, Harold, earl of Stockton (1894–1986), publisher and statesman 378
MacPherson, James (1736–96), translator 51, 56, 65
Madox, Thomas (1666–1727), legal antiquary and historiographer royal 110
Maine, Sir Henry James Sumner (1822–88), jurist 16, 18, 162, 169, 217–18, 258–9, 262
Maitland, Frederic William (1850–1906) 14–15, 99–122, 176, 178, 214, 401–2
Malcolm, Sir John (1769–1833), Indian administrator and diplomat 266
Malinowski, Bronislaw (1884–1942), ethnologist 274, 274n., 277, 286
Mallock, William Hurrell (1849–1923), author 260
Malthus, Thomas Robert (1766–1834), political economist 211, 218
Manning, Henry Edward (1808–92), cardinal-priest 146, 168
Marcks, Erich (1861–1938) 320, 329–33, 341, 368
Mark Twain (1835–1910), author 125n., 292
Marriott, Sir John Arthur Ransome (1859–1945) 338, 351
Marshall, Alfred (1842–1924), economist 18, 211–12, 214–15, 220–1, 221n., 224–6, 338n., 349

Martineau, James (1805–1900), unitarian divine 137–8
Marvin, F. S. 352
Marx, Karl (1818–83) 11, 161–2, 171, 179
Maurenbrecher, Wilhelm (1838–92) 183
Maurer, Georg Ludwig von (1790–1872), jurist 115, 180
Maurer, Konrad von (1823–1902), scholar of Scandinavian antiquity 259
Medley, D. J. 348
Meinecke, Friedrich (1862–1954) 80, 104, 283, 341, 368, 370
Meiners, Christoph (1747–1810) 61, 68
Mela, Pomponius (1st century AD), Roman geographer 74
Mendelssohn, Moses (1728–86), philosopher 59
Menger, Carl (1840–1921), economist 212
Merle d'Aubigné, Jean Henri (1794–1872), theologian 129
Metternich, Klemens Wenzel von (1773–1859) 202, 205
Meusel, Johann Georg (1743–1820), lexicographer 69
Meyer, Eduard (1855–1930) 34, 276, 369
Meyer, Jürgen Bona (1829–97), philosopher 237
Michelet, Jules (1798–1874) 93, 123, 124n., 161, 172, 280
Milford, Sir Humphrey Sumner (1877–1952), publisher 359–60, 364
Mill, James (1773–1836) 211, 267
Mill, John Stuart (1806–73) 123, 125, 211, 216, 218, 230, 232–3, 235, 237, 244–5, 261
Milman, Henry Hart (1791–1868), dean of St Paul's 9, 124n., 134–6, 138, 140, 143–4, 150, 157
Mitford, William (1744–1827) 147
Momigliano, Arnaldo Dante (1908–87) 74, 402
Mommsen, Theodor (1817–1903) 34, 36, 70–2, 74, 77, 98, 167, 174, 182, 186, 329
Montelius, Oscar (1843–1921) 268n.
Montesquieu, Charles de Secondat, baron de (1689–1755) 4, 8, 54, 64
Morgan, F. 342, 354
Morgan, Lewis Henry 20, 275–6, 278

Morley, John, Viscount Morley of Blackburn (1838–1923), statesman and man of letters 235
Mosheim, Johann Lorenz (1694/95–1755) 75
Mühlmann, Wilhelm Emil (1904–88), ethnologist and sociologist 274n.
Muir, John Ramsay Bryce (1872–1941), historian and politician 348, 355
Müller, Friedrich Max (1823–1900), orientalist and philologist 124, 142, 151, 259
Müller, Johannes von (1752–1809) 266
Müller, Karl Otfried (1797–1840), classical philologist 92, 126n.
Murray, George Gilbert Aimé (1866–1957), classical scholar and internationalist 342–3, 351–2, 354–5
Mussolini, Benito (1883–1945) 375, 388

Namier, Sir Lewis Bernstein (1888–1960) 357, 362
Napoleon Bonaparte (1769–1821) 147, 159, 162, 170, 198, 388
Nerva, Marcus Cocceius (AD 30–98), Roman emperor 62
Neumann, Karl Johannes (1857–1917) 80
Newman, John Henry (1801–90), cardinal 139, 143, 168
Newton, Arthur Percival 315, 317, 319
Niebuhr, Barthold Georg (1776–1831) 9–10, 16, 35–6, 70, 74–7, 76n., 79–80, 83–98, 123, 126n., 139, 160, 238, 253, 265
Niebuhr, Carsten (1733–1815), explorer 265
Niebuhr, Reinhold (1892–1971), theologian 395
Nietzsche, Friedrich (1844–1900) 10n., 341, 347, 359n., 364
Nightingale, Florence (1820–1910), reformer of hospital nursing 124
Nipperdey, Thomas (1927–92) 402
Nissen, Heinrich (1839–1912) 186
Nitze, Paul 395
Noorden, Karl von (1833–83) 180n.
Norman, Edward 382
Northcliffe, Viscount (1865–1922), journalist and newspaper proprietor 362
Novalis [Georg Philipp Friedrich, baron Hardenberg] (1772–1801), poet 54

Oncken, Hermann (1869–1945) 320, 323, 341, 358, 368
Ovid (43 BC–AD 17), Roman poet 83
Owen, Sir Richard (1804–92), naturalist 263

Paley, William (1743–1805), archdeacon of Carlisle 263
Pallas, Peter Simon (1741–1811), physician and explorer 267
Palmerston, Henry John Temple, 3rd viscount (1784–1865), statesman 141
Papencordt, Felix 127, 129, 144n.
Pareto, Vilfredo (1848–1923), economist and sociologist 212
Pattison, Mark (1813–84), scholar 91–2
Paul III (1468–1549), pope (1534–49) 135
Paul IV (1476–1559), pope (1555–9) 37
Pauli, Reinhold (1823–82) 14, 176–7, 179–81, 183
Peel, Sir Robert (1788–1850), statesman 384–5, 397
Perizonius, Jacobus 75, 89
Petty-Fitzmaurice, Henry, 3rd marquis of Lansdowne (1780–1863), statesman 145
Pickthorn, Sir Kenneth William Murray (1892–1975) 380n.
Pigou, Arthur Cecil (1877–1959), economist 226
Pitt, William, 1st earl of Chatham (1708–78), statesman 331
Pitt, William (1759–1806), statesman 330–2
Pius V (1504–72), pope (1566–72) 127, 137
Pius IX (1792–1878), pope (1846–78) 141, 168
Plato (427–348/47 BC) 91
Pliny (AD 23–79), Roman writer 74
Poe, Edgar Allan (1809–49), author 146
Pollard, Albert Frederick (1869–1948) 391n.
Pollock, Sir Frederick, 3rd baronet (1845–1937), jurist 401
Popper, Karl (1902–94), philosopher 10n.
Powell, Frederick York (1850–1904) 103
Powicke, Sir Frederick Maurice (1879–1963) 117–19, 178

Index of Names

Powys, John Cowper (1872–1963), novelist and miscellaneous writer 343
Primrose, Archibald Philip, 5th earl of Rosebery (1847–1929), statesman 356–7, 363
Prothero, Sir George Walter (1848–1922) 16, 180, 349–51, 363, 365
Prutz, Hans (1843–1929) 33, 35, 40
Pusey, Edward Bouverie (1800–82), scholar of Hebrew 21, 89

Radcliffe-Brown, A. R. 274
Rait, Sir Robert Sangster (1874–1936), principal of Glasgow University 354
Raleigh, Sir Walter Alexander (1861–1922), critic and essayist 354
Ramsay, Sir William Mitchell (1851–1939), classical scholar 338n.
Ranke, Clara (née Graves) 137–8
Ranke, Leopold von (1795–1886) v, 10, 12–13, 16–18, 26, 34, 38, 46–8, 80, 111, 115, 123–57, 161, 164, 170–1, 177, 179, 181n., 182–5, 187, 192, 199, 201–2, 207, 238, 253, 255, 260, 262, 267, 273, 279, 326–8, 330–1, 388, 390, 401
Ratzel, Friedrich (1844–1904), geographer 280, 282, 284–5, 287
Raumer, Friedrich von (1781–1873) 179
Raymond, Ernest 374
Raymond, John 387
Redlich, Oswald (1858–1944) 179
Reeve, Henry (1813–95), man of letters 140n., 144n.
Reicke, Georg (1863–1923), author and mayor of Berlin 366
Reid, Thomas (1710–96), philosopher 50
Renan, Joseph Ernest (1823–92) 157, 157n.
Rhodes, Cecil John (1853–1902), imperialist 256, 315, 330
Ricardo, David (1772–1823), economist 211, 218
Richards, Sir H. Erle 353
Richelieu, Armand-Jean du Plessis, duke of (1585–1642), statesman and cardinal 153
Ritter, Carl (1779–1859), geographer 256, 278–80, 287
Ritter, Heinrich (1791–1869), philosopher 40–1, 41n., 47–8
Ritter, Moritz (1840–1923) 80

Robertson, Sir Charles Grant (1869–1948) 349, 357
Robertson, William (1721–93) 4, 5n., 6, 8, 51–2, 58–9, 64, 269
Robinson, Henry Crabb (1775–1867), diarist 136, 138, 142
Ronge, Johannes (1813–87), founder of the Deutschkatholiken 138
Roscher, Wilhelm (1817–94), economist 17–18, 193, 195–6, 206–9, 216–18, 228
Rose, John Holland (1855–1942) 341, 350
Rosebery, Lord, see Primrose
Rothschild, Lionel Nathan de (1808–79), banker and philanthropist 140n.
Rotteck, Karl von (1775–1840) 198–9
Round, John Horace (1854–1928) 107–8
Rousseau, Jean-Jacques (1712–78) 54, 58
Ruge, Arnold (1802–80), politician and publicist 19
Russell, Bertrand (1872–1970), philosopher and author 109

Salisbury, see Cecil
Samuel, Raphael (1934–96) 407
Sanday, William (1843–1920), theological scholar 345, 354
Savigny, Friedrich Carl von (1779–1861), jurist 14, 18, 114, 162, 217, 259
Say, Jean Baptiste (1767–1832), economist 222
Schäfer, Dietrich (1845–1929) 22n., 34, 36, 294–5, 315, 319–26, 333–4, 367–9
Schelling, Friedrich Wilhelm Joseph von (1775–1854), philosopher 132, 138, 263
Scherer, Wilhelm (1841–86), Germanist 245n.
Schiller, Friedrich von (1759–1805) 29, 32, 35, 49, 62, 66, 68, 95, 161
Schlegel, Friedrich von (1772–1829), cultural philosopher 132n., 259
Schleiermacher, Friedrich Daniel Ernst (1768–1834), theologian and philosopher 140
Schlosser, Friedrich Christoph (1776–1861) 123, 239n., 270–1
Schlözer, August Ludwig (1735–1809) 60, 195–9, 267, 272

Index of Names

Schmidt, Julian Heinrich (1818–86), Germanist 133n., 245n.
Schmidt, Wilhelm (1868–1954), ethnologist 282, 282n., 285n.
Schmoller, Gustav von (1838–1917), economist 208, 212, 226, 228, 276, 276n., 277n., 320, 322, 401
Schultze, Walther 186
Schurz, Carl (1829–1906), politician and publicist 283
Schuster, Sir Claud (1869–1956), civil servant 360
Scott, David Dundas 125, 143
Scott, Sir Walter (1771–1832), novelist and poet 89, 110–11
Scruton, Roger 382
Seeley, John Robert (1834–95) 9, 12–13, 16, 21, 97, 169, 182–4, 236n., 246, 255–8, 294, 302, 306–12, 308n., 314–16, 318–19, 321, 324, 326–8, 331, 333
Shelley, Percy Bysshe (1792–1822), poet 84
Sherriff, Bob 374
Sidgwick, Henry (1838–1900), philosopher 108–9, 116, 214, 258
Sieyès, Emmanuel Joseph, Abbé (1748–1836), revolutionary and politician 162
Sime, James (1843–95), author and journalist 184
Simpson, Richard (1820–76), Roman Catholic writer 161, 233, 247n.
Sinclair, Sir John 51
Sixtus V (1521–90), pope (1585–90) 155
Smith, Adam (1723–90), political economist 50, 54, 103, 211, 217–19
Smith, Arthur Lionel (1850–1924) 118, 349, 356
Smith, Goldwin (1823–1910), controversialist 169, 233–4, 314
Sohm, Rudolf (1841–1917), jurist 180
Solinus, Gaius Julius (around AD 250), Roman author 74
Sonnenschein, Edward Adolf (1851–1929), classical scholar 356
Spencer, Herbert (1820–1903), philosopher 20, 230, 246, 251–2, 260–4, 276n.
Spengler, Oswald (1880–1936) 285n.
Spinoza, Benediktus de (1632–77), philosopher 167

Spittler, Ludwig Timotheus (1752–1810) 8, 69–70, 197
Sporschil, Johannes 81
Spring-Rice, Sir Cecil Arthur (1859–1918), diplomat 348
Stählin, Karl (1865–1939) 294–6, 309, 329, 334
Stalin, Josef W. (1879–1953) 375
Stanley, Arthur Penrhyn (1815–81), dean of Westminster 88, 91, 94, 138, 140, 142, 157, 157n., 185n.
Stein, Heinrich Friedrich, baron (1757–1831), statesman 256, 258, 328
Stendhal [Marie Henri Beyle] (1783–1842), writer 145n.
Stephen, Sir Leslie (1832–1904), man of letters 108–9, 235n., 260
Stern, Alfred (1846–1936) 176
Steuart, James 50
Strabo, Walahfrid (808/809–849), poet 74
Strauss, David Friedrich (1808–74), theologian 91, 94
Stubbs, William (1829–1901) 13–16, 99–122, 151n., 177, 179–80, 182, 185, 236n., 246, 248, 254–6, 258–9, 262, 299–300
Sudermann, Hermann (1857–1928), author 366
Sulpicius, Publius (b. 124), Roman tribune 96
Sybel, Heinrich von (1817–95) 16, 33, 40, 42, 45, 166, 193, 239–40, 313, 314n.
Symonds, John Addington (1840–93), author 145, 154, 156

Tacitus, Publius Cornelius (c. 55–after 115) 74, 95, 113, 258
Tait, James (1863–1944) 108, 116
Tanner, Joseph Robson (1860–1931) 102
Tawney, Richard Henry (1880–1962) 351, 391n.
Taylor, Alan John Percivale (1906–90) 338n., 375, 375n., 376n., 380
Thackeray, William Makepeace (1811–63), novelist 126, 130
Thirlwall, Connop (1797–1875) 9, 83, 86, 88, 139
Thompson, Edward Palmer (1924–93) 377, 380, 402, 407
Thompson, Kenneth 395
Thurnwald, Richard 274n.

Index of Names

Thursfield, Sir James (1840–1923) 361
Tillemont, Sébastien Le Nain de (1637–98) 69–70
Tirpitz, Alfred von (1849–1930), admiral of the fleet 323, 327
Tocqueville, Alexis Clérel de (1805–59), political philosopher 208
Toland, John (1670–1722), deist 9, 89
Tout, Jonathan (1713–85), philologist 108, 118
Toynbee, Arnold Joseph (1889–1975) 213n., 215–16, 218–19, 282n., 362–3, 375, 375n., 380n.
Treitschke, Heinrich von (1834–96) 3, 34, 38–9, 45–7, 119–21, 174, 178, 183, 188, 193, 206, 257, 276, 294, 311–13, 319, 321–2, 326, 329, 334, 340–1, 347, 356–7, 359n., 364
Trevelyan, George Macaulay (1876–1962) 21, 102, 342, 351, 360
Trevelyan, Sir George Otto (1838–1928) 178
Trevor-Roper, Hugh Redwald (1914–) 382n.
Troeltsch, Ernst (1865–1923) 11, 191, 195
Turner, Frederick Jackson (1861–1932) 21, 291–3, 295–7, 303
Twesten, Karl (1820–70), positivist 238, 238n., 242n.
Tylor, Sir Edward Burnett (1832–1917), anthropologist 269, 276, 278

Ulrici, Hermann (1806–84), philosopher 237
Unwin, George 111
Urban VIII (1568–1644), pope (1623–44) 139

Vegetius, Publius Flavius, Roman author 74
Velacott, Paul 386
Vico, Giovanni Battista (1668–1744) 201, 270
Victoria (1819–1901), queen of the United Kingdom and empress of India 105
Villiers, George William Frederick, 4th earl of Clarendon (1800–70), diplomat 140n.
Vincent, John 382
Vinet, Alexandre (1797–1847), theologian 172

Vinogradoff, Sir Paul Gavrilovitch (1854–1925) 112–13, 355, 359n., 360
Virchow, Rudolf (1821–1902), pathologist 277, 284
Voltaire [François-Marie Arouet] (1694–1778) 4, 8, 53, 58–9, 64, 80, 265
Vorländer, Franz (1806–67), philosopher 237

Wachler, Ludwig (1767–1838) 28n.
Wachsmuth, Kurt (1837–1905) 80
Wagner, Adolph (1835–1917), economist 228
Waitz, Georg (1813–86) 14, 112, 115, 174, 180, 193, 259, 314n.
Waitz, Theodor (1821–64), anthropologist 261, 277
Wallas, Graham (1858–1932), political psychologist 339–40
Walras, Marie Esprit Leon (1834–1910), economist 212
Warburg, Aby (1866–1929) 407
Ward, Sir Adolphus William (1837–1924) 16, 176, 178, 351, 364
Webb, Sidney (1859–1947) and Beatrice (1858–1943), social reformers 117
Weber, Georg (1808–88) 239n.
Weber, Max (1864–1920) 133, 191, 207–9, 283, 313, 329, 408
Wegele, Franz Xaver von (1823–97) 27, 27n., 39
Welcker, Karl Theodor (1790–1869), jurist and politician 198
Whately, Richard (1787–1863), archbishop of Dublin 9
Wheatstone, Sir Charles (1802–75), man of science 232
Whewell, William (1794–1866), scholar 246n.
Wiegand, Theodor (1864–1936), archaeologist 367
Wieser, Friedrich von (1851–1926), economist 212
Wilamowitz-Moellendorff, Ulrich von (1848–1931), philologist 31, 71–2, 367
Wilberforce, Samuel (1805–73), successively bishop of Oxford and Winchester 91, 246
Wilda, Wilhelm Eduard (1800–56), jurist 116

438 Index of Names

Wilde, Oscar (1854–1900) 157
William II (1859–1941), German emperor 345, 367n.
Wilkinson, Henry Spencer (1853–1937) 354–6
Wolf, Friedrich August (1759–1824), classical scholar 35, 90–2, 92n.
Wolf, Gustav 177
Wolfers, Arnold 395
Wordsworth, William (1770–1850), poet 124, 137

Worthington, J. W. 130
Wundt, Wilhelm (1832–1920), philosopher 286n., 358
Wuttke, Adolf (1819–70), theologian 271

Young, George Malcolm (1882–1959), scholar 380n.

Zimmern, Sir Alfred Eckhard (1879–1957), scholar 362